Gestalt is more than an effective psychotherapy; it is a way of seeing and knowing, an action approach that emphasizes dynamic awareness rather than introspection.

Here is the classic volume which introduced this revolutionary approach to psychology, together with a complete program for unblocking the barriers erected by society, language, education and ourselves.

GESTALT THERAPY explains in clear prose the core concepts of Gestalt, such as figure/ground formation, contact and retroflection. It offers amazing techniques for getting in touch with our bodies, our emotions, ourselves . . . for helping us live more fully and freely in the Here and Now.

W9-CKJ-554

GESTALT THERAPY

*Excitement and Growth in the
Human Personality*

Frederick S. Perls, M.D., Ph.D.
Ralph F. Hefferline, Ph.D.
Paul Goodman, Ph.D.

GESTALT THERAPY

*A Bantam Book | published by arrangement with
Crown Publishers, Inc.*

PRINTING HISTORY

*Julian Press edition published 1951
Bantam edition | February 1977*

ISBN 0–553–10217–6

Published simultaneously in the United States and Canada

*Bantam Books are published by Bantam Books, Inc. Its trade-
mark, consisting of the words "Bantam Books" and the por-
trayal of a bantam, is registered in the United States Patent
Office and in other countries. Marca Registrada, Bantam
Books, Inc., 666 Fifth Avenue, New York, New York 10019.*

CONTENTS
VOLUME ONE

CONTENTS
VOLUME TWO

AUTHOR'S NOTE

Gestalt Therapy is now coming of age even though I wrote the original manuscript roughly twenty years ago. The years in between have produced many changes both social and psychological; however, the Gestalt experiments included in this volume are as valid today as they proved to be the first time we conducted classes in awareness expansion.

The overall accent, however, has changed from the idea of therapy to a gestalt concept of growth. I now consider that neurosis is not a sickness but one of several symptoms of growth stagnation. Other symptoms of growth stagnation are the need to manipulate the world and control madness, character distortion, reduction of the human potential, and lack of "response-ability," and most important of all, the production of holes in a personality.

Maturation is a continuous process of transcending environmental support and developing self-support, which means an increasing reduction of dependencies.

The unborn baby is dependent in every respect upon the mother—for getting the material for physical growth, oxygen, warmth, transportation; immediately after birth he must provide his own oxygen. Soon he must contribute to his own food intake by sucking the milk and providing a considerable amount of warmth for himself. As time goes on, he becomes more and more self-supportive, learns to communicate, to crawl and walk, to bite and chew, to accept and reject. So the development continues and the child realizes some part of his potential for existence. Unfortunately in our time the average person uses only about 10 to 15 percent of his potential; a person who uses 25 percent is already called a genius.

To mobilize his potential and to ensure proper maturation, the child has to overcome many frustrations. In the healthy child these frustrations will mobilize the resources which are innately available.

When either the frustrations are too great for the child to cope with or he is spoiled and deprived of the opportunity to "do for himself," he will develop his own individual brand of psychopathology. He will start to manipulate the environment by phony behavior (role playing) or by taking control to ensure that those intolerable frustrations will not occur again. He will form a specific character and write a life-script that guarantees his survival. The most important frustrations occur of course when demands are made upon him from the environment at a stage when he cannot cope, when for instance he is spoken to in a language of concepts and abstractions at a time when he can think only in concrete terms. At that time he may develop a feeling of utter stupidity. In a case like that his life-script will demand an overcompensation of omniscience.

The basic principle underlying these disturbances is the environmental demand to be what he is not, the demand to actualize an ideal rather than to actualize himself. He becomes lopsided. Some of his potential is then alienated, repressed, projected. Other characteristics are put on as phony behavior, requiring strain with self-support, exhaustion without satisfaction.

Finally this deep split between our biological and our social existence leads to more and more conflicts and "holes." The holes are the main characteristics of the incomplete personality. Some of us have no heart or no intuition, some have no legs to stand on, no genitals, no confidence, no eyes or ears.

If a person has a hole where other people have eyes, he finds that his eyes are projected into the environment, and he will lead a life of self-consciousness, permanently persecuted by the idea that he is looked at, judged, admired, accused, etc. The worst hole I can think of is a person having no ears. This is usually found in people who talk and talk and expect the world to listen. They use other people's sentences merely as jumping boards for repartee, if they listen that much. They certainly don't listen to the voices of their environment; at best they abstract the content and stay on an empty intellectual level. We have a peculiar polarity in this world: listening versus fighting. People who listen don't fight, and people who fight don't listen. If the warring factions in our society—marriage partners, business dependencies—would open their ears and listen to their opponents, the hostilities in our environment and among nations would greatly diminish.

The "I'm telling you what you need" would be replaced by "I'm listening for what you want," and the basis for rational discussion would be opened.

This applies as much to our inner conflicts as it applies to the world situation in general.

But how do we open the ears and the eyes of the world? I consider my work to be a small contribution to that problem which might contain the possibility of the survival of mankind.

F. S. Perls

August 1969
Cowichan Lodge, B.C.

INTRODUCTION

This book began as a manuscript written by Frederick S. Perls. The material was developed and worked over by Paul Goodman (Volume II) and put to practical application by Ralph Hefferline (Volume I). However, as it stands now it is truly the result of the co-operative efforts of the three authors. What began as the work of one author ended up as that of three —each of us equally responsible.

We have had in common one purpose: to develop a theory and method that would extend the limits and applicability of psychotherapy. Our differences were many, but by bringing them forth rather than politely concealing them we many times arrived at solutions that none of us could have anticipated. Many of the ideas in the original manuscript have been retained in this book, but just as many have been added in the co-operative effort of the three authors in the writing of the book, and more importantly, they take on a new meaning in the context of the book as it has been completed.

* * *

The insights of Gestalt Psychology have been fruitful in the approach to art and education; and in academic psychology the work of Wertheimer, Koehler, Lewin, etc. is now fully recognized; however, following the interest in behaviorism, which is for the most part motorically oriented, academic circles now overemphasize the perceptual aspect of the Gestalt. The magnificent work of Goldstein in neuropsychiatry still has not found the place in modern science that it deserves. The full application of Gestaltism in psychotherapy as the only theory that adequately and consistently covers both normal and abnormal psychology has not yet been undertaken. The present work is an attempt to lay the foundation for that.

*   *   *

Indispensable—both for the writing and the thorough understanding of this book—is an attitude which as a theory actually permeates the content and method of the book. Thus the reader is apparently confronted with an impossible task: to understand the book he must have the "Gestaltist" mentality, and to acquire it he must understand the book. Fortunately, the difficulty is far from being insurmountable, for the authors have not invented such a mentality. On the contrary, we believe that the Gestalt outlook is the original, undistorted, natural approach to life; that is, to man's thinking, acting, feeling. The average person, having been raised in an atmosphere full of splits, has lost his Wholeness, his Integrity. To come together again he has to heal the dualism of his person, of his thinking, and of his language. He is accustomed to thinking of contrasts—of infantile and mature, of body and mind, organism and environment, self and reality, as if they were opposing entities. The unitary outlook which can dissolve such a dualistic approach is buried but not destroyed and, as we intend to show, can be regained with wholesome advantage.

One of the themes of the book is assimilation. The organism grows by assimilating from the environment what it needs for its very growth. Though this is obvious to everyone in regard to the physiological processes, the stages of mental assimilation have, for the most part, been overlooked. (An exception is Freud's concept of introjection, which at least provides a partial account.) Only by thorough assimilation can heterogeneous substances be unified into a new Whole. We believe that by assimilating whatever valuable substance the psychological sciences of our time have to offer we are now in the position to put forward the basis for a consistent and practical psychotherapy.

Why, then, as the title suggests, do we give preference to the term "Gestalt" when we take equally into account Freudian and para-Freudian psychoanalysis, the Reichian armor theory, semantics and philosophy? To this we have to say: we were not benevolently eclectic; none of the disciplines mentioned have been swallowed wholesale and artificially synthesized. They have been critically examined and organized into a new whole, a comprehensive theory. In this process it emerged that we had to shift the concern of psychiatry from the fetish of the unknown, from the adoration of the "unconscious," to the problems and phenomenology of awareness: what factors operate in awareness, and how do faculties which can operate successfully only in the state of awareness lose this property?

Awareness is characterized by *contact*, by *sensing*, by *excitement* and by *Gestalt* formation. Its adequate functioning is the realm of normal psychology; any disturbance comes under the heading of psychopathology.

Contact as such is possible without awareness, but for awareness contact is indispensable. The crucial question is: with what is one in contact? The spectator of a modern painting may believe that he is in contact with the picture while he is actually in contact with the art critic of his favorite journal.

Sensing determines the nature of awareness, whether distant (e.g., acoustic), close (e.g., tactile) or within the skin (proprioceptive). In the last term is included the sensing of one's dreams and thoughts.

Excitement seems to be linguistically a good term. It covers the physiological excitation as well as the undifferentiated emotions. It includes the Freudian cathexis notion, Bergson's *élan vital*, the psychological manifestations of the metabolism from Mongolism to Basedow, and it gives us the basis for a simple theory of anxiety.

Gestalt formation always accompanies awareness. We do not see three isolated points, we make a triangle out of them. The formation of complete and comprehensive Gestalten is the condition of mental health and growth. Only the completed Gestalt can be organized as an automatically functioning unit (reflex) in the total organism. Any incomplete Gestalt represents an "unfinished situation" that clamors for attention and interferes with the formation of any novel, vital Gestalt. Instead of growth and development we then find stagnation and regression.

* * *

Configuration, structure, theme, structural relationship (Korzybski) or meaningful organized whole most closely approximate the originally German word *Gestalt,* for which there is no exact English equivalent. As a linguistic example: pal and lap contain the same elements, but the meaning is dependent upon the order of the letters within their Gestalt. Again, bridge has the meaning of a game of cards or a structure joining two river banks. This time the meaning depends upon the context in which "bridge" appears. The color lilac looks bluish against a red background, red against a blue background. The context in which an element appears is called in Gestalt psychology the "ground" against which the "figure" stands out.

In neurosis, and much more in psychosis, the elasticity of figure/ground formation is disturbed. We often find either a rigidity (fixation) or a lack of figure formation (repression). Both interfere with the habitual completion of an adequate Gestalt.

In health the relation between figure and ground is a process of permanent but meaningful emerging and receding. Thus the interplay of figure and background becomes the center of the theory as presented in this book: attention, concentration, interest, concern, excitement and grace are representative of healthy figure-ground formation, while confusion, boredom, compulsions, fixations, anxiety, amnesias, stagnation and self-consciousness are indicative of figure/ground formation which is disturbed.

Figure/ground, unfinished situation and Gestalt are the terms which we have borrowed from Gestalt psychology. Psychoanalytical terms such as super-ego, repression, introjection, projection, etc. are so commonly used in any contemporary psychiatric book that we shall not presently concern ourselves with them. They will be discussed in detail throughout the book. Semantic and philosophical terminology has been kept to a minimum. The cybernetic, dianetic and orgone theories will find little or no discussion in the text. We consider them to be at best half-truths as they deal with the organism in isolation and not in creative contact with the environment. A critical appreciation of dianetics, however, will be found in the introduction to J. A. Winter's book on this subject. Cybernetics has a unitary outlook in the all-or-nothing principle (first mentioned by Alfred Adler as a general neurotic attitude), in the yes/no attitude of the electronic tube (covered in this book in the discussion of the ego-function of identification/alienation) and in the optimum efficiency of balanced systems; but as long as Wiener's robots do not grow and propagate by themselves, we prefer to explain his machines by human function rather than vice versa.

Reich's orgone theory successfully extends *ad absurdum* the most doubtful part of Freud's work, the libido theory. On the other hand, we are deeply indebted to Reich for having brought down to earth Freud's rather abstract notion of repression. Reich's idea of the motoric armor is doubtless the most important contribution to psychosomatic medicine since Freud. We are at variance with him (and Anna Freud) at one point. We regard the *defensive* function of the armor as an ideological deception. Once an organismic need is condemned, the self turns its creative activity as aggression against the disowned impulse, subduing and controlling it. A person would have to engage in a lifelong nerve-wracking struggle with his own instincts (many nervous breakdowns bear witness to that) were it not for the organism's ability to form automatically functioning *cordons sanitaires*. The ego is as defensive as Hitler's Ministry for Defense in 1939.

However, in shifting the accent from the recovery of the "repressed" to re-organizing the "repressing" forces, we wholeheartedly follow Reich, though we find that in the recovery of the self there is much more involved than the mere dissolving of the character armor. When we try to make the patient aware of his "means whereby" he suppresses, we find an astounding inconsistency. We find that he is aware and proud of it when he uses many of his energies against himself, as in self control, but we also notice—and this is the therapeutic dilemma—that he is for the most part unable to relinquish his self-control.

The Freudian tells his patient to relax and not to censor. But this is precisely what he cannot do. He has "forgotten" how he is doing the inhibiting. The inhibiting has become routine, a patterned behavior, just as in reading we have forgotten the spelling of the single word. Now we seem to be only slightly better off than Reich. First, we were unaware of *what* was repressed; now we are largely unaware of *how* we repress. The active therapist seems to be indispensable: he either has to interpret or to shake the patient.

Again a Gestaltist outlook comes to our rescue. In an earlier book (Perls: *Ego, Hunger and Aggression*) the following theory was put forward. In the struggle for survival the most relevant need becomes figure and organizes the behavior of an individual until this need is satisfied, whereupon it recedes into the background (temporary balance) and makes room for the next *now* most important need. In the healthy organism this change of dominance has the best survival chance. In our society such dominant needs, for example, morals, etc., often become chronic and interfere with the subtle self-regulating of the human organism.

Now we have again a unitary principle to work with. The neurotic's survival outlook (even if it appears foolish to the outsider) requires that he become tense, that he censor, that he defeat the analyst, etc. This is his dominant need, but as he has forgotten how he organized it, it has become routine. His intentions not to censor are as efficient as an alcoholic's New Year's resolution. The routine has to become once more a fully aware, new, exciting need in order to regain the ability to cope with unfinished situations. Instead of pulling means out of the unconscious we work on the upper-most surface. The bother is that the patient (and too often the therapist himself) takes this surface for granted. The way the patient talks, breathes, moves, censors, scorns, looks for causes etc.—this to him is obvious, is constitution, is nature. But actually it is the expression of his dominant needs, e.g., to be victorious, good and impressive. It is precisely in the obvious that we find his unfinished personality; and only by tackling the obvious, by melting the petrified, by differentiating between blah-blah and real concern, between the obsolete and the creative, can the patient regain the liveliness of the elastic figure/ground relation. In this process, which is the process of growth and maturing, the patient experiences and develops his "self," and we intend to show how he comes to this "self" via the means at his disposal: his available amount of awareness in experimental situations.

*   *   *

The greatest value in the Gestalt approach perhaps lies in the insight that the *whole determines the parts,* which contrasts with the previous assumption that the whole is merely the total sum of its elements. The therapeutic situation, for instance, is more than just a statistical event of a doctor plus a patient. It is a *meeting* of doctor and patient. If the doctor is rigid and insensitive to the specific requirements of the ever-changing therapeutic situation, he will not be a good therapist. He might be a bully or a businessman or a dogmatist; but he is not a therapist if he refuses to be a part of the on-going processes of the psychiatric situation. Likewise, the patient's behavior is dictated by many variables of the interview, and only the 100% rigid or the insane (oblivious of the context in which they operate) will behave in the consulting room as they do outside.

Neither the full understanding of the organismic functions nor the best knowledge about the environment (society, etc.) covers the total situation. Only the interplay of organism and environment (a partial account of this is given in the theory of interpersonal relations of Harry Stack Sullivan) constitutes the psychological situation, not the organism and environment taken separately. The isolated organism and its abstractions—mind, soul and body—and the isolated environment are the subjects of many sciences; e.g., physiology, geography, etc.; they are not the concern of psychology.

The overlooking of this limitation has thus far prevented the creation of an adequate theory for both normal and abnormal psychology. As there is no doubt that associations and reflexes exist, most previous theories, even to a great extent Korzybski's, concluded that the mind consists of a mass of associations or that behavior and thinking consist of reflexes. The creative activity of the organism is as little explained by associations, reflexes and other automatisms as the planning strategy and the organizing of war is explained by the automatism of the disciplined soldier.

Sensing and moving are *both* outgoing activities, not mechanical *re*sponses, whenever and wherever the organism meets novel situations. The *sensoric* system of *orientation* and the *motoric* system of *manipulation* work interdependently, but as reflexes only in the lower layers which are fully automatized and require no awareness. Manipulation is our (somewhat awkward) term for all muscular activity. Intelligence is adequate orientation, efficiency adequate manipulation. To regain these, the desensitized and immobilized neurotic has to recover his full awareness; i.e., his sensing, contacting, excitement and Gestalt formation.

In order to do this, we change our outlook toward the therapeutic situation by acknowledging that every non-dogmatic approach is based upon the trial and error method of nature. That way the clinical becomes an experimental situation. Instead of putting explicit or implicit demands upon the patient—pull yourself together, or: you must relax, or: do not censor, or: you are naughty, you have resistances, or: you are just dead—we realize that such demands would only increase his difficulties and make him more neurotic, even desperate. We suggest graded experiments which —and this is of the uppermost importance—are not *tasks* to be completed as such. We explicitly ask: what is going on if you repeatedly try this or that? With this method we bring to the surface the difficulties of the patient. Not the task, but what interferes with the successful completion of the task becomes the center of our work. In Freudian terms, we bring out and work through the resistances themselves.

This book has many functions. To those who work in the field of education, medicine and psychotherapy, we bring an opportunity to give up a sectarian attitude that their specific point of view is the only possible one. We hope to show that they can look at other approaches without going to pieces. To the layman we bring a systematic course for his personal development and integration. To derive the full benefit, however, the reader should tackle both parts of the book together, possibly in the following way: do the experiments as conscientiously as possible; a mere reading will achieve little. It might even leave you with a feeling of confronting a big and hopeless task; whereas, if you actually do what is suggested, you will soon feel that you begin to change. While you are working on the practical part, read the second part of the book once without bothering about how much you will understand. You may find the reading often exciting and stimulating, but as the total picture will be much at variance with the usual way of thinking, you cannot assimilate it at once unless you are well acquainted with Korzybski, L. L. Whyte, Kurt Goldstein and other Gestaltists. After a first reading you will have decided whether you have benefited enough from your first approach and you can start on a systematic chewing through of the theoretical part. Finally, if you are a patient or a trainee in psychoanalysis whose going to therapy is more than a mere dummy, you will find that the work here will not adversely interfere with your therapy but rather will stimulate it and help to overcome stagnation.

VOLUME ONE

MOBILIZING
THE SELF

PART 1

Orienting the Self

I

THE STARTING SITUATION

The first half of this book invites you to invade your own privacy, and it offers a technique for doing this which many before you have found workable. What may be accomplished by such a venture is a question which you will ask at once, but the answer cannot be delivered in a neat verbal package. As a matter of fact, a crucial part of the answer is non-verbal and must remain such; if you are to obtain it, it will have to come from doing work of the sort set forth here. But since we cannot expect you to initiate what appears to be a time-consuming and probably difficult course of action simply in the blind faith that it will in the end prove worth the trouble, we endeavor in the remarks which follow to present something of the general human situation as we see it and our grounds for believing that we have something important to share with anyone who genuinely wants to improve his lot.

What we propose to help you do for yourself cannot but smack at first of the blandishments and unctuous phrasings that have been used to hawk Messianic literary wares, for, baldly stated, it is this: to assist you to discover your self and to mobilize it for greater effectiveness in satisfying your requirements both as a biological organism and as a social human being.

Self-discovery may sound like "old stuff"—one more futile muttering of the "lift-yourself-by-your-own-bootstraps" school of thought—but, as we employ the term, self-discovery is an arduous process. Far from being a sudden flash of revelation, it is more or less continuous and cumulative—and need never end so long as one is alive. It involves the adoption of a rather

3

special attitude toward your self and observation of your self in action. To observe your self in action —ultimately, to observe your self *as* action—calls for techniques strikingly different from those you may have tried already and found wanting; in particular, introspection.

If self-discovery sounds not unavailing but ominous, we shall not contest this reaction, however reminiscent of the psychiatric mumbo-jumbo of the movies. To suppose that you do have a secret or hidden self but that it is sinister and better left alone is an attitude you have not always had and need not retain indefinitely. It comes from your having in the past in time of stress rejected parts of your self that were causing too much trouble. As the circumstances then were, these parts *were* sinister and, to live on in the situation which then existed, you had to get rid of them. Perhaps it was something like the predicament of a wild animal caught in a trap by one leg; under such conditions the leg becomes a menace, and the animal will sometimes gnaw it off and thereby escape, though he spend the rest of his life a cripple.

Your life as it now stands is far different from what it was when you rejected part of your self, and this cast-out part, unlike the animal's leg, can perhaps now be salvaged. Whether the original grounds for rejection still hold or have now long since disappeared would seem, at the very least, to merit your investigation. In what is to follow we supply a method by which you may conduct a systematic examination and reconstruction of your present situation. The procedure is arranged so that each step lays the necessary groundwork for the next. How much of the task you can accomplish within a stated interval depends both on how much of your self you have cast out and on what you are at present up against in your life-situation. You will set your own pace. In any event, you will not go one step faster or further than you wish to.

We have in store for you no "easy steps to mastery," no moral uplift program, no guaranteed rules for breaking bad habits which you are actually determined to keep. We undertake to do nothing *to* you. Instead, we state some instructions by means of which, if you so desire, you may launch yourself on a progressive personal adventure wherein, by your own active efforts, you may do something for your self—namely, discover it, organize it and put it to constructive use in the living of your life.

Paradoxes in the above statements we leave until later. For the moment let us merely say that, in separating "your" and "self" instead of saying "yourself," we have not wished to plague the proofreader in you but to emphasize the possessiveness of the possessive pronoun "your." It is *your* self. Also, please note in passing that the "you" we speak of—the "you" that must do any discovering that is done—is at one and the same time obviously a part of "your self." It is the part that is accessible to us as we address you now. It is the part that is subvocally repeating these words as it reads them.

No suggestion is made that this undertaking will be easy. The directions as stated may appear easy—so easy, in fact, that it is quite possible for you to claim to the end that there is nothing to them. You may breeze through, get no results you did not foresee, and call it a day. If, on the other hand, you contact a bit more closely the experimental situations which you will set up, you will find that, in a peculiar way, they present the hardest, the most exasperating work you have ever tackled—but also, if you follow through, the most fascinating.

In these pages we try to talk to you as if we were face to face. Of course, you do not, as in ordinary conversation, have a chance to take the floor, talk back, ask questions, or supply precise details about your personal situation; and we, on the other hand, have the disadvantage of not knowing you personally. If we did know particulars about you—your age, sex, schooling, work, or your successes, failures, plans, fears,—then, while this would not change in any fundamental way what we wish to communicate, we could add or delete, change emphasis here and there, put things in different sequence, and perhaps effect short-cuts on the basis of such information. Nevertheless, we believe that practically everything we shall deal with is applicable, in some degree or in some respect, to every human being living in our times under the conditions of Western civilization. For you to make whatever application is appropriate to your personal situation constitutes your work in this joint undertaking.

Since many of our views on the manner in which the self functions differ from currently accepted notions of human nature, it is important to realize that what we present is not something "dreamed up" overnight, but is, rather, the fusion of several lines of approach to the problem of the human personality. To make this clear, we must say something about the present status of the science of psychology.

Psychologists—and by this term we mean all those who conduct systematic investigations directed at the understanding of human behavior—may be roughly divided into two groups. The members of one group take pride in following what has traditionally been called the "experimental approach," while the others, regardless of their various self-christenings, are regarded—particularly by the experimentalists—as following the "clinical approach." Common to both is the basic problem of understanding human behavior, but, because of divergent assumptions on how to go about the job, they have until recently had relatively independent development.*

Toward the end of the Nineteenth Century, when psychology was separating from philosophy and attempting to establish itself as a science, its leaders were eager to be accepted as true scientists. Accordingly,

---

*In separating this group of workers into two mutually exclusive subgroups we lay ourselves open to the same charge of "false dichotomizing" that we bring to bear against others throughout this book. Actually, psychologists as a group constitute what the statistician would characterize as a "bimodal distribution." We are here deliberately abstracting what we regard as typical of "clinicians" and of "experimentalists" when considered as distinct and contrasting subgroups, even though we are quite aware that this distorts the case in greater or lesser degree for those many workers who occupy intermediate positions.

they did their best to copy in their own field the same methods which had won prestige for the older and more advanced science of physics. To correspond with the physicist's atom as the most elementary unit of matter, these early psychologists endeavored to identify "atoms" of behavior—that is, irreducible elements of human activity which might serve as building-blocks for more complicated reactions. They tried to do this by employing as nearly as possible those methods of experimental analysis which were used in physics. By present standards these early efforts were crude, but, despite increased sophistication, present-day experimentalists still tend to be ultra-conservative in the selection of problems upon which to do research. Since they are fearful of turning up data not at once countable or measurable by techniques *already at hand,* they have relatively little to contribute as yet to such full-scale human problems as emotion and personality. Psychology, they say, needs perhaps another fifty or a hundred years of development before it can deal adequately with such complicated matters.

A little later we shall have to come back to the position taken by the experimentalist, particularly because of its bearing on the problem of proof. As you work along with us, you will be inclined from time to time to question statements that we make, and you will demand, "Where is your proof?" Our standard answer will be that we present nothing that you cannot *verify for yourself in terms of your own behavior,* but, if your psychological make-up is that of the experimentalist as we have portrayed him, this will not satisfy you and you will clamor for "objective evidence" of a verbal sort, *prior to* trying out a single non-verbal step of the procedure.

Failure to provide proof for their theories is the heaviest charge laid at the door of those who follow the "clinical approach." The clinician, unlike the experimentalist in his laboratory, was forced from the beginning to deal in some fashion with the full complexity of human behavior, for his work was that of attempting to heal, and his patients lacked the grace to bring him simple problems. While the human urgency of his cases kept him centered on emotional crises of living and protected the vital level of his work from sinking ever to the depths of what may be performed in the name of experimental science—namely, to grub away at safe tasks for the sake of adding items to one's list of publications—nevertheless, the clinician was swamped by the very richness and profusion of his case material. Usually pressed for time, inured by necessity to playing hunches, often unaware or contemptuous of the experimentalist's passion for verification, he spun theories which were bizarre blendings of keen insight and ungrounded speculation. Nonetheless, his work has been so fruitful that it carries the present potential of freeing the species from man's age-long distortion of man.

Because of differences in temperament, training and objectives, experimentalist and clinician have viewed each other with mutual distrust. To the experimentalist the clinician has seemed, as a scientist, an untamed wild man, careening drunkenly through areas of theory and practice; while to the clinician the experimentalist has appeared an untreated obsessional, miserably bound to his counting mania and, in the name of pure science, learning more and more about less and less. Recently, as they have converged on problems of mutual interest, they have manifested increased respect for each other and their sharper differences are being resolved.

We must go to the core of the issue between experimentalists and clinicians, for this is not just a family quarrel within psychology but one which reflects the selfsame division in beliefs and attitudes which exists in some degree within the personality of everyone reared in our society. Since the self-development procedures which we shall present constitute an informal but genuine joining of experimental technique to a clinical type of material, it is essential that we be clear about what we are doing. We must, for instance, face the fact that we blandly commit what to the experimentalist is the most unpardonable of sins: *we include the experimenter in the experiment!** To justify anything so preposterous, we must now consider further the fact that experimentalist and clinician alike are seeking, each with his own standards of rigor and workability, an understanding of human behavior. Let us examine their respective positions more closely and the extent to which their views and methods overlap, for it is in this area that we shall do our work.

In a court of law the ordinary witness is permitted to give testimony only with respect to what he has seen, heard, or otherwise directly experienced. He is denied the privilege of stating any inferences or conclusions which he may have drawn from such experience, for, in the eyes of the court, his "opinions" are "irrelevant, immaterial, and incompetent." The expert witness, on the other hand, is allowed to offer as testimony his opinions on those aspects of the case which lie within the area of his special competence. Unfortunately, the trial may then degenerate into a battle of opposed experts.

A similar situation develops when human beings are asked to report on their own psychological processes. These reports differ widely from person to person, and there is no way of checking on which of them, if any, is correct. As a result, the experimentalist has long since outdone the courts in excluding unreliable testimony, and for him there exists *no* acceptable expert witness of events which are private. It follows inevitably, of course, that in excluding the single witness who is in a position to report on them, he also thereby excludes from his science all concern with private events as such.

In his continuous stress on psychology's need to be

---

*Many investigators acknowledge, to be sure, that in some particular study they have not managed to keep the experimenter out of the experimental picture. To the extent, however, that his presence has influenced the results, this is regarded as contamination, and attempts are then made, by statistical manipulations perhaps, to "partial out" his influence and thus purify the data.

objective and to banish eternally from the realm of science whatever is *subjective,* the experimentalist says, in effect, that whatever can be placed publicly on display for inspection by competent observers is admissible as scientific data; whatever is by its nature limited to a private showing, while it may outside of working hours be granted to exist, cannot be acceptable as part of the stuff of science because of its inaccessibility to other observers for confirmation. In the older terminology, what may be pointed to in the "external world" in such fashion that others may come and view it and say yea deserves our confidence, whereas what one reports as being "in his mind" is wholly untrustworthy.

Such a dichotomy between public and private has much to commend it, for the fallibility of testimony is notorious. The clinician, by a curious turn, is here in stride with the experimentalist, for, although he listens endlessly to what his patient has to say, he declines to take it at face value. The patient in his view is utterly incapable of telling a straight story, even to himself. To his own vocalizations the doctor may, perhaps, be a bit more likely to accord a clean bill of health.

The experimentalist's conviction that in public display there is safety—or, at any rate, less risk—is, to be sure, not his exclusively. In all undertakings where much is at stake and where effort is expended to establish fact securely or to make binding for the future such formal commitments as promises, confessions, or depositions, we see the insistence upon signatures, attestations, multiple records, affixing of seals, and so on —to the extent that it provides a livelihood for notaries public. One says to a friend, "Whatever you do, don't put it in writing," or, if it is the friend who is trying to hold someone to something, this changes to, "Make them give it to you in black and white." When such mistrust is rampant and even rational in everyday transactions, why should the scientist be immune?

Experimentalists subscribe to this further safeguard: an investigator must publish his findings with such detailed specification of apparatus, steps of procedure, and so on, that any competent fellow investigator, dubious of his conclusions, may repeat the study. Though this is seldom done and, in many instances might be impracticable, nevertheless such a proviso presumably has combated temptation to "cook the data" for more positive results. In contrast to such formality in making public the conditions under which an experiment has been performed and which, if reestablished, make feasible its redoing, consider how impossible it is to stipulate conditions under which the deliverances of private "minds" might be subject to recheck.

Restriction of studies to situations capable of being reproduced constitutes a stifling limitation from the point of view of those habituated to thinking of psychology in terms of the nuances of personality. The experimentalist's reply would be that science can never concern itself with the unique. It seeks rather to specify the circumstances under which a given event may be reliably predicted. Should it become possible to do this in sufficient detail, then prediction changes into control and the event may then be made to occur at will. Those events which are of great complexity may stubbornly remain outside the range of direct control and not pass beyond the stage of somewhat increased accuracy of prediction.

Let it be noted in passing that if the object of study be human beings, then any prediction or control of their behavior in the experimentalist's sense must be in the hands of someone empowered to act as stage-manager in their theatre of action. *For the stage-manager to be a part of the person himself adds nothing except change of locus of the control, and is but a special case under the more general formulation.*

Experimentalists who are eager to make the widest practical applications of their findings assert that we are on the brink of an era of "human engineering." Already this is on an organized basis in such matters as propaganda, public relations, sales promotion, personnel management, and the proclivities of assorted "action groups." The pity, say the experimentalists, is that such applications so often are not "in the social interest"; but, they add, when a new tool is forged it is not the fault of the tool or the toolmaker if it is misused. The problem is to extend the "human engineering" to the point where it controls the motives of the user of the tool. This implies a hierarchy of controllers of controllers, with much dependent on the top "human engineer."

With respect to the individual, he is encouraged to be to an extent his own "human engineer." By manipulating the situations in which he has found that he is likely or unlikely to come forth with various desired or undesired reactions, he may learn to trigger off or bottle up according to plan. That such devices of "self-control" are perfectly feasible is well shown in the case of the "self-conqueror," who will come in for discussion later. The darker side of the picture is that this "human engineer" in the personality would have to be *one part in charge of the rest,* operating it according to what he conceived to be *his own* best interests, and these, by the very nature of such a set-up, would be, as we shall try to show later, arbitrary and discordant with the animal needs of the species.

The "human engineering" proposals are reminiscent of the Huxleyan "Brave New World." There, even with the benefits of Utopian technology, it may be remembered that, as a precautionary measure, it was deemed advisable to lock up in a vault the works of Shakespeare and other such inflammatory relics lest the social equilibrium so laboriously attained be set once more awry.

Now let us have a further look at the situation from the standpoint of the clinician. His work, as we said before, has always been concerned with therapy, but we shall not review here the history of psychological healing. (Its practice as an art is as old as civilization, and its methods as varied as man's ingenuity or folly. We deal only with the modern, highly developed form of psychotherapy wherein doctor and patient time after time confront each other in private and talk. This is the situation we have visualized in speaking of the "clinical approach," although this does not cover the term's full range of application.)

The name most frequently connected with interview therapy is, of course, that of Sigmund Freud. Psychoanalysis has since been modified, expanded or variously transformed, particularly by auxiliary techniques which go far beyond what was available in the early years. The orthodox followers of Freud would, if they could, restrict application of the term "psychoanalysis" to their own practice, and have the various offshoots, derivatives, or innovations named otherwise; but control of the term has been irretrievably lost in the welter of loose usage. On the other hand, those groups who believe that their methods have moved so far ahead of what Freud called "psychoanalysis" that this term, applied to their own practice, is an antiquarian misnomer, are in no better plight. The generic appellation, especially in its elided form of "analysis," has passed into the public domain and may be slow to be sloughed off.

By many "clinical approach" has been regarded as the antithesis of "experimental approach." It has lacked rigor and quantitative evaluation of results. It has wallowed in "subjective" findings and remained unregenerate when sharply called to task. It has been unruffled by the unreproducibility of its data. It has coined words with abandon and been indifferent to problems of operational definition. In short, while there are now very few indeed who would defend the thesis that the whole psychoanalytical movement has been simply a tremendous hoax, from sundry quarters voices ask, "But is it science?"

The answer, obviously, depends on how one chooses to define "science." If the term be restricted to what is done under full laboratory rigor, then certainly clinical practice is not science. By the same criterion, however, the designation of "science" would have to be withheld from many other areas of study, notably the social "sciences." Should this be done, their work would proceed as usual, though at a lower level of prestige.

It is the current prestige of the *word* "science" that makes this tedious discussion necessary. What is "scientifically established" *must* be believed, and what is "unscientific" *must* be distrusted. Even the family doctor, for generations proud to regard himself as "practicing the art of medicine," gives indication of climbing on the bandwagon with a new self-styling of "medical scientist."

Psychoanalysis might today enjoy better standing in the scientific family had it made use of that brand of "human engineering" called "public relations." It would then, perhaps, have been less truculent when attacked, and where it saw a spade and called it such it might, when admonished to be more mannerly, have announced that, on second look, it was, indeed, a shovel. One thing it would never have done upon advice of counsel was to assert that no one who had not himself been psychoanalyzed was in any position to evaluate it with respect to method or theory. Among the protests which this called forth one of the more temperate was to the effect that "it is not necessary to eat the whole egg to tell if it is bad."

Perhaps we can clarify, although not resolve, this altercation. Petty criticism of psychoanalysis, which expresses nothing but spite or repeats hearsay, we do not attempt to contend with. What we are concerned with is serious, informed criticism, from men of scientific attainment, who have evaluated psychoanalysis as a logical system and found it wanting. First we must ask: from what basis of contact with it do they render judgment? The answer would seem to be that their acquaintance has been with its verbal formulations, notably the writing of Freud, and it is to these verbal formulations that they allude when they apply the term "psychoanalysis."

On the other hand, when that same term is uttered by those who practice psychoanalysis and those who have encountered it as patients, they are not referring to the *writings about psychoanalysis*. They speak, instead, of what has over a long period of time become a way of functioning that has modified their whole organism. Their over-all processes of seeing and doing have in varying degree undergone transformation. Correspondingly, what they say on the subject comes from sources which are not themselves exclusively verbal.

This differs in no way from what happens in the behavior of a person who becomes skilled or expert in any specialty. Let us cite the case of the experimentalist reading the formal publication of a study done by a fellow-investigator in a field related to his own. The diagrams or pictures of apparatus, which would stop the novice in his tracks, he readily comprehends. He has handled similar pieces, and has through arduous technical training come to appreciate the necessity for their seemingly over-complicated design. The procedures are clear to him as stated, the results openly displayed, and the conclusions follow in logical order. If, to his practiced eye, nothing is amiss, the experimentalist accepts the new findings and will, if occasion warrants, use them as a jumping-off place for further investigations of his own.

But suppose, to his dismay, the conclusions reported damage a cherished theory of his own. What shall he do? He can go vigorously into print attacking the study which has upset him, exploiting to the utmost whatever talking-points he can ferret out. Or he can—and if he is a confirmed experimentalist he will—disdain the area of verbal polemic and take to his laboratory for a complete rechecking of the troublesome study. This is the only way he can solve his problem. A spate of words directed against the published words of his rival cannot suffice, for those words arose from non-verbal operations—and it is in the validity of those non-verbal operations that the words must find or lose their sanction.

But we must also inspect the other side of the coin. To the extent that psychoanalysts have shrugged off criticism when it came from those who were not members of the esoteric brotherhood, they have defended themselves by a neat but infuriating twist of the wrist that has parried sound criticism together with the rest. But, however that may be, recent developments in clinical practice suggest that much that has been controversial can finally be relegated to the past.

We return to the matter previously broached: the assumed antithesis of "experimental" and "clinical." Putting aside the separate origins of these two approaches, Newtonian physics and the art of healing, let us look again at the actual activities of those engaged in each.

"Experiment" derives from *experiri,* to try. An experiment is "a trial or special observation made to confirm or disprove something doubtful, esp. one under conditions determined by the experimenter; an act or operation undertaken in order to discover some unknown principle or effect, or to test, establish, or illustrate some suggested or known truth; practical test; proof."

According to such a definition, interview therapy is experimental. Consider the tremendous control of "variables" introduced by the deliberately simplified setting of the therapeutic situation as compared with the full complexity of everyday living. The doctor and patient are alone in an atmosphere cleared of distractions. The customary admonitions of the clock are in abeyance and, for the duration of the session, time is open for whatever may come to pass. For a period society is diminished to two persons. It is a genuine society, but, for this hour, there is respite from ordinary social pressures, and the customary penalties for "misbehavior" are humanely withheld. As the experiment of therapy proceeds, the patient dares more and more to be himself. He voices the statement that elsewhere he could only think, and thinks the thought that elsewhere he could not acknowledge even to himself. Fluid and changeable, differing from hour to hour or from stage to stage of the total process, such phenomena are not fortuitous and they are not imaginary. They are predictable when the setting is arranged with skill and the sessions expertly conducted.

Apart from these larger aspects, the therapeutic interview is experimental from moment to moment in the sense of "try it out and see what happens." The patient is taught to *experience himself*. "Experience" derives from the same Latin source—*experiri*, to try—as does the word "experiment," and the dictionary gives for it precisely the sense that we intend here, namely, "the actual living through an event or events."

Our view of the therapist is that he is similar to what the chemist calls a catalyst, an ingredient which precipitates a reaction which might not otherwise occur. It does not prescribe the form of the reaction, which depends upon the intrinsic reactive properties of the materials present, nor does it enter as a part into whatever compound it helps to form. What it does is to start a process, and there are some processes which, when once started, are self-maintaining or autocatalytic. This we hold to be the case in therapy. What the doctor sets in motion the patient continues on his own. The "successful case," upon discharge, is not a "cure" in the sense of being a finished product, but a person who now has tools and equipment to deal with problems as they may arise. He has gained some elbow-room in which to work, unencumbered by the cluttered odds and ends of transactions started but unfinished.

In cases handled under such a formulation, the criteria of therapeutic progress cease to be a matter of debate. It is not a question of increased "social acceptability" or improved "interpersonal relations," as viewed through the eyes of some extraneous, self-constituted authority, but the patient's own awareness of heightened vitality and more effective functioning. Though others, to be sure, may also notice the change, *their* favorable opinion on what has happened is *not* the test of therapy.

Such therapy is flexible and itself an adventure in living. The job is not, in line with widespread misconception, for the doctor to "find out" what is wrong with the patient and then "tell him." People have been "telling him" all his life and, to the extent that he has accepted what they say, he has been "telling" himself.

More of this, even if it comes with the doctor's authority, is not going to turn the trick. What is essential is not that the therapist learn something about the patient and then teach it to him, but that the therapist teach the patient *how* to learn about himself. This involves his becoming directly aware of how, as a living organism, he does indeed function. This comes about on the basis of experiences which are in themselves nonverbal.

That this can be done has been incontrovertibly demonstrated in recent years by developments in the advanced wings of clinical practice. It is not the work of one man or any single group of men, and it has by no means reached the summit of its trajectory.

However, since face-to-face therapy is expensive and time-consuming, it has been restricted to the few who could afford it as a luxury or who had to buy it as a necessity. This has limited it to those who were out-and-out "neurotics." But what about that major bulk of the population which, while not malfunctioning by ordinary medical standards, not incompetent to the extent of being unable to hold a job, not in need of help in the sense of being emergency cases, still rates as under par from the standpoint of well-being and satisfaction in living?

The question eventually comes into full focus as to whether the aforementioned miniature society of two, doctor and patient, cannot, for the sake of more widespread dissemination throughout the community of its benefits, be, for general purposes, reduced to one person—the reader of printed instructions and discussion. This question we put to a test a year ago. Using the material which is presented in this book in more developed form, we found that the answer to our question was a decisive *yes!*

The material was put into the hands of undergraduate students in psychology at three universities. At one of these, where the students ranged in age from eighteen to nearly seventy, and where many of them were working part- or full-time at a variety of occupations, it was handled simply as part of the "homework" for an otherwise standard course. Written reports were obtained at intervals over a period of four months, the length of the school term. The next time the course was given an increased number of students worked with a revised and expanded form of the material. Permission was obtained from nearly one hundred to use their reports in any way that would not disclose their identity, with the result that excerpts are available in their own words to give some indication of the range and kind of reactions elicited by this program. For many persons four months is all too short an interval —hardly a warming-up period for anything beyond superficial effects—but we have statements from a number of cases which were followed up to the effect that the development begun while registered in the course continues at an accelerated rate even when the material is no longer a part of their "homework." There is every reason to believe this can be the case for you.

The basic endeavor is to assist you to become aware of how you are now functioning as an organism and as a person. Since you are the only one who can make the necessary observations, we shall, of course, be dealing with what we discussed previously as "private events." The locus of such events is, in the ancient terminology which thus far has survived repeated and determined attempts to scotch it, the "mind." We certainly shall not defend this term in its traditional meaning of a disembodied something which transcends organic functioning. In fact, we are on the side of the scotchers—with a difference. It will be strongly stated later on that we deny *independent* status to "mind," "body" and "external world." What these words apply to are artifacts of a dualistic tradition which has sought to build them right into the functioning of man's organism. If they are relinquished, and a unitary language developed which reports what exists for non-dualistic observers, then nothing important will have disappeared from the picture.

Meantime, by making such dogmatic statements, we stand in danger of losing friends in both directions.

Those who cherish their "minds" and intend to cling to them to the end will, at the very least, decline our suggested procedures if we show so little understanding of how they genuinely experience themselves—that is, as non-physical "mind" operating a physical "body" in an "external world." This way of experiencing oneself is the fruit of the socialization process which we all undergo as children. Further consideration of this we leave until later, and merely say here that for those who refuse to go a step further without their "mind," they will find that, in their terms, work along the lines that we suggest will broaden and extend the domain of "mind."

Those who espouse the strict experimentalist position will cheer us on if we attack "mind," but turn on us belligerently if we tamper with "external world." Their insistence that we be "objective," that we stick to matters which have public rather than private manifestation, is a plea that we place everything in the "external world." But does "external" have significance except as the counterpart of an implied "internal"?

Now, in a sense, the "internal" does exist for them, too, if come upon from the outside, that is to say, "externally." How can this be done? Well, there are electroencephalographs for tapping in on the electrical activity of the brain, and electromyographs for picking up the so-called action potentials of contracting muscle, and sensitive galvanometers for determining changes in skin resistance to the passage of an electric current. Such physiological events are universally accepted scientifically as correlated with what the human being so investigated verbally reports about his "mental activity." For the experimenter this is not "mental." It is "covert behavior," the hidden responding of the organism which may be invisible to the naked eye but detectable by suitable instrumentation. In contrast there is "overt behavior," the obvious movements of the organism in "external space." Please note, however, that what is here accepted by experimentalists as "internal" is so accepted only when it is located in *their* "external world"—the tapes and dials and counters of their recording instruments.

Let us inspect a bit more closely this "external" and "internal" which even the experimentalist concedes to whatever organism he works with. What he means here, obviously, is inside or outside the skin, not inside or outside the "mind." When he reports that his experimental subject, of whatever species, responds to changes in the environment, he is saying usually that when he, the experimenter, presents stimuli of certain kinds under certain conditions, the subject may do something which reliably indicates that the stimuli have had an effect. These stimuli may be visual, auditory, olfactory, etc., or various groupings of them. For them to have an effect the organism must, of course, have appropriate receptors, or "sense-organs," which it does have in eyes, ears, nose, etc. However, it has become increasingly necessary, as work has proceeded, to acknowledge that responses are not under the exclusive control of stimuli from outside the skin, which the experimenter can manipulate with relative ease, but that, in addition to the exteroceptors, the organism possesses additional receptors inside the skin. One group of these, the interoceptors, seems largely restricted to the alimentary canal, appropriate stimuli for their excitation being distention or flaccidity of the hollow viscera; for example, the "hunger contractions" of the stomach, fullness of the bladder, etc.

A further class of receptors inside the skin is the proprioceptors, embedded in muscles, joints and tendons. In more "subjective" days psychologists spoke of their function as "kinesthesia" or "muscle-sense." In current literature "proprioception" now dominates this area as being more "objective." It is interesting in this connection to note the derivation of "proprio-" from the Latin *proprius,* meaning "one's own."

Since any movement of an organism or even increased tonus (tension) in a muscle gives rise to proprioceptive stimuli, these are spoken of by experimentalists as "response-produced" stimuli. Their importance in controlling the behavior of the organism is more and more appealed to by experimentalists as they attempt to account for "verbal behavior," which for them largely replaces what the old-time "subjectivist" alluded to as "the higher mental processes," including "consciousness" itself.

We could stud this section with bibliographical references, showing the rapid advance being made along these lines, but that would take us far afield from what is our intention here, namely, to orient with respect to its scientific aspects the technique which we shall introduce. In passing let us merely mention a recently devised "alertness indicator," which has been built around the fact that to be awake the human organism must have the proprioceptors which are spread throughout the muscles of the body functioning above a certain minimum level. If he relaxes further—that is to say, reduces muscle tonus still more—proprioception diminishes below the critical level and he is asleep. Now, by attaching electrodes to the forehead of the person and picking up action-potentials from the frontalis muscle, it becomes perfectly feasible to arrange a relay which will operate when the volume of potentials falls below a predetermined point and close the circuit of, say, a loud buzzer, and startle the dozer back into alertness. Paradoxically, by going to sleep he wakes himself up. For pilots, long-haul truckers, or whoever else compels himself or is compelled to stay awake when it is time to go to sleep, such a device might on occasion be a lifesaver.

However illuminating or useful within limits such an approach to the behavior that goes on inside the organism's skin may be, notice the emphasis on getting control of that behavior *from the outside*. It is as if the knowledge so painstakingly acquired is to be directed toward making the organism behave in prescribed ways in spite of itself. This statement still holds even though, in the human case, the prescriber may be a part of the person himself.

If the prescriber of behavior could act with unlimited wisdom, then such "human engineering" might lose something of its aspect of arbitrary demand on the organism, but with such unlimited wisdom the prescriber might resign as such and give the organism a chance to regulate itself. That it could do so is attested by the fact that it did succeed in evolving to the point of having approximately the same form and functional properties as modern man prior to the time of the invention of language itself. If the claim be made that the human organism could not be trusted to regulate itself unguided amidst the complexities of present civilization, the counterclaim is just as valid that a self-regulating human organism would not tolerate civilization as it is.

Neither claim is to the point, however, for, if the human organism does not regulate itself, what does? If one wheedles, bullies or otherwise manipulates himself into doing what he otherwise would not do, then wheedler and wheedled, bully and bullied, manipulator and manipulated, are both still living flesh, no matter how sunk in civil war. If the question be raised of how it comes about that the human organism should be so divided against itself if this is not an inevitable state of affairs, the answer must be a somewhat speculative one as to the origin and historical development of our present society. This has no place here, but a brilliant discussion along these lines may be found in L. L. Whyte's "The Next Development in Man."*

Our problem is with the unmistakable facts that human beings *are* so divided in their functioning, that they did not as babies start off their life at war with themselves, and that, specifically, they may, if not indifferent to the further vicissitudes of their lives, demonstrate this split more clearly to themselves and, in this very process, begin to heal it. The way, from the strict experimentalist's viewpoint, looks superficially like a relapse into "subjectivism," but this is not the case. Once beyond a certain stage, one recognizes that "subjective-objective" is a false dichotomy.

---

*L. L. Whyte, *The Next Development in Man,* Henry Holt and Company, New York, 1948.

To clarify this further, let us return still again to the supposed polar opposition of experimental and clinical approaches. What is the crux of their difference? We have suggested it before, and now bring it to a head. We believe it consists in this: experimentalism, sired in method and outlook by physics, which deals with the inanimate, has, as nearly as possible, tried to deal with the living as if it were inanimate. Disregarding the flesh and blood humanity of the investigator, who has tried desperately to make himself nothing more than a disembodied eye, it has studied the living as if from the viewpoint of an impersonal, but highly intelligent, recording instrument. It has seen the organism as activity, which it certainly is. It has found activity which regulates other activity, which it certainly does. But, no matter how far it goes, it finds nothing but more of the same. We venture to say that from the viewpoint of some de-humanized observer—and this, to repeat, is what experimentalism strives for as its scientific ideal —no matter how far research might be pressed, this is all that there would ever be. Furthermore, within the stated purpose of many sciences, including a portion of psychology, there is, both with respect to theory and application, no possibility of and no wish for anything beyond this! This is *knowledge,* sound and tested under conditions of controlled observation. It contributes mightily to man's actual and potential control over the conditions of his living.

But it is not his living!

In contrast, the clinician has sought ever more intimate contact with the activities of the human organism as *lived* by the human organism. His patient comes to him with a view of himself which is a conglomerate of fact and fiction. But it *is* what he notices about himself and his world. It is not impersonal. Rather, it is intensely personal. What he seeks from the doctor is not knowledge in the sense of *verbal statements* which report correctly what his situation is, how it came about, and what would be the processes which would have to be modified to produce beneficial change. No! What he is after is relief—and this is not a verbal matter.

To the limit of his ability, and everyone is limited, the clinician empathizes with his patient—feels the patient's experience by means of his own experience. He, too, is a human being living a life. When the patient talks about himself, his doctor does not say, "Please be more objective in your remarks or I shall have to discharge your case." Far from that, and especially with a patient who is a "verbal" type, the therapist works to get him to be less and less reserved, impersonal, detached, stand-offish with respect to himself. He strives to help him to remove the barriers which he has erected between his official self, the facade he presents for the scrutiny of society, and his more intensely "subjective" self—the feelings and emotions that he has been told and has later told himself that he ought to be too manly or too mature to have. These shut-off parts have immense vitality, which needs to be reclaimed and put to better "subjective" use —and it takes more vitality to *keep* them shut off. This, too, needs to be rechanneled.

The view here taken of the human organism is that it is *active,* not *passive.* For instance, inhibition of certain behaviors is not merely absence of these behaviors in one's overt performance; instead, it is, as the Latin source has it correctly, an in-holding, or, put less awkwardly, an active holding in. If the inhibition is lifted, what was held in does not then passively emerge. Rather, the person actively, eagerly brings it forth.

In the "objective" account of human behavior, the organism is an instrument operated by a kind of remote control. The control may variously be called cause-and-effect relationships, influence of environment, social pressures, or whatever, but, in any case, the organism is regarded as the unconsulted heir to an unasked-for legacy. So strong has become this attitude as to make modern man almost a bystander in his own life. The extent to which he himself produces his own situation—if a patient, produces his symptoms *actively* —is ignored or denied. While certainly something may be gained by being "objective" about oneself in the sense of trying to see how one's behavior might look to an outsider, it also does aggravate the tendency to talk to and about oneself as if this talker somehow transcended the status and limitation of one's organic life.

It reverts to the ancient problem of responsibility. To the extent that one holds one's own life at arm's length and inspects it, as it were, from the outside, then the question of controlling it, regulating it, shaping it in one way or another, becomes a matter of technology. If the technology fails, then, whatever the disappointment or relief, one is freed of personal responsibility, for it can be said, "In the present state of our knowledge, we haven't found out yet just how to handle this kind of personal difficulty."

One cannot on any rational ground take responsibility for what one is not in contact with. This applies to happenings in distant places of which perhaps one has never heard, but it also applies equally to events taking place in one's own life if one is not aware of them. If one makes contact with them and becomes intimately aware of what they are and how they figure in one's functioning, then one becomes responsible for them—not in the sense of now having to assume some burden that was not there before, but rather in the sense of now recognizing that it is oneself who determines in most instances whether they shall or shall not continue to exist. This is quite a different concept of responsibility from that which has at its core the notion of moral blame.

If we have in the above discussion made the point convincingly that the crucial difference between experimentalist and clinician is that the former strives for an *impersonal* formulation of processes neutrally at work in the universe whereas the latter strives to formulate and work with *human* experience—this being, by the dictionary, "the actual living through an event or events"—then the issue becomes one of whether these two approaches must remain mutually exclusive, as has largely been the case so far, or, while reluctantly tolerant of each other, must agree to disagree, or whether they can, at least for the area of study concerned with how human beings regulate each other and themselves, join forces in the solution of a common problem. On this matter much is still shrouded in fog, but a few points are already clear.

Clinical practice in its advanced forms gets results by "subjective" methods which are quite susceptible to measurement and evaluation by "objective" standards acceptable to the strictest experimentalist. For example, studies of the level of chronic muscular tension in the human being as determined before, during and after treatment by "subjective" methods have yielded positive findings by "objective" techniques.

The whole content of the clinician's talks with his patient could reasonably be subsumed under the experimentalist's time-honored and still unsolved problem of "instructions to the subject." Should he conduct his experiment without giving verbal instructions to his human subjects, he finds later that they have not operated in a void, but have given themselves "self-instructions." As a makeshift, he now presents highly formalized instructions, perhaps printed on a card. He also has begun to perform experiments solely to determine the effect of variations in instructions—their clarity, timing, quantity, kind, etc.—and this type of work might effectively be extended to clinical practice and education in general.

In contrast to these suggested aids which experimentalism is giving or may give to clinical practice, it will be interesting to see what happens to experimentalists when they begin to try out on themselves the sort of informal experimentation described in the pages to come. To the extent that it changes them as persons, it will also change them in their professional role as scientists, and perhaps make them more vividly aware of the fact that science, no matter how pure, is the product of human beings engaged in the exciting business of living their personal lives.

The language for talking about personal experience is necessarily less precise than that available for describing public objects and activities. If a child has been taught that his pet quadruped is a "doggie" and later wins approval by saying "doggie" in the presence of a similar quadruped, there is nothing so far to prevent his saying "doggie" whenever he sees a four-legged animal of whatever kind. But suppose that, in attempting to call his mother's attention to a horse, he cries, "Oh, mummie, look at the big doggie!" She will reply, "No, honey, that's a horsie," and proceed to point out characteristics which differentiate horse from dog. By and by he will have acquired a precise vocabulary in this and other areas where what is named can simultaneously excite his exteroceptors and those of a tutor well-versed in standard language.

Private occurrences, though they do acquire a vocabulary of a sort, cannot be so precisely named, for they are not subject to correction when misnamed. A child learns to say, "It hurts," even when nothing shows by which someone else might notice and name the hurt. In such case the ability to report in standard language what is purely private derives from previous instances, such as falls, bumps, scratches, experienced by the child, in which some solicitous person has told him, "It hurts, doesn't it?" But there can be no such thing as saying, "Here, take a feel of my headache," and have it make sense. Furthermore, since such a private event is safely private, it may, given appropriate motivation, be played down or exaggerated as one pleases, without fear that the deception will be unmasked.

Experience is largely reported in metaphorical terms, and its effective sharing with others has traditionally been the province of the poet and novelist. A child may do this well before his verbal expressions become emasculated by convention. A small boy, walking with his mother on a hot sidewalk, announced, "I like the shadows better. The sun makes a noise in my stomach."

Even were we poetically gifted, however, poetry would be an inadequate medium for conveying to you what we have to say about the functioning of your self. Poetry undoubtedly can be profoundly moving and enlightening, but it can also fail to achieve any effect whatsoever or can, on the other hand, produce effects which were entirely unintended. We must thus eschew any wild flights of language and remain quite pedestrian. For whatever help it can give us, we shall make use of terminology developed by gestalt psychology.

A generation ago gestalt psychology, an importation from Germany, made a scientific stir in this country. By ingenious experiments it demonstrated many previously overlooked aspects of "visual perception." Scouting the notion that in seeing something one collects visual fragments and assembles them into the object seen, it insisted that seeing is organized from the start —that is, it is a gestalt or configuration. One's visual field is structured in terms of "figure" and "background." ("Background" became elided to "ground," and in what follows we shall employ the shorter term.)

"Figure" is the focus of interest—an object, pattern, etc.— with "ground" the setting or context. The interplay between figure and ground is dynamic, for the same ground may, with differing interests and shifts of attention, give rise to different figures; or a given figure, if it contains detail, may itself become ground in the event that some detail of its own emerges as figure. Such phenomena are, of course, "subjective," and it was this aspect of gestalt psychology which limited its development when introduced into American psychology. The latter was at the time repudiating the "subjectivism" of Titchener by an uncritical espousal of the "objectivism" of Watson's behaviorism and Pavlov's reflexology. In the light of the foregoing discussion, it is significant to observe that while gestalt psychology today is formally taught in the psychology departments of no more than a handful of American colleges and universities, it is vigorously applied throughout the country in the teaching of art, creative writing—or, in general, "the humanities."

The gestalt movement did exert a lasting influence on psychology by wounding mortally the tendency to "atomistic," building-block constructions, and by getting into the language of psychology the concept of

the "organism-as-a-whole." That its influence was not
greater is attributable in part to the gestalt psychologists themselves, who, in capitulation to the epidemic
demand for "objectivity," vitiated what was new and
promising in their approach by prematurely or un-
wisely installing quantitative measures and excessive
experimental restrictions.

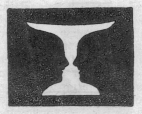

Figure 1

Since we shall make extensive use of the gestaltist's
concepts of figure and ground, we present several illus-
trative visual examples. Figure 1 is a well-known
textbook example of the figure-ground phenomenon.
In this drawing the figure may be seen as a white
chalice on a black ground; or, if the white area be
taken as ground, then the figure becomes two heads
in profile silhouette. One may, upon continued inspection of this ambiguous picture, become adept at shifting
from one way of organizing it to the other, but one
can never organize it both ways at once. Furthermore,
please note that when a change in what is seen occurs,
it is not a consequence of some modification in what is
"objectively" given on the printed page—that was fixed
once and for all when the book went to press—but is,
rather, brought about by the activity of the seeing organism. Also, notice the three-dimensional quality of
the two-dimensional picture. When one sees the white
figure, the black ground is *behind* it. Likewise, a similar
depth effect occurs when the two heads are seen as if
outside a lighted window.

Figure 2 again presents an ambiguous picture, this
time one in which there is more detail. In glancing at

this, you will probably see at once a young woman in three-quarter view to the left. On the other hand, you may be that one person in about five who immediately sees an old hag facing to the left and forward. If you do

Figure 2

not for a time spontaneously reorganize what you first saw—that is, destroy it as such and use its parts to make the new picture—there are ways in which we can assist you, and these, essentially, are the same ways that will be employed in the experiments to follow.

First, though, there are several important points that we can make with the situation as it stands. Unless we had told you that there was a second picture, you certainly would not have suspected it or looked for one. You would have been quite satisfied with the correctness and adequacy of what you saw at first glance. What you now see, whichever picture it is, *is* correct. It solves for you, in terms of the way your seeing is at the moment organized, the question of "What is this a picture of?" In the context of our present discussion of figure and ground, you are probably willing to concede that we are not trying to dupe you and that the alternative organization, if it has not by this time been achieved by you, will shortly be yours and you will see the other picture just as clearly as you now see the first one. In another context, you might regard

someone who claims to see something that you do not
as mistaken, or "nuts," and pass on.

If you see a young woman where we say there is an
old woman, you might, if a compliant type, decide to
submit and say what we say. If we greatly outnumber
you—if we, for instance, are "society" and you an "individual"—then, if you will yield and agree with us,
we shall reward you by acknowledging that now you
are behaving "normally." Please note, however, that in
such case your acceptable behavior will have been imposed upon you and you will not be living it *on your
own*. You will be in agreement with us only on a verbal
basis, not on the basis of *seeing,* which is *non-verbal*.

This picture has been constructed so that various of
its details have a dual function. The long promontory
which is the old hag's nose is the whole cheek and
jaw-line of the young woman. The hag's left eye is the
young woman's left ear, her mouth the young woman's
velvet neckband or choker, her right eye a bit of the
young woman's nose, etc. If we could trace these for
you it would be more helpful, but by now you probably have seen the second picture. It will have come
suddenly, perhaps startling you into a little exclamation of surprise. This is what gestalt psychologists call
the "aha!" experience. Their formal name for it is insight.

To give further illustration of what is meant by
insight or sudden reorganization of behavior, we present Figures 3, 4 and 5. The first is "easy," the second
"harder," and the last "very hard" for most persons,
although this order by no means holds in all cases.
These are not ambiguous pictures. They are incomplete
objects, with much of the detail which would ordinarily
be present left out. However, the bits which are present
are in their proper positions, and the work which must
be done to see and name the object involves a kind of
"subjective" filling in of the blank spaces in such a way,
as the gestaltists put it, as to effect "closure." Staring
fixedly at what is given, or deliberate attempts to force
meaning on the hodge-podge of parts, usually blocks
the spontaneous process of reorganization. That this

must be spontaneous, as opposed to something deliberately decided upon, is shown by the failure of any attempt to "will" to see the old hag or the young woman. Freely shifting your gaze from one part to another and taking, if you can, an attitude of eager curiosity rather than vexed impatience, is the most favorable approach. If the pictures still do not come, they will at some later time when you examine them afresh.

In the experiments to follow, when we talk of figure and ground, it may or may not be in a visual sense. We have used visual examples here because they are the only kind we can present in a book, but later we shall request you, for example, to examine bits of muscular tension which you may find here and there in your body, tinglings, itches, or even blank spots, and

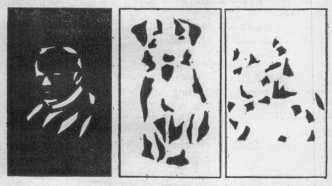

Figures 3, 4, 5

From Street, Roy F., Gestalt Completion Test. *Bureau of Publications, Teachers College, Columbia University, 1931. Reprinted by permission of the publisher and the author.*

to see whether they will perhaps suddenly come together as a gestalt—in this case a motor gestalt which is the beginning pattern of action of something that you want to do. This will be difficult, time-consuming, exasperating. When you fail to get quick results, you may abandon the whole program, condemning it as a stupid waste of valuable time, or, at the very least, complaining that the instructions should have made the work clearer, quicker and easier. These can be and will be improved. In fact, you can contribute to their improvement by reporting your difficulties to us, addressing us through our publisher. But we cannot do the work for you. Like seeing the other picture in the example given above, you must do this for yourself if it is ever to be done.

I I

CONTACTING THE ENVIRONMENT

EXPERIMENT 1: Feeling the Actual

Our first move is directed at helping you to heighten your feeling of what is actual. Most people admit that at times they are only half there, that they daydream, lose track of things, or otherwise wander off from the present situation. They also comment about others: "He doesn't stay on the spot," or "He doesn't keep his eye on the ball"—or, in general, "He doesn't make good contact."

Contact does not imply a constant state of pop-eyed alertness. This would indicate chronic apprehensiveness, which usually rests on a *mis*apprehension of actuality. There are occasions when it is appropriate to let go, grow hazy, and bask in animal comfort. That few of us can do this fully is a curse of our times—a consequence of "unfinished business"—but the ability to do so, which for the most part we now know about only from envious watching of our household tabby, is one that we can reacquire.

Apart from such moments of occasional bliss, when we can afford to let alertness dissolve and give place to a diffuse glow of well-being, there are other times when sharp awareness of actuality runs counter to the organism's best interests. While the dentist is extracting an infected tooth, only that patient who needs to pose as a hero will spurn the anesthetic. Nature herself sometimes acts as anesthetist when she makes a creature swoon with pain. The situation is far different, though, when one buys patented "pain-killers" at the drugstore. Here one attempts to trick the organism into losing its feeling of actuality—throbbing headache, agony of an abscessed tooth, fatigue from overwork, insomnia as an indicator of "unfinished business." These are warning signals—they indicate something amiss which needs attention—and the problem is falsely solved when one merely turns off the signal.

Obviously, there is no virtue in enduring the continuation of a warning signal after it has been heeded. If one has a toothache and has made an appointment with the dentist for the earliest possible time, then the "pain-killer" comes in handy as a way of avoiding *suffering that can do no good.* With headaches, fatigue, insomnia, the case is not so clear. Sometimes the family doctor can despatch them as readily as the dentist repairs or pulls the ailing tooth, but often even the specialist shakes his head and says he can find nothing organically wrong—though, if up-to-date, he may hint darkly of something "psychosomatic." Even so, he will be chary of recommending psychological treatment, for it is long, expensive and often unsuccessful. Frequently he will ease the patient out of his office with advice to "forget it" or "take some aspirin."

That pharmacological "pain-killers" are a means of partially blacking out one's actuality—in this case, the actuality of pain—is well-known to everyone. That comparable "pain-killers" of a behavioral sort exist and are used still more widely is less often recognized. They are not taken in pill or tablet form, and the person using them, not being aware of what he is doing, will deny that his actions have this function. Furthermore, once he has become dependent on them, it would be cruel to wrest them suddenly from him, if this were possible, just as it would be cruel to deprive an addict abruptly of his drug. But, because this is behavior which the person himself controls, whether he knows it or not, there is no way—even were it desirable, as is *not* the case—to strip it from him by force. On the other hand, should he wish to uncover such self-defeating behavior and to change it gradually, staying always within the limits of what he cares to tolerate, that is another matter.

As a first step in this direction we propose something

that will seem fatuously simple. We state it in the few indented lines below. The indentation is our device for indicating that what is set off in this fashion we wish you to take as definite instructions. In what follows there will be many such passages. Whenever possible, try them out at once before you read further. If you read on, you may by the discussions which you encounter, cheat yourself of something you might have discovered for yourself.

> Try for a few minutes to make up sentences stating what you are at this moment aware of. Begin each sentence with the words "now" or "at this moment" or "here and now."

Now, having survived this first, brief testing of the water and found it neither too hot nor too cold, let's talk about it a little. Then we shall ask you to do it again.

Whatever is actual is, as regards time, always in the present. Whatever happened in the past *was* actual then, just as whatever occurs in the future *will be* actual at that time, but what *is* actual—and thus *all* that you can be aware of—must be in the present. Hence the stress, if we wish to develop the feeling of actuality, on words such as "now" and "at this moment."

Likewise, what is actual for *you* must be where you are. Hence the stress on words like "here." You cannot at this moment experience any event—that is, live through it at first-hand—if it takes place beyond the range of your receptors. You may imagine it, yes, but that means picturing it to yourself, and the picturing will be *here* where you are.

It has been customary for psychoanalysts—for instance, in the interpretation of dreams—to speak of the present as including the recent past—say, the past twenty-four hours. But whenever we speak of the present, we shall mean the immediate, here-and-now present—the time of your present attention-span, the time that is *right now!*

Remembering and anticipating are actual, but when

they occur, they occur in the present. *What* you remember will be something seen or heard or done in
the past, but its recapture or review is in the present.
What you anticipate will be something which, if it
happens, will happen at some time in the future, but
such *fore*-seeing is the *present* seeing of a picture which
you here and now construct and label "future."

These considerations may seem so trite as to need no
further pounding home. But examine, for instance,
these remarks from an intelligent student: "I feel that
we are all living too much in the present and disregard
to a painful degree the memories and lessons of the
past. Similarly there is too much preoccupation with
the present and not nearly enough consideration of the
results of our current activities and their effect upon
the future." What is missing here is a clear comprehension that the aim of this experiment is not to get us to
live more exclusively *for* the present, blind to what the
past should have taught us or foolhardy about what
lies ahead and needs to be prepared for, but, rather,
to get us to live *in* the present. Living fully in the
present includes taking note of present reminders of
past lessons and thus making more adequate present
responses; and it includes taking note of present har-
bingers of things to come and adjusting our present
behavior accordingly. The healthy person, with the
present as reference-point, is free to look backward or
ahead as occasion warrants.

A point that could bog us down in metaphysical
mires if we did not meet it and dispose of it is raised
by this statement from a student: "Others may be
able to remain in the now, but, unfortunately, I find it
completely impossible. There can be no constant now
for me. At this very moment I have just passed now."

The wish to seize the present and pin it down—to
mount it, as it were, like a butterfly in a case—is
doomed to failure. Actuality forever changes. In
healthy persons the feeling of actuality is steady and
continuous but, like the view from a train window, the
scenery is always different. We shall see later that
when actuality seems fixed, permanent, unchanged and

unchangeable, this is a fictional actuality which we *continuously build anew* because it serves some present purpose of our own to preserve the fiction.

Actuality, as you experience it, is *your* actuality. You cannot experience what is actuality for someone else because you cannot tune in on his private receptors. If you were able to, you would *be* that person. You can share an experience with someone in the sense that you and he may experience similarly some situation which you and he have in common, but what he experiences is *his* and what you experience is *yours*. When you say to a friend in trouble, "I feel for you," you do not mean that literally, since he is doing his own feeling and no-one else can do it for him, but simply that you, by imagining yourself in his place, construct a vivid picture of what the situation would be like—and then react to that.

Now let us go back to the experiment once more. As you again produce sentences stating what you are aware of, put a pedantic emphasis on the words "now," "here," and "at this moment." While this will be merely a verbal artificiality which we do not expect you to continue for the rest of your life, it will assist you not only to realize (make real) the nowness of your experience, but also to verbalize what you are doing or about to do, thus sharpening your awareness that it is *you* who experience whatever it may be. Feel the meaning of the now-here as *your own* now-here; thus, "Now I, with my breathing body sitting *here* in the chair, the chair in the room, the room in the neighborhood—*now* in the afternoon, this particular day, in this Twentieth Century—I *now-here* am doing so and so." To repeat:

> Try for a few minutes to make up sentences stating what you are immediately aware of. Begin them with the words "now" or "at this moment" or "here and now."

Next we go to a very important part of the experiment. As you perform it, what difficulties do you encounter?

This question may come as a surprise. A common remark at this point is, "Difficulties? There aren't any difficulties. It's pretty dull, but—no difficulties." Then let us ask this: why did you terminate the experiment just when you did? We are not suggesting you should have continued longer, but simply asking if you are aware of what immediately preceded your stopping. Were you tired? Had you gone blank and ceased forming sentences? Or did you, perhaps, quit without being aware that you were quitting?

Let us review some difficulties reported by others. These may not be your particular stumbling-blocks. We mention them to give you some notion of the range of reactions to this experiment, to show you that nothing extraordinary is expected and also that you need not be disappointed if at this stage you do not already "feel like a different person." If you are dissatisfied with the work so far, admit it. If you begrudge the waste of your time, then be aware of your resentment toward us for having misled you into this. One student said, "I was told this would seem fatuously simple. Well, it did—and it still does!"

When this experiment is conducted in the doctor-patient situation, the patient in many ways can go through the motions in a fashion which observes the letter but not the spirit. For instance, an obsessional case, a Mary-Mary-quite-contrary, produced sentences like these: "Now yesterday I saw my friend" and "At this moment I shall see my friend tomorrow." This illustrates how easy it can be to win petty victories by carrying out instructions in a way that defies or nullifies their intent. To some extent most people have such a need for personal triumph over someone, and it is important to be on the lookout for this motive in doing these self-awareness experiments. While certainly you may not respond in this particular way, you may somehow feel that we are challenging you to a kind of tug-of-war, in which you must defend yourself against us. If so, you have the decisive advantage, for, so long as you feel that way, we cannot budge you. What we wish to do is to ally ourselves with you and help you to budge yourself. Should you succeed to the end in demonstrating that you can do these experiments and still remain unmoved, over whom would you have won a victory?

Let us suppose that, far from being defiant, you are, instead, a good, well-behaved type who swallows indiscriminately whatever is offered. If you are such an "introjector," you will find later experiments on chewing difficult but useful. Your initial reaction, though, may be one of enthusiastically talking about this program to your friends but neglecting to chew your way into it with your own teeth.

Or you may be a person who does not want to get close enough to his experience to feel it vividly. A student reported: "I gave considerable practice to the 'now' and 'here' awareness process, but concluded that these things are only actions and reactions which have become conditioned responses. It is convenient, probably necessary, that they be relegated to the level of automatic habits." Habit, certainly, conserves time and energy, and our organized ways of dealing with things would be disrupted if we had to give close attention to every detail. When routine matters are truly routine, they are best handled in ways so standardized as to require the very minimum of attention. What makes this best, though, is that attention is thereby freed to deal with what is novel and non-routine. To make a point of maximizing automatic functioning and minimizing awareness in one's life is to welcome death before its time. It is the goal of the cybernetics workers in reverse—instead of trying, as they do, to make robots which are more and more like men, it is an attempt to make oneself more and more a robot.

Again, you may be a person who is abashed, when you try to feel your actuality, to discover what a commonplace, lackluster actuality it is. Students have reported, "I am ashamed to say that I was not able to be aware of anything very remarkable. It was just such dull stuff as, 'Now my nose itches' and 'Here and now I scratch it.'" But what impossible kind of actuality are you demanding if you require that, at any given moment when you try to feel it, it must be wondrous and exotic? If nothing more exciting is at hand to give attention to, what could be more healthy than to become aware of an itching nose and to scratch it? On the other hand, should you find your actuality chronically dull and uninteresting, what is to keep you from doing something to liven it up? What hindrances in this direction are you aware of?

We are not at the moment suggesting that, in connection with whatever you become aware of, you rush pellmell into action. Manipulation of actuality we shall deal with later. Here we focus exclusively on the topic, "What *is* your actuality? Can you genuinely *feel* it? Can you feel that it is *yours?*"

Although the instructions for this experiment are as clear and simple as we can make them at this time, there is nothing we can do to keep you from reading in additional instructions of your own and then attributing them to us. For instance, a student, without being aware that these were his own instructions to himself rather than those given on the printed page, concluded that what this experiment called upon him to do was to search for something that was missing in his feeling of actuality. He stated, "I looked and looked but didn't find anything that was missing." His procedure is akin to making a roll-call by requesting all those not present to shout out their names. What one *can* do is bit by bit to extend one's awareness by discovering and dissolving the resistances in oneself which have prevented this, but one cannot command what one is unaware of to march obediently into awareness.

Nevertheless, we know from clinical practice that there may be a gross neglect of areas of awareness which may be corrected simply by pointing it out. For instance, one patient may make sentences only about what he is aware of by means of exteroceptors, while another may report awareness of no events other than those taking place inside his skin—the beating of his heart, the pulsing of his arteries, the aches, the tensions. Are we to suppose from this that, for the first person, actuality is limited exclusively to what may be seen and heard, and that, for the second, no "external" events exist? No, but we can say that these patients differ radically in where they direct their attention and in what they exclude from attention. If they were running a newspaper, we would say that they favor some available news-sources to the exclusion of others, and our advice to them would be, "Whether you choose to print it or not, take notice of the range and kind of information that is pouring into your editorial office. Maybe you're passing up some good bets."

You may react to the experiment—this one or others to come—as if it were some kind of test of your potency; that is, you will do it, prove to yourself that you can do it—and leave it at that. But of course you *can* do it! Anybody can, to a degree. The point, though, is to achieve a result that makes it worthwhile —a genuine change in your perspective of events, the feeling that you are a *continuous flow* of processes. We may suspect that something less than this had been obtained by a student when he claimed, "I tried the experiment. Really, I was completely successful in that I got just the feeling that the writers wanted and which I also wanted." Proving one's potency in this manner is perhaps the most dangerous of all self-deceptions.

Some persons, confronted with these experiments, undertake to decide in advance how or whether they will have any effect; for instance, "I have spent hours trying to decide how and to what extent the experiments on self-awareness would change my sensory and conscious thought-experiences. First, I wanted to know if the sought-after end-result would bring about a change that I would welcome. Second, I wanted to know if the time and effort would be worthwhile. . . . At the present time I have not achieved any miraculous sense of awareness." Words are wonderful tools in their place, but why would anyone sit for hours with a meal prepared before him trying to reach a verbal decision as to whether it would taste good and be worth the effort of eating? Or, having taken a bite or two, why expect something "miraculous"? If one waters a plant, does it instantly burst into bloom?

Perhaps, after these comments from others who have worked at the task, you are ready to try again. This time, maybe, you can notice more clearly when and if you leave the present. And if so, where do you tend to go? Some people suddenly find that it is as if they were *in* the past or *in* the future, without awareness that it is now and here that they reminisce about the past or anticipate the future. Other people, or these same people at other times, find that, while they maintain present tense, they do not stay *here*. It is as if they were outside themselves, observing their own experience as an onlooker rather than being the immediate experiencer. As one student put it, "I take a man-from-Mars view of myself." Whatever you discover in this regard, don't try to compel yourself to change it and somehow force yourself to stay in the here-and-now. Just notice what you do in as great detail as possible.

Make up sentences about what you are immediately aware of. Begin them with "now" or "at this moment" or "here and now."

Discussion of this experiment has been unusually prolonged because it is the first. Many of the points made will apply as well to all subsequent experiments, but will not be repeated there. Let us conclude by considering the here-now procedure in comparison to the approaches of Freud and Adler.

These two men, each expressing what was characteristic of his own personality, laid stress, respectively, on past and future. In their work with neurotics they indulged, each in his own way, the patient's wish to dig into the past or to safeguard the future. Delving into the past serves the purpose of finding "causes" —and thus excuses—for the present situation. That the present is an outgrowth of the past no-one will deny, but it does not, for instance, solve present problems to blame one's parents for the way they brought one up.

Suppose, as an example, that you treasure memories of how your father has frustrated you. Such memories are important for you in actuality only insofar as you *now* feel that what you expected from your father is *still* to be fulfilled or that your resentment at its non-fulfillment is *still* to be expressed—in short, that your relationship with your father still *presents* a problem to be attended to and solved. Otherwise, your brooding on the past is a mere pretense of attacking your problems and is actually a convenient refuge from them.

If, instead of carping about the past, one clings to it as "the good old times" or one's "golden childhood," one is again escaping present frustrations or even neglecting present enjoyments by sentimentalizing or glamorizing what is past.

Adler, contrary to Freud, encouraged his patient in a futuristic attitude. He asked him to dwell upon his life-plan or prospect, his ambition, his final goal. Such a procedure aggravates what is already the usual tendency—to try to be, however impossible, always a step ahead of actuality. People who live futuristically never catch up with the events for which they have prepared and do not reap the fruits of their sowing. They rehearse for even the most unimportant interview and then have no ability to act spontaneously when it arrives. Situations for which they have failed to prepare catch them utterly at a loss.

If your view of the future is not apprehensive but rosy, why do you so paint it? Are you consoling yourself for some present frustration with daydreams, resolutions and promissory notes? Is your hope for tomorrow a means of putting off doing something today? Now, as you know very well, the future course of events can rarely be predicted with much accuracy. Do you, perhaps, count on this real uncertainty so as to avoid involving yourself in what is certain—namely, the present—or even adopt such an attitude as a secret way to disappoint and punish yourself?

Let us emphasize strongly here that we do not wish our experiments to foster new repressions, to rouse guilt feelings, to make the personality shrink still further. On the contrary, the aim is to expand or, better, to heighten awareness of what you are doing and how you are doing it. For instance, in this experiment on actuality, what present grudge, gratitude, remorse, or excuse makes you anticipate the future? Our method is not to suppress that grudge or that ambition, but simply for you to become aware that, in terms of the way you are now *structured,* this is how you behave! With awareness this structure will change in line with changes in your functioning, and your escapes into past and future will diminish. Do not moralize to yourself about escapist tendencies, but simply *describe* them in terms of the actuality—that is, as behavior that is going on.

The relationship of past and future must be continually re-examined in the present. A useful way to begin is to *describe* the scene and situation you are in. Suppose, for example, you omit the reading which you ordinarily do in the subway on the way to work and instead look around and commence an internal monologue: "At this moment I am riding in the subway. Now the train is swaying. Now people are beginning to move toward the exit. Now this man is looking at me. Now I am concerned with how I impress him." Stay aware of the two parts of the experiment: (1) to use "now" or an equivalent in *every* sentence, and (2) to discover your resistances to doing so—for instance, that you get bored or annoyed or, more likely, lose ("flee from") the sense of actuality.

The theory of these two parts is this: *To the extent that your feeling of actuality has been split off from your workaday personality, the effort to experience actuality will rouse anxiety (masked, perhaps, as fatigue, boredom, impatience, annoyance)—and what specifically rouses your anxiety will be the particular resistance by which you throttle and prevent full experience.* We shall discuss this in more detail later. In this experiment we are concerned only with your discovering the *actuality of such resistances* to what, on the face of it, is a "fatuously simple" procedure.

For the most part you will not notice the transition from contacting your environment to wandering off into thoughts about past and future. You may simply have the experience of catching yourself fleeing, or waking up with a start from daydreaming, or, on the other hand, of fearing to lose yourself in "thoughts" lest you thereby miss your station.

A by-product of this experiment on the feeling of actuality—the use and meaning of the words "now" and "here"—will be to increase your sense of the concreteness of experience and to sharpen the difference between the concrete and the abstract (generalized). Both concrete immediate experience and abstract generalizing, classifying, etc., are healthy functions of the personality, but they are *different modes* of behaving. To confuse them means to regard actual things and persons as stereotypes, as vague and irrelevant furniture, or, on the other hand, as mere bogeymen who do not really exist. The feeling of actuality dissipates such vagueness, and to this we shall return in a later experiment.

To over-emphasize the abstract is characteristic of so-called intellectuals. With some of them one feels that what they say derives solely from other words—the books they have read, the lectures they have attended, or the discussions they have engaged in—without much flesh-and-blood contact with the nonverbal. For such persons the attempt to become aware of their immediate experience may be disturbing at first and feel like strenuous work. We quote from a student's report:

"I went through the first experiment for what seemed about fifteen minutes. Increasing impatience was the main reason for stopping. It was an unusual experience. The word 'now' is very successful in bringing about the feeling of the immediateness of being. This gave me a sense of fear, that I can describe only as breathing very deeply while feeling a constriction in the chest. On the other hand, an instant's experience was much richer than ever before, and I could actually see things in the environment at which I had only *looked* before. I was in my room, and as I went through the experiment I felt a drive to straighten out and put in order whatever was amiss. It was like seeing the things in it for the first time or after a long absence. The objects had an identity of their own, stood around me, but were in no way continuous with me. A tendency to go off into abstract thinking kept creeping in.

"The second time I tried the experiment I noticed the recurrence of the same sense of fear at the realization of the actuality of being alive, and also the tendency to indulge in adding modalities, qualifications, adjectives, to the objects observed rather than concentrating on the experience of the act of observing, which I found mentally tiring and disturbing.

"On a third occasion I practiced the experiment on the subway. The experience was rich and penetrating. The sense of fear was still present but to a slighter degree, perhaps because of other people around me. My ability to see seemed multiplied a hundredfold and this gave me strong pleasure. After a while it was like playing an amusing game, but one exacting much energy."

To reacquire the full feeling of actuality is an experience of tremendous impact, moving to the core. In the clinical situation patients have cried out, "Suddenly I feel like jumping into the air!" and "I'm walking, really walking!" and "I feel so peculiar—the world is there, *really there!* And I have eyes, *real eyes!*" But there is a long road from this present experiment to such a full experience.

EXPERIMENT 2: Sensing Opposed Forces

In the previous experiment we asked what difficulties you encountered, and these we called "resistances." Now we must try to understand who or what does the resisting. As a clue, which you may easily verify, consider what happens when instructions for the actuality experiment are put to a healthy child. He finds in them nothing strange, artificial, or an affront to his dignity, and, if you are his friend, he straightway obliges with a copious flow of here-and-now sentences. In fact, at a certain stage in language development, he delivers spontaneous monologues which are play-by-play accounts of his aims and actions. Compared with ours, his resistances to the actuality experiment are negligible.

It would thus appear that the resistances are not present to begin with. If we can understand how we acquired them, this should give some pointers on how to get rid of them. But in the present experiment we merely take the first step toward realizing that they—the resistances—belong to us, are *ours,* just as much as whatever they resist. This is difficult, for it involves discovering that we ourselves interfere with our own activity—in short, that, without being aware of it, we launch counterattacks against our own effort, interest, or excitement.

As an approach, let us consider the concept of equilibrium. At its core is the notion of a balance of forces. In the chemistry laboratory a student who has been instructed to use five grams of a certain compound determines this quantity by first putting a standard weight—a bit of metal known to weigh five grams —into one pan of his balance. In the other pan he adds the compound until both pans hang in the air, with precise balance indicated when the pointer on the scale stands at zero. Any tendency for it to move in one direction is exactly counterbalanced or canceled by the equal and opposite tendency to move in the other.

The car of an elevator hangs in its shaft in such fashion that the cables supporting it run over pulleys at the top of the shaft and down to heavy metal plates which weigh just about as much as the car. For the car to rise the motor needs to exert a force only slightly greater than that which is necessary to counterbalance the weight of the passengers or freight; conversely, for the car to descend the motor must expend a force somewhat less than the weight of the cargo. This illustrates the fact that where large forces are truly in balance it requires but little additional force, added to one side or the other, to produce large changes.

A moving body does not come to rest until it meets opposing forces sufficient to counteract its further progress. A bullet fired from a gun does not, of course, go on forever, but it comes to rest much sooner if aimed, say, into the trunk of a hardwood tree than if discharged into a bale of cotton. Likewise, as is now well known, a feather, released in a vacuum jar, falls just as heavily to the bottom as a chunk of lead.

Moving on from such simple equilibria, now consider some that require constant rebalancing. The total life-processes of an organism demand continual rebalancing, but let us for the moment limit ourselves to the single activity of riding a bicycle. For the beginner this is an impossible feat. When he wobbles too far to one side, either he fails to compensate adequately by shifting weight or steering, or, in desperation, overcompensates—and then falls off on the other side. If, despite setbacks and bruises, he persists in trying to ride, eventually he handles the continuous adjustments, originally so troublesome, almost automatically. He does not reach a static equilibrium on his bicycle. Rather, he becomes expert in correcting disequilibria before they go too far—but this, far from seeming burdensome, provides much of the fun of riding.

To attain and maintain a healthy equilibrium in his activities a person must be able—like the poised rider of a bicycle—to appreciate and act upon differences in his situation as they occur. These may be subtle or so striking that they cannot be overlooked. For anything to be noticed at all, however, it must somehow be distinguishable from its background. It must differ from it in a way, as someone has said, "that makes a difference." If, to a pure white surface you add a patch of white, it goes unnoticed because, literally, it doesn't make any difference. A patch of black, on the other hand, provides maximum contrast and is seen as blacker and the white whiter than would be the case if either were seen by itself.

Many phenomena could not exist if their opposites did not also exist. If day were indistinguishable from night, no such distinction would ever have been made and we would lack the corresponding words. Now, as a first step in this experiment:

Think of some pairs of opposites in which neither member could exist were it not for the real or implied existence of its opposite.

You may be dissatisfied with a number of the pairs of opposites you produced. Some, you may feel, are not genuine opposites, and others are opposites only in a very specific context. With some pairs you may have found that there were additional phenomena which fitted intermediate positions. For instance, "beginning —end" has an in-between term, "middle"; "past— future" has "present"; "desire—aversion" has "indifference." The middle term in such pairs is especially interesting, since it often constitutes a "neutral-" or "zero-" or "indifference-point" along some kind of dimension or continuum. On an algebraic scale numerical values diminish one by one until zero is reached; beyond zero they increase again, but as negative values. The gear-shift on many devices has extreme positions labeled "forward" and "reverse" and an intermediate position "neutral," in which, with the motor running, the device remains stationary or "idling."

The pilot of a carrier-based plane must take off from a short runway. Unless he can attain speed sufficient to support him in the air by the time he reaches the end of the deck, he will simply drop off into the water. To minimize this hazard he first "revs up" his engine, while his brakes, fully applied, hold him stationary. Then, when his motor is whirling the propeller at such a rate that the plane shakes, throbs, strains at the brakes, he suddenly releases them and flashes into the air. Until this point the pilot, identifying himself with his ship, might verbalize his sense of the opposed forces by saying, "I feel the tremendous urge to fly, but also the equal and opposite tendency to hold back. If I kept this up for long, it would shake me to pieces." And, of course, the whole maneuver would be completely senseless if there were not the clear intention, when the right moment came, to release the brakes and take off.

Note the difference between idling in "neutral," where no force is applied forward or backward, and straining forward with the brakes set. The first is a situation of "resting," while the second is one of extreme conflict. In the case of the plane, the opposition is not forward—backward, but moving—not moving. A mechanical example of forward—backward conflict would be the situation where a ferry boat, coming into its slip too fast, reverses its engines to slow its forward momentum.

"Creative pre-commitment" is the situation of being at the "indifference-point" of a continuum, poised between but *aware of and interested in the potential situations which extend in either direction.* One feels the beckonings to action, but is not yet committed to either side.

Now, to return to the original problem, just what does all this have to do with resistances? Situations in which you encounter blocks in carrying out tasks which you have set for yourself are conflict-situations —and, furthermore, *the conflict is between one part of your personality and another.* Of one part you are aware, the part which sets the tasks and tries to carry them through. Of the other part, the resister, you are less or not at all aware. To the extent that you run up against resistances, they frequently seem, far from being of your own creation, to be imposed and inflicted on you from outside.

If these experiments simply sent you about your ordinary business, you would experience little conflict, for in those situations you know very well how to avoid conflict. Instead, this work is designed with the express purpose of making trouble for you. It is intended to make you aware of conflicts in your own personality. If this were the full scope of the program, you could justly charge us with malevolence. But there is this further plan: to show you how, by appropriate action, the *re*sister can be reclaimed from unawareness and transformed into a most valuable *as*sister. The resisting part of your personality has vitality and strength and many admirable qualities, so that, while it is a long and arduous job to achieve full reintegration of these disintegrated parts, to settle for less when it is unnecessary is to ratify the permanent loss of parts of your personality. The brighter side of the picture is that, before you have proceeded far, you are likely to feel that you have already salvaged priceless potentialities and energies.

In these theoretical remarks we have split you as a person into two warring camps. If you are incredulous about this, we strain your incredulity a bit further by asking you to accept, as your own, the conflict between these factions.

How are you to go about acquiring a sense of the opposed factors in your make-up? Well, along the lines just mentioned, would we not have to infer that the wishes and inclinations of this resister, of whom you are so little aware, must be *the opposite of the ones you feel that you bring to the task?* And would it not follow, then, that you might get some notion of how things look to the resister if you tried to imagine the direct opposite of whatever you, as the aware person, believe to be the case? If this seems worth a trial, do the following:

Consider some everyday life-situations, objects or activities as if they were *precisely the opposite* of what you customarily take them to be. Imagine yourself in a situation the reverse of your own, where you have inclinations and wishes exactly contrary to your usual ones. Observe objects, images and thoughts as if their function or meaning were the antithesis of what you habitually take them to be. Furthermore, confronting them thus, hold in abeyance your standard evaluations of good or bad, desirable or repugnant, sensible or silly, possible or impossible. Be satisfied to stand between them—or, rather, above them—at the zero-point, interested in both sides of the opposition but not siding with either.

A benefit which comes from developing your ability to see things in reverse—to be uncommittedly interested in the opposites—is *the power to make your own evaluations*. Psychoanalysis has brought about many reversals. What used to be considered good—for instance, sexual inhibition—is now judged to be bad; what used to be rejected is now accepted. When patients came to Freud with concealments, he urged them to reveal. When he noticed that dreams were new synthetic unities, he set about to analyze them into separate elements. But, if all this is to be evaluated as good, by what criterion is it to be so evaluated?

How is the patient to know that his analyst's evaluation of sexual inhibition is better than his own? If the analyst uses knowledge and authority to impose *his* evaluation—meanwhile disparaging the patient's opposite evaluation as resistance, negative transference, or irrational conscience—he may, by convincing the patient that he is wrong, foist on him a new compulsive morality *in the opposite direction!* But if, instead of this, the patient can come to feel within his own personality the actual clash of opposite evaluations without being swept off his feet or compelled, then, instead of being a person who feels himself as always *being judged,* he will begin to feel (as will be clearer later on) what actually is the case—that, ultimately, *he himself is the person who does the judging*.

Perform the reversal experiment in a playful spirit. Never mind what amusing or tragic aspects the reversed situation may assume. As Socrates pointed out, the comic and tragic are not far apart, and the same event from different points of view may be comic or tragic. The mischance of a child or adolescent is comic to an adult—for instance, "he looks so cute when he cries" or "he's suffering from puppy love." And adult woes are comic to the gods. Change places, for once.

Reverse such details as the "p" to "q" in a line of type, or turn the "p" upside down to "b". Reverse other letters which change meaning when rearranged. Notice what happens if you spell words backward, for instance, "lap" and "pal." Inability to notice such reversals is an important part of the reading difficulties and mirror-writing of some children.

Imagine the *motions* around you as if they occurred the other way around, as in a reverse-motion moving-picture film, where a diver sails gracefully from the springboard into the water and then with equal ease flies back up from the water to the springboard.

Reverse *functions*. Under what circumstances might a chair be used to eat from and a table as something on which to sit? Instead of looking through a telescope at the moon, make the man in the moon look at you. Take the white ceiling and blue walls of your room and imagine them the other way around. Turn the pictures upside down. Allow submarines and fishes to fly through the air. Let loose the schizophrenic possibilities of your imagination—for most of them are no more strange than the bitterly held conviction that persons, and society as a whole, act in an obviously sensible way.

Freud made a significant observation when he said that if we find people standing on their heads, we have to turn them upside down to put them back on their feet. Take, for instance, the extremely common way in which the "need to be loved" is mistaken for "loving." The neurotic claims to be full of love and kindness, but then it turns out that what he does for the beloved stems mainly from fear of rejection. Similarly, we often meet our "dear friends" with feelings of disgust and hostility. You may have noticed (in others) that all over-compensations are reversals of the original tendency. Compulsive modesty covers greed and cockiness hides inner shakiness.

Consider what the situation would be if you hadn't got out of bed this morning. What would happen in a certain situation if, for once, you said "no" instead

of "yes"? What if you were four inches taller? Or
twenty pounds leaner? What if you were a man instead of a woman or vice versa?

Every credit is a debit, a transfer from somewhere.
Nature does her bookkeeping by double-entry. Every
addition is somewhere a subtraction. The food we
wrest from the soil impoverishes the soil, and by disregarding this obvious reversal man has made barren
areas and dustbowls. So, think of something you have
acquired and consider where it has been lost somewhere else. What if you had failed to get it? And, with
regard to something you didn't obtain, what would
now be the situation if you had?

Reactions to this experiment fall roughly into two
classes. For a majority it is a release from the "strait-
jacket" of the actuality experiment and a chance "to
use the imagination." For others it is a "foolish mess-
ing around with what all the time you know isn't so,"
or an uncalled for interruption of the tried and true
policy of "letting sleeping dogs lie." For instance:

". . . .In any event, I had too many years when my
opinions were dispassionately formless; all I can say
is that I felt like a lost soul. With accumulation of experience I began to have my own opinions formed on
empiricism and for the first time began to feel some
sense of direction. In other words, I became 'hide-
bound.' All right! But that's better than feeling like an
amoeba. It seems more important to consider the accuracy of decisions an individual makes, rather than
demand a chronic state of analysis. What is accurate?
Evidently, what is considered eminently sensible by
the society, a consensus of opinion. Has society any
monopoly on truth? Probably not, but you cannot de-
part publicly too radically from the consensus. After
all, despite the lack of funds and the over-crowded
conditions of state hospitals, there is only so much
bizarre behavior you can get away with before you
find yourself committed."

Can we venture a guess at the premise which must
underlie such statements? At the very least, they imply
that one had better toe the mark of conventional be-

havior pretty carefully, on pain of being shut away in a psychiatric hospital. To be sure, bizarre behavior *can* lead to commitment—and thought is a form of behavior. But is it reasonable to view what you have been asked to do in this experiment as bringing you dangerously close to the brink? Or may we say that here is a man who feels obliged to summon up pretty frightful bogeymen to keep himself walking a chalk-line?

Some persons make difficulties for themselves by demanding that they be able to find something that is, in literal detail, the exact opposite of something else. For example:

"I am typing. What is its opposite? Now I'm balked. What is the opposite of typing? Not typing. But that is just negation and doesn't leave anything. So I try various situations as opposites to typing, but none fits. Is canoeing the opposite of typing? Is conducting an orchestra its opposite? True, they're not typing, but they're also not its opposite."

Now, for any highly differentiated activity or structure there is no reason at all to suppose that by looking around one can find another activity or structure which would be for it a perfect match in reverse. But, to stick with typing, consider what you do. You put words on paper. What is the opposite? You take them off— that is, you erase. Or, again, what are you typing? Perhaps a letter accepting a job. What is its opposite? A letter of resignation. Or, to shift the context again, the opposite of typing is to get someone else to do your typing. That the validity of opposites depends upon appropriate context is a point to which we shall return shortly.

For some it is the height of absurdity to suppose that altering the position or sequence of letters in a line of type should pose a problem for anyone, but consider the following:

"When reversing such details as "p" to "q", etc., I found that disturbing, too. It was the same reaction I get when seeing a person opening a can or a package of cigarettes upside down. For me things have to be precisely as they ought to be—that is, the correct way. When I get in bed at night I can't go to sleep if I know that a drawer is open or the door to the closet is not shut. It's something that's wrong, something that should not be."

Another student had still greater trouble with the letter-reversals:

"When I turned letters around I became nervous. My heart began to beat faster and my eyes began to water. Since I was just looking at words on a page and trying to imagine how they would look twisted around, I thought maybe somehow I was straining my eyes to do it. So I tried writing them down in reverse and then looking at them—but after that my eyes watered so much I couldn't even look at them! That's crazy! What are you doing to us with these experiments?"

"Creative pre-commitment" can be misconstrued to be a state of chronic indecisiveness, rather than the phase of orienting to diverse possibilities and actualities, or even, after trying out one unsuccessful plan of action, of returning to the zero-point to reorient with respect to other possibilities. A student said, "The attitude of seeing both sides ultimately results in an aloofness from reality." Perhaps he is referring to the trick of pitting one argument against another as an excuse for not taking action and, if so, we would agree with him that this involves "aloofness from reality"; but we would say that it is the need to be aloof which gives rise to and supports this stratagem rather than the other way around.

In trying to reverse one of his important life-situations a student reports as follows:

"The real situation is this: my sweetheart is coming home soon, after being over in Europe for nearly nine months, and when she does we're going to get married. I have the just-can't-wait feeling about it all.

"Now if I try to imagine having opposite 'wishes and inclinations' I come up with something like this: I don't want her to come home; I don't love her; I'd rather run around with lots of new girls for another few years. Now that I've written this, I see there's a little truth in the last thing I said.

"That leads me to criticize what you said about the numbers that algebraically approach zero and then increase again, only this time negative in value. This is a pretty complicated way to say something unimportant. Furthermore, it's wrong, because the truth about a situation is spread pretty well over the whole continuum. One side is not all positive, or all negative, and therefore what you said is misleading. . . . Then again, perhaps only to me."

We can use the above excerpt to illustrate several points. The first paragraph states this young man's official position with respect to his coming marriage —namely, he was completely sold on it. Then, in the very process of typing statements expressing the opposite situation, he recognized that he also possessed some contradictory feelings where previously he had suspected none. With little reading between the lines it may be inferred that he then became angry with us for having led him to this unwelcome insight, for he at once attacked some of our statements. Finally, having expressed his aggression appropriately—that is, directly to the very ones who roused it in him—the air was cleared and he could in the end acknowledge that perhaps his objections were highly personal.

Another man, a prospective father, by the reversal-experiment foresaw that the little "credit" who was on the way would also entail some debits:

"My wife and I are planning a family, and I look forward with great eagerness to the prospect of having a child. To picture a situation where I could not stand such a prospect, I dwelt upon—and was surprised at how readily they occurred to me!—the loss of freedom, disturbances in the middle of the night, medical expense, and all the other possible disad-

vantages. I genuinely realized the truth of the statement, 'There are no credits without debits.' "

Some reversals have a nightmarish quality. A zoolo-
gy student reported, "I am not dissecting the fetal pig.
Now it is dissecting me!" If you will notice your
dreams, you will discover that you can make sense of
a great many by treating them as reversal experiments
spontaneously performed! In dreams, the resister gets a
chance to express himself more openly, but he does it in
a language which you, the awake personality, find
largely incomprehensible.

Daydreams, too, are spontaneous reversal experiments, and their meaning is usually much more obvious. What we fantasy ordinarily is the reverse of a
present frustration. If broke, we fantasy winning the
sweepstakes. If jilted, we wallow in fantasied revenge.
If we feel like a nobody, our daydreams put the world
at our feet. There is nothing baneful in daydreams
provided they do not crowd out "real life" efforts. If
given to daydreaming, you can learn from their content what the areas are in which you feel yourself
frustrated—that is, you can learn more clearly the
direction of your needs.

If, for instance, you daydream about being in love
with a famous film star, this may indicate, not that
you need the film star, but that you would find it re-
warding to cultivate your acquaintance with that attractive person who lives down the street. If you daydream about becoming a famous author, you probably
have latent talents in this direction worth developing.
When you follow up in a practical way the suggestions
of daydreams, the outcome, while less grandiose than
the fantasy, will be much more adequate in ministering
to your genuine needs.

A student reversed some situations in which she had
become angry at people. She reports, "Some of them
made me laugh out loud. There was relief, as if now I
was through with them."

Some persons report disturbance when they attempt
to imagine hating someone they love. Others cannot

conceive of such a possibility. One man, who tried to imagine hating his wife and could not, commented, "Perhaps this is a form of 'shrinking from completing the experiment'—but, after all, it's still less than a year since I was married!"

There are several reversals which are especially likely to produce blocking and going blank. One is the attempt to imagine oneself as being of the opposite sex. Another, which might be a good one for you to try, is to attempt to reverse roles with your parents. A student, who tried out reversals in company with her mother, states that things went swimmingly, each of them suggesting situations for the other to reverse, until the mother suggested reversal of the mother-daughter relation. "At this point," the student said, "my imagination dried up completely."

Some persons imagine situations so vividly that they can feel the beginnings of what would be the appropriate overt behavior:

> "I worked as a waitress last summer. For this experiment I thought of myself as a waitress who sat down at a table while a customer waited on me. Even though realizing the irreality, I could feel the muscles of my legs become tense in the effort to inhibit the impulse to get up and correct the situation."

Now let us look a little more closely at what you do when you treat two situations as contrasting opposites. Whether aware of it or not, you put them in some context which includes both. So, having acquired the knack of reversing, try to sharpen the exactness of the oppositions by thinking up the precise context. For instance, "fresh" has an antithesis "rotten" in the context of eggs, but "modest" in the context of character, and "seasoned" in the context of lumber or of college slang ("frosh"). Producing the precise context will give you improved orientation. You will begin to notice without effort important connections where previously you had to search for them. Most important, the contrasts themselves will begin to appear as functional relations between the opposites—that is, they will begin to generate their own explanations. For instance, mirror-images may be understood as reversed from left to right because of the nature of the reflection, whereas camera-images are reversed both from left to right and also from top to bottom by the action of the lens.

Notice how the quality of a situation—happy or tragic, attractive or repellent—depends on the context. If to think of the loss of something you have makes you sad, try to think of someone—for example, an enemy—whom it would make glad. Once again take note of the main purpose of the experiment—to discover the circumstances or the persons that make it difficult for you, even in fantasy, to make reversals. Where do you find that you set in motion resistances to your own free activity? Do you love your parents? Then imagine in what circumstances you would hate them. Does your friend bully you? Then imagine bullying him. Can you do it? Watch for the point where anxiety, fear, or disgust comes to the foreground and makes you shrink from carrying through the experiment.

For the most part, our "obvious" preferences and "natural" ways of looking at things are mere hand-me-downs. They become routine and "right" because we hold back from even imagining the opposite. Where people lack imagination it is always because they are *afraid* even to play with the possibility of something different from the matter-of-fact to which they cling for dear life. The ability to achieve and maintain an interested impartiality between imagined opposites, however absurd one side may seem, is essential for any new creative solution of problems.

Perhaps we can make sure that this point is clear by taking a look at the behavior of political parties in a democracy with respect to some national issue. Since each party-position is espoused by a large portion of the population, it is most improbable that complete wisdom on the matter rests with either side. Neither of the "solutions" offered is likely to be a creative solution in which nothing valuable is lost. Yet each party is so immersed in its vote-getting and other obligations that it cannot be interestedly impartial, cannot think of the opposition in its precise context, cannot change the context. Almost surely this means that there are ambitions and vested interests that *are not allowed* to come into the foreground of awareness.

EXPERIMENT 3: Attending and Concentrating

The preceding two experiments were opposites. In trying to heighten your feeling of actuality you narrowed down interest to your now-here, while, on the other hand, any success in getting the sense that there are in your personality forces opposed to each other depended on widening your perspective beyond your accustomed interpretations and evaluations of things. But the aim of both was the same: namely, to help you become aware of resistances (blanknesses, counter-emotions, and other behavioral difficulties) encountered in trying seriously to carry out the experiments.

If these resistances have been severe enough to make you feel somewhat helpless and inadequate to the tasks, there is no need to be despondent. When you blocked or went blank, you may have complained, "It's because I can't concentrate," and with this we would agree, but not in the conventional sense. Inability to concentrate comes from years of carefully learning to hold parts of your personality at bay as if otherwise they would ferociously eat you up. Then, when these parts are needed for something you try to do, you cannot beckon them back by the mere crooking of a finger. It does no good for people to insist that you "pull yourself together." It does not make it any more feasible even if it is a psychoanalyst who says, "Just relax, don't censor, and remember the details of your childhood." *Except very superficially, these things cannot be done by deliberate decision!*

What can be done is what you have started to do in these experiments—that is, to become aware of your efforts and reactions and to acquire toward them an attitude of "creative pre-commitment."

First, let us distinguish between what is habitually called concentration and what is genuinely healthy, organic concentration. In our society concentration is regarded as a deliberate, strenuous, compulsive effort— something you *make yourself* do. This is to be expected where people are forever neurotically commanding, conquering and compelling themselves. On the other hand, healthy, organic concentration usually is not called concentration at all, but, on those comparatively rare occasions when it does occur, is named attraction, interest, fascination or absorption.

Watch children at their games and you will see that they are concentrating on what they are doing to such a degree that it is difficult to draw their attention away. You will notice also that they are excited about what they are doing. These two factors—*attention* to the object or activity and the *excitement* of satisfying need, interest or desire through what one is attentive to—are the substance of healthy concentration.

In deliberate concentration we "pay" attention where we feel we "ought to," at the same time withholding attention from other needs or interests. In spontaneous concentration what we are attentive to attracts to itself and includes the full range of our present interests. When we "have to" undertake a particular task, we are fortunate if deliberate concentration can turn into spontaneous concentration and draw freely on more and more of our powers until the task is finished.

Where the personality is divided with respect to a given situation, so that the part which attempts the task is confronted with a sabotaging resister, one's full power cannot flow freely to the object of attention, for part of it is already fixed on something else—perhaps precisely on interfering with and preventing the completion of the "chosen" task. Such interference the deliberately concentrating person will experience as "distraction," and he then has to use a portion of his deliberately available energy to reduce to a minimum the disruptive influence of the distraction. Carefully note what happens here in terms of his total energy as an organism. His total energy is suffering a three-way division: part goes to the task, part goes to energizing the resister, and part goes into fighting the resister. Also note that what, to the deliberately concentrating person, constitute *"dis*tractions," to the resisting part are *at*tractions elsewhere—toward something other than the task or toward fighting rather than accomplishing the task. As more and more of one's total energy gets committed to the battle over the "attractive distracter," and less and less of it remains available for proceeding along the deliberately chosen line, one experiences mounting irritability and temper until one either abandons the task as a bad job or explodes.

In other words, when one forces oneself to attend to what does not of itself draw one's interest, excitement accumulates, not toward this "chosen" object of attention, but in the struggle over the "distraction" which might really fire one's interest. (When this mounting excitement finally explodes as anger, one often turns it against some innocent bystander, as if *he* were the distracter.) Meantime, as more and more of the excitement of attentiveness becomes committed to suppressing the disturber, what one is deliberately concentrating on is correspondingly more and more drained of interest. In short, it is boring.

Boredom occurs, then, when attention is deliberately paid to something lacking interest. The situation that *could* become interesting is effectively blocked. The result is fatigue and, eventually, trance. Suddenly attention switches from the boring situation to daydreaming.

The sign of spontaneous attention and concentration is the progressive forming of a figure/ground, whether the situation be one of sensing something, making a plan, imagining, remembering, or practical activity. If both attention and excitement are present and working together, the object of attention becomes more and more a unified, bright, sharp figure against a more and more empty, unnoticed, uninteresting ground. This form of unified figure against an empty ground has been called a "good gestalt."

But the gestalt-psychologists themselves have not, on the whole, been sufficiently interested in the meaning of the ground. The ground is *everything* that is progressively eliminated from attention in the experienced situation. In the figure/ground what is included in figure and what in ground does not remain static, but changes in the course of a dynamic development.

Consider such a simple experience as observing some visual shape—for instance, a square on a blackboard. When the square becomes sharp and clear, the "everything-eliminated" comes to include the blackboard, the room, one's own body, any sensations other than this particular seeing and any interest other than this momentary interest in the square. For the gestalt to be unified and bright—a so-called "strong gestalt" —all this varied background *must* become progressively empty and unattractive. The brightness and clarity of the figure is the energy of the excitement-of-seeing-the-square which is freely being drawn from the emptying background.

A crude analogy might be to think of one's diffuse attentiveness at the start of the figure/ground process as similar to light transmitted through a pane of glass and shining on a relatively large area. No part of the area is more brightly lighted than the rest. Then, if it were possible for the pane of glass gradually to form itself into a lens, the area as a whole would darken while the spot on which the lens was focused would gradually brighten. No more energy in terms of light units would be required, but the rays would more and more converge from the periphery into the bright spot and intensify the energy there. Where this analogy obviously falls short of the figure/ground situation is that we have hypothesized nothing which would select the particular spot for the lens to focus on or the sharpness of its focus. In the organism/environment situation it is, of course, the relevance of environmental objects to the organism's needs which determines the figure/ground process. In this connection, our example of a square on a blackboard is trivial unless we think up some extraordinary circumstances. We use it only to indicate that the figure/ground process is not reserved for what is unusual or dramatic.

What we have said above about the formation of a gestalt we suggest that you verify and practice as follows:

For a brief period pay attention to some visual object—for example, a chair. As you look at it, notice how it clarifies itself by dimming out the space and objects around it. Then turn to some other nearby visual object and observe how this, in turn, begins to have quite a different background. Likewise, attend to some sound that is occurring and notice how other sounds form a background. Finally, attend to some body-feeling, such as a twinge or itch, and observe how here, too, the rest of your body-feeling recedes into the background.

The dynamic, free-flowing relation between figure and ground can be interrupted, obviously, in either of two ways: (a) the figure can become too fixedly attended to so that new interest is not allowed to enter into it from the ground (this is what occurs in compulsively deliberate attentiveness); or (b) the background can contain points of powerful attraction which cannot be emptied of interest, in which circumstance they actually distract or must be suppressed. Let us experiment with each case in turn:

(a) Stare fixedly at any shape, trying to grasp precisely this shape by itself and nothing else. You will observe that soon it becomes unclear and you want to let your attention wander. On the other hand, if you let your gaze play around the shape, always returning to it in the varying backgrounds, the shape will be unified in these successive differentiations, will become clearer, and will be seen better.

Just as when stared at, an object is unclear when it has gained attention by brute excitation of a receptor; for example, the continued howling of a siren. It is not the physical violence that causes "fatigue" but the essential lack of interest—one's inability to draw some-

thing more into the figure from the ground. If a com-
poser wishes to maintain a fortissimo—perhaps far
louder than the siren—he keeps attention by varying
the timbres and the harmony. Similarly, in spontaneously studying a picture or piece of sculpture, we let
our eyes drift across it or we move around it. If we do
not permit free change and play of observation, awareness is dulled. Thus, in deliberate concentration
which does not tend to become spontaneous, there is
fatigue, flight, and, to make up for it, *staring*.

During the war a number of fliers complained to us
of intense headaches during night landings. This was
due to staring. When taught to allow small eye-move-
ments by looking here and there about the landing
strip—that is, when they stopped staring—they found
they no longer had headaches and their vision was
sharpened. When staring is persisted in up to the point
of complete disappearance of the figure/ground, the result may be blotting out of awareness altogether; that
is, hypnotic trance.

(b) The opposite difficulty in freely forming a
figure/ground is the inability to empty the ground,
with the result that the figure falls short of becoming
unified. The extreme of this would be the experience of
chaos. To experience your environment as chaos is
not easy, because, for practical living, you must always
find differentiated unities (gestalts). Possibly you have
this feeling of chaos, though, in experiencing some
works of modern art which do not, in terms of your
past training, provide points of attention. You then
flee from the chaotic feeling because you find it painful or ludicrous. The experiments below should help
you to confront such experiences with a more free-
floating attentiveness and acceptance, so that the
meaning of the art-work can develop itself and not be
rejected only because you steadfastly cling to previous
notions:

Select an impatience-situation; for example, when
you are waiting for someone or waiting for a bus. Let

yourself freely see and hear the figures and grounds in the environment as instructed in the experiments above—that is, shift about from one to another. You will notice that the amount of excitement involved in the still-continuing impatience-situation (for instance, your mounting anxiety at the lateness of the hour) will diminish the amount of interest you can invest in attention to other matters. Persisting, nevertheless, in noting what is about you (but without forcing an artificial concentration on any one thing), let yourself begin to feel the chaotic meaninglessness of the environment. As always, notice your resistances, blanking out, daydreaming.

The environment as such is not, of course, meaningless. If you have by now acquired a good sense of actuality, you will be able to say, "Here and now there are people and things to be observed. Waiting for the bus is now part of the background. I am now impatient." Then, since nothing is to be gained from the impatience itself—it will not make the person or the bus arrive—you may as well make use of the time and achieve a creative pre-commitment in the actual situation.

Often, under the most favorable of life-situations, there are occasions where the ground contains strong attractions of which we may or may not be aware, but where we must, nevertheless, deliberately concentrate on some task. In this case, the mistake is to have too rigid an attitude toward the duty and to suppress too sternly the distracters—for then the foreground will become less and less clear and attractive. If we are more lenient with ourselves, we are more likely to work up an efficient interest in the task. For instance, a student who had tremendous difficulty in cramming (a kind of "learning" which by definition excludes interest) managed the job by interrupting himself from time to time and deliberately allowing a few minutes of daydreaming.

Let us now, in the context of the theory of psychotherapy, consider the two obstacles to spontaneous concentration—the too-fixed figure and the too-charged ground. *In therapy the aim is to shift the "inner conflict," that between impulse and the counter-attacking resistance, into an open, aware conflict.* Suppose that, as therapist, we concentrate and ask the patient to concentrate on his resistances. These are stubborn and combative, and the attempt to keep them under surveillance will have to be forced and a kind of staring. But such forced concentration—peering at and staring at what does not want to be seen—is itself disintegrative and compulsive. It teaches the patient, for instance, to be "morbidly introspective."

Instead of admonishing the patient to concentrate on resistances, suppose we follow the older Freudian method of free-floating attention, free-association, and the like. This is spontaneous and unforced, and it reveals the hidden impulses (the charged background) in complexes, etc. But such "free" techniques lead to a flight of ideas; they avoid what are precisely the critical points—the conflicts with the resistances—and the technique of free-association becomes a training in free-dissociation. The therapist is led a merry chase. The thoughts and symbols produced all seem relevant to the hidden problem, but they deceptively go round and round and in every direction.

What is necessary is for the therapist to find some definite *context,* and then, keeping always to this, to allow a freer play between figure and ground—avoiding staring at the resistances, yet not allowing the patient to wander everywhere. In orthodox psychoanalysis such a definite context is regarded as given in the "transference," the erotic attachment to and hatred for the therapist, for this is an observable and more or less controllable life-situation. In our method we use, instead, the experimental situation of the therapeutic session as the context. On what is a more general and a better basis, you may use as context your actuality—your present-day situation, its needs and aims. The more complete the felt-contact between you and your environment, and the more honestly you feel and express to yourself your feelings of desire, loathing, coldness, boredom, disgust, with the persons and things you come in touch with, the more you will have a relevant context in which the "inner conflict" will emerge during the experiments.

The following will facilitate your felt-contact with the environment:

Let your attention shift from one object to another, noticing figure and background in the object—and in your emotions. Verbalize the emotions each time, as, "I like this" or "I dislike this." Also, differentiate the object into its parts: "It is *this* in it I like, but *that* I dislike." And, finally, when this much comes naturally to you, differentiate your emotions, thus: "For this I feel disgust" or "For this I feel hatred," etc.

The resistances you are likely to encounter in yourself during this experiment are embarrassment, self-consciousness, the feeling of being too harsh, presumptuous, nasty, or perhaps the wish to be *paid* attention rather than *give* attention. If, with respect to the persons you are in contact with, these resistances should become too strong to tolerate and tempt you to abandon the experiment, restrict yourself for a time to animals and inanimate objects.

In reporting on the first parts of this experiment most persons express relief that "here at last is something tangible." With respect, however, to differentiating figure and ground in their emotions, the results vary. Many insist that they "get no emotional effects at all," and a few claim that "it would take a lot more than this to get me emotional." On the other hand, some make statements such as this:

"As for differentiating emotions, I don't think I'm quite ready to do this. When I think of a person and try to say that I hate him, I feel too guilty. This happens even with inanimate objects. When I tried to acknowledge that I hate a certain modern painting, I felt I was being unfair—not giving it a chance. I also felt bad because it was done by my friend's father."

Some had difficulty because for them anything that goes by the name of emotion must attain Wagnerian intensity. As we shall later try to show in the experiment which singles out emotions for special attention, there is continuity in the emotional life, although admittedly there are great fluctuations in its forcefulness.

One student used an ingenious approach which you might find worth trying:

> "I found it very difficult to verbalize likes, dislikes, and emotional effects in general to inert objects. I got a feeling of doubt that *any* object could engender this sort of experience. Some objects seemed to be just utterly neutral in their affecting properties.
>
> "Then, getting no results, I finally began assigning emotions arbitrarily to each object. After I did this I started to feel these emotions as genuine and I almost forgot that the assignment of them had been arbitrary. It sort of scared me to see how easily I could fool myself into believing that I was having emotions."

What do you consider more likely here—that the emotions which felt genuine were only faked or that the original assignment of emotions was not so arbitrary after all?

The following illustrates a common phenomenon— the surprise at discovering that one's emotions are what they are rather than what one supposed them to be:

> "The emotional differentiation was performed in a crowded subway car, and I uncovered considerable aggression toward the other passengers. Instead of feeling ashamed or abashed about this, I confess I rather *enjoyed* it and actually felt the desire to tell them what I thought of them. Later, in a less annoying environment, I reviewed it—and *then* I experienced the blocks (shame, desire to dilute these feelings, etc.) which I would have expected to have in the original situation but didn't."

From still another comes a statement worthy of consideration as showing the common tendency to condemn emotion in one's usual behavior and to take pride in being emotionally unmoved:

> "The 'intolerable' resistance I was supposed to encounter in my felt-contact with the environment simply *did not occur*. Only once did anything of the sort emerge. Once, trying the experiment while talking in a group, I became aware of the wish to be paid attention rather than to give attention. But all that resulted was a smile, and I quickly forgot it."

Where one recognizes unfriendly emotion in oneself, there is a strong urge to assign it to something which one may quickly "discount and forget," as in the following:

> "I was sitting near my father-in-law. I began to notice the figure and background and then to verbalize (to myself) the emotions. 'I like him . . .' but, as I said it, I felt some sort of anxiety arise which could be expressed in these words, 'I dislike something in this figure.' It seemed to be a vague fear. At this point I terminated the experiment and only after later reexamination considered it definitely to be a fear reaction. Upon further pondering of this point and taking into consideration that my relationship with my father-in-law had been always on the best of terms, I looked a little further for this reaction and its reason. One (perhaps 'the') reason is that through my wife and her sister I have often heard tales of their father's strictness when they were younger. This may have built up a prearranged reaction, although based on nothing concrete."

If this father antagonized both his daughters when they were growing up, is it not probable that he is still a person who might be disliked directly rather than by hearsay?

The following is an example of what happens when one tries to divide one's attention among several persons who are competing for it:

> "When I permitted the 'chaos of divided attention,' I felt angry and frustrated. My husband insists that I

listen to him when he is holding forth on some theory, even at times when the children are concocting some situation which, if consummated, will be serious. I am torn between self-pride—the wish to answer him intelligently—and wanting to protect the children. This conflict quickly becomes intolerable, and is then resolved by shifting my full attention to the children."

Sometimes we fail to notice and express our emotion because it might give someone too much pleasure. Can you detect this in the following final excerpt:

"Today I concentrated on a friend's Cadillac, which he has owned and been tremendously proud of for over a year, and which I've frequently ridden in. I had always been a trifle scornful of his great pride of ownership. For the first time I really noticed the beautiful lines and curves of its construction, and its magnificent functional capabilities. I received an esthetic emotion that I never would have expected a car would arouse. My pleasure from this was exceeded by my friend's when I made a sincere and spontaneous comment on the car's beauty. A small incident, perhaps, but I found it indicative of the new areas of experience that true awareness can open for me."

EXPERIMENT 4: Differentiating and Unifying

When spontaneous attention is directed to an object, so that it brightens as figure and the background darkens, the object simultaneously becomes more unified but also more detailed. While more and more details are noticed and analyzed one by one, at the same time they become more organized in their relations to each other. In contrast, forced attention gives a skimpy figure and divided attention gives chaos.

The object of spontaneous concentration seems increasingly concrete and just itself. Correspondingly, it grows more "meaningful" in the sense that it becomes more and more the carrier of functions and importances that are matters of excited concern to the organism. For a classic example, consider (if you are in love) the person with whom you are in love.

Spontaneous concentration is *contact with the en-*

vironment. The actual situation is organized in a way that is detailed, structured, vivid, concernful.

In the following experiment, while maintaining here-and-now actuality as your context, you are to let your attention freely play about an object. The continuously shifting figures and grounds will sharpen your appreciation of the difference between staring and looking, between dulling trance and alive participation.

For an illustration, let us consider such an ordinary object as a pencil. (You will later go through the same procedure with objects of your own spontaneous selection.) Notice first that the pencil is *this unique thing.* There are other pencils, to be sure, but not this very one. Say its name, "pencil," and realize vividly that *the thing is not the word!* The pencil as thing is *non-verbal.*

Next, notice as many as you can of the qualities and properties that inhere in and constitute this thing—the cylinder of black graphite, the reddish wood, the weight, hardness, smoothness; the way it is sharpened, the yellow it is painted; the fact that its wood forms a hexagonal prism; the trade-mark, the rubber eraser and the metal which crimps it to the wood.

Next, review its functions and possible roles in the environment—for writing, for pointing out a passage, for wetting with one's tongue or biting on, for sale as a piece of merchandise. Also, think of its more "accidental" roles—to burn if the house burns, to dig into a child's eye if he runs with it and falls; also, its more far-fetched and fantastic uses—to send to someone as a Christmas present or to feed hungry termites.

As you abstract from this unique thing, *this* pencil, its many qualities and functions, note how in detail they go together or cohere as a structure—for example, the wood firmly holds and protects the graphite and is gripped by the writing hand.

Now try this out on something of your own choosing.

In principle this is the experiment that the philosopher Descartes carried out on an object formed by a piece of wax melted from a candle. Since this was malleable between his fingers, the shape was more "accidental" than that of our pencil. He concluded that certain properties of the thing—for instance, its mass and spatial extension—were absolutely permanent in it. These he called "primary." Other properties, such as the color, he deemed "secondary." We are not presently concerned with metaphysics, and the soundness of his conclusions is therefore not in question. What we are interested in is to realize, by freely attending to them, the various levels of abstraction—the "thisness" of the thing, this shade of yellow as distinguished from all other yellow paint in the world, the more obvious and "intended" functions, the more accidental, farfetched and fantastic uses—and to make as many as possible of these *come together and cohere in the present experience.* Thus, if consideration of an object should lead to a fantasy, keep the fantasy always returning to and connected with the present experienced object.

Although the unique thing is non-verbal, as we stated above, nevertheless, its importance and concern for you are given in properties and functions that you *can verbalize*—that are "abstractions" from unique things and, as words, cover many cases besides the present unique thing. You might write with many other things besides *this* pencil; the merchant who sold it makes a profit as well on many other kinds of merchandise. This pencil, because its properties, qualities, importance, are shared by so many other objects, is not an object which can give rise to limitlessly rich, spontaneous concentration or fascination. On the other hand, a beloved person or a great painting seem unique *both* in their "thisness" and in their properties and functions. With them one gets into "closer contact," and it is less easy to abstract.

Suppose you try the experiment with a painting you like. Notice the lines and the drawing apart from the objects painted and the colors; for example, trace the outlines of the main figures and observe the pattern they form. Examine the pattern formed by the *empty spaces* between the outlines of the main objects. See the pattern produced by each color in turn—abstract the patch of blue, of yellow, of red. If the picture gives an illusion of three-dimensionality, follow the receding planes—the pattern of the foreground, of the middleground, of the background. Trace out the pattern of lights and shadows. Note the way that material is indicated by the texture of the brushstrokes. Last of all, look at the story or scene portrayed, for this is where most people *begin* to look at a painting and *become fixed*.

If you do as suggested and have liked the painting to start with, you will find that it suddenly begins to swim toward you with a new beauty and fascination. All kinds of new relations among the parts suddenly seem "inevitable" or "just right." You will begin to partake of some of the *constructive* joy of the artist. Now you will be aware of the painting with spontaneous concentration—the details and their unity will be evident without painfully taking them apart and putting them together. This *single, immediate* grasp of the differentiated unity means that you are in contact with the painting.

Try the same experiment with a piece of music. If not musically trained and if you regard yourself as "unmusical," notice first how difficult it is for you to keep in contact with the music at all; the sounds soon degenerate into chaos and you into trance. In this case (what is best is to play a record over again and again) abstract first the appearances of a single instrument. Then pay attention to the rhythm only; the timbre only. Detect what seems to be the melody and what the accompaniment. Often you will find that there are other "inner" melodies that you had not expected. Abstract the harmony as you feel it; that is, notice when the harmony seems unresolved, seems to call for something more to come after it, and when, on the contrary, it seems to resolve and "close." Provided you do this seriously, suddenly all music will come alive for you.

As your next experiment:

Pay attention to someone's voice. How does it sound? Monotonous? Varying? High pitched? Strident? Melodious? Too soft in volume? Careless in articulation and hard to understand? Too loud? Flowing or faltering? Forced? Easy? Now ask yourself two questions: first, what is your own emotional reaction to the particular qualities of that voice? Are you, for instance, irritated at the too-soft tone, frozen by the loudness? Second, what is the emotional background in the other person that produces the particular qualities in his voice? Is he whining, oily, sexy, angry? It often happens that, quite unaware of what he is doing, and often *in contradiction to what he is saying*, this other person is *trying* to produce in you, with his voice quality, precisely the reaction that he *does* produce! His words may be of a calm, take-it-or-leave-it kind, but his voice cajoling. Or the words may be wooing words, but the voice angry and freezing.

Can you now try to pay attention to the sound of your own voice? This is very difficult, as shown by the fact that our voices heard for the first time on records seem quite alien to us. But be aware of the difficulties you encounter in the attempt.

The Stoic emperor, Marcus Aurelius, recommends an experiment similar to ours with the pencil. In his words:

"Make a particular description and delineation, as it were, of every object that presents itself to thy mind, that thou mayest wholly and thoroughly contemplate it, in its proper nature, bare and naked; wholly and severally: divided into its several parts and quarters; and then by thyself in thy mind, call both it and those parts of which it doth consist, and in which it shall be resolved, by their proper names and appellations. For there is nothing so effectual to get true magnanimity [what we would call "largeness of personality"] as to be able truly and methodically to examine and consider all things, and so to penetrate into their natures" (*Meditations*, III, ɪɪ).

Notice that the process we have been describing, by which one arrives at differentiated unity, is one of taking things apart and putting them back together—a kind of *aggressive destructiveness and reconstructive-*

ness! It is the destructive aspect which scares away people who have been taught to regard anything that goes by this or any kindred name as unwarranted, cruel, brutal, wrong. They must not interfere with things, but must let them stand unquestioned and unexamined. Those who follow such a concept imply that such investigation as was necessary to establish an evaluation that is to be correct for all time has presumably already been made by other and wiser persons, and to look into matters afresh from the standpoint of one's personal experiencing of them is presumptuous and worthy of condemnation.

What is neglected in this petrified attitude is the fact, quite obvious in minor matters, that for any kind of creative reconstruction to occur there must first to some degree be a *de-structuring* of what already exists. The present parts of a given object, activity or situation must be recombined in a fashion more adequate to the requirements of the here-and-now actuality. This does not necessarily involve a *devaluation* of any of the present parts, but rather a *re-evaluation* of how they need to go together. Apart from detailed analysis and taking apart (destruction), there can be no close contact, excited discovering, and true love for any object (which, as we use the term, always includes persons).

When we spoke earlier of abstracting detail after detail from a painting, this was the preliminary destruction of the painting prerequisite for heightened appreciation. Destruction and reconstruction refer here, not to literal reduction to fragments of the *physical object,* but to *our own behavior with respect to the object.*

Close friendship is possible only if certain barriers can be destroyed so that the persons can "come to an understanding." Such coming to an understanding requires that the other person be explored in a fashion somewhat similar to your study of the painting, so that his parts become reconstituted in relation to one's own background needs, and these, precisely in contact with the other person, now become foreground and figure. To put this in terms to which we shall return later, there can be no assimilation without prior destruction (de-structuring); otherwise, the experience is swallowed whole (introjected), never becomes our own—and does not nourish us.

Now, just as you did for seeing and hearing, but in a more sketchy way, try the experiment of detailed abstraction with your "closer" senses of touch, smell, taste and the proprioception of your own muscular actions. With these closer senses you will find that emotional factors very quickly become involved and that you soon resist or flee from the experiment. Upon discovering this, do not force yourself to continue, but proceed with the next experiment.

By way of approach to a full awakening of your closer senses, suppose you do an experiment on your eating. We shall at this point suggest no changes other than that you concentrate on your food. (As a rare exception, you may do this already.)

Take stock of your eating habits. Where do you tend to concentrate while eating—on your food? On a book? On the conversation (perhaps talking and forgetting to eat)? Do you taste your first bite only or do you keep in contact with the taste through the whole course? Do you chew thoroughly? Do you tear the food off? Do you bite through it? What are your likes and dislikes? Do you force yourself to eat what partly disgusts you (perhaps because you have been told it is good for you)? Do you adventure with new foods? Does the presence of particular persons influence your appetite?

Notice the relation between the taste of your food and the "taste" of the world. If your food tastes like straw, the world probably seems equally dull. If you relish your food, then the world, also, very likely seems interesting.

Do not in the course of this inventory of your eating habits attempt to rectify any of them other than to eliminate such severe distractions as reading. It is only man who ever comes to regard eating as a necessary evil or an emergency refueling. After all, it is a very important biological and (although we are not emphasizing this aspect here) social function. One certainly would not be tempted to read during the important biological and social function of sexual intercourse. Eating, sexuality—and, as we shall see later, breathing—are *decisive* in the operation of the organism and are *worth attending to*.

Against concentration on eating you are most likely to mobilize the resistances of impatience and disgust. With both of these we shall deal later in connection with "introjections." Just now try to achieve what seems so simple and is, nonetheless, so difficult—awareness of the fact that *you are eating when you are eating!*

This experiment on differentiated unity, which concludes a series of four devoted to improving your contact with the environment, is the first one to which the reaction of nearly all persons is, at least to some extent and in some areas, positive. Comments range from the claim that what is involved here is nothing more than a systematic approach to what the person has already been doing all his life to statements such as: "After all these years of going to concerts and taking music lessons, for the first time I *hear* music!"

Fairly frequently criticism is made of our use of the word "destruction" in a favorable or approving sense. For instance: " 'Destruction' has a wanton and antisocial connotation. Why don't you find some word which means 'taking apart for the purpose of putting together again in a better way'? I can readily see that to reconstruct necessitates a prior 'destruction,' as you call it, of what is to be reconstructed, but why use such an offensive name for it?"

No alternative word has thus far been proposed. What has been offered several times is a long sequence of words which practically duplicates the dictionary's definition of "destruction." What could be done, of course, is to coin a new term which would mean precisely what we intend, but then there would arise the louder hue and cry about "scientific gobbledy-gook" and the irritated query: "Why don't you speak English?"

All this could be and is said just as cogently about such a word as "aggression." This, to the editorial writer, means "unprovoked attack." But, while this specialized meaning dominates current usage of "aggression" in everyday life, its broader meaning, as intended by the clinician, for example, includes everything that an organism does to initiate contact with its environment.

We believe that if new words were made up for what clinicians intend by "destruction" and "aggression," these, too, would eventually acquire the same offensive connotations, because, in our early training for full membership in the tribe, we are taught to condemn in others and ourselves not only "wanton destruction" and "unprovoked aggression," but also forms of destructiveness and aggressiveness which are *necessary to the health of the organism*. Were this not the case, our social scene could change more rapidly and convincingly in the direction of "the good life."

All in all, is it not perhaps advisable to retain strong, efficient words like "aggression" and "destruction," and meanwhile perform some "aggressive destruction" on the barriers which tend to restrict them to the specialized meaning of something obviously and unquestionably to be condemned?

Our emphasis on the importance of the eating function meets with indignant rejection from almost everyone except a few who take themselves to be the "rare exception" who already concentrate on their food. A number of persons inform us that they wouldn't even consider wasting meal-time on *just eating!* Others point to the bad food and unpleasant surroundings of the typical city worker's luncheon and demand: "Would you have me concentrate on *that?*" Granted that atrocious eating conditions do exist, would they continue to be tolerated were there not such a general devaluation of the eating function? For those who insist that reading "goes naturally" with eating but who also assure us solemnly that reading would be impossible during sexual intercourse, we can only cite the case of the man who delayed *ejaculatio praecox* by imagining during intercourse that he was reading the evening newspaper.

We cite the following from a student who took the eating experiments seriously:

"My lunches for years have been mere excuses for business discussions. I found that what I had previously boasted about—my catholic taste in food and the fact that 'I could eat anything'—was actually based on a nearly complete unawareness of what I was eating. I would read while eating, and bolt my food at a rate to be described only as alarming.

"Almost immediately upon applying the 'here-now' test to my eating, I experienced heightened pleasure in my food. Although I spent several years in California, I am convinced that I never really tasted orange-juice until yesterday morning. I still have a long way to go—you can't change the habits of many years in a few days—and I frequently forget to remain aware.

"I ask myself if these bad habits are not responsible for the digestive difficulties (ulcers, diarrhoea, acid stomach) from which I've suffered in the past few years. In the last few days, since beginning to go to work on this eating business seriously, I've had none of the typical stomach disturbances I've grown to expect. It's still too soon, of course, to know whether this is or isn't something ephemeral."

We conclude this beginning group of experiments with summary statements made by several students:

"I'm interested in the way the experiments tend to blend in with each other. I don't know if this is their ultimate purpose, but the 'here-now', 'reversal', 'figure/ground' and 'differentiated unity' experiments all seem to come to me at once or in various combinations. I seemed to be operating all of them simultaneously tonight while watching several dance sequences on a television show. I felt that never had I seen a performance so clearly, and at the same time been able to observe so sharply the center of interest without being disturbed by non-essentials in the ground."

*   *   *

"Feeling of actuality, sense of opposed forces, concentration and differentiated unity are so interdependent that if, in contact with my environment, I have one of these, then I have the others too."

*   *   *

"As I continue with these experiments there seems to be a greater and greater integration of *all* of them. Each contributes more and more to the opening motif—to attain a feeling of actuality. This last one in particular has continued this trend, but I by no means intend to say that anything revolutionary has been revealed to me with the concept of differentiated unity. The most novel effect has come when destruction and reconstruction of personalities is attempted—but I find it difficult to distinguish this destruction and reconstruction from the previous three experiments, for everything is merging, boundaries dissolving.

"Nevertheless, I find a strong tendency not to indulge in the 'self-awareness' technique, beneficial as it may be. To get full benefits from the approach I think I shall have to practice it first in theory—and subvocally—before I dare to do much of it right out loud in the company of others. Some of it already is beginning to be 'second nature'—for instance, my growing tendency to think in terms of 'here and now' no longer surprises me or seems like something special. It's getting to be part of me."

I I I

TECHNIQUE OF AWARENESS

EXPERIMENT 5: Remembering

The four experiments of the preceding group were intended to increase and sharpen your contact with your environment. Probably they have seemed to have little to do with personal problems of any sort. If so, we agree that we have not so far dealt directly with the "inner conflicts of your mind," but rather with improving the orientation of your receptors—mostly, your exteroceptors—so that you might gain heightened awareness of *where you are*.

We hope that you have by this time realized and will not merely give lip-service to what we now state: *You* and your *environment* are not independent entities, but *together* you constitute a functioning, mutually influencing, total system. Without your environment you—your feelings, thoughts, tendencies to action—would not organize, concentrate, and have direction; on the other hand, without you as a living, differentiated organization of awareness, your environment would be, for you, non-existent. *Your sense of the unitary interfunctioning of you and your environment is contact,* and the process of contacting is the forming and sharpening of the figure/ground contrast, which is, as we have seen, the work of spontaneous attention and mounting excitement. For you as a living being contact is, then, ultimate reality.

In touching, smelling and tasting the sense of contacting is fairly well preserved for most persons. With the more distant senses of seeing and hearing, however, most modern people feel that they are being invaded by external stimuli—that what they see and hear is imposed on them willy-nilly from the outside —and they respond more or less according to the pattern of the "defensive reflexes." Such behavior is a symptom of paranoid projection, a matter which we shall discuss later on. What people in general are only dimly, if at all, aware of is that their seeing and hearing is a reaching out, an active stretching toward whatever is interesting and likely to fulfill their needs. With such awareness blacked out they feel that the environment attacks them—rather than its being, as must be the case for all healthy organisms, the other way around. Therefore, since their needs must obviously be satisfied by and in the environment, they, without being aware of it, *want the environment to attack them!* To put this another way, for it is an exceedingly difficult point for modern man to understand and accept, the organism and its supporting world must be in intimate contact for growth, development and life; but if —and this is what we shall have to prove—the organism, by virtue of fears and trepidations acquired in previous functioning, does not dare to initiate and take responsibility for the necessary contacts, then, since they *must* occur for life to go on, the initiative and responsibility are thrust upon the environment. Persons differ with respect to what part of the environment they expect to do this work. It may be, for instance, "my folks," "the government," "society," or "God." Such agencies are supposed to "supply me with what I need" or else "*make* me do what I ought to do."

At this point many of you, we know, are objecting. For instance, to say that a person experiencing what he sees and hears as imposed upon him by the environment thereby manifests a symptom of paranoid projection is certainly to use strong language. Genuine exceptions immediately present themselves. On occasion the environment *does* attack and, were this not the case, the healthy defenses of the organism—which we wish to strengthen and supply with more effective weapons—would be superfluous.

With respect to one's most intimate sense, proprioception—the feeling of one's own movements—people tend to be aware of and to accept only what is supplied by deliberately instituted movements—that is, what they do "on purpose." Their spontaneous muscular interactions with gravity, with solidity, and with much else besides, are performed without awareness.

What must be reacquired is the realization that it is *you* who are seeing, hearing, moving, and that it is you who are focused on the objects, whether they be interesting or dull, desirable or hostile, beautiful, ugly or plain. So long as you take your environment as something "given" or foisted on you and, at best, to be "put up with," you tend to perpetuate its present undesirable aspects. This holds especially for your close-up environment, but also to some degree for what is more remote and "public." Consider the importance of this, for instance, in the civic question of the layout of streets; if people regarded such environment as their concern and *their* environment, we would soon have better cities. Only the attitude of, "Well, at any rate, *I* can't do anything about it," this helpless (?) acquiescence in the status quo, staves off the necessary destruction and reconstruction.

The basic barrier to full, healthy experiencing is the tendency to accept as one's own only what one does deliberately—that is, "on purpose." Of all one's other actions one tends to be studiously unaware. Thus, modern man isolates his "will" from both his organism and his environment and talks about "will power" as if this were something that he somehow ought to be able to invoke in a fashion that would transcend the limitations of flesh and worldly circumstance. So, to increase the area of your awareness, begin now to attend to your spontaneous self and try to get the feeling of the difference between your deliberate and your spontaneous functioning.

When you first attempt the following experiment, you will be unable to distinguish true awareness from introspection, and you will probably conclude that we intend for you to introspect; however, this is not the case. Awareness is the spontaneous sensing of what arises in you—of what you are doing, feeling, planning; introspection, in contrast, is a deliberate turning of attention to these activities in an evaluating, correcting, controlling, interfering way, which often, by the very attention paid them, modifies or prevents their appearance in awareness. Habitual introspection is pathological; occasional introspection, as practiced by psychologist or poet, can be a useful technique but is very difficult.

Awareness is like the glow of a coal which comes from its own combustion; what is given by introspection is like the light reflected from an object when a flashlight is turned on it. In awareness a process is taking place in the coal (the total organism); in introspection the process occurs in the director of the flashlight (a split-off and highly opinionated *part* of the organism which we shall call the deliberate ego). When you have a toothache, you are aware of it without introspection, but you may also, of course, introspect it—bite down on the sore tooth, wiggle it with your fingers, or, deliberately neglecting it, force attention stoically away from it.

In this awareness experiment let your attention move about freely and allow the figure/ground to form. Previous experiments were limited largely to exteroception—the experiences given by receptors at the surface of the body, such as those for vision, hearing, smell, taste, touch—but now we are going to add the experiencing of the "body" and "mind," which is given by proprioception and for which the receptors are in the muscles, joints and tendons. At first you will almost surely merely introspect these self-feelings—and block them. When you do, attend precisely to such blockages (resistances) and the conflicts—opposition of forces—of which they are a part.

Our technique of awareness may strike you as being a variant of Yoga. It is, but its goal is different. In the West we have for centuries devoted ourselves mainly to exteroception of the "external world," while the Indians have turned the other way to heightened awareness of "body" and self. We want to surmount this dichotomy altogether. The Indian tries to overcome suffering and conflict by deadening sensation and thus insulating himself from the "environment." Let us, on the other hand, not be afraid to enliven feeling and response to stimulation and stir up such conflict as may be necessary in order in the end to achieve *a unitary functioning of the whole man*. Our emphasis is on self-awareness, not because this is the ultimate attainment of living (though it *is* a good thing), but because this is where most of us are handicapped. Whatever lies beyond this one finds out for oneself in one's own creative adjustments, when one has available the awareness and the energy to make creative adjustments.

Select a place where you will not be disturbed by intruders. Sit or lie comfortably in an easy chair or on a couch or bed which is, preferably, not too soft. *Do not try to relax,* although, if relaxation comes spontaneously, do not try to prevent it.

Forced relaxation is as unsound as forced concentration. The muscular tensions which prevent relaxation constitute important parts of the very resistances that we want to attend to, so we must not drive them out of the picture to begin with. As you proceed with the experiment you will find that in some respects you spontaneously relax further, but you will also begin to notice how you are preventing relaxation—for instance, by holding your breath or clutching the sides of the couch with your hands. Sometimes, when you notice a tension, you will relax it; at other times you will be taken with a strong anxious discomfort, an inability to be comfortable at all, and an imperious need to get up and terminate the experiment. Notice these things and the precise points where they arise.

When we say, "Do not relax," this is to prevent your attempting the impossible. Forced relaxation can be achieved sometimes in one or more places but only at the price of tightening up somewhere else. At this stage in our experiments, it is possible to become aware of resistances to relaxing but not possible to bring about general relaxation of tensions. Unless we emphasize this, you would very likely tackle the impossible —and be resigned in advance to failure. Our society frequently demands the impossible from us. Without the growth, training, or experience necessary for acquisition of many socially esteemed qualities, we are told to *be* strong, to *have* will power, to *be* kind, forgiving and patient. Since such requirements are so insistently and universally pressed upon us, we feel that they *must* make sense—consequently, we force ourselves to go through what we think would be the appropriate motions!

In the first experiment we noted that, while it is pathological to live in the past or future, it is healthy, from the vantage-point of the present, to remember past occurrences and to plan for future events. We now present instructions for an experiment designed to strengthen your ability to remember:

> Select some memory which is not too distant or difficult; for example, in fantasy revisit the house of a friend. Close your eyes. What do you actually see? The door—somebody opening it? Furniture? Other people? Do not try to ferret out what is in your "mind"—what you think ought to be there—but simply keep going back to the remembered place and noticing what is there.

It is a basic tendency of the organism to complete any situation or transaction which for it is unfinished; therefore, if you stick to the selected memory-context, the figure/ground will form quite without your deliberate intervention. Above all, do not think or reason like this: "There must have been chairs. Where were they?" Simply *see*. Use the technique of the last experiment—detailed abstraction—on what you fantasy. Treat the images as if they were present here-and-now to your senses. Very soon forgotten details will appear of themselves. But you will also quickly come upon resistances—for example, the annoying feeling of just not quite being able to catch sight of something that you know is there or to say what seems to be on the tip of your tongue. Again, do not force yourself. See if you can leave that item alone. It may appear before long in a sudden flash. However, some items needed to fill out the scene will not present themselves because your resistances are too strong; others will not be remembered because they never were of sufficient interest to be included in the figure which you experienced in this situation in the first place.

With respect to visual memory, persons vary from those who "have none" to those who, like Goethe, have an eidetic (photographic) memory. Eidetic memory is "infantile." You had it as a child and perhaps animals have it. Few of us preserve this ability to re-view situations in such vividness, with figure and ground easily shifting. The conventional demands of our "education" that we abstract only useful objects and verbal knowledge from situations which are full of life so suppress the eidetic power that most of us experience it only in dreaming.

Like any other asset, eidetic memory can be used well, as it was by Goethe, or misused, as in the case of a patient who could read off whole pages remembered with photographic exactness and thus pass examinations on material he had not in any way understood or assimilated (a case of perfect introjection).

If you at present have little or no visual memory—the ability to see vividly "in your mind's eye"—this is probably because *you have erected a wall of words and thoughts between yourself and your environment*. Your world is not genuinely experienced, but is contacted only to the extent necessary to activate your previously acquired systems of abstractions. Intellect has superseded alive participation. We shall come later to a valuable experiment on acquiring ability to live in a non-verbal region, a situation of internal silence. Meantime you must proceed *as if* you were in fact visualizing. While you will for the most part experience merely the shadows of the events you try to remember, now and then you are likely to get a brief flash of vision.

The resistance is largely tension of the muscles of the eyes, as in staring. It may help to close your eyes and pretend that you are asleep. Though often you will then actually fall asleep, you may be able with practice to hold to the borderline between sleep and waking, the state in which the so-called hypnagogic images appear. When they occur, these will be of a schizophrenic, incoherent sort; but tolerate them—for they do not mean that you are going crazy—and do not pooh-pooh them because of their senselessness. They can be a bridge to the recovery of your ability to visualize and remember.

The same sort of training can be applied to the auditory and other senses. Notice your resistance in trying to recall the voices of people. If you fail altogether in this, you can be sure that you never really listen to other people when they speak. Perhaps you are preoccupied with what you are going to say when you get the chance, or perhaps there was more dislike of the speaker than you realized.

Smells, tastes, and movements are not so easy to re-experience in this vivid way, which amounts to a kind of healthy hallucinating. But if you can re-experience any of them, you will discover that these close senses are charged with emotion. Emotion is a unifying gestalt of exteroceptions and proprioceptions, as we shall consider in more detail later. Seeing and hearing, because they are "distant" senses, can with relative ease be disconnected from alive participation with the "body" and become feelingless—except in our responses to painting and music, which tend to get through our muscular blocking. Taste and smell, which are "close" senses, may retain feeling-tone—although the dead palate and the stopped-up nose are quite common resistances.

Now do a memory experiment as before, but this time, instead of stressing merely vision, attempt to integrate as many senses as possible—not only what you saw, but also what you heard, smelled, tasted, touched, felt in your movements—and try also to recapture the emotional tone that went with the experience.

Do you avoid recalling any particular person? Do you notice that you can remember inanimate objects, or photographs of people, but not the persons themselves? Do your remembered situations remain static, or is there movement? Is there drama—motivation—in the scene? Do you get quick glimpses only, or can you follow up, the details without losing the whole? Do the images tend to recede or become hazy?

In sampling a few reactions to this experiment we start with one which may serve as a reminder that the "proof of potency" is the most self-defeating of all resistances:

> "I find no difficulty in the assigned task. I can remember with perfect clarity: scenes, events, situations, people, both recent and remote. I notice no particular tensions or blocks in memory flow."

In their recall-experiences some individuals found that, while they had highly developed imagery of a visual sort, they were almost totally lacking in auditory imagery. For others it was the other way around.

> "The remembering experiment was the most fruitful of any so far, since it provided me with a dramatic insight into a shortcoming. I had been rather smug in my feeling that I was already master of what was involved in figure/ground, concentration, actuality, and so on, with the result that when I tried this experiment the result was all the more shocking.
>
> "I've always known that my ability to see and, in memory, to re-see, is exceptionally good, but I didn't know the extent to which it dominated my awareness and perhaps—alas and alack!—compensated for what I was deficient in. On occasion, since I'm a fine arts enthusiast, I've remarked to friends, 'Fine arts are for me what music is for other people.' By this I implied that most people are blind to visual figure/ground

relations but appreciative of auditory figure/grounds, as witness the difficulty encountered by modern abstractionistic painters in getting their work accepted by a public blind to visual figure/ground. What I didn't know was that I myself was practically deaf to auditory figure/ground.

"The naked truth is that in the remembering experiment I was utterly incapable of recalling an auditory experience. Since then I've been listening extra hard—and I'm just beginning to realize for instance, that there's something more to dancing than a mere shuffling of the feet."

Many report difficulty in re-seeing what is animate and moving, and a number, unable to remember color, visualize only in black and white. Photographs of persons may be remembered when the persons themselves are not. In many cases the simple survey involved in this experiment and the discovery that something was missing in one's own private life which other people possessed initiated the corrective measures of giving more interest and attention to the under-aware sense.

"Before I read the instructions and discussion for this experiment I somehow had always thought that to talk about images was just a kind of figure of speech. I guess I thought that all we remembered was a result of what we had verbalized. I'm beginning to have a little success now, with some hazy images and occasionally a fairly clear memory-flash. Oddly enough, it's easier for me to remember voices than memory-pictures."

The personal significance of the event recalled affected, of course, the vividness of the memory. For instance:

"Voices either did not come through at all or they came through with such penetrating realism I became almost scared. These were the voices of my mother and my step-father. When I heard them, my mind began to drift and sleepiness came over me."

Another report contained the following:

"I found it much easier and relaxing to remember good occurrences than bad ones. One thing I recalled produced an automatic movement of my legs. It involved a situation where I had to jump back quickly or be cut by a broken beer bottle. I surprised myself to see that in the recall I had almost relived the happening. I realized that the speeded breathing and heartbeat were associated with this."

As a last personal statement, we quote the following:

"With the auditory tests I must report absolute failure. I was horrified to discover that I could not even recollect my parents' voices. I think that I have an average ear, and I am very quick to notice accents and peculiarities of pattern in a voice. But I found it impossible to recall them unless I did so within a few minutes of the person's departure. Any attempt to recall them as much as a day later met with failure.

"I have refrained above from mentioning the one attempt when I did manage to hear a voice. Previously I had recalled only pleasant scenes. This time I deliberately set out to recall an unpleasant one. At first I was unsuccessful, but with perseverance I was able to remember it. It suddenly returned to my mind with extraordinary clarity. It seemed to me that I had recaptured it down to the minutest detail. Then I seemed to hear a voice. It was that of the man I had intended to marry. The impression was very fleeting, and I was suddenly seized with a restlessness which made further work on it impossible."

EXPERIMENT 6: Sharpening the Body-Sense

Our strategy for developing self-awareness is to extend in every direction the areas of present awareness. To do this, we must bring to your attention parts of your experience which you would prefer to stay away from and not accept as your own. Gradually there will emerge whole systems of blockages which constitute your accustomed strategy of resistance to awareness. When you are able to recognize them in your behavior, we shall turn to direct concentration on them in their specific forms and attempt to rechannel the energy with which these blockages are charged into the constructive functioning of your organism.

Our present group of experiments is concerned with undirected awareness, as opposed to the directed awareness which will come later. The following general instructions are for setting up the appropriate context:

(1) Maintain the sense of actuality—the sense that your awareness exists now and here. (2) Try to realize that *you* are living the experience; acting it, observing it, suffering it, resisting it. (3) Attend to and follow up all experiences, the "internal" as well as the "external," the abstract as well as the concrete, those that tend toward the past as well as those that tend toward the future, those that you "wish," those that you "ought," those that simply "are," those that you deliberately produce and those that seem to occur spontaneously. (4) With regard to every experience without exception, verbalize: "Now I am aware that . . ."

From the philosophical point of view this is a training in phenomenology: the realization that your sequence of thoughts, your surface experience—whatever else it is and whatever it stands for—is first of all something that exists in its own right. Even if something is "only a wish," it *is* something—namely, the event itself of wishing. It is, therefore, as real as anything else.

As long as you are awake, you are at every moment aware of something. When absent-minded or in a trance-state, awareness is very dim; the figure/grounds do not develop and the processes involved—vision, fantasy, or whatever—do not precipitate strong experiences in the form of memories, wishes, plans, actions. Many persons live in a permanent trance so far as non-verbal experience is concerned, and since nearly all that they are aware of is a tremendous amount of verbal thinking, they take such verbalizing as being nearly the whole extent of reality.

Insofar as this applies to you—and it does apply to all of us in varying degrees—you are aware, at least, of this verbal existence and also have, perhaps, a dim sense that this is not all there is. Very much of what you are only dimly aware and almost unaware can be brought into awareness by giving it the requisite amount of attention and interest—so that a gestalt can be formed that is strong enough to precipitate an experience. It is true, of course, that there are the "repressed contents" as well as those objects which we cannot bring to awareness simply by "attending to what is not there"—but these we shall take up when we attempt to dissolve the blocks to awareness.

To verbalize, "Now I am aware . . ." with every experience is similar to Freudian free-association, which also is intended to loosen habitual modes of experiencing and to make available, as indicated by one's ability to verbalize it, experience characteristically unnoticed and unfelt. But free-association loses the context of actuality and often becomes free dissociation, or a means of by-passing what is important and practical in solving present problems. Furthermore, free-association generally restricts itself to "ideas," "thoughts," "mental processes." Our attempt, in contrast, is to recover *all* experiences concomitantly—whether they be physical or mental, sensory, emotional, or verbal—for it is in the unitary functioning of "body," "mind," and "environment" (these are all abstractions) that the lively figure/ground emerges.

The greatest barrier to this is one's tendency to interfere with and thus falsify the unitary flow of experience by holding back ("censoring") or by forcing. Since our interest lies not in recovering some particular item like a childhood incident but in extending and increasing integrated functioning, we have no need to force expression of anything—for example, embarrassing material—any more than we try to force relaxation. Forcing oneself to do anything could not take place unless there simultaneously existed the counter-tendency to hold back, and the latter, as the opposed force, is just as genuinely you and worthy of consideration as the forcing. To grind ahead despite resistances—by-passing embarrassment, for instance, by being brazen—is as inefficient and wearing as to drive a car with the brakes set. Our approach is to attain first a realization that behind the embarrassment and holding back there is a concealed conflict which does not appear in awareness now because it would produce too much anxiety. It is sufficient at this point simply to note carefully any evidences of such conflicts.

"Now I am aware . . ." applied to all your experiences will, unless yours is a very conscientious, obsessional character (in which case you will nullify the experiment by some other means), lead invariably to your wandering off into daydreaming, "thinking," reminiscing, or anticipating. As you deviate thus from the experiment you will lose awareness that *you* are *now* doing so, and you will wake in chagrin that such a simple task should be so hard to perform. Don't expect at the start to be able to carry on for more than a few minutes without slipping. But come back again and again to verbalizing, "Now I am aware . . ." until you get the feeling that "I," "now," and the object of awareness constitute a unified experience.

So, stick to this formula and, further, keep to the surface and the obvious. Do not try to become aware of the extraordinary and arcane. Do not guess at interpretations of the "unconscious." Remain solidly with what is. Without preconceptions, without models of any sort, without an official road-map of whatever kind, *come to yourself*. In doing this you get the chance to identify yourself with what is your spontaneous experience in addition to your customary identification with deliberate—"on purpose"—actions. The aim is to extend the boundary of what you accept as yourself to include *all organic activities*. By slowly but persistently doing this, you will gradually become able to do without effort much that was previously impossible no matter how great the effort.

So we proceed in such a simple fashion as this: "Now I am aware that I am lying on the couch. Now I am aware of the wish to do the awareness-experiment. Now I am aware of hesitating, of asking myself what to do first. Now I am aware that the radio is playing in the next room. That reminds me . . . No, I am aware that I meant to listen to that program. I am aware that I have stopped myself from wandering. Now I feel lost again. I am remembering the advice to stick to the surface. Now I am aware that I am lying with my legs crossed. I am aware that I have a pain in the back. I am aware of wishing to change my position. Now I am doing that," etc.

Notice that processes are going on and that you are involved in and concerned with these processes. To realize such continuous involvement is extremely difficult, and most persons escape by accepting as their own—by identifying themselves with—only those processes which are deliberate. But bit by bit you are to take increasing responsibility for all your experience (we do not mean *blame* for it!)—including your blocks and symptoms—and gradually to acquire both free acceptance and control of yourself. The notion that "thoughts" on their own initiative and without any help from you "enter your mind," must give place to the insight that *you* are thinking the thoughts. At present it is sufficient to notice that thoughts are not like objects floating in space, but that they are processes which have some temporal span.

Now, still accepting and identifying yourself with all your awareness, begin to differentiate as follows:

Try first to attend mainly to external events—sights, sounds, smells—but without suppressing other experiences. Then, in sharp contrast, concentrate on internal processes—images, physical sensations, muscular tensions, emotions, thinking. Then, one by one, differentiate these various internal processes, by concentrating, as exclusively as you can, on images, then on muscular tensions, etc. Follow these through, as previously, by detailed recognition of the different objects or activities and, if possible, of whatever moving dramatic scene they may be components.

The rest of this experiment and the following two are devoted to helping you to differentiate "body," "emotions" and "thinking."

Almost all persons in our society have lost the proprioception of large areas of their body. The loss was not accidental. It was, when it occurred, the only means of suppressing intolerable conflict. The issues which were then at stake, if now gradually reintroduced into awareness, can be worked through on a basis which actually resolves and puts an end to the conflict. Then what was lost—one's power to manipulate himself and his environment in various constructive ways, to enjoy feelings and satisfactions now beyond the bounds of awareness—can be restored through remobilizing what are now "missing" parts of the organism. The following is to start you along this road:

Concentrate on your "body" sensation as a whole. Let your attention wander through every part of your body. How much of yourself can you feel? To what degree and with what accuracy and clarity does your body—and thus you—exist? Notice pains, aches and twinges ordinarily ignored. What muscular tensions can you feel? Attending to them, permit them to continue and do not attempt prematurely to relax them. Try to shape their precise limits. Notice your skin sensations. Can you feel your body as a whole? Can you feel where your head is in relation to your torso? Where are your genitals? Where is your chest? Your limbs?

If you believe that you have had complete success with the above experiment, you are almost certainly mistaken. Most persons, lacking adequate proprioception of parts of their body, substitute in place of this visualization or theory. For instance, they *know* where their legs are and so *picture* them there. This is not *feeling* them there! With a picture of your legs or a map of your body you can deliberately walk, run or kick after a fashion; but for free, unforced, spontaneous functioning of these parts you need felt-contact with your legs themselves. This you must get directly from proprioception of their tensions and tendencies to movement. To the extent that there is a discrepancy between the verbal concept of the self and the felt awareness of the self—and it exists to some degree in practically everyone—*this is neurosis*. So notice the difference as you slip from one to the other, and *do not deceive yourself* that you actually feel more than you do. It is helpful to verbalize somewhat as follows: "Now I am aware of a tightness in my chest—but now I am visualizing the relation of my throat and chest —and now I merely know that I want to vomit."

Experimenting in body-awareness is universally difficult and awakens resistance and anxiety. But it is profoundly important and worth spending many, many hours in doing—*in moderate doses!* Not only is it the basis for dissolving the "motor armor" (muscular tensions in which resistances are anchored) but it is also the means of curing all the psychosomatic ailments. Miracle-cures which are reported—such as the dissolving of an acute neurotic symptom within a few minutes —will seem natural to you once you feel the bodily structure of such symptoms. The neurotic personality *creates* its symptoms by *unaware manipulation of muscles*. Unfortunately, however, the neurotic personality cannot grasp that here symptom is figure and personality is ground—that this is a symptom/personality instance of the figure/ground of experience. He has lost contact with the ground of personality and only the symptom is in awareness. To the extent that this applies to you, much reintegration will be necessary before you clearly sense *what* you yourself are doing, *how* you are doing it, and *why* you are doing it. But this and later experiments in body-awareness, if seriously performed, take you directly on your way. What is important now is not to "succeed," but simply to go ahead sincerely and without straining. If you take the attitude that you "ought" to be able to do whatever is put before you, you will at once *limit* what you may become aware of to *what you now already know and expect*. As much as you can, be accepting, experimental and curious—for what you discover about yourself in this way is fascinating and vitalizing knowledge! So, once again:

> Walk, talk, or sit down; be aware of the proprioceptive details without in any way interfering with them.

Do not be dismayed when you find this very difficult. You are so habituated to superficial "corrections" of your posture or way of speaking or whatever, that you find it nearly impossible to go ahead walking in a way that is "wrong" or speaking "in a bad tone," even though you fully realize that any quick, deliberate readjustment will be as ineffective and ephemeral as most New Year's resolutions. And, in fact, your notion of what is the "right" way is likely to be unsound, since based perhaps on an incorrect military norm or on some actor's voice.

In doing this experiment you may suddenly become aware that *you are divided into a nagger and a person nagged at*. If so, notice this as vividly as you can. If possible, feel yourself in each role—as nagger and as "naggee." Finally:

> As you sit or lie comfortably, aware of different body-sensations and motions (breathing, clutching, contracting the stomach, etc.), see if you can notice any combinations or *structures*—things that seem to go together and form a pattern—among the various tensions, aches, and sensations. Notice that frequently you stop breathing and hold your breath. Do any tensions in the arms or fingers or contractions of the stomach and genitals seem to go with this? Or is there a relationship between holding your breath and straining your ears? Or between holding your breath and certain skin sensations? What combinations can you discover?

Since difficulty in doing the body-awareness experiment is reported by almost everyone, we begin our citation of various personal reactions with several which are exceptions:

"Concerning awareness of bodily sensations, I was apparently able to do what was asked for. My general reaction to it all was, 'So what?'"

This type of reaction we have previously commented on as "the proof of potency." It can take the form, as here, of doing the experiment and being finished with it—before one has actually started!

"When I concentrate on the body, I become aware of insignificant twinges and aches, particularly in the extremities, which I do not usually notice in the normal flood of ongoing activity."

We question the term "insignificant." Anything may be evaluated as insignificant if one does not permit it to develop and reveal its significance. The wish to regard these phenomena as insignificant—and therefore not a matter of concern and responsibility—is readily understood. One can also understand resistance which rationalizes itself as precaution against becoming hypochondriacal:

"Since early childhood I have been sickly, and I have been taught and have taught myself to disregard my bodily aches and pains. I've played around with this experiment a little bit, and I've been able to feel, slightly, my body and all its quirks and tensions. That's as far as I'm going to take it, for, after spending my earlier years 'unlearning' my body, I'm leery of allowing its aches and twists to take too much of my mind's attention."

If it were our ultimate intention to acquaint you with the present malfunctioning of your organism and then to go off and leave you high and dry with no further effective course of action, this man's position would be unassailable. What we have tried to stress is that this is preliminary work, designed to give you better orientation with respect to your organism-environment situation as it now exists. Specifically, in this experiment, the aim is to have you explore the chronic, "meaningless" tensions which exist within your body. Once you yourself genuinely feel the need to change it on the basis of such *direct awareness* of the situation, *then* it becomes practical to present corrective procedures.

In doing the experiment many did experience vividly the splitting of their personalities into a nagger and a person nagged.

"I found that when I was aware of talking, sitting, or walking, I was forever trying to correct or readjust what I was doing."

A few were able to identify themselves a little more strongly with the "naggee"—take his side for once—than was their ordinary practice:

"Rather than finding it difficult to avoid correcting my posture and speech, I found it wonderfully exhilarating! I was able to ignore that part of me which was nagging about correctness."

We come now to several statements from persons who were rather astonished and disturbed by what they found going on in their bodies:

"In the beginning my feelings about this experiment were uncomplimentary in the extreme. It was about three weeks before I got any results. I then suddenly became aware of muscular tensions. All at once it seemed to me that I was a mass of knotted muscle. In fact, even as I write about it, it feels as though parts of me are in knots. The most severe tensions seem to be in the small of the back, the back of the neck and in the upper part of the legs. I also noticed that as I did these experiments my mind would focus itself on a small irritation or pain, and then, as I became increasingly aware of this minor irritation my whole consciousness would become directed toward it, obscuring every other part of my body. These tensions made me realize that resistances and tensions are part of the same thing—or maybe *are* the same thing! I have some insight into the reason for some of the tension, but so far have had no success in relaxing it to any degree."

The "insight" spoken of here is largely of the verbal and theoretical type which, while it may be perfectly correct so far as it goes, does not in itself contain the felt-significance which is prerequisite to genuine relaxation of the tension.

"Normally—that is, before I let my 'attention wander through my body'—I was aware of my body sensations merely as a general hum, a kind of poorly defined sense of general vitality and warmth. However, the attempt to subdivide this into component sensations was a source of genuine amazement. I became aware of a series of tensions in various parts of my body: knees and lower thighs as I sit in a chair; the region of the diaphragm; the eyes, shoulders and dorsal neck region. This discovery was quite astonishing to me. It was almost as if my feeling had entered a foreign body with tensions, rigidities, and pressures entirely different from mine. Almost immediately upon discovery I was able to relax these tensions. This, in turn, caused me to be aware of a sense of looseness and even elation; a very sudden freedom, pleasure and readiness for anything to come. Aside from these pleasurable sensations I was not aware of any emotions, anxieties, fears, connected with these tensions and their relaxation. In addition, despite the fact that I had bared the existence of these tensions and succeeded in relaxing them, they invariably returned, and later sessions repeated this discovery-relaxation-satisfaction cycle."

The elated relaxation attained by this person is by no means to be sneered at. It is comparable to the effects of massage or the training in "progressive relaxation" given by Edmund Jacobson. What is missing is the final resolution of the conflicts producing the tensions. As stated, "they invariably returned." However, since they yielded so readily, the conflicts involved in these particular tensions were presumably superficial, and, had the tensions been concentrated upon instead of being prematurely and repetitiously relaxed, they might fairly quickly have yielded up their meaning and been disposed of once and for all.

"The sense-of-body experiment was quite dramatic. With little trouble I was able to capture tensions of the abdominal muscles. It was very frightening at first. Leg and arm tensions came through clearly, as did a stiffness and tension of the upper jaw, above the back teeth. It was very strong, like an intense toothache, but without pain. The only other time I can remember experiencing it was at a chug-a-lug beer party just before I got sick. Along with this tension was a tension of the neck muscles which made me feel as if I were going to be sick. I wonder if there is any connection."

There is! What was present in both instances was the beginnings of, and the resistance to, the vomiting-reflex.

"There is an extreme tendency to flee this exercise. Sleep overcomes me frequently. I notice a rigidity in my neck and jaw. I observe my respiration and find myself taking exaggeratedly deep breaths to assure my ability to breathe completely. I have some ability to visualize the relationship of parts of the body, but generally have to contract my muscles to continue the exercise. Throughout this experiment my jaw and neck are rigid, legs are tense, my fingers partially relaxed and back slightly arched."

Instead of being as generalized as this, the holding-back tensions may seem highly focal, as in the following:

"I was doing the awareness of internal muscular tensions on a train, and I was therefore seated the first time I did it. Since then I've tried this particular phase lying down, standing still, and even when walking, but I can't vouch for the correctness of all findings after the first one, for what I noticed then was to me so surprising that now whenever I try to see if that tension is still there, I invariably find it. The point is, though, how do I know that my very concentration on it is not what's calling it up?

"Here's what happened: I was feeling around my insides when I finally got around to the region of my rectum, and there I noticed what seemed to me a silly tension, something of which I felt completely unaware before. There I was sitting with the muscles of my rectum as tightly clenched as possible.

"It was as if I was holding my breath with the lower part of my colon, if that analogy makes any sense. I called this tension silly because when I examined myself I found that I didn't feel like defecating, but there I sat with the sphincters just about as tense as if I did. Corresponding with this I found a tension band extending across my belly in the region of my navel, not so strong, it seemed, as that of the rectum.

"Since then, while I'm lying down, I suddenly switch over to my rectal muscles to see if they're tight, and, sure enough, they are! I don't deliberately lie down to test this tension (for then I'd surely find it there) but rather look for it when I find myself on the bed, etc. At other times, when I'm sitting, I don't set out to find it, but I just switch over to it from whatever else I'm doing. I always find it now. This might be purely a natural, physical tension, one that should be there, but, at any rate, I've never noticed it before."

This particular tension is well known. As much as a generation or so ago Ferenczi spoke of it as the very "manometer of resistance." It is present in all who are chronically constipated, and its release puts an end to this psychosomatic symptom.

"When I read the sentence: 'Notice the pains and aches that you ordinarily ignore', I thought that, quite on the contrary, it is when you have pains that you start being aware of the aching part; however, I was later surprised to find that when deliberately paying attention to the way I was sitting I first of all noticed a pain in the under part of the knee—which, it seemed, had been there before, although I was really unaware of it."

The above points up a verbal difficulty. To speak of a pain of which one is unaware sounds like a contradiction in terms; to be exact we need to speak of some unaware condition which, if it becomes aware, does so as the experience of pain.

"A much better way of achieving body-awareness would be to prescribe exercise and sports."

Athletes are not outstanding for body-awareness, but gymnastics, dancing, and other activities which emphasize balance and coordination do tend to keep alive or even to revive body-awareness. Similar aids are massage, an electric vibrator, soaking in the bathtub, and applying a hot water bottle to areas of tension.

"I find suddenly I have nothing to do with my arms. I am aware of awkwardly crossing them on my chest. I put them in my pockets. I am aware of being uncomfortable. I keep shifting around and I'm suddenly aware of feeling confused. I get up almost immediately and walk about. My wife calls me for dinner and I am glad to leave the experiment."

When attention centers in this fashion on parts of the body, but none of the behavior which you then produce gives satisfaction and ends the restlessness, these various abortive behaviors may sometimes be correctly construed as distractions designed to prevent your becoming aware of what it really is that you want to do with these parts of your body.

"Even in reading about this experiment I found myself conscious of rigid muscle tensions (especially in my extremities), and I was constantly holding my breath during intensive efforts of concentration. All of this occurred despite my interest in the material involved."

Shall we say that here, despite the interest, there is apprehensiveness and some tendency to run away?

"My thoughts suddenly stop. I find myself slightly clenching my fists now. My chest seems to be building up as if to make me yell something. I can't think what, even when I try."

The yell broke surface a month later in the form of an effective "telling off" of the fiancée's meddling parents!

"On certain parts of my body there was merely the feeling of blankness or dullness. I knew that the 'middle of my back' was there, but yet I couldn't feel it. Then an extremely ludicrous group of sensations occurred. Whenever I couldn't contact the 'middle of my back,' I immediately experienced some unusual sensations and twinges in the areas surrounding the uncontacted area. It felt extremely unusual, as if there were a void in one part of my body—a blank, insensitive spot which couldn't be felt."

Others experienced blank spots between head and torso—that is, they had no felt-neck—or toes, genitals, stomach, etc.

Some reported that after working on this experiment they were fatigued. Others reported a terminal feeling of exhilaration. Some reported fatigue on the first attempts, exhilaration on later ones. Where the latter occurred, it was usually after some "meaningless" tension had become invested with significance.

"After repeatedly tracing out this same pattern—neck particularly stiff, lower lip strained out and protruding, heavy breathing—I found there were certain situations I could recall that seemed automatically to bring on this whole business. These were all situations where I had to hold in resentment. The clearest instance came when I was going over my notes preliminary to typing this up. At the same time that I found myself breaking into a broad grin, I was aware that I'd been having this particular pattern of tensions and—again all at the same time—I was aware of how put-upon and martyrized I was feeling about having to do these experiments and report on them. It seemed

that the resentment toward you had finally arrived!
After that, when I've done the body-awareness experiment for any period of time I've ended up feeling, not
all pooped-out the way I did at first, but sort of refreshed and pulled-together."

As a final example, we quote the following:

"After many repetitions I was successful in the
proprioceptive experiment, although there were many
resistances. I plan to carry on with this, for already I
have noted some benefits. I have succeeded in a limited
way in making contact with most parts of my body,
and I now find it very pleasant to do so, although at
first it disturbed me. I find that the wisest procedure is
to do it more frequently and for shorter periods of
time than I first attempted. Becoming aware of my
muscular tensions was a most alarming experience at
first. There were so many of them, that my first impression was, 'Boy, am I a mess!' But further awareness has made them much less alarming, and, though I
am making no conscious effort to relax the tensions,
I now find contacting them almost pleasant. The main
tensions I felt were in the muscles of the arms, legs,
across the chest, the back of the neck, the jaw, across
the temples, and a tension in the solar-plexus, which I
believe to be in the region of the diaphragm. In my
last proprioceptive work-out I concentrated particularly on my stomach, and I am convinced that I made
strong contact with it. I felt a connection between
certain activities there and the muscle tensions in my
diaphragm, across my chest, and, strangely enough,
across my temples."

EXPERIMENT 7: Experiencing the Continuity of Emotion

The first experiments centered on exteroception, the
basis of your awareness of the "external world." Then,
in the experiment immediately preceding this, the focus
was on proprioception, which affords awareness of
your "body"—its actions and tendencies to action.
Such separate stress on "outer" and "inner" was, however, merely preliminary, for each of these is but an
abstraction from your whole experience, which includes

both. In the present experiment we ask that you give special emphasis to neither but instead try to be aware of the gestalt that forms when you no longer *insist* on assigning separate, independent existence to "inner" and "outer."

When the deliberate dichotomy between "external world" and "body" is not made, what you then experience is the organism/environment field—the differentiated unity which comprises you-in-your-world. This ever-changing gestalt is never neutral but is of vital concern to you, for it is, actually, your life in the process of being lived. Its concernfulness, importance, relevance to your welfare, is omnipresent. Experiencing the organism/environment field *under the aspect of value* is what constitutes *emotion*.

By such a definition emotion is a *continuous* process, since every instant of one's life carries in some degree a feeling-tone of pleasantness or unpleasantness. However, because in modern man this continuity of emotional experience is, for the most part, suppressed from awareness, emotion is regarded as a kind of periodic upheaval, which occurs unaccountably in one's behavior on those very occasions when one would most like to "exercise control." Such eruptions—which are so "unreasonable"!—tend, of course, to be dreaded and guarded against. Whenever possible, one endeavors to stay out of situations which might bring them about.

Most students of behavior, while apparently going along with the notion that the term "emotion" should apply only to such volcanic instances, are fully cognizant of other phenomena which are highly similar though less violent. These are usually referred to as "feelings," and scholarly attempts to give a full account of this area repetitiously adopt the title: "Feelings and Emotions." We believe that this practice attempts to break in half what actually is a continuum. What determines the place of a given emotional experience on this continuum depends upon the extent to which the organism's concern in experiencing the organism/environment gestalt has emerged from ground into figure.

Emotion, considered as the organism's direct evaluative experience of the organism/environment field, is not mediated by thoughts and verbal judgments, but is *im*mediate. As such, it is a crucial regulator of action, for it not only furnishes the basis of awareness of what is important but it also energizes appropriate action, or, if this is not at once available, it energizes and directs the search for it.

In primitive undifferentiated form, emotion is simply excitement, the heightened metabolic activity and increased energy mobilization which is the organism's response to experiencing novel or stimulating situations. In the newborn this response is massive and relatively undirected. Then, as the child gradually differentiates the parts of its world—the constellations of events which confront it jointly from within and without on various occasions—it correspondingly differentiates its early, global excitement into selective, situationally-polarized excitements. These acquire names as specific emotions.

Emotions *per se* are not vague and diffuse, but are just as sharply differentiated in structure and function *as is the person who experiences them*. If a person experiences his emotions as confused and crude, then these terms apply also to *him*. From this it follows that emotions in themselves are not something to be rid of on such trumped-up charges as being impediments to clear thought and action. On the contrary, they are not only essential as energy-regulators in the organism/environment field, but they are also unique deliveries of experience which have no substitute—they are the way we become aware of our concerns, and, therefore, of what we are and what the world is.

This function of emotion is grossly maligned in our society. As stated previously, it is regarded as arising only in crises, and even then only if the person "loses control of himself" and "gets emotional." Calmness is prized as the very antithesis of emotion, and people strive to appear "cool, calm, and collected." Yet calmness is not without emotional tone, for it is born of the directly evaluative experiencing of this particular situation as one which can be effectively handled, or, at the other extreme, as one about which nothing can be done. It is the fluid, open-ended situation, where one feels that he has much at stake and where his own actions may swing the balance, that is truly exciting. To affect calmness in such a situation is a "front," achieved by suppressing manifestations of concern. To fool others in this way may be worthwhile if they are enemies, but to fool yourself is to mistake yourself for a foe and to deny yourself awareness of "what's up."

Certain "negative feelings" are customarily denied emotional significance. Yet such things as frigidity and boredom, for instance, are actually very strong feelings—they are not mere absence of feeling! One feels ice as surely as one feels fire. Numbness—the absence of feeling where feeling is expected—is, paradoxically, an overpoweringly strong feeling, so strong that it is soon excluded from awareness. That is why, in these experiments, it is so difficult to seek out blind-spots and restore sensitivity.

Because of the discomfort which they produce in grown-ups who are working hard to squelch awareness of their own emotions, the emotions of children are not permitted to undergo natural development and differentiation. What the "adults" do not guess and bitterly resist having revealed to them is that their impatience in getting the child to "control his emotions" is rooted squarely in the fact that in their own childhood, too, "the authorities" had this same warped, apprehensive attitude toward emotion. They themselves, since they were never allowed on the basis of unforced experience to differentiate adequately and thus outgrow childish emotionality, to a large extent never did. They merely suppressed it—*and are still doing it!* When the child behaves spontaneously, it stirs the same latent tendencies in the grown-ups and threatens the precariously maintained "maturity" of their own conduct. As a consequence, the child, too, must be coerced as quickly as possible into the suppression of strong feeling and into putting on once and for all the false-face of conventional "self-control."

This is largely achieved by emphasizing the "external world" and its demands as *reality,* while the promptings of organismic needs, as made aware by proprioception, are, to a great extent, pooh-poohed as being "only in the mind." The child "adjusts" to this unremitting pressure by dulling his body-sense and then devoting to the "external world" whatever interest he can still whip up.

This whole crusade for "control of the emotions" is, of course, itself emotionally grounded, and it is prosecuted in a most emotional fashion. It does not fail to get results, but the results achieved are not those which were offered in justification of the program. It does not *eliminate* "undesirable" emotions from the person, for it cannot repeal *the way nature designed organisms to function*. What it does succeed in doing is to complicate further the already intricate organism/environment field by setting up a great number of situations which, *unless avoided, are immensely emotion-arousing!*

For instance, if a "properly-trained" person should, in certain types of situations, "lose control of himself" and spontaneously discharge what he has been bottling up, then *this* becomes a situation which gives rise to such intensely painful emotions as shame, chagrin, humiliation, self-contempt, embarrassment, disgust, etc. To forestall recurrence of such a demoralizing experience, he will tighten up his self-control to a still more suffocating degree of constriction.

This constitutes whatever apparent success one may have in "getting over being emotional." What happens is that certain emotions, before they can get far in organizing action, or perhaps even get into awareness, are stifled and immobilized by the counter-emotions which they arouse, with the whole resulting deadlock more or less effectively excluded from awareness. To become aware of this unattractive set-up within one's own personality brings back painful conflict, turmoil, anxiety and "dangerous" excitement. But, unless one is willing to accept this as the existing state of affairs, it is relatively immune to modification and hopelessly self-perpetuating.

In the present experiment we ask nothing heroic of you, but merely that you make a first approach to increased awareness of your emotions. If you have not made yourself too insensitive to your bodily posture and functioning, perhaps you can, by means of the following instructions, demonstrate to yourself that emotion is, as we have stated, the concernful experiencing of extero- and proprioception in combination.

Attempt to mobilize some particular pattern of body-action. For instance, tighten and loosen the jaw, clench the fists, begin to gasp. You may find that this tends to arouse a dim emotion—in this case, frustrated anger. Now, if to this experience you are able to add the further experience—a fantasy, perhaps—of some person or thing in the environment which frustrates you, the emotion will flare up in full force and clarity.

Conversely, when in the presence of some frustrating person or thing, you may notice that you do not *feel* the emotion unless or until *you accept as yours* the corresponding body-actions; that is, it is *in* the clenching of the fists, the excited breathing, and so on, that you begin to feel the anger.

The celebrated James-Lange theory of emotion as a reaction to bodily movements—for instance, running away gives rise to fear or weeping gives rise to sorrow —is half right. What needs to be added is that the bodily actions or condition are also a relevant *orientation to,* and a *potential manipulation of,* the environment; for example, it is not just running, but running *away,* running away from *something,* running away from something *dangerous,* that constitutes the situation of fear.

It is only in the recognition of your emotions that you can be aware, as a biological organism, either of what you are up against in the environment or of what special opportunities are at the moment presented. It is only if you acknowledge and accept your longing for someone or something—the assessment of the strength of your urge to seek out this person or thing as you confront the distance or obstacles that separate you —that you obtain orientation for appropriate action. It is only if you acknowledge and accept your grief— the sense of despair and not knowing where to turn as you confront the loss of someone or something of great concern to you—that you can weep and say good- bye. It is only if you acknowledge and accept your anger, feeling the posture of attack as you confront persons or things which frustrate you, that you can mobilize your energies effectively for surmounting these obstacles in your path.

Psychotherapy has often been called a "training of the emotions." If it is to deserve this description, we can readily appreciate from the foregoing that it must employ a unitary method which concentrates *both* on orientation in the environment (analysis of the present situation, sensation, fantasy, memory) and on loosen- ing the motor blocks of the "body." Undue emphasis on either side can produce only pseudo-cures. The first puts too much weight on what is called "adjusting to re- ality," which largely means complying more fully with the status quo as conceived and defended by "the au- thorities." On the other hand, if the therapist works with the "body" alone, he may get the patient to simu- late and express in the therapeutic session various feel- ings, but these, unfortunately, will not match up with or will be actually irrelevant to what he experiences his situation to be when he is away from the therapist. Only if the "outer" and the "inner" can be harmonized and integrated can the patient ever be discharged as "cured."

To sharpen your awareness of emotion, try the fol- lowing:

Lie down and try to get the feel of your face. Can you feel your mouth? Your forehead? Eyes? Jaws? When you have acquired these feelings, ask, "What is the expression on my face?" Do not interfere, but simply permit the expression to persist. Concentrate on it and you will see how quickly it changes of itself. Within a minute you may feel a number of different moods.

So long as you are awake you are aware of something, and that something always carries an emotional tone of some sort. Anything which is a matter of complete indifference, lacking in concern for you—that is, devoid of emotion—simply does not set the figure/ground process in operation to an extent sufficient to enter into awareness.

It is all-important that you become aware of the *continuity* of your emotional experience. Once emotion is understood to be not a threat to rational control of your life but a guide which furnishes the only basis on which human existence can be ordered rationally, then the way is open to the cultivation of continuous awareness of its wise promptings. To suppose that this would take extra time and attention is not correct. The analogy is crude, but consider the case of the skilled driver of an automobile. For him to be continuously aware that his motor is running smoothly is no burden, for this is not the focus of attention. That the sound of the motor is part of the dynamic figure/ground of his driving, however, and that it is something with which he is concerned, is indicated by the speed with which it becomes some figure and claims more attention if it develops some slight, but significant, irregularity. Another driver—perhaps one who *does not want to be bothered* —will not hear the anomalous sound, or, if he does, will not recognize its meaning and will drive on for as long as he can, oblivious to the damage that may be occurring. To be continuously aware of emotion is possible only when you are willing to be aware of whatever is of genuine concern in your life, even if this be at variance with what others say or what you have previously *told yourself*.

Many people feel that their lives are empty when in fact they are merely bored and blocked from doing what would eliminate their boredom. Boredom is, though, a condition which can be rather easily tackled, so let us turn to its remedy.

In the experiment on concentration we saw that boredom results when deliberate attention is paid to something uninteresting and resolutely withheld from what would fire one's interest and allow spontaneous formation of the figure/ground. Nature's remedy is fatigue, the tendency to fall asleep or go into a trance where, once the deliberateness is relaxed, spontaneous interests can come to the fore as fantasies. If you will accept this as a natural process instead of fighting it, you can use the fantasies as a means of recognizing what it is that you would like to be doing. This is very simple when you are alone. Just close your eyes and permit a bit of dreaming. This will frequently precipitate a clear notion of what you want to do. In the company of others— where there are considerations of duty, keeping up appearances, trying not to hurt people's feelings, fooling the boss, and so on—the situation is harder to handle. Even so, to admit to yourself that you are not interested may help you to find points of interest—if you cannot escape. But situations which chronically bore you you must either modify or abandon.

You have noticed how differently you feel when you are with different people. One person bores you, another irritates you, one makes you feel stimulated and another depressed. You prefer, of course, whomever makes you feel at ease, happy, or important. In these reactions of yours there is often a considerable degree of "projection" (you are putting your own attitude into the other person and then saying that this person *makes* you feel thus and so); nevertheless, the following is often true: when you have a pronounced reaction to a particular person, it may be that person's aware or unaware *intention* to produce this reaction in you. The melancholic may *want* to depress you, the fawner to inflate you, the tease to hurt you, the nagger to annoy you. Conversely, the animated person wants to interest you; the happy person wants to have you share his enjoyment. It is by developing sensitive awareness of one's own reactions that one becomes a "good judge of personality."

When one has overcome the tendency to project his own unwanted and disowned feelings and attitudes into other persons—that is, when he has come to respond to the other person rather than to himself as projected into the other person—he can detect when someone wants to drown him with words and facts, to hypnotize him with his monotonous voice, to put him off guard or bribe him with flattery, to depress him with whining and wailing. You can develop this helpful kind of intuition if you first ascertain just how you react to every person in your environment and then see whether or not your reaction is confirmed by his other behavior. In doing this you will also begin to make the separation between what is the projection of your own unaware tendencies and what is true intuition of the other person.

Imbalances of the personality are remedied, not by reining in and suppressing the hypertrophied side, but by concentrating on and lending additional weight and differentiation to the hypotrophied side. An overbalance of sensation is likely to produce hypochrondria; of emotion, hysteria; of thinking, compulsion and frigid intellect. But such overbalances are always accompanied by underbalances in other spheres. The reestablishment of harmony and integration comes about through unblocking what is blocked. This previously impoverished side of the personality will then claim its due share of energy and attention and the hypotrophy will disappear.

Another experiment for becoming sensitive to your emotional experiences is the following:

Visit a gallery of paintings, preferably of wide variety. Take simply one quick look at each picture. What emotion, however faint, does it stir in you? If a storm is depicted, do you feel in yourself a corresponding turbulence? Do you quail a bit before the malevolence of that face? Do you feel annoyance at this garish splash of color? Whatever may be your quick impression of the painting, do not stay to make a dutiful inspection, but move on to the next. Notice the exquisite variety of emotional effects as you flash a glance at this canvas, then at that, and so on. If your response seems very faint and fleeting—or even just not there—do not take this as an unalterable state of affairs, but simply repeat this or similar experiments on other occasions.

If a gallery is not easily accessible, use a book of reproductions.

The next experiment will be a genuine chore, for it asks you to seek awareness of emotions which we all prefer to avoid, the very ones we use to scare ourselves into self-control. Such unwanted emotions, however, must be brought to awareness and discharged before we become free again to enter situations where we have experienced them. Suppose that a man is afraid to speak in public because on one occasion when he tried it he "flopped" badly. Suppose that a girl is afraid to fall in love because once upon a time she was jilted. Suppose one is afraid to get angry because on a previous show-down with someone he was badly beaten. All of us have had numerous experiences which are now available to be conjured up to frighten us off from making fresh approaches to interesting situations where we have suffered mishaps in the past. These old experiences are "unfinished business," which block us from undertaking attractive "new business." You can begin to finish them by repeatedly re-experiencing them in fantasy. Each time you go through one of these painful episodes you will be able to recover additional details and to tolerate in awareness more and more of the blocked-off emotion which they contain.

In fantasy relive over and over again, each time trying to recover additional detail, experiences which have carried for you a strong emotional charge. What, for instance, is the most terrifying experience you can recall? *Feel* it through again, just as it happened. And again. And again. Use the present tense.

Perhaps in the fantasy some words will come up, words which you or somebody else uttered on that occasion. Say them over and over aloud, listening to yourself say them, and feeling yourself forming and expressing them.

On what occasion were you most humiliated? Relive this repeatedly. As you do so, notice whether you tend to recall some still earlier experience of the same kind. If so, shift to it and work it through time after time.

Do the same for as many other kinds of emotional experience as you can find time for. Do you, for instance, have an unfinished grief situation? When someone dear to you died, were you able to cry? If not, can you do it now? Can you in fantasy stand beside the coffin and express farewell?

When were you most infuriated, most ashamed, embarrassed, guilty, etc.? Can you feel the emotion now? If not, can you feel what you do to block it?

In reporting reactions to the experiment of feeling their faces a number of students announce the discovery that theirs is a poker-face. Some express pride that they can cover up in this fashion—and say they have absolutely no intention of foregoing what they take to be the advantages of hiding behind a screen. Does this imply that they see all of their interpersonal relations as one never-ending game of poker? If, as they say, they don't take off the poker-face even in private, against whom, in this case, are they playing?

Almost all find it difficult to perform the experiment, as indicated in the following typical example:

"The emotion-awareness experiment has so far aroused too much resistance in me to give significant results. The main resistances were a feeling of uncomfortableness and boredom. I was unable successfully either to locate my facial expression or to note whether or not it was changing. The only expression I did note was one in which my lower lip pressed upward and outward in relation to the upper one. This I related to impatient cynicism, when I am hearing something (usually in a business way) that I don't quite believe. At other times I noticed a frozen quality to my face. This disturbed me to the extent of making me stop the experiment as soon as I became too acutely conscious of it. I have also become aware of my face under the influence of anger. Once again I found awareness of this particular expression too disturbing to linger on for too protracted a time."

Some stated their expression did not change, but remained rigid, while others said that it changed so rapidly and constantly they could not name it. Some said that just as soon as they labeled what they felt in their features they immediately recalled situations for which it was appropriate; while others said that the only way they could get any expression into their face was by first thinking of some emotional situation and then noting what happened in their facial muscles.

Discovery that their faces were relatively inexpressive gave some students new grounds for nagging themselves:

"I found, for the most part, that my face did not seem very expressive and often felt rather oafish. My mouth was frequently open and my eyes squinted. Both are habits which I can break only if I maintain an awareness of how I use my face.

"When excited, I found that my face was much more expressive. If I can control this I'm sure that I'll be a more interesting person."

This reflects the universal tendency to try to work on a symptom directly rather than on its underlying basis. To control the features deliberately is not expressiveness, but play-acting, and, unless one is a good actor, is likely to be just "making faces." In the training of actors it is recognized that one can play a stage role adequately only if one has had somewhat similar experiences in one's personal life and can again sense effectively the facial expressions and other behavior which accompanied these experiences. In the Stanislavski method of training actors (as described, for instance, in *An Actor Prepares*) great emphasis is laid on the cultivation of "sense-memory" and "affective-memory." What we are after, however, is not to teach you to play stage-roles convincingly, but, rather, to *act yourself!*

EXPERIMENT 8: Verbalizing

To verbalize means "to put into words." If we describe objects, scenes or activities, what we do is say their names along with other words which have to do with their arrangement, relationships, special properties, and so on. We verbalize what they are as based on seeing, hearing, or otherwise directly experiencing them. If we reason about them, we manipulate the sets of words that describe them. This may be without further direct experience, for, once anything is named, its name can for many purposes serve as proxy. Maneuvering names instead of the named objects may be tremendously labor-saving and efficient—as, for instance, in planning how to move a heavy piano. But note! Moving names around does *not* in and of itself *actually move what is named*.

Healthy verbalizing usually takes off from what is non-verbal—objects, conditions, the state of affairs—and terminates in the production of non-verbal effects. This is not to say that verbalization may not on occasion be useful when it is about what is already verbal—books, plays, what someone said—but this tendency to talk about talk is in our times a disease! When one fears contact with actuality—with flesh-and-blood people and with one's own sensations and feelings—words are interposed as a screen both between the verbalizer and his environment and between the verbalizer and *his own organism*. The person attempts to live on words—and then wonders vaguely why something is amiss!

In the "intellectual" there is this hypertrophy of verbalizing. He attempts in compulsive and obsessive ways to "be objective" about his personal experience—which largely means to theorize in words about himself and his world. Meanwhile, and *by* this very method, he avoids contact with the feeling, the drama, the actual situations. He lives the substitute life of words, isolated from the rest of his personality, contemptuous of the body, and concerned with the verbal victories of righteousness, arguing, making an impression, propagandizing, rationalizing—while the genuine problems of the organism go unattended.

But this word disease is not limited to the intellectual. It is universal. Partial awareness of the disorder leads people to write books bearing such titles as *The Tyranny of Words,* and the general effort of semantics in recent years has been to reconnect words to at least the environmental non-verbal reality by insisting that each word refer to a non-verbal something. Our experiments on actuality and abstraction have been in this direction. But the semanticists often use their precision with regard to the "things out there" to exhaust their time and attention and thus avoid getting around to the semantic problems of what is "in here." They rarely mention the biology of language—its sensory-motor roots.

Our technique for exposing and becoming aware of the pathological aspects of verbalizing is, as with other functions, to regard it first of all as an existent activity. This applies whether the words are spoken aloud or whether they are "merely thought," that is, occur as subvocal speech. Speaking aloud comes first—that is how a child is taught the language—but one can later put this publicly acquired language to private use as thinking. As such, in the integrated personality thinking is a useful, active instrumentality in handling the complex relationships of aware need, imagined means of fulfillment, and the overt behavior which makes concrete what has been imagined. Most adults, however, look upon thinking as independent and prior: "It is easy to think, but hard to express the thoughts." This is due to a secondary block, one's fear of how others will react to one's thoughts if they are voiced. Once a person gets to speaking at a good pace, warms up to his subject, loses the fear of committing himself, and stops rehearsing his statements before uttering them, it becomes obvious that, when there is nothing to fear, speech and thought are identical.

In order to integrate our verbal and thinking existence, we must become aware of it. The means of orientation with regard to speaking is listening:

Listen to your own production of words in company. If you have an opportunity, have your voice recorded. You will be surprised, perhaps chagrined, at how it sounds. The more your concept of your self differs from your actual personality, the more unwilling you will be to recognize your voice as your own.

Next, recite aloud a poem that you know, and once again listen to yourself. Do not interfere by trying to speak more loudly, clearly, or expressively. Just repeat the recitation, however it comes, and listen until you can feel the integration of speaking and listening.

Next, recite the same poem internally—"in your mind." By now it should be easy to hear yourself saying it. Also, in doing your ordinary reading listen to yourself reading subvocally. At first this will slow you up and make you impatient, but before long you will be able to listen as quickly as you can read—and the practice will vastly improve your memory by increasing your contact with the material read.

Finally, begin to listen to your subvocal thinking. At first, when listened to, you as the internal speaker will go dumb, but after a while the babbling will start up again. You will hear incoherent "crazy" bits of sentences floating around. If this produces too great anxiety, talk to yourself deliberately a little: "I am now listening to myself. I don't know what to think. I shall do the now-I-am-aware experiment silently. Yes, it sounds just as it did aloud. Now I have forgotten to listen . . ." etc.

Notice the modulation of your internal voice. Is it angry, wailing, complaining, bombastic? Do you harangue? Does your voice sound childish? Does it go on pedantically explaining matters in detail even after the meaning has been grasped?

Persist until you get the feeling of the integration —the going together, the belonging together—of listening and talking. This internal dialogue is what Socrates called the essence of thinking. If you can come to feel the functional unity of the talking and listening, your thinking will become much more expressive. At

the same time the part of your thinking that is not
expressing anything, that is simply like gears which
whir around without meshing and pulling a load, will
tend to disappear.

In your ordinary conversation and that of your com-
panions, take note of the number and kind of super-
numerary expressions: "don't you think?"; "right?";
"well . . ."; "maybe"; "you know"; "I mean"—as well
as meaningless grunts, all of which serve only to prevent the slightest amount of silence in the vocal flow.
Once you have observed these face-savers and plead-
ers-for-attention, they will begin to vanish from your
speech and leave it smoother and more to the point.

When you have mastered internal listening, proceed
to the decisive step—the production of *internal silence!*
This is very difficult. Most people cannot endure even
external silence. Do not mistake internal silence for
blankness, trance, cessation of "mind." Only talking-
and-listening are in abeyance—all other awareness persists.

> Try to keep internally silent, to refrain from sub-
> vocal talking—yet remain awake and aware. At first
> you will be able to do this for no more than a few
> seconds at a time, for the thinking will obsessively start
> up again. So, to begin with, be content simply to notice
> the difference between internal silence and talking, but
> let them alternate. An excellent way to do this is to
> coordinate them with your breathing. Try to be with-
> out words while you inhale. Then, on the exhalation,
> let whatever words have formed speak themselves
> subvocally. If you are alone, you will find it helpful
> to say the words in a way that is intermediate between
> vocal and subvocal—that is, *whisper* them. If you per-
> sist in your performance of this experiment, what you
> visualize will become brighter, your body-sensations
> more definite, your emotions clearer, for the attention
> and energy used up in pointless talking will now be
> invested in these simpler and more basic functions.

Poetry, the art of expressive speech, resides in the
ability to maintain silent awareness of need, image,

feeling, memory, at the very time that the words are welling up, so that, instead of being banal stereotypes, the words when uttered are plastically adapted to a richly experienced figure. Such words express what had a non-verbal beginning.

Listen to and interpret your subvocal speaking—its rhythm, tone, catch-phrases. To whom are you speaking? For what purpose? Are you badgering and nagging? Cajoling? Do you turn the phrases as if you were holding back something, you know not what? Are you trying to impress? Is your thinking tentative and bewildered? Is it a bluff? Do you admire the way the words roll along? Is there always an audience?

Much of what you customarily feel as evaluation and moral judgment is your subvocal speaking in such internal dramatic situations. If you can stop the internal talking and maintain internal silence, you will arrive at a simpler appreciation of the facts and your reactions to them.

We shall now quote a few comments from students about this experiment on verbalizing. Most reported disappointment with the sound of their recorded voices, for it was higher, thinner, less forceful, and so on, than had been supposed; a few, however, were agreeably surprised. The significance of this experienced discrepancy was, in several cases, strongly disputed.

"That people's conception-of-self differs from their actual personality I would agree, but inability to accept one's recorded voice as one's own is no measure of this. What about the fact that the more one comes to hear one's recorded voice the more one comes to recognize it as sounding like one's own voice? Are we to gather that this would mean that one's concept-of-self was coming to be more nearly like one's actual personality? I think not!"

Although the above quotation concerns a relatively minor issue, let us briefly consider it. One can distort an indicator when it points to something that is unwelcome. If a man stepped on a scale to weigh himself, disliked the figure at which the pointer stopped, and then, to correct matters, bent the pointer, this would certainly not constitute a valid gain or loss in weight, but, provided he could in addition blot out awareness of the fact that he had worked directly on the indicator rather than on what it indicated, he could fool himself into believing that what he had disliked had now been corrected. If, after the initial shock of hearing one's recorded voice, one rationalizes about the differences in bone conduction of sound versus air conduction, the imperfections of the recording medium, etc., one can readily reconcile himself to the travesty which the recording instrument makes of what he *still believes* to be his true voice. Nevertheless, to come to accept one's recorded voice as actually one's own does, at least in some degree, bring closer together one's self-conception and one's actual personality.

Listening to subvocal speaking brought forth a variety of comments:

"There was a badgering quality to my subvocal tone. It seems as if I'm not really satisfied with things as they exist, and I'm forever at myself in an angry, snarling way."

* * *

"I became aware that I was not merely speaking to myself, but it was as if I were delivering long sermons to an invisible congregation. Some of it was non-sensical—didn't hang together logically—but all of it was in the same aggressive, forcefully persuasive manner that I find I consider necessary to good public speaking. It was slow and very deliberate."

The attempt to produce internal silence aroused the greatest interest and diversity of reports.

"I find it utterly impossible to develop what you call 'internal silence.' In fact, to be quite frank, I'm pretty sure that such a thing is impossible, and, if it's really true that you get people reporting that they attain it, are you quite sure they aren't just pulling your leg?"

* * *

"I succeeded in maintaining internal silence for short intervals, but it was boring and a complete waste of time. This is a momentary, unnatural state of affairs because the thought intrudes that one must return to normal activity because there are things that have to be attended to and accomplished which are of interest and consequence."

* * *

"In trying to achieve inner silence I feel my throat muscles getting so tense that I feel I have to stop this silly business or I'll scream."

* * *

"I found that keeping 'internally silent' made me very nervous and restless. After doing it for about three minutes I was nearly ready to jump out of the window. It reminded me of the child's game of seeing who could stay under water longest."

* * *

"The internal silence experiment is something I can't take. It was as if I wasn't breathing and I gasped for breath to be out of it. But I know it is this lack of internal silence that keeps me awake for a couple of hours every night after I go to bed; this inner voice keeps droning on and won't stop."

* * *

"I hadn't really expected to be able to produce any complete silence and was all the more pleased, though puzzled, to see that after all it was possible and that it created a delightful, somehow 'complete' feeling."

* * *

"This is amazing! I can do it only for short stretches, but when I manage it, it is really wonderful, and what a relief from all that incessant, internal jabbering!"

* * *

"I can't keep from talking with one or more inner voices at once. This silence that I'm after happens for a duration that I really can't reckon, but it's practically no time at all. Then what happens is that I start making notes on my mental scratch-pad—that is, I start rehearsing a competent description of when and why the silence breaks, and this, of course, constitutes a break in itself. For instance, first there's silence. Then I notice the sound of rain and a label sneaks into the silence: rain. Mental scratch-pad makes a note that the first thing to creep in was the name of something, and very soon the whole business deteriorates into my usual subvocal ranting."

*   *   *

"I had no luck at all with internal silence until last Sunday when I was walking in the park with my husband. For a while I was not preoccupied with the usual 'troubles' which clutter up my 'mind.' Suddenly I pinched the poor man and exclaimed: 'It happened!' This, of course, ended the silence, but, for quite a while, without any thinking, I had been experiencing the landscape, the wind, the rhythm of walking, and other such things. If this is the experience of internal silence, to call it 'wonderful' is understatement."

*   *   *

"The most exciting and difficult experiment was my attempts to produce inner silence. Most of the time I did not succeed, but on occasions when I did for a few seconds I was amazed at the result, which was a feeling of tremendous potential power and relaxation. Unfortunately, as soon as a few seconds had passed, I began to speak internally about this very success—which, of course, immediately sabotaged it."

EXPERIMENT 9: Integrating Awareness

If you have seriously worked through the preceding experiments—on body-sensations, emotions and verbalizing—you may already begin to feel more alive and more spontaneously expressive. We hope you are gradually recognizing that much of the constant effort you supposed necessary to hold yourself together is actually unnecessary. You do not fall apart, go to pieces, or "act crazy," if you let up on your deliberate holding back, forcing attention, constant "thinking" and active interference with the trends of your behavior. Instead, your experience begins to cohere and to organize into more meaningful wholes. This, in contrast with forced, deliberate, pseudo-integration, contrived and maintained by determined suppression of some behavior and effortful squeezing out of other responses, is genuine self-integration.

When you relinquish your determination to make your behavior fit the arbitrary, more or less fixed pattern that you have taken over from "the authorities," aware need and spontaneous interest come to the surface and reveal to you what you are and what it is appropriate for you to do. This is your nature, the very core of your vitality. Energy and attention have gone into forcing yourself, because of a mistaken feeling of "oughtness," along lines that run counter to your healthy interests. To the extent that you regain and redirect this energy, the areas of restored vitality will progressively increase. It is nature that cures—*natura sanat*. A wound heals or a bone knits by itself. There is nothing the physician can do but to clean the wound or set the bone. It is the same with your personality.

Every method ordinarily used in psychotherapy is, as single and isolated, relevant, but also inadequate. Since physical and social environment, body, emotion, thinking, speech, all exist in a unitary functioning which is the total organism/environment process, to give attention to *any one* of these components is appropriate for promoting personality integration. Those methods which abstract from the living unity one of these parts and concentrate on it more or less exclusively—for example, on the body-sensations and muscular-tensions, *or* on the interpersonal relationships, *or* on emotional training, *or* on semantics—should in the long run prove efficacious. Even if the method limits itself to a part, the effects tend to spread through the total unity of functioning. But it is reasonable to conclude that such partial methods, since they have the status of being merely abstractions from the concrete actuality, are in isolation not the essence of therapy, but only various approaches with therapeutic intent.

The danger in the use of any one of them exclusively is that the effects will not spread sufficiently to those areas which the particular method neglects. If any partial approach is pursued, in isolation from the others, the unaware resistance in other components of total functioning will increase to such a degree as either to make further progress in the selected approach impossible unless or until other kinds of material are admitted, or else to achieve a "cure" in terms of a new, arbitrary pattern. This will be whatever the "therapeutic authority" sets up as a model—for instance, the "spontaneous physical man," or the "adjusted personality," or the "psycho-person," or what not. Since you are working with the concrete actuality and not merely with an abstracted version of yourself, fitting yourself to one of the Procrustean beds is not the maximum that you can achieve.

Have you thus far begun to develop a feeling for, and an acceptance of, the unitary functioning of the organism/environment field? Can you begin spontaneously, not just on the basis of verbal logic, to see, for instance, the interconnectedness of the human sciences —biology, sociology, psychology, anthropology, linguistics, and so on—and, likewise, of the arts?

Our experiments so far have given special attention to various areas of your experience. Since these areas, when separately considered, are abstractions from your total functioning, let us now work on shifting from one area to another and note that, as you shift, your situation remains the same but that you express yourself differently, depending on which aspect of the situation receives your attention.

On the basis of whatever awareness you now have, try to form sentences that, with more or less adequacy, express the same situation successively in terms of the body, the feelings, the speech-habit, the social relations. As an example: "I am clenching my jaw and tensing my fingers. . . . In other words, I am angry, but not letting much of my anger express itself . . . In other words, my voice has a quivering edge but is soft and restrained . . . In other words, in our society the possibility of continued contact among persons depends on certain limitations of overt behavior."

Each of these formulations is a relevant and essential insight into the living situation. Practice passing easily from one to another, for this will deepen and broaden your orientation with respect to where you are and what to do.

We quote a few excerpts from students' reports to give some notion of the range of reactions to this experiment on shifting:

"My greatest disappointment with myself in the experiments is that I have thus far been unable to make spontaneous interrelations of the various functions . . . I have been able to reconstruct all my reactions to a given situation in retrospect, but never at the time they were occurring. I can only say that I have confidence that by continuing the experimenting I will eventually achieve the desired integration of function."

* * *

"This so-called experiment is ridiculous! All this verbal ritualism contributes nothing. Awareness is too sharp, acute, and complex a thing to be expressed in these—quite likely fallacious—'in other words' sequences. To say one thing is *not* to say another. This is a hopeless technique for expressing different aspects or facets of the total awareness. It only distracts and corrupts."

* * *

"Having worked through all the experiments so far I do feel a certain amount of self-integration and aliveness. It is a good feeling!"

* * *

"I feel I am just beginning to get a feeling of what's really going on. I'm beginning to feel some sense of what it is to live as a part of the world. . . . As far as being able to integrate the various areas is concerned, it will take a lot more work."

*　　　　　*　　　　　*

"If the material were presented with more understanding of the difficulties of the layman and with a clearer presentation of just what is required, I think it would be more beneficial."

*　　　　　*　　　　　*

"There must be something I've missed. I can't feel an integrated awareness. It's as though I don't want to, as though I were trying very hard to avoid it, to escape from it, not face it. Why, why, why?"

*　　　　　*　　　　　*

"I honestly think my experience begins to cohere in more meaningful wholes. As a matter of fact, there's no doubt about it at all, but for some obscure reason I'm reluctant to admit that you've helped me."

*　　　　　*　　　　　*

"Recently I've several times felt the rare elation associated with a sudden functional unity, the elation of dawning awareness, and this sudden insight when it has come has made me all the more anxious to continue with these experiments. My original doubts about putting any trust in your procedures are gradually fading away."

*　　　　　*　　　　　*

"This experiment was fascinating, partly because the results were so different from what I had expected after reading the instructions. After doing the previous experiments I thought that just putting them together would be simple. Actually, it took a lot of practice. But what I came up with was this: when you talk about shifting from one area to another, it's not really a shift. For instance, when I formed sentences that would differentiate, say, the body-situation from the feeling-situation, I found that they are the *same*. The body, no less than the feelings and the speech-habit, is a part of something—it's an integral part of a *functioning something*. And when one is able to give his attention to the different aspects of the same situation, then all the aspects combine to produce the total felt-meaning of the situation. What you've done here, without saying so, is to give us the very same experiment as No. 4, only this time the unity to be differentiated, instead of being a painting or a piece of music, is to be ourself."

I V

DIRECTED AWARENESS

EXPERIMENT 10: Converting Confluence into Contact

Thus far, in developing awareness-technique, we have limited ourselves to helping you to improve the orientation of your self with respect to environment and physical organism. We have worked on the senses, fantasies and memories, pains and body-sensations. Awareness has been undirected, in the sense that we were not asking you to seek anything in particular, but only to notice and acknowledge anything and everything that "caught the attention." We come now to directed awareness, in which we narrow and sharpen our focus in an attempt to single out and become aware of particular blocks and blind-spots. To do this, more stress must be laid on the self's manipulation of the body and environment. Your problem is to become aware of how you yourself manipulate yourself and your world. More attention must be given to the motor —specifically, the muscular—system. As you approach what is hard to observe, you will have to facilitate and manipulate figure/ground processes through active use of your muscles.

It is reasonable to correlate orientation (extero- and proprioception) with the sensory system, and movement and manipulation with the muscular system. This is the usual distinction between receptor- and effector-function. It is important to remember, however, that in all healthy behavior, senses and muscles work in functional unity. For instance, seeing is impossible without continual small movements of the eyes. Similarly, the spastic who has lost proprioception from his limbs and can execute none but the crudest and most graceless of movements, still draws on a good deal of sensory experience—gravitational pulls, directional cues, and so on.

Despite this genuine functional unity of senses and muscles, to approach our problems with initial emphasis placed on sensory orientation offers a tactical advantage. What we merely notice and register requires no conspicuous muscular action on our part and does not attract the attention of others. It is, rather, in the big, overt movements which we make in our environment that we run our greatest risks of incurring humiliation, suffering embarrassment, or in various ways bringing down punishment on ourselves. It is, therefore, easier and more sensible to work first to improve our orientation. But once we have a certain confident awareness of where we are, we can begin to move our muscles and, without unbearable anxiety, feel what we do in our larger actions.

Also, in working initially with orientation and then with manipulation, we retrace in proper order the steps by which symptoms and blocks have developed. What usually has happened is that, first, as a child we inhibited overt muscular approaches and expressions when they made too much trouble for us in our social environment. Gradually we became unaware that we were deliberately inhibiting them. In other words, since their suppression was chronic and the situation held no promise of changing in a fashion that would render the suppression unnecessary, this suppression was transformed into repression. That is, by no longer holding our attention (which requires change and development), it became "unconscious." Then, since constriction of muscular action tends to constrict the senses and make them inefficient, we began to lose our orientation. In these experiments we reverse the process and sharpen our sense of where we are and what we feel. With some degree of orientation recovered we can then begin to regain ability to move about and manipulate ourselves and our environment constructively.

We emphasize that in all types of activity, whether it be sensing, remembering, or moving, our blind-spots and rigidities are in some aspect aware and not completely buried in an inaccessible "unconscious." What is necessary is to give whatever aspect *is* aware more attention and interest so that the dim figure will sharpen and become clear against its ground. We can, at least, be aware that there *is* a blind-spot, and, by working alternately on what we can see or remember and on the muscular manipulations by which we *make* ourselves blind, we can gradually dissolve the blocks to full awareness.

Every healthy contact involves awareness (perceptual figure/ground) and excitement (increased energy mobilization). Every block conversely necessitates the performance of actual work to prevent contact. This work consists precisely of manipulating one's orientation—that is, limiting or distorting receptor-functions—in such a fashion that figure/ground does not form and, instead of there arising these two differentiated parts of the field, what would be figure and what would be ground simply flow together indistinguishably. In other words, there is "confluence," the condition to which we devote ourselves in the present experiment. If, despite all efforts to counteract it, figure/ground tends to form anyway, the process will be accompanied by its usual excitement. This poses an additional problem in the prevention of contact: since it is not intended to apply the energy in the excitement as would be the natural next step in making and living through the contact, it must be suppressed. Suppression of excitement produces the *breathing difficulty* which is *anxiety*—the problem to be dealt with in our next experiment.

A sensing and the object sensed, an intention and its realization, one person and another, are confluent when there is no appreciation of a boundary between them, *when there is no discrimination of the points of difference or otherness that distinguish them*. Without this sense of boundary—this sense of *something other* to be noticed, approached, manipulated, enjoyed—there can be no emergence and development of the figure/ground, hence no awareness, hence no excitement, hence no contact!

It is only where confluence is maintained as a means of *preventing* contact that it is unhealthy. *After* contact has been achieved and lived through, confluence has an entirely different meaning. At the *end* of any successful experience—one that is not interrupted but allowed to complete itself—there is always a confluence of energy or energy-producing materials. For example, when food has been savored, chewed and swallowed, one is no longer aware of it. The contact-functions have finished their work. Whatever novel operations were necessary to make this particular food assimilable are finished, and the further work can be handed over to the standard, automatic and unaware digestive apparatus which has phylogenetically evolved. The stored energy of the food is assimilated—literally, made similar to—what is already present in the tissues and organs of the body. It is no longer foreign, different, but has been "naturalized." It is now new strength added to the resources of the organism. It and the organism flow together—that is, what was food and what was organism are now in confluence.

The process of acquiring new knowledge has exactly the same form. What is new must attract attention by its being different from what one already knows, and must excite interest as something to be accepted, rejected, or partly accepted and partly rejected. It may be a potential extension of one's existing knowledge, or possibly a replacement or substitute for something one has hitherto believed. To assimilate it one must inspect it, try it for fit, work it over, and to some extent work oneself over. In this way the already-known and the new knowledge are actually *assimilated to each other*. The range and scope of what one can understand and do are thereby increased. If assimilation is not carried through to completion, one may accept the new knowledge on a tentative basis as something to "be applied" in such and such circumstances. With complete assimilation the knower and his knowledge are one. There is no "application of knowledge" to a situation, like ointment to a wound or cold cream to the face, but only the person-in-action. The person and his knowledge are in healthy confluence.

Should a way of thinking, believing, or doing which one has fully assimilated come later on any grounds to seem inefficient or be challenged by something which offers itself as possibly more adequate, it will raise a problem, come fully into awareness again, be worked through once more, and then be reaffirmed, modified, or discarded in favor of what proves itself to be better. It is only what one has been told he *should* believe, only what one has felt compelled to accept as what he *ought* to do—in other words, what one has not fully accepted as *his own* and *assimilated to himself*—that one feels himself unable to question, even though all present circumstances warrant it. Too much guilt and anxiety would be roused if he thus interrupted his confluence with "the authorities"!

Pathological confluence is the situation where component parts, previously differentiated and separated from each other, have been brought together and then kept together by being isolated from the play of further experience. This "binds the energy"—literally ties up the actual and potential activity—of both parts in a way that makes them of no further functional use to the organism. Consider, for example, the structure of some chronic inhibition. Suppose one inhibits sobbing by deliberate contraction of the diaphragm and this becomes habitual and unaware. Then the organism loses both activities—that is, the man who manipulates his functioning in this way can neither sob nor breathe freely. Unable to sob, he never releases and gets finished with his sadness; he cannot even properly remember what loss he is sad about. The tendency to sob and the contraction of the diaphragm against sobbing form a single stabilized battle-line of activity and counter-activity, and this perpetuated warfare is isolated from the rest of the personality.

The task of psychotherapy, obviously, is to bring back the boundary of demarcation—the awareness of the parts as parts, and, in the specific instance, of the parts as consisting of crying and diaphragm-contraction. Crying is a genuine need of a human organism which has sustained loss. Aggression against crying —in this instance, tightening of the diaphragm—has become a need only through the establishment of confluence with "the authorities" who say "big boys don't cry." To dissolve the inhibition requires that the confluent, bound energy of the opposed parts be again differentiated into sobbing and aggression-against-sobbing, that the conflict be revived under present, more favorable circumstances, and that it be resolved. The resolution must include not just one but *both* sides of the conflict. The sadness will be released by crying it out once and for all. The aggression-against-sobbing —contrary to one's own natural functioning—will be redirected outward against anti-biological "authorities."

Useful habit sets attention free for what is novel and interesting. There would certainly be no point in making wholesale changes in one's ways of doing things simply to demonstrate ability to change. However, many of our habits were not freely developed and are not maintained because of their efficiency, but are confluences with someone who taught them to us, with a model of some sort, or with some abstract conception of duty, propriety, or utility. We take for granted that they were spontaneously acquired, but any attempt to change them brings us up against resistances so strong as to be unmistakable evidence of unhealthy confluence.

Notice some of your habits—the way you dress, the way you brush your teeth, the way you open or close a door, the way you bake a cake. If they do not seem as efficient as they could be, or if some alternative seems just as good and has the advantage of offering variety, try to change. What happens? Do you take pleasure in learning the new way? Or do you encounter strong resistances? Does changing some item in your usual schedule throw off the rest of your routine? What happens if you watch someone perform a task similar to one of your own? Do you get annoyed, irritated, indignant at small variations from your own procedure?

Shortly after awakening in the morning one slips into a feeling-tone that is habitual and a sequence of actions which unquestionably neutralize much of one's available attention and energy.

Before arising think of feeling or acting differently. Do not make resolutions to be grimly carried through, but simply visualize in a vivid way the execution of some simple and easily practicable alterations in your usual routine.

Persons who live in unhealthy confluence with one another *do not have personal contact*. This, of course, is a common blight of marriages and long friendships. The parties to such confluence cannot conceive of any but the most momentary difference of opinion or attitude. If a discrepancy in their views becomes manifest, they cannot work it out to a point of reaching genuine agreement or else agreeing to disagree. No, they must either restore the disturbed confluence by whatever means they can or else flee into isolation. The latter may emphasize sulking, withdrawing, being offended, or in other ways putting the brunt upon the other to make up; or, despairing of restoring the confluence, it may take the form of hostility, flagrant disregard, forgetting, or other ways of disposing of the other as an object of concern.

To restore interrupted confluence one attempts to adjust oneself to the other or the other to oneself. In the first case one becomes a yes-man, tries to make up, frets about small differences, needs proofs of total acceptance; one effaces his own individuality, propitiates, and becomes slavish. In the other case where one cannot stand contradiction, one persuades, bribes, compels or bullies.

When persons are in contact, not in confluence, they not only respect their own and the other's opinions, tastes, and responsibilities, but actively welcome the animation and excitement that come with the airing of disagreements. Confluence makes for routine and stagnation, contact for excitement and growth.

To be sure, there may be a healthy confluence in marriages and old friendships—when it means the secure taking-for-granted of the other as "like oneself." But this assumption must prove itself, as must any other healthy habit, by its flexible utility in fostering satisfaction and growth.

A most important case of personal confluence is unaware identification (which we shall later discuss further as an introjection). All social solidarity depends on identifications with our intimates, our vocational roles, party, language, etc. They constitute the "we" that enlarges the "I." Like anything that is assimilated, identifications become unaware and they are healthy only if, should occasion arise, they *can* again be noticed and then be once more affirmed or else modified or discarded.

Consider as many of your traits as you can—speech, dress, general behavior—and ask yourself from whom you acquired them by imitation. From friends? From enemies? If you approve of a trait, can you feel grateful to the source?

Interpersonal confluence is an instance of trance or hypnosis. We are all suggestible in this way, but the safeguard is the availability of the suggestion to awareness and the ability to evaluate the emotional attachment to the other person.

Observe your reaction at a movie or play. Notice how, unaware, you identify with the characters. With which characters? Are there characters with whom you find it hard to identify?

Ability to evoke such identifications from the audience is crucial to an art-work's success in establishing its "reality"—that is to say, its illusion of reality. Popularity of the work stems largely from this. Yet works of art which accomplish only this have no great value, for it is a cheap experience (in no sense a re-creation) to drain off emotions by habitual channels, whether real or fantasied. An art-experience is worth your while only if it leads you to a difficult identification, some possibility in yourself different from what is customary in action or wish—a larger vision or a subtler analysis. Furthermore, since from the standpoint of the serious artist, the handling, style and technique is of highest importance, remember that you cannot grasp this by simply sinking into the characters but only by concentrating on *how* they are being created. As you become aware of the style along with your awareness of the characters and plot, you will be identifying with the artist and will share something of his joy of creation.

Before concluding this discussion of confluence we should like to have you consider guilt and resentment as symptoms of disturbed confluence. If a confluence between Persons A and B is interrupted, A will think that either he or B interrupted it—and is, therefore, guilty. If he feels that he himself has done it, then he must make restitution to B in order to restore the confluence; but if he regards B as guilty, then he feels resentment, feels that B has to pay him something, which may range from an apology to a willingness to accept punishment. In German, *Schuld* means either guilt or debt; to apologize is *sich entschuldigen*—to indebt or "en-guilt" oneself.

The aim of these inconclusive attitudes of nagging oneself or nagging the other party—guilt and resentment—is to restore the upset balance and mend the intolerable situation of broken confluence. What is avoided in such cases is *actual contact with the other person as a person,* whether this contact were to take the form of an explosion of anger, a generous act of understanding and forgiveness, enjoying the other's pleasure, being frank about oneself, or any one of a number of other actions which would be possible and appropriate if first consideration were not given to slavish restoration of the status quo.

Notice with whom you feel guilty or resentful. Would the same action rouse the same feeling if performed by another person? Now consider your other relationships to this person. How much do you assume is taken for granted that is perhaps by this person *not* taken for granted? Do you want to change the status quo? Then, instead of nagging yourself with guilt or resentment, think of ways of *enlarging the area of contact!*

The guilty and the resentful are, for the most part, clingers. They hang on. (We shall return to this mechanism in discussing suckling, biting, and chewing, in the experiments on introjection.) Such persons fear that, should a particular confluence be broken, then, no matter how contactless and unnourishing this emotional tie has actually been, they will be utterly and irredeemably starved!

Many students regard the invitation to notice their habits as sheer nonsense, being quite certain that they have experimented with various ways of performing a task and then chosen the one most efficient and desirable. Why bother, then, to try something else as an alternative, since it is sure to mean loss of time and inconvenience? Several point to the tragic fate of the centipede which stopped to consider which leg came after which.

A few went through several customary performances in an uncustomary way, found this possible, and thereupon concluded that they were not "a slave to habit." Others varied all the way from the admission that slight changes in routine—in shaving, for instance—were irritating, to bewildered confession that in some quite ordinary activities they couldn't diverge by one iota without getting considerably upset.

One man found that he could introduce novelties into his behavior only at the price of feeling very "unlucky." He discovered, furthermore, that many of his interpersonal relations were strained by his need to conceal the extent of his superstitiousness. With respect to his "lucky" daily route, he said:

"If someone else is with me and wants to go a different way, I force myself to go his way because I wouldn't want him to know that I believe so helplessly in good and bad luck. But, although I've known that when I do this—that is, go the other fellow's way—I feel miserable and mad at myself, I never realized until now that I get mad at the other fellow and feel that he owes me a lot for my willingness to go his way when I secretly feel it's unlucky for me."

Some say that they can with complete equanimity watch others do things in a way contrary to their own. Others feel annoyed or anxious. We quote a few examples:

"My wife was ironing one of my shirts, a practice with which I myself am not unfamiliar. But of course when I iron a shirt, I don't use the same care and patience as she. My system stresses speed and, as a result, I got annoyed after watching her for a while, as if I could *feel myself straining* in an attempt to push the iron faster."

*   *   *

"I take pride in my proficiency in driving a car, but I'm very rigid about it. It has made me quite intolerant of other drivers—either in my car or in theirs. I'm irritated when any fellow-driver on the road violates any 'rule' which I myself follow, even though the violation involves no hazard to me or anyone else. My wife incenses me highly if she deviates even slightly from what I consider proper technique, such as staying in low gear for a fraction of a second longer than I would."

*   *   *

"I'm beginning to realize that I frequently experience anxiety when an alternative course of action is offered me."

*   *   *

"I have what amounts to a compulsion to close doors that I find someone has left open. If I try to ignore these doors, I sit in agony, restless until the door is shut. I've attempted to ignore this, but I can't. The discomfort of getting up to close a door is much less than that of waiting until someone else sooner or later does it."

* * *

"I'm very disturbed when people do a job in a way different from the way I'd do it. I'm sure they're going to botch it. This feeling is so strong that I have to go someplace where I can't see what they're doing, or, if I stay there, I have to tell them how to do it—and sometimes I even take it right out of their hands and do it myself."

A more extended statement goes as follows:

"I find that I'm a slave to my concept of efficiency. It has been my lifelong habit to reduce all necessary actions to systems of habits (I comb my hair before shaving so that moisture won't later roll down my face after talcum is on it), presumably so that I'll have more time for the serious business of 'thinking.' Since studying the literature on psychotherapy I have, of course, become aware of the mechanism of compulsive tidiness and I have managed to rid myself of a good many habits which had become inappropriate and ritualistic. In the present experiment I have tried changing my habits (tentatively) even when I was convinced that the habit was the most efficient possible. This *does* create anxiety. Awareness that the new procedure is an experiment and can be abandoned at any time alleviates the feeling of uneasiness to a degree, but my 'superego' (me) keeps bothering my 'ego' (me) until we (me) do something about it.

"In the case of observing others performing tasks which I do in a certain (most efficient) stylized manner, I am indeed disturbed when they 'go off the beam.' I find it most difficult to keep from coaching them, even when their actions do not affect me and when unsought advice would be resented. I usually resort to fantasy for relief: 'Stupid bastard isn't worth fooling with!' "

Far from feeling bound to any fixed routine in their daily life, a few reported a "deplorable" lack of any regular and effort-saving system for handling routine matters.

With regard to the experiment of imagining, while still lying in bed, feeling or acting differently, some declare that when they first wake up they are much too sleepy to do anything of this sort; others state that "the seemingly small changes which result" may make quite a difference in their day.

> "For years I've tried to make myself get up a little earlier so that there wouldn't be this exasperating last-minute rush to get off to work. Last week, instead of turning off the alarm and snoozing for fifteen more minutes, one morning I lay there and visualized what would happen if I renounced this small luxury. It wouldn't make any appreciable difference in my total amount of sleep, and it would give me a chance to start the day without pressure. The funny thing that happened, when I looked at it this way, was that I didn't feel that I had to *make* myself do it, but, instead, I *wanted* to do it. The result has been that I don't feel rushed, I'm less groggy all morning, and much more relaxed."

Most persons admitted to identifying rather fully with some particular character-type in movies or plays. Those who identified themselves with the hero or heroine assumed that everyone else did this too, but there were many who preferred to imagine themselves the under-dog, the top-dog, the saintly, the sinful, regardless of whether their preferred role was that of the hero or not. One man stoutly affirmed: "I'm always—but always—the villain!"

Except for bits of outstanding behavior, few were aware of having copied personality traits from others.

> "One striking bit of behavior that I know I've imitated from my father is that of being the 'sage,' the solver of other people's problems, the one friends rely on to fix things. I'm uneasy about this, because I don't believe it rests on sound foundations—that is, I don't have this understanding of all kinds of problems.

While I get true pleasure from helping close friends where I can—and so does my father—I don't feel grateful to him for teaching me to be the center of the troubles of all and sundry."

In connection with guilt and resentment, our suggestion to "think of ways of enlarging the area of contact" brought forth a chorus of impatient questions on how to go about doing this. A few, on the other hand, reported that they had started "enlarging the area of contact."

"Recently I had some trouble with my girl. For once I put my pride in my back pocket and enlarged the area of contact by a frank discussion of my grievance. Presto, she stopped kicking me!"

Another said:

"For the last thirteen years my relations with my parents have been strained. I don't enjoy being with them, and usually I manage to make myself so unpleasant that they surely can get little enjoyment out of being with me. I feel resentment, primarily because I think they've been too strict. Probably I feel guilty, too, but this I'm not aware of.

"I don't know whether they sense my animosity, but I assume they still love me in spite of my rebellious behavior. I do respect them, for they have many fine qualities. I've never mentioned my feelings to them. By God, I think I will! It *can't* make matters worse.

"If I were to air how I feel (and, of course, also enumerate the things which I do admire in them), the worst thing that could happen would be to bring my 'war' out into the open where it could be waged more intelligently. And we *might* even come to a better understanding and find that we have much more in common than I now let myself believe. It's certainly worth a try.

"In the light of these experiments, my behavior at present is silly, childish, and unadaptive. I hope my present enthusiasm for this long overdue project lasts, for I won't be able to put it into operation until I see my folks a month from now."

EXPERIMENT 11: Changing Anxiety into Excitement

Relief from guilt and anxiety has always been one of psychotherapy's chief ends. Guilt (and resentment) we have discussed as a function of confluence. Guilt is the self-punitive, vindictive attitude toward oneself when one assumes responsibility for interruption of confluence; resentment is the demand that *the other person feel guilty*. Both constitute a resistance to contact, awareness, and differentiation; they are a clinging to the object in isolation from the rest of experience. Both pervade all neurosis. (Further complications of guilt as the result of "conscience" we shall discuss in later experiments on projection.)

Anxiety is the neurotic symptom par excellence. Even if the person does not feel it because it is repressed, it will manifest itself to anyone with an eye for it in such signs as restlessness, increased pulse, or impaired breathing. Since therapists encounter it as the basic symptom in all patients, they have theorized about it *ad infinitum*. Birth-trauma, choking by the mother's large breast, "converted" libido, inhibited aggression, the death-wish—all these and others have seemed to one theorizer or another to be the central phenomenon in anxiety. With respect to certain striking cases perhaps each theory is correct, but what they have in common has been overlooked. It is a very simple psychosomatic event. *Anxiety is the experience of breathing difficulty during any blocked excitement.* It is the experience of trying to get more air into lungs immobolized by muscular constriction of the thoracic cage.

We use the term "excitement" to cover the heightened energy mobilization which occurs whenever there is strong concern and strong contact, whether erotic, aggressive, creative or whatever. In excitement there is always an upsurge in the metabolic process of oxidizing stored food-substances—and hence an imperious need for more air! The healthy organism responds in simple fashion by increasing the rate and amplitude of breathing.

The neurotic, on the other hand, invariably attempts to control excitement—and his chief method is to interfere with his breathing. He attempts to create the illusion for himself and others of being unmoved, of remaining "calm and collected," self-controlled. Instead of spontaneously deepening his breathing, both exhalation and inhalation, he deliberately tries to continue the breathing which was adequate before the excitement with its stepped-up oxidation rate. Then, in spite of himself, he narrows the chest to force exhalation, to rid the lungs of carbon-dioxide (by-product of oxidation), to create a vacuum into which fresh air can rush. Anxiety (from *angustia,* narrowness) comes with the involuntary constriction of the chest. It develops in all situations, neurotic or otherwise, where the organism is deprived of adequate oxygen. It is, thus, not in itself a symptom of the neurosis, but it occurs in neurosis as an emergency measure produced by the conflict between strong excitement and fearful self-control.

Anxiety and fear are to be sharply distinguished, yet the connection usually felt between them is easily understood. Fear is experienced with respect to some formidable object in the environment which must be either tackled or avoided. Anxiety, on the other hand, is an intra-organism experience without direct reference to external objects. To be sure, the excitement of fear, if suppressed, produces anxiety, but so does the suppression of any other excitement. It is a fact that many situations give rise to fear, but in our society no "strong" person wishes to reveal fear by panting or gasping, and this establishes the close connection between fear and anxiety.

A pleasant prospect may be accompanied by anxiety—when, for instance, we say we are "breathless with anticipation." The anxiety occurs when we try to rein in the excitement within the limits of decorum.

This is what Freud called "instinct-anxiety," caused precisely by over-controlling necessary functions of the organism. Another frequent instance of non-fearful anxiety is stage-fright. The audience is not something to be actually tackled or avoided and it presents no real danger unless it is the tomato-throwing kind. The actor is keyed up with excitement, without which his performance would be frigid and lifeless. Once he has overcome his breathing difficulty, he warms up and enjoys the excitement. Before the performance begins he may generally be seen pacing restlessly up and down. While this is better than standing still, what would be more profitable would be to exhale deeply and gasp. The complication of this situation by "self-consciousness" is a matter which we must discuss later, but essentially it involves the actor's apprehensiveness that something will go awry, that he will give a bad performance and thus interrupt the confluence between himself as the actual performer and his ideal of himself as someone who never lets the audience (himself) down.

Although any anxiety will have its particular quality, determined by what kind of excitement is being blocked, most often, as we said before, anxiety is toned with fear. Since sexual and aggressive excitement are especially dangerous and punishable, the fearful control of such excitement in various ways interferes with normal breathing. To control a burst of rage or angry shouting one holds one's breath. This has the double function of denying the excitement its fuel, oxygen, and also of choking back what would be expressed if one permitted free exhalation. During masturbation or intercourse one may, for the sake of concealment or in shame of one's animality, suppress excited, noisy breathing. The pompous he-man chest, symptomatic of the need to exhibit a powerful torso, gives insufficient air, for, fearful that this facade will collapse since there is nothing much behind it, one maintains it rigidly. In artificial concentration and staring one holds one's breath as part of the suppression of the feared distracter.

There is nothing pathological in the momentary arrest of respiration which occurs when a strong stimulus abruptly presents itself. Observations throughout the animal kingdom indicate that, suddenly alerted, an organism halts overt movements, including breathing. It is as if, when full attention is needed to orient oneself to what is novel, the very sounds and sense of muscular movement that go with breathing are sources of distraction. We try to get rid of these distractions, either by breathing more shallowly or by suspending breathing altogether for a few seconds. What is pathological is to extend this emergency behavior indefinitely.

Breathing is not just inhaling; it is the full cycle of exhaling-and-inhaling. Under normal conditions exhaling does not require effort, since it is simply letting go and allowing the muscles which lift the ribs and lower the diaphragm to relax. But exhalation is, of course, just as important as inhaling, for it cleanses and empties the lungs so that fresh air can enter. The amount of air that can be exhaled obviously depends on how much has been inhaled, and it is to the inhalation phase that health cultists give emphasis. If there is interest and excitement and physical exertion of a meaningful sort, depth of inhalation takes care of itself quite adequately without resort to artificial setting-up exercises.

Although unrestricted breathing dispels anxiety, the neurotic who suffers anxiety-states simply cannot follow the advice to exhale and inhale—that is, simply to breathe. This is precisely what he cannot do—namely, breathe—for, unaware of what he is doing and therefore uncontrollably, he maintains against his breathing a system of motor tensions, such as tightening the diaphragm against tendencies to sob or express disgust, tightening the throat against tendencies to shriek, sticking out the chest to appear substantial, holding back the aggression of the shoulders, and a number of other things which we shall discuss later under retroflection. He is utterly incapable of a complete, unforced exhalation. Instead, his breath comes out in uneven spurts—staircase breathing—and it may stop, as if bumping into a wall, long before thorough emptying of the lungs. After hitting such a wall, he may then, by forced contraction, expel more air, but this is artificial and continues only as long as the deliberate effort.

The cure of anxiety is necessarily indirect. One must find out *what* excitements one cannot at present accept as one's own. Since they arise spontaneously, they must be related to genuine needs of the organism. Ways must be discovered to fulfill these needs without jeopardizing other functions of the organism. One must also find out just *how,* by various patterns of muscular contraction, one arrests full exhalation.

While, as stated, the cure of anxiety is roundabout, involving awareness of what the excitement would express and overcoming the resistances to accepting this as one's own, a partial relief of any given instance of anxiety can be obtained, paradoxically, by tightening even further the narrowness of the chest instead of resisting it. In other words, give in to and go along with the motor impulse that you feel (but do not add others). A basis for achieving deeper and more lasting relief from anxiety is presented in the next two experiments on muscular-concentration and development.

If you are prone to anxieties and aware of them, try out and confirm for yourself the suggestion made above. A student comments as follows:

"I have experienced one mild anxiety attack during the past four months. This was while studying for an exam in physiology. The harder I worked, the less I seemed to know. To fail the exam threatened my self-esteem unbearably. I tried the business of tightening my chest even more and practiced the exhalation suggestion. It seemed to help. At least, I was then able to reconcile myself to failing the test (I passed it, after all). My main point here is that I was able to think with greater perspective after I relieved the physical tension of not-breathing."

*   *   *

"After reading about anxiety I attempted to dispel my own anxieties when they arose in later situations by the breathing exercises mentioned. By freer exhalation-inhalation, relaxation of the diaphragm, etc., I was able to end the tautness and semi-paralysis of anxiety, leaving myself much freer to act and think in that situation (and others, since anxiety aroused by one incident or stimulus seemed to expand to others and to remain for a time after the precipitating stimulus had been removed). However, the anxiety invariably returned, since nothing was done to correct the originally provoking incident or stimulus."

*　　　　　*　　　　　*

"When I read the discussion of anxiety I can't say I was very much impressed. I forgot all about it until I went for an interview a few days later, an interview that I was very much interested in having turn out well. During the time while I was kept waiting I tried reading a magazine, but when I found I didn't know what I was reading, I realized I was displaying just those symptoms of anxiety that the experiment had described. I was breathing rapidly but very shallowly and I was getting more and more keyed up every minute.

"So I tried breathing deeply. At first it was very difficult, because I actually rebelled against slowing down my breathing and taking it easy. However, I kept at it, and soon I could feel that I was getting a grip on myself. At the same time I noticed that the cold perspiration that was standing out on my neck and arms was stopping. I felt less and less like a lamb about to be slaughtered and more like a person going in to have an interview with a man who was no less a human being than myself. I was truly amazed by discovering that I could do something about a thing that I had previously considered completely out of my control."

A few misinterpreted entirely what had been said, as in the following statement: ". . . I'm not sure that deep breathing is the answer to anxieties." Of course it isn't! The breathing procedure of this experiment was introduced with the explicit statement that it was no magic cure-all but merely a means of obtaining relief from acute attacks, with permanent changes in anxiety-proneness dependent on modification of the underlying basis—that is, on release of the *blocked excitements*.

"Breathing is related to anxiety, undoubtedly. But even now, as I breathe in and out, I still feel an overwhelming anxiety. I feel like crying, but I can't. I only gasp and feel myself tense all over. My hands clench and unclench, my lower jaw is tight, and I shrug my shoulders and think, 'It can't be helped; I'll just have to make the best of it.' I can feel everything that you say in your description of breathing except 'exhalation is simply the effortless elastic return of ribs and muscles to the resting condition which preceded inhalation.' My exhalation certainly is not effortless. It is as though I were pushing the breath out with strong resistance from some part of me, the breath ending in a suppressed sob. Funny, I had never noticed that before. Now I am trying to exaggerate that and, much to my surprise, it does bring relief, just as you said it would. Also, when I have felt extremely keyed up I have forced myself to breathe in and out, preferably outdoors, and have found that that helps too."

Some prefer to keep their investigations of breathing in the anxiety-situation at the verbal level:

"About this conception of anxiety, are you serious? It's a cute idea, but I don't know enough physiology to judge. Anyway, I would think a little evidence in order."

A number of references could be given to relevant physiological researches. We are not in this work, however, attempting to say everything that is relevant to this subject, particularly where it would involve unnecessary technicalities; instead, we are limiting ourselves, for the most part, to what you yourself can validate in terms of your own experience. On the present issue, if you discover in your own functioning that anxiety does indeed arise when excitement is blocked and, conversely, is dispelled if you can lift these self-imposed restrictions on breathing, what better evidence could you want?

Whether you are at present aware of anxiety or not, we recommend that you begin to notice your breathing. Think of yourself and feel yourself as a breather. Remember that the very term "psychology" derives from a Greek word which came to mean "soul" after it had originally meant "the vital breath." At first it will be simpler for you to notice the breathing of others: the rate, amplitude, irregularity, stoppages; the yawns, gasps, sighs, coughings, chokings, sniffs, sneezes, wheezings, and so on. Then, in your own breathing, see if you can differentiate the parts of this complicated process. Can you feel the air going into your nose, down through your throat and neck, into the bronchi? Can you feel your ribs spread apart as you inhale, the stretching of your back, the increase in the amount of space you occupy as you expand your chest? Can you feel exhalation as simply the effortless, elastic return of ribs and muscles to the resting condition which preceded inhalation?

Yawning and stretching are usually associated with drowsiness. We yawn and stretch in the morning when not yet fully aroused from slumber or at night when tired and ready for sleep. Unless they are suppressed in the name of good manners, yawning and stretching occur spontaneously on many other occasions; for instance, when we are bored, but feel that we have to pay attention, or, on the other hand, when tensely alert, perhaps while waiting for an examination to begin or just before walking onto the stage or meeting someone. All these instances have this in common: the organism needs to limber itself up and to change the existing situation.

To see yawning and stretching at their luxurious best, watch a cat which has just awakened from a siesta. It arches its back, extends to the utmost legs, feet and toes, drops its jaw, and all the while balloons itself up with air. Once it has swelled until it occupies its very maximum of space, it permits itself slowly to collapse—and then is ready for new business.

The morning yawn-and-stretch restores working tonus to muscles gone slack during sleep. All other occasions for this vigorous puffing up and then subsiding are apparently spontaneous efforts of the organism to break loose from the constriction of deliberately holding something back. Not much yawning occurs at night if one can tumble into bed without delay. It is when one feels obliged to stay awake despite wanting to go to sleep that he is beset by a succession of yawns.

Boredom is a state of suspense. In clock-watching situations one knows boredom will disappear as soon as one is set free and able to go about doing what he finds more interesting. In a situation where one is apparently free, but says, "I don't know what to do with myself," he is himself blocking his needs from coming through to awareness. In waiting for the examination to begin or for one's cue to go out on the stage, one is keyed-up but must await the starting-signal.

All of these are situations of suppressed excitement. The suppression is achieved by contracting one's muscles, breathing shallowly, and thus immobilizing the organism. To eliminate this constriction, or at least to soften its severity, it is the spontaneous and healthy tendency of the organism to yawn and stretch. The suppression of this, too, has been enforced by those who, rightly or wrongly, assumed that such an action on the part of *anyone* indicated boredom *with them!* However, even if one still, in "polite company," chooses to follow this tenet of good breeding, he can, at least on other occasions, make it a steadfast practice to yawn and stretch to his organism's delight.

Make it a habit to yawn and stretch frequently. Take the cat as your model. When you start your yawn let your jaw drop as if you were going to let it fall right off. Draw in fresh air as if you had not just your lungs to fill but your whole body. Let your arms, bent at the elbows, come up and push your shoulders back as far as they will go. At the peak of your stretch and your inhalation, let go and allow the built-up tensions to collapse.

PART 2

Manipulating the Self

V

THE MODIFIED SITUATION

All experiments thus far have been concerned with becoming aware of processes which are basic to the integrated functioning of the human organism. They apply to everyone. Now we come to experiments dealing with processes which occur chronically only when the organism is malfunctioning. They are "abnormal." It is their prevalence in a person's behavior that justifies calling him "neurotic" or "psychotic." However, granted certain kinds of upbringing and certain life-situations (which, in varying degree, have been encountered by every one of us) they are *inevitable*.

This is not equivalent to saying that since they are so common, we need not be concerned about them. Those writers of abnormal psychology textbooks who draw a sharp line between "normal" and "abnormal" —they are virtually extinct at last—reveal themselves to be confluent with "the authorities," whose concept of "normal" is so impoverished as to be synonymous with "conspicuously respectable."

There is now nearly universal agreement that every person in our society has his "neurotic trends," "unresolved conflicts," or "areas of maladjustment." Where the informed disagree is not with respect to the ubiquity of neurosis but in regard to what should or can be done about it. The orthodox Freudian, following hard upon what the master set down in *Civilization and its Discontents,* resigns himself to repression as the price we must pay for civilization. Others, more optimistic as regards the long-view, can, nevertheless, foresee nothing more hopeful than many generations of slow amelioration. Because of the lack of widely available therapeutic techniques and anything more

163

than drop-in-the-bucket methods of social prophylaxis, they use pussyfooting manners of speech for fear of being, as they think, unduly alarmist and upsetting. Were a tested remedy at hand which could be applied wholesale, we may be sure that they would more frankly publicize the epidemic status of the disease.

Still others, with Messianic fervor—and this present work will not fail to be classified as such—bring forth from time to time some simple nostrum and say, "Do this, and the world is saved!"

A major problem for all forms of psychotherapy is to *motivate the patient to do what needs to be done*. He must return to "unfinished business" which he left unfinished in the past because it was so painful that he had to flee. Now, if he is encouraged to go back and finish it, it is still painful; it reactivates his misery, and from the short-run view, it is still to be avoided. How can he be kept at the task—ultimately, how can he keep himself at the task—when there is such a quantity of unpleasantness to live through?

To this question no positive answer exists today for most persons. An unknown number, perhaps a majority, believe they would have no troubles if the world would just treat them right. A smaller contingent does have, at least at times, a vague recognition that they themselves are responsible for the ills that beset them, at any rate in part, but they lack techniques for coping with them other than the old threadbare resolutions "to do better," or moral maxims. Or they displace problems from their true arena to a spurious one which allows a great show of busyness and suffices, at least, to let off steam. A very small number take their troubles to an "expert," hopeful that some magic formula will be uttered and their personal devils exorcised.

Of those who start treatment most do not continue. Their cases are not discharged by the therapist but are self-terminated. Many, when magic is not forthcoming from one therapist, try another, then another, and another. Among myriad ways of expressing dissatisfaction with one's doctor a very common one is to the effect: "He doesn't understand my case." Perhaps he does not, and there may be merit in shifting. But most patients, perhaps all, wish in some degree to prescribe to the therapist how he shall cure them—and this prescription does not include that they shall suffer in the process!

For surgical and pharmacological forms of medical treatment the patient can be perfectly passive, and it is better if he is. He may receive an anesthetic and wake up with the operation over. The notion that treatment should be administered to a passive patient generalizes to notions of how it ought to be possible to cure a neurosis. The latter, however, is not "organic" but "functional." While the patient is not so naive as to suppose there can literally be surgical removal of his symptoms, he is likely to feel that little more should be necessary on his own part than to bring the body. Once he presents himself, the doctor—perhaps with the aid of hypnosis—ought to be able to fix him up.

Since it is, nevertheless, the patient himself who must change his own behavior and thus effect his own cure, all methods of psychotherapy give rise to what, in professional jargon, are called "disappointment reactions." These usually stem from realizing after a time that the therapist actually expects one to do hard work and undergo pain. As a matter of fact, without being fully aware of it, one may have sought out the therapist in the hope of acquiring exactly the opposite, namely, a better way of escaping work and avoiding pain. To discover that therapy involves concentrated doses of what one sought to be relieved of seems as absurd as to take the ailment and apply it as treatment.

In the fortunate case what happens is that, before the patient develops a disappointment reaction strong enough to make him terminate treatment, he learns that the hard work is not mere drudgery. However far removed it may at first seem from what he thinks is urgent and therefore the place to start, he gradually gains orientation and perspective. He comes to see particular symptoms as merely surface manifestations of a more general and complicated system of malfunctioning which underlies and supports them. Though now, in a way, the job looks bigger and will obviously take longer than originally supposed, it does begin to make sense.

Likewise, with respect to the pain involved, he comes to see that this is not pointless, needless pain. He begins to appreciate the rough-hewn wisdom of the advice to get back on a horse, when thrown, and successfully ride him off. The patient's situation is different in that he has, perhaps, avoided his particular horse for a long time; years, perhaps, or even most of a lifetime. Nevertheless, if healthy functioning requires that he learn to ride and manage a certain kind of horse that has thrown him in the past, the only way he can possibly do this is to make approaches to the horse and then, sooner or later, get into the saddle.

Although the therapist keeps leading the patient back to that which he wishes to avoid, he usually is milder and more considerate with him than the patient himself or than his friends and relatives. Their attitude is one of demanding that he snap out of it, stop pampering himself, and take the hurdle, whatever it is, in a blind, compulsive rush. The therapist, on the contrary, is at least as much interested in the avoidance itself as in what is avoided. Whatever the superficial appearances, where there is the tendency to avoid something, this tendency exists for good and sufficient reasons. The job is to explore and become fully aware of these grounds for avoidance. This is called "analyzing the resistance." How the patient experiences and verbalizes these grounds will change, perhaps dramatically, as therapy progresses. With the change, not just in how he talks, but in how he feels himself and experiences his problems, he can make further and further "approaches" as he feels the initiative and strength to do so until he settles his neurotic difficulties once and for all.

The strategy of motivating the patient to continue therapy is usually not particularly taxed at the very beginning. There is at that time the so-called "honeymoon period," when what is uppermost is the satisfaction of having made a start after an interval of vacillation, the opinion that one's therapist is wonderful, the conviction that one will be the brightest, the fastest-moving, in short, the most remarkable patient he has ever had, and that one will now blossom forth as that radiant, inimitable personality that one has always felt himself potentially to be.

It is when the "honeymoon" is over that the motivation problem becomes critical. One has worked so hard, been so cooperative, been the model patient, and yet —well, there is so little to show for it! The glamor is gone, and the road still stretches far ahead. In Freudian analysis this is likely to be the time of "negative transference." The therapist, who at first seemed so all-knowing and all-powerful, has revealed his feet of clay. All he knows is more of the same, and the same is getting tiresome. In fortunate cases such discontent with one's doctor breaks into the open as reproaches, disparagement, or even wrathful denunciation. When this occurs, it usually clears the air, and the case may then settle down for the long haul. If it does not—if the patient is "too polite," "too considerate," "too understanding" to attack the therapist outright—the case is likely to clog up with unexpressed resentment and be terminated by the patient.

For the most part, the patient's progress in therapy is not aided and abetted by the persons he sees in everyday life. He may, of course, be fortunate enough to have friends and acquaintances who have themselves benefited from therapy, in which event it is not so difficult for him to maintain belief in the value of continuing. If, on the other hand, he lives with relatives who construe his action as a reflection on the wholesomeness of the family relationships, who view it as "weakness" to be treated for something "mental," or who, to the extent that he progresses, find it less and less easy to domineer, exploit, overprotect, or otherwise be in neurotic confluence with him, he will have to struggle against veiled or open pressures to make him cease and desist from this "foolishness." Many patients succumb to such emotional blackmail levied upon them by "normal" associates.

As the effectiveness of psychotherapy has come to be more generally recognized, this situation has improved somewhat. Nevertheless, even though one may have a verbal understanding of what is involved in psychotherapy and a naturalistic conception of its rationale so that one does not boggle over giving it lip-service at a distance, when it comes close enough to interfere with one's own life—for instance, through changes forced in one's relationship to a friend or relative who is in therapy or through the heightened "temptation" to try it out oneself—then, to the extent that one is neurotic, one *must* fight it—*for it is aggressive toward the neurotic way of life!* The neurotic's resistance to psychotherapy, whether he is actually a patient or simply someone entertaining an opinion on the subject, constitutes his counter-aggression against psychotherapy. He feels threatened by it. And, *as a neurotic,* so he is! What could be more natural—and, with certain qualifications, healthy—than that he should fight back?

All that has been remarked above has centered around formal psychotherapy—that is, the situation where therapist and patient confront each other face-to-face. Now how does the matter stand with respect to your continuing to do the work involved in these experiments? They provide you with instructions whereby, if fully followed through, the crux of what goes on in formal therapy may be reenacted by the single person. But it is difficult to keep going!

Perhaps already, in the foregoing work on orienting the self, you have uncovered strong resistances against continuing. You are certain to encounter stronger objections to doing experiments still to come, for they involve going a step further and taking decisive action in your life-situation.

As you have found out already, this work leads you to the discovery that the human organism functions in a manner which is at odds with conventionally held notions about human nature. These traditionally established opinions, however, have been so deeply trained into all of us and have been so invested with feelings of moral rightness that their modification—even when our own first-hand experience confronts us with this necessity—seems wrong and worthy of condemnation.

There will be times in the work to come when, if you let it break through, your anger will flare against us for intimating that you possess feelings and entertain fantasies which, by your lifelong standards of what is proper, will seem despicable. At such moments you will be tempted to cast aside these experiments in disgust—and should you actually do so, certainly no-one could say that it was not your privilege. On the other hand, if your occasional assumption that we are "dangerous crackpots" does not lead you to such a summary breaking off of our relationship, we are certain that you will sooner or later arrive at a more positive evaluation, for you will have acquired new values without the loss of any of the old ones which were of any real importance to you.

During your moments of wrath against us it would be best if you could express it to us face to face. Since that is not practicable, the next best thing will be for you to fire it off to us in written form via our publisher. If "too polite" for that, then write the letter anyhow, even if you then consign it to your wastebasket. Whatever you do, try to get it off your chest!

We are personally responsible for whatever discomfort you experience in doing these experiments in the sense that, in recommending them to you, we commit an aggressive act aimed at your present status quo and whatever complacency it affords. That we act "with the best of intentions" or "for your own good" is beside the point. A certain highway is said to be paved with good intentions, and your life has been cluttered with meddlers who claimed to act for your own good.

In the experiments to come we shall make use of a formulation of behavior which, briefly stated, is as follows: various excitements, colored with pleasure, aggression or pain, energize the organism to make contacts and creative adjustments in its environment. It is by feeling and contact that the organism grows and expands its boundaries. Every neurotic mechanism is an interruption of some kind of excitement—a prevention of its further development. As explained previously, anxiety is the consequence of such interruption. Rather than risk the new, unknown contact, the neurotic withdraws into a contactless (unaware) confluence with his "safe" habitual functioning.

Three important mechanisms with which we shall work are retroflection, introjection and projection. These could be considered as defining three different types of "neurotic character," since they have their beginning in different life experiences and are rooted in different physiological functions. However, even if one of these mechanisms should predominate in us over the others, we all use every one of them. Since our approach is an all-round one, you need not, hypochondriacally, ask yourself whether you are a typical "retroflector," "introjector," or "projector" for, by proceeding with *all* the abstract possibilities of environment, sensation, body, feeling, speech, and the various characteristic resistances, you will, regardless of what your particular "diagnosis" may be, develop areas of integrated functioning that will then facilitate still further integration.

V I

RETROFLECTION

EXPERIMENT 12: Investigating Misdirected Behavior

To retroflect means literally "to turn sharply back against." When a person retroflects behavior, he does to himself what originally he did or tried to do to other persons or objects. He stops directing various energies outward in attempts to manipulate and bring about changes in the environment that will satisfy his needs; instead, he redirects activity inward and *substitutes himself in place of the environment* as the target of behavior. To the extent that he does this, he splits his personality into "doer" and "done to."

Why did he not persist as he started—that is, directing outward toward the environment? Because he met what was for him at that time insuperable opposition. The environment—mostly other persons—proved hostile to his efforts to satisfy his needs. They frustrated and punished him. In such an unequal contest—he was a child—he was sure to lose. Consequently, to avoid the pain and danger entailed in renewed attempts, he gave up. The environment, being stronger, won out and enforced its wishes at the expense of his.

However, as has been demonstrated repeatedly in recent years by a number of experiments, punishment has the effect, not of annihilating the need to behave in the way that met with punishment, but of teaching the organism to *hold back* the punishable responses. The impulse or the wish remains as strong as ever and, since this is not satisfied, it is constantly organizing the motor apparatus—its posture, pattern of muscular tonus, and incipient movements—in the direction of

171

overt expression. Since this is what brings punishment, the organism behaves toward its own impulse as did the environment—that is, it acts to suppress it. Its energy is thus divided. Part of it still strains toward its original and never satisfied aims; the other part has been retroflected to hold this outgoing part in check. The holding back is achieved by tensing muscles which are antagonistic to those which would be involved in expressing the punishable impulse. At this stage two parts of the personality struggling in diametrically opposite directions are in a clinch. What started as conflict between organism and environment has come to be an "inner conflict" between one part of the personality and another part—between one kind of behavior and its opposite.

Do not jump to the conclusion that we imply that it would be fine if we could all without further ado "release our inhibitions." In some situations holding back is necessary, even life-saving—for instance, holding back inhaling while under water. The important question is whether or not the person has *rational grounds* for presently choking off behavior in given circumstances. While crossing a street it certainly is to his advantage if he quells any urge to contest the right-of-way with an oncoming truck. In social situations it is usually advantageous to suppress a tendency to go off half-cocked. (But if fully cocked, aimed and ready, it may be quite a different matter!)

When retroflection is under aware control—that is, when a person in a current situation suppresses particular responses which, if expressed, would be to his disadvantage—no-one can contest the soundness of such behavior. It is only when the retroflection is habitual, chronic, out of control, that it is pathological; for then it is not something done temporarily, perhaps as an emergency measure or to await a more suitable occasion, but is a deadlock perpetuated in the personality. Furthermore, since this stabilized battle-line does not change, it ceases to attract attention. We "forget" it is there. This is *repression*—and neurosis.

If it were true that the social environment remained

adamant and uncompromising—if it were just as dangerous and punishable to express certain impulses now as it was when we were children—then repression ("forgotten" retroflection) would be efficient and desirable. But the situation has changed! We are not children. We are bigger, stronger, and we have "rights" which are denied children. In these drastically changed circumstances it is worth having another try at getting what we need from the environment!

When we suppress behavior, we are aware both of what we are suppressing and the fact that we are suppressing; in repression, on the contrary, we have lost awareness both of what is repressed and the process by which we do the repressing. Psychoanalysis has stressed recovery of awareness of what is repressed—that is, the blocked impulse. We, on the other hand, emphasize recovery of awareness of the blocking, the feeling that one is doing it and *how* one is doing it. Once a person discovers his retroflecting action and regains control of it, the blocked impulse will be recovered automatically. No longer held in, it will simply come out. The great advantage of dealing with the retroflecting part of the personality—the active repressing agent—is that this is within fairly easy reach of awareness, can be directly experienced, and does not depend upon guessed-at interpretations.

Theoretically, the treatment of retroflection is simple: merely reverse the direction of the retroflecting act from inward to outward. Upon doing so, the organism's energies, formerly divided, now once more join forces and discharge themselves toward the environment. The impulse which has been blocked is given the chance at last to express and complete itself and is satisfied. Then, as is the case when any genuine need of the organism is fulfilled, there can be rest, assimilation and growth. In practice, however, the undoing of a retroflection is not so straightforward. Every part of the personality comes to its defense as if to head off catastrophe. The person is overcome with embarrassment, fear, guilt and resentment. The attempt to reverse the self-aggression, to differentiate the clinch of the two parts of the personality, is responded to as if it were an attack on his body, his "nature," on his very life. As the clinched parts begin to loosen and come apart, the person experiences unbearable excitement, for the relief of which he may have to go temporarily into his clinch again. These are unaccustomed feelings which are being resurrected and he has to make approaches to them and gradually learn to tolerate and use them. At first he becomes anxious and would rather retreat into his deadened state of unawareness.

A main reason for the fear and guilt in reversing retroflections is that most retroflected impulses are aggressions, from the mildest to the cruelest, from persuasion to torture. To let these loose even into awareness is terrifying. But aggression, in the broad sense of its clinical usage, is indispensable to happiness and creativity. Furthermore, reversing the retroflection does not manufacture aggression that was not already there. It was there—but applied against the self instead of against the environment! We are not denying that aggression may be pathologically misused against objects and other persons, just as it is pathologically misused when directed steadfastly against the self. But until one can become aware of what one's aggressive impulses are and learn to put them to constructive use, they are *certain* to be misused! As a matter of fact, it is the act of repressing them—the setting up and maintenance of the grim clinch of the musculature—that makes these aggressions seem so wasteful, "anti-social," and intolerable. Once they are allowed to develop spontaneously in the context of the total personality, rather than being squeezed and suffocated in the remorseless clinch of retroflection, one puts quite a different and more favorable evaluation upon his aggressions.

What is also feared in releasing a blocked impulse is that one will then be completely frustrated—for retroflection does give at least partial satisfaction. A religious man, for instance, unable to vent his wrath on the Lord for his disappointments, beats his own breast and tears his own hair. Such self-aggression, obviously a retroflection, nevertheless *is* aggression and it *does* give some satisfaction to the retroflecting part of the personality. It is aggression that is crude, primitive, undifferentiated—a retroflected childish temper-tantrum—but the part of the personality that is attacked is always there and available for attack. Self-aggression can always be sure of its victim!

To reverse such a retroflection in one fell swoop would mean that the person would then attack others in ways just as ineffectual and archaic. He would rouse the same overwhelming counter-aggression that led him to retroflect in the first place. It is some realization of this which makes even the imagined reversal of retroflections productive of so much fear. What is overlooked is that the change can be made in easy stages which gradually transform the whole situation as they proceed. One can, to start with, discover and accept the fact that he does "take it out on himself." He can become aware of the emotions of the retroflecting part of his personality—notably, the grim joy taken in administering punishment to himself. This, when he achieves it, represents considerable progress, for vindictiveness is so socially disesteemed as to be most difficult to acknowledge and accept even when supposedly one spares others and directs it solely against oneself. Only when accepted—that is, when it is reckoned with as an existing, dynamic component of one's functioning personality—does one reach the possibility of modifying, differentiating, redirecting it into healthy expression. As one's orientation in the environment improves, as one's awareness of what one genuinely wants to do becomes clearer, as one makes approaches which are limited try-outs to see what will happen, gradually one's techniques for expression of previously blocked impulses develop also. They lose their primitive, terrifying aspect as one differentiates them and gives them a chance to catch up with the more grownup parts of the personality. Aggression will then still be aggression, but it will have been put to useful tasks and will no longer be blindly destructive of self and others. It will be expended as the situation demands, and not accumulated until one feels that he sits precariously atop a seething volcano.

Thus far we have spoken only of behavior which the person was unsuccessful in directing toward others and which he consequently retroflected against himself. Retroflections also include what one *wanted from* others but was unsuccessful in obtaining, with the outcome that now, for want of anyone else to do it, one gives it to himself. This may be attention, love, pity, punishment, almost anything! A great deal of what originally was done for one by others—notably, by his parents—he takes over and does for himself as he grows up. This, of course, is healthy, provided it does not include trying to gratify for oneself what are genuinely *interpersonal* needs.

This kind of retroflection combines the absurd and the pathetic. For instance, the story is told of a college student who, though living in a dormitory, was unable to make contact with his fellows. From outside the window of his lonely room he would frequently hear the occupants of adjacent quarters being summoned forth to join their friends. One night he was discovered standing beneath his own window repeatedly calling his own name.

Let us take a look at some typical retroflections. There are those that are simple linguistic reflexives. When we use such verbal expressions as "I ask myself" or "I say to myself," what is involved? In previous experiments we have often suggested: "Ask yourself . . ." Doesn't this seem logically peculiar? If you don't know something, why ask yourself, and, if you do know it, why tell it to yourself? Such ways of talking (and we employ them all the time) simply take it for granted that the personality is divided into two parts, as if two persons lived within the same skin and could hold conversations with each other. Do you regard this as a mere peculiarity of our language, or can you get the feeling that this quite common manner of speaking stems from being a person divided and having parts functionally in opposition to each other?

Try to get a clear understanding that when you "ask yourself" something, this is retroflected questioning. You don't know the answer or you wouldn't have to ask. Who in the environment does know or, so you feel, ought to know? If you can specify such a person, can you then be aware of wanting to ask your question, not of yourself, but of that person? What keeps you from doing so? Is it shyness, fear of a rebuff, reluctance to admit your ignorance?

When you "consult yourself" about something, can you be aware of your motive? Many are possible. It may be a game, a teasing, the administering of consolation, or the making of a reproach. Whatever it may be, for whom are you substituting yourself?

Consider self-reproach. Here you will find no true feeling of guilt, but the mere pretense of guilt. Reverse the reproach by finding that Person X among those you know at whom you are really leveling your reproach. Whom do you want to nag? Whom do you want to reform? In whom do you want to rouse the guilt that you are *pretending* to produce in yourself?

At this stage the important thing is not for you to attempt the full undoing of the retroflection by immediately rushing out and confronting Person X with whatever you hold against him. You have not yet explored and accepted enough of yourself nor examined the interpersonal situation sufficiently. Let the detailed content of any particular problem go for the moment and content yourself with trying to realize the *form* of your behavior as a retroflector. Gradually you will begin to see the role you also play in your interpersonal relations. You will start to see yourself as others see you. If you are forever making demands on yourself, you also, explicitly or implicitly, make demands on others —and this is how you appear to them. If you feel angry with yourself, you will feel angry even with the fly on the wall. If you nag yourself, you may be perfectly sure that there are others, too, whom you nag.

A person who retroflects aggression takes the attitude: "If I'm mean to myself, it doesn't hurt anybody else, does it?" It wouldn't, if his retroflection were complete and if he lived in a capsule, isolated from others. Neither is true. He lives with others, and much of his behavior—of the same general type as that which he retroflects—escapes retroflection. For instance, specific aggressions which have not been specifically punished and turned inward do find their mark in the environment. He is not aware of these, for his self-concept excludes "hurting others." Since he makes his attacks on others in a random, unconsidered way, rationalizing his motives, such actions, just as much as his retroflected aggressions, will be crude, primitive, and relatively ineffectual. Self-aggression can be more easily accepted as genuine aggression—one feels less guilt for hurting himself than for hurting someone else —but aggression toward others exists also in one who retroflects, and it must in the end be made aware and accepted before it can be developed into aggression which is rational and healthy rather than irrational and neurotic.

When a retroflection has been truly realized, reversed, and allowed spontaneously to develop with its proper objects, the meaning of what was retroflected always undergoes changes—for instance, *re*proach turns into *ap*proach. In the long run any interpersonal contact is better than retroflection. We do not mean by interpersonal contact "mixing with people," "being with others," or "going out more"—for such activity, while masquerading as "social contact," may be nothing more than contactless confluence. Making genuine contact sometimes involves what conventionally would be regarded as breaking or avoiding contact. For instance, suppose someone invites you to a gathering in which you haven't the slightest interest. You would greatly prefer to spend the time otherwise. But if you frankly say so, the common view would have it that you are declining "social contact." This is "bad," for we are taught early and late that some special virtue is inherent in gregariousness, even when it consists of nothing more than meaningless, insincere, time-wasting chitchat. But we say, "Yes, I'd be delighted," instead of, "No, thank you, I'd rather not." Thus we avoid breaking confluence with prevailing stereotypes of what constitute good manners. But we must then be *rude to ourselves* and treat with high-handed disregard otherwise possible activities which *are* matters of spontaneous interest and concern for us. When we say, "Yes, I'll come," and thus commit ourselves to what we do not wish to do, we are, in effect, saying "No" to alternative ways of spending the time which are of more importance to us. By preening ourselves on having a "positive personality"—being yes-man for every Tom, Dick or Harry—we retroflect the negative and say "No" to ourselves.

Let us look again at the nature of the retroflecting process. In deliberate suppression one identifies oneself with both the suppressed and the suppressing behavior. As a very simple example, consider the suppression of urination. Suppose one feels the urge to void his bladder at a time and place which is inappropriate. He simply contracts the urethral sphincter to offset the contraction of the distended bladder. This is a temporary retroflection. He has no intention whatever of making it permanent, and he does not disown—alienate or reject from his personality—either side of the conflict. As soon as convenient he reverses the retroflection. This consists, obviously, of merely relaxing the sphincter and allowing the bladder to press forth its contents. The need is satisfied and both tensions released. Persons differ, of course, with respect to how much tension of this sort they will endure before seeking relief. If their attitude toward eliminative functions is that they are "not nice," they may be too embarrassed to excuse themselves from a social group.

In contrast to a simple suppression like this, where both contenders in the conflict are aware and accepted by the "I" as belonging to it—"I want to relieve myself, but I prefer to wait"—one may identify with and accept as his own only one side of the conflict. In forced concentration, as noted in a previous experiment, one identifies himself only with the "chosen" task —that is, he identifies himself with the taskmaster who insists that he do whatever the job consists of. He dis-identifies with—alienates and disowns—those counter-interests which he calls distractions. In terms of the structure of the conflict this is similar to the simple suppression cited above; the difference is in the attitude adopted toward one side of the conflict. Although various needs are pitted against each other and working at cross-purposes, the "I" is not split in this situation because it refuses to include in itself (refuses to identify itself with) those background needs which run counter to the task. Not much gets accomplished; it frequently would clear the ground if the "I" could identify with the more urgent of these "distracters," give them priority, get them out of the way, and then come back to the task. However that may be, what we are trying to point out here is that in the type of retroflection which constitutes fighting the "distracters" in forced concentration, the "I" feels itself to exist only in the efforts to get the task done.

Sometimes in retroflections the "I" plays both parts —it is identified with both the active, retroflecting part of the personality, and also the passive part which is the object of the retroflection. This is especially true in self-pity and self-punishment. Before discussing these further, suppose you examine instances of self-pity or self-punishment in your own life and find out what answers you can obtain to the following questions:

Whom do you want to pity? Whom do you want to pity you? Whom do you want to punish? Whom do you want to punish you?

"Pity," "sympathy," and "compassion" are grossly synonymous, and all are in good standing as "virtuous" words. They have shades of meaning, however, which, while subtle from the linguistic standpoint, are profoundly significant from the psychological. The dictionary distinguishes them as follows: "Pity is feeling for another's suffering or distress, and sometimes regards its object as not only suffering, but *weak or inferior*. Sympathy is fellow-feeling with others, esp. in their grief or affliction; the word implies *a certain degree of equality* in situation, circumstances, etc. Compassion is deep tenderness for another, esp. under severe or inevitable suffering or misfortune." (Italics ours) These words, all expressive of attitudes toward the sufferings of others, are graded in terms of the amount of actual participation in, or closeness to, or identification with, such sufferings. Pity is the most remote, and we contend that most of what passes muster as pity is actually *disguised gloating*. Tennyson speaks of "scornful pity," and most of us have heard the recipient of pity shout, "I don't want your damned pity!" Such pity is condescension. We apply it to those who are in such low estate that they are not or have ceased to be our own serious rivals. They are "out of the running." By pitying them we emphasize the discrepancy between their lot and ours. Such an attitude, we believe, motivates much so-called charity.

When concern for the sufferings of others is genuine and not a mask for stand-offish, jubilant self-congratulation, it entails the urge to help in a practical fashion and to assume responsibility for changing the situation. In such cases we are more likely to speak of sympathy or compassion, an entering into and an active participation in the sufferer's situation. These attitudes enmesh themselves with the actuality and are too engaged in it for the luxury of sentimental tears. Tearful pity is mostly a masochistic enjoyment of the misery.

When this is retroflected we have the situation of self-pity. A part of oneself is now the object, but the pitying attitude is still one of scornful, aloof condescension. If the split in the "I" (the division into pitier and pitied) can be healed, the stand-offish enjoyment of the punishment being administered changes into the active urge to help, whether the object of succor be someone else or *neglected portions of oneself*. This new orientation leads to the task of manipulating the environment to bring about appropriate changes.

The *desirability* of self-control in our society goes unquestioned; on the other hand, there is little *rational consideration* of what it involves. This whole program of experiments attempts to develop self-control, but on a much broader and more comprehensive basis—in fact, on quite a different basis—from what is envisioned in the usual, naive, frantic seeking after it. When a person demands, "How can I make myself do what I ought to do?" this can be translated into, "How can I make myself do what a strong part of me doesn't want to do?" In other words, how can one part of the personality establish an ironclad dictatorship over another part? The wish to do this, together with more or less successful attempts to bring it about, is characteristic of compulsion neurosis.

The person who treats himself in this fashion is a domineering bully. If he can and dares to behave like this with others, he may sometimes be an efficient organizer; but where he must accept direction from others or from himself he becomes passively or actively resistant. Usually, therefore, the compulsive accomplishes very little. He spends his time preparing, deciding, making sure, but he makes little headway in the execution of what he has so laboriously planned. What happens within his own behavior is similar to what occurs in a shop or office where the boss is a slave-driver; the "slaves," by slow-downs, errors, sickness, and the myriad other techniques of sabotage, wreck his best efforts to coerce them. In the compulsive, the "I" identifies with rigid objectives and tries to ram them through; the unconsulted other parts of the personality, whose interests are disregarded, retaliate with fatigue, excuses, promises, irrelevant difficulties. In the compulsive, the "ruler" and the "ruled" are thus in a continuous clinch.

Although few of us would be diagnosed as compulsive neurotics, all of us have some degree of compulsiveness, for it is the outstanding neurotic symptom of our times. To the extent that we do, it will color most of our behavior. If the doing of these experiments is taken as an example, it is undoubtedly true that at times they feel like an onerous task imposed from outside and the issue is merely to get through them as expeditiously as possible. You respond with irritation, annoyance, or rage if all does not go according to the cut-and-dried order of your preconceptions. To wait for spontaneous developments is the last thing that the slave-driver in you will tolerate.

Reverse a situation in which you compel yourself. How would you set about compelling others to perform the task for you? Would you try to manipulate the environment with magic words? Would you bully, command, bribe, threaten, reward?

On the other hand, how do you react to your own compelling? Do you turn a deaf ear? Do you make promises you do not mean to keep? Do you respond with guilt and pay the debt with self-contempt and despair?

When you try to force yourself to do what you yourself do not want to do, you work against powerful resistances. The prospect of reaching your goal brightens if, instead of compelling yourself, you clear the ground of whatever obstacles you can find standing in your way (or of yourself standing in your own way). This is the great principle of the Tao-philosophers: make a void, so that nature can develop there; or, as they also express it, *stand out of the way*.

What obstacles, for instance, can you find to doing these experiments? If you say, "I must do them," who is supplying the "must"? You, apparently, for you are not compelled from outside. What if you didn't do them? No blow would fall. Your life would continue in its customary pattern uninterrupted. Suppose you say, "I want to do them but some part of me objects." What is the objection? Waste of time? Are you equally severe toward other ways of wasting time? If you saved the time that you spend on these experiments, would you have some urgent, "important" task to which you are sure that you would then devote the time?

Suppose you object to the lack of a guarantee that these experiments are going to "do you some good." Are you able to get such a guarantee on other things that you do?

Whatever your objections, don't blame yourself for them. Blame whomever or whatever you think is responsible for the way you feel. After discharging some of this aggression that you have been turning against yourself, you may respond to the situation quite differently.

Another extremely important retroflection to consider is self-contempt, feelings of inferiority—everything that Harry Stack Sullivan called the weak self-system and considered the essence of neurosis. As he put it, when one's relations with oneself are disturbed, all interpersonal relations are likewise disturbed. One is on chronically bad terms with himself when he has the habit of forever taking stock of himself, evaluating himself, and, on the basis of comparative judgments, dwelling all the time on the discrepancy between his actual performances and those which would meet his high-flown specifications. If he reverses the retroflection, he will let up on himself and then start evaluating the persons in his environment. Once he ventures to do this, he will soon come to regard such verbal evaluations, whether applied to others or himself, as of secondary importance. He will realize that his retroflected evaluations were merely a mechanism for dwelling on himself. When he directs the same kind of elaborate evaluating to others, he may soon see the futility of it and stop. Then he will notice persons with simple awareness of what they are and what they do, and will learn either how to manipulate them in a genuinely satisfying way or to adjust himself to them.

What do you doubt about yourself? Mistrust? Deprecate? Can you reverse these attitudes? Who is the Person X whom you doubt? Who makes you suspicious? Whom do you wish to pooh-pooh and take down a peg? Can you feel your inferiority as concealed arrogance? Can you undo self-effacement and recognize it as the retroflected wish to wipe out Person X?

Still another important type of retroflection is introspection. When you introspect, *you peer at yourself*. This form of retroflection is so universal in our culture that much of the psychological literature simply takes it for granted that any attempt to increase self-awareness must of necessity consist of introspection. While this, definitely, is not the case, it probably is true that anyone who does these experiments will *start* by introspecting. The observer is split off from the part observed, and not until this split is healed will a person fully realize that self-awareness which is not introspected can exist. We previously likened genuine awareness to the glow produced within a burning coal by its own combustion, and introspection to turning the beam of a flashlight on an object and peering at its surface by means of the reflected rays.

Examine your procedure when you introspect. What is your aim? Are you searching for a secret? Ferreting out a memory? Hoping for (or fearing) a surprise? *Do you watch yourself with the sharp eye of a stern parent to make sure you don't get into mischief?* Are you trying to find something that will fit a theory—for instance, the theory developed in these pages? Or, on the other hand, are you seeing to it that such corroboratory events do not take place? Then try directing these attitudes toward persons in the environment. Is there someone whose "insides" you would like to search? Is there someone on whom you would like to keep a strict eye? Who is it that you feel bears watching?

Apart from the aim of your introspecting, what is your manner? Do you dig? Are you the brutal police officer who pounds on the door and bellows, "Open up there?" Are you timid or furtive with yourself— that is, do you sneak your glances? Do you stare at yourself unseeingly? Do you conjure up events simply to fulfill your expectations? Do you falsify them by way of exaggeration? Or do you soft-pedal them? Do you abstract only what coincides with your immediate aims? In short, notice *how* your "I" is functioning. This is far more important than the specific content.

The extreme case of introspection is hypochondria —the search for symptoms of illness. Reverse this and search for symptoms in others. You may be an inhibited physician or nurse. What is the aim of such searching? Is it sexual? Have you ever been told that masturbation produces a tell-tale appearance of the eyes? Have you searched your own eyes or those of others for such a symptom? Do you introspect your body for signs that punishment has started for your "sins"?

A few students, in reporting their reactions to this experiment, expressed indignation over what they took to be its "insulting insinuations" and launched themselves upon a defense of the "goodness" of their personal motives.

> "You assume that all of us have an innate desire to pity or punish someone, and likewise to be pitied or punished. I must reject such a position as utterly preposterous."

> *   *   *

> "When I pity someone, I vehemently deny that there is any disguised gloating in it."

> *   *   *

> "You certainly talk as if you regarded us as a bunch of 'abnormals.' Or is it that you're 'abnormal' yourself?"

> *   *   *

> "You make it sound as if I ought to hold myself responsible for the situation I'm in. That may hold for some, but not for me. You just don't know how I've been treated!"

> *   *   *

> "Some of the statements you make seem to me quite unnecessarily harsh."

Most reports, on the other hand, indicated attempts to grapple frankly with whatever was turned up.

> "I don't want ordinary kinds of pity, but I want people to pity me when I've made some important sacrifice."

> *   *   *

"I have had to acknowledge that what I took to be my kind-hearted pity for my step-sister does involve a considerable amount of secret gloating."

*   *   *

"My pity goes to those who, as you say, are 'out of the running.' "

*   *   *

"I've discovered that I actually want to punish my girl. This bothers me, because I really love her. Fortunately, it's not all the time, but just when I'm blue and down in the dumps."

*   *   *

"I couldn't believe that the wish to punish or be punished applied to me. But then I thought of the dreams I'm forever having of punishing someone, usually female, and doing it in a rather violent way. When I was younger the dreams were of someone punishing me physically. I enjoyed it. My parents didn't punish me physically, but by the threat of withdrawing their love. This would go on for quite a while, and I thought how much better I would like it if they actually beat me and got it over with."

Rather than cite short comments from a number of students on the various other parts of the experiment, we give the following rather extended quotation from a single report:

"While there is no-one I would constantly want to shower with pity, there are times when I would like to pity my sister, for I feel she has embarked on an undesirable marriage. But when I see her and have to realize that she is very happy, I know my pity is misplaced. . . . I am very happy, for I am deeply in love with my fiancé. I am very fond of his parents, and they've been wonderful to me.

". . . At times I would like to punish my father for venting his anger on my mother. If I had to choose someone to punish me, it would be my mother. She is so lenient and good-hearted that the punishment would not be severe. I would like to avoid punishment by my fiancé, because he is so stubborn that the punishment, though it would probably be nothing more than pro-longed silence or absence would be worse than any sort of fast, violent punishment.

"When I try to compel myself, I make promises to myself. I promise that I'll never let my affairs get into such a mess ever again where I have to put myself under pressure. I also promise that, after doing a certain amount of work, I'll give myself the chance to relax. This works pretty well when the relaxation period doesn't go on and on, as it does tend to do.

". . . . What I doubt most about myself, and this doesn't recur too frequently, is whether I'm entirely ready for marriage. I still have a wonderful, romantic picture of marriage which doesn't include washing dirty socks and economizing on the groceries. I doubt whether my sister, although she is married, is ready for that. She doesn't have her own apartment yet, and hasn't been faced with these things.

". . . The terms you use are particularly strong. There is no one I would like to 'wipe out.' If my sister were Person X, I certainly would have no wish to destroy her. Before she got married our relationship was a particularly close one, but I can't say I am jealous of her husband for separating us. . . . For the first time I've become really antagonistic toward you. Something inside me seems to be asking, 'What are they driving at; what are they trying to find out?' It is almost as if you had me backed against a wall with a strong spotlight on me. There is a certain anxiety; it is as if some cobwebs were being pushed aside, but I can't identify what is beyond. I only know that it is disturbing.

". . . . When I introspect, it is as if I were waiting for something to turn up—something that is elusive. I'm not sure if it is pleasant, but I think not, for it makes me slightly anxious. . . . If there is one person who bears watching, that is my fiancé's mother. She is a wonderful person, and has been more generous and gracious to me than most future mothers-in-law would be, but there are times when I am with her when I fear that she will come to dominate me as completely as she does her husband and daughter. My fiancé, for-tunately, has gone through the period of revolt and been almost completely successful in getting out from under her thumb.

". . . When introspecting, I first stare at myself, unseeingly. Then, almost furtively, I try to sneak glances. . . . If the events I hit upon are distasteful, I tend to soft-pedal them, or they become blocked out by other thoughts.

"The symptom for which I found myself searching was a sexual one. It probably can be traced to a particularly disgusting French film of which I saw only the smallest part. I suddenly got the idea that women who had had intercourse sat with their legs spread, rather than crossing them at the knees. I looked for this in my sister when she came to visit us. The symptom was there. It has been three weeks since I saw the picture, but it still, from time to time, comes into my mind."

EXPERIMENT 13: Mobilizing the Muscles

In this experiment we come to grips with the mechanics of retroflection. When your approaches to objects and persons in the environment are frustrated or evaluated as too dangerous to continue, so that you turn your aggressions inward against yourself, the muscular motions by which you do this may retain their form or be modified to conform to the substitute objects. If with your fingernails you scratch your own flesh, this is precisely what, without the retroflection, you would do to someone else. On the other hand, when you control an urge to pound someone with your fist by contracting the antagonistic muscles and thus immobilizing your arm and shoulder, the retroflection does not consist of pounding yourself; it is, instead, a statically maintained counteraction. It is a doing of one thing and also its opposite at the same time in such fashion as to achieve a net effect of zero. So long as the conflict endures, the use of the arm for other purposes is impaired, energies are squandered, and the state of affairs is the same as the military situation of a stabilized battleline. Here the battleline is within the personality.

Retroflections are manipulations of your own body

and impulses as substitutes for other persons and objects. Such self-manipulation is unquestionably useful and healthy when it constitutes withholding, biding your time, adjusting yourself to the surroundings, in situations where you need to exercise prudence, caution, selectivity, in the service of your own over-all best interests. The neurotic abuse is when you have once and for all *censored* a part of yourself, throttled and silenced it, so that it may no longer lift its voice in your aware personality. But no matter how squeezed, choked off, clamped down upon this censored part may be, it still exerts its pressure. The struggle goes on. You have simply lost awareness of it. The end-result of such censoring, whether recognized or not, is invariably a more or less serious psychosomatic dysfunction: impairment of powers of orientation or manipulation, ache, weakness, or even degeneration of tissues.

Consider how ineffectual is retroflection in the following example. A patient undergoing treatment may display an extraordinary frequency and amount of weeping, perhaps several outbursts in a single session. The crying occurs whenever one might expect the patient to come forth with a reproach or some other kind of attack. What happens is this: the patient feels like attacking, but, not daring so, retroflects the attack against himself, feels hurt, and bursts into tears as if to say, "See how harmless and how abused I am." The original aim, of course, is to make some Person X, perhaps the therapist, cry. When this cannot be achieved, the crying spells and the chronic resentment persist until the aggression can be reorganized and turned outward.

Other cases may have frequent headaches which are, as the Freudians would say, "converted" crying. Here the mystery of the "conversion-process" is readily solved when one recognizes that the headaches, like most other psychosomatic symptoms, are retroflected motor activity. They are produced by *muscular tensing against a swelling impulse*.

If you open a water tap slightly and attempt with a

finger to hold back the water against the pressure in the pipe, you find this increasingly difficult. There is a strict analogy between this and many internal conflicts where you squeeze or hold back an urge to defecate, to have an erection or to become tumescent, to vomit or belch, etc. If you clench your fist hard, after a while it will ache from cramp. The "psychogenic" headache —or, as it used to be well called, the "functional" headache—is the same type of phenomenon. In a given instance, you start to cry, but then you control the impulse by squeezing your own head so as not to be a sissy or to give others the satisfaction of seeing they have made you cry. You would like to squeeze the life out of Person X who has so upset you, but you retroflect the squeezing and use it to hold back your crying. Your headache is nothing but your experience of the muscular straining. If you de-tense the muscles, you will start to cry and, simultaneously, the headache will disappear. (Not all headaches, of course, are produced in this way; also, crying may be inhibited by tensions other than those in the head—for example, by tightening the diaphragm against the clonic movements of sobbing.)

We repeat once more our opposition to premature relaxation. Suppose you manage to relax the muscles of your neck, brow, and eyes and burst out crying. This by no means solves the original conflict. It merely by-passes it. An important part of the symptom— namely, the tendency to aggressive squeezing—goes unanalyzed. When someone has hurt you, there is the wish to retaliate by hurting him. This tendency gets some expression—you do some hurting—even if it is but the retroflected squeezing which makes you the victim of your own aggression as well as of that of the other person. If, instead of reversing the retroflection, you simply give up the retroflecting behavior—in this case, your self-squeezing—you can succeed only by somehow also getting rid of your proneness to be hurt. This requires a technique more serious than retroflection, namely, desensitization. Not wanting to hurt depends on not being hurt, which depends on ceasing to respond emotionally to the environment. This process can go as far as depersonalization. Admittedly, one may be *hyper*sensitive and "have one's feelings hurt" by almost everything; one has, correspondingly, a heightened urge to "hurt back." The solution for this condition is reorganization of the personality, not further disorganization in the form of going numb. *The healthy organism, when genuinely attacked, fights back in a way and to a degree appropriate to the situation.*

Furthermore, when muscles are willfully relaxed, they are less at your disposal even for behavior not involved in the conflict. You lose agility, grace, and mobility of feature. This accounts for the relaxed facelessness of some "analyzed" persons. They have "mastered" their problems by becoming aloof—too aloof to be fully human.

In the healthy organism the muscles are neither cramped nor relaxed (flaccid), but in middle tone, ready for the execution of movements which maintain balanced posture, provide locomotion, or manipulate objects. In beginning the motor-muscular work of this experiment, do not relax. Later we shall amend this by saying do not relax until you can cope with the excitement which will thereby be released. If relaxation occurs prematurely and you are surprised and frightened by unblocked excitement, you will clamp against it harder than ever and experience great anxiety. With correct concentration, however, on the motor manipulation of yourself, slowly and methodically adjusting to pressures as you feel yourself exerting them, the loosening of tension will often take place as a matter of course.

From the beginning be prepared for sudden urges to break out in rage, to cry, vomit, urinate, behave sexually, etc. But such urges as you experience at the start will come from near the surface of awareness and you will be quite able to cope with them. Nevertheless, to spare yourself possible embarrassment, it is advisable at first to perform the muscular experiments in solitude. Furthermore, if you are prone to anxiety attacks, before attempting intensive muscular concentration, work through what you are going to do by internally verbalizing it.

While lying down, but not deliberately relaxing, get the feel of your body. Notice where you have an ache —headache, backache, writer's cramp, belly-cramp, vaginism, etc. Realize where you are tense. Do not "give in" to the tension, nor do anything about it. Become aware of the tensions in your eyes, neck, around the mouth. Let your attention wander systematically (without making a fetish of system) through your legs, lower trunk, arms, chest, neck, head. Should you find that you are lying in a crooked position, adjust it accordingly. Do not move jerkily, but let the self-sense develop softly. Notice the tendency of your organism to regulate itself—the tendency to pull back into a better position in one place, to stretch out in another.

Do not fool yourself that you are feeling your body when you are merely visualizing or theorizing it. If prone to the latter, you are working with a concept of yourself, not yourself. But this concept is imposed by your "I" and its resistances; it is not self-regulating and spontaneous. It does not come from the felt-awareness of the organism. By waiting, refusing to be put off by visualizations and theories, can you get the glow of awareness which arises directly from the parts attended to?

As you proceed, consider what objections you may have to each particular bit of self-awareness. Do you despise physical functioning? Are you ashamed of being a body? Do you regard defecation as a painful, dirty duty? Are you frightened by a tendency to clench your fist? Do you fear that you will strike a blow? Or that you will be struck? Does the feeling in your throat disturb you? Are you afraid to shout?

In parts of your body where it has been difficult for you to get any feeling at all, what you are likely to experience first as feeling is restored is a sharp pain, a painful numbness, a cramp. When such pangs occur, concentrate on them.

(It goes without saying that we are dealing here with

functional or "psychogenic" pains, not those resulting from "physical" lesions or infections. Try not to
be hypochondriacal, but, if doubtful, consult a doctor.
Get one, if possible, who has an understanding of
functional symptoms.)

An extremely useful method of grasping the meaning
of particular aches or tensions is to call up appropriate
expressions of popular speech. These invariably contain
long-tested wisdom. For instance:

> I am stiff-necked; am I stubborn? I have a pain in
> the neck; what gives me a pain in the neck? I stretch
> my head high; am I haughty? I stick my chin out; am
> I leading with it? My brows arch; am I supercilious?
> I have a catch in my throat; do I want to cry? I am
> whistling in the dark; am I afraid of something? My
> flesh creeps; am I horrified? My brows beetle; am I full
> of rage? I feel swollen; am I ready to burst with anger?
> My throat is tight; is there something I can't swallow?
> My middle feels queasy; what can't I stomach?

Now, assuming that you have begun to rediscover
your bodily existence, your tensions, and their characterological and interpersonal significance, we must take
the next step. What you have been doing—searching
and softly adjusting so as to orient yourself further—
must now give way to the other functions which are
latent in contracted muscle. With orientation we must
begin to integrate overt expression, to change the muscular contractions into controllable behaviors available for manipulation of the environment.

The next step in solving the problem of chronic
muscular tensions—and of every other psychosomatic
symptom—is to develop adequate contact with the
symptom and accept it as your own. The notion of
accepting the symptom—precisely what you feel you
want to be rid of—always sounds preposterous. So
let us try, even at the risk of unnecessary repetitious-
ness, to get this perfectly clear. You may ask, "If I
have a symptom that is painful or some characteristic
that is undesirable, should I not try to get rid of it?"

The answer is, "Certainly!" The issue then is reduced to the selection of a means which will work and the abandonment of any means which superficially looks as if it ought to work—but actually doesn't. The direct means of condemning the symptom, of regarding it as something which has been imposed upon you, of appealing to others for help in making it disappear, will not work. The only way that will work is an indirect one: become vividly aware of the symptom, accept both sides of the conflict as *you*—this means to re-identify yourself with parts of your personality from which you have dis-identified yourself—and then discover means by which both sides of the conflict, perhaps in modified form, can be expressed and satisfied. Thus, for your headache it is better to take responsibility than aspirin. The drug temporarily dulls the pain, but it does not solve the problem. Only you can do this.

Pain, disgust, repulsion, are all disagreeable, but they are functions of the organism. Their occurrence is not accidental. They are nature's way of calling attention to what needs attention. You must, where necessary, learn to face pain and to suffer, in order to destroy and assimilate the pathological material contained in the symptom. Reintegration of dissociated parts always involves conflict, destroying and suffering. If, for instance, you are on guard against some "infantile" behavior, you must, nevertheless, learn to accept it as yours in order to give it a chance to grow up and find its proper place in the general integration of your personality. *If not allowed to claim attention and do its work, whatever this may be, it cannot be altered. Given attention and allowed to interact with the rest of your behavior, it is sure to develop and change.*

To gain confidence in this hard task, start with "mistakes" that you are prone to. In playing a piece of music perhaps you keep making the same mistake. If so, instead of being upset about it and trying to block it out, become curious and repeat it deliberately to find out what it means. Possibly your "mistake" is a natural fingering of a passage and the "correct" fingering quite wrong.

Repeated <u>mistakes</u> or acts of clumsiness are often retroflected annoyance. If someone has annoyed or upset you, instead of striking back at him, you upset the next glass of water and upset yourself still further.

For a while allow your pronouncements of moral judgment on yourself to remain in abeyance. Give yourself a chance. When the impulses which you customarily alienate on moral grounds can learn to speak in their own voices, you frequently will find that you change your evaluations of the right and wrong of the matter. Do not, at least, be any more harshly critical of yourself than you are of others. After all, you are a person, too!

Soon you will discover that facing neurotic pain or some "immoral" tendency is not as bad as you feared. When you have acquired the technique for dissolving the pain and reintegrating the "immorality," you will realize that you are freer, more interested, more energetic.

Apply to a headache or some other symptom the method of the concentration-experiment. Give it your attention, and let its figure/ground spontaneously form. If you can accept the pain, it serves as a motivating interest; it is a concernful sensation. The important thing in dissolving the pain is to wait for development. Permit this to occur of itself, without interference or preconceived ideas. If you make contact, you will get a clearer figure and be able to dissolve the painful conflict. For a considerable period after you have started work on this technique the changes that occur may be so subtle—especially if you are expecting heavy drama from the outset—that you lose patience.

The pain will shift about, expand or contract, alter in intensity, transform itself in quality and kind. Try to feel the shape, size and direction of particular muscles which you contract. Be on the alert for any trembling, itching, "electricity," shivering—in short for any signs of biological excitement. Such excitement-sensations, vegetative and muscular, may come in waves or be constant, may swell or subside. When an itch develops, see if you can keep from prematurely scratching or rubbing it away; concentrate on it and wait for it to develop further. Allow the excitement to come to the foreground. Correctly carried through, this procedure should leave you with a sense of well-being. The same technique is applicable not only to psychosomatic aches and pains, but to fatigue depressions, unspecified excitements, and attacks of anxiety.

In the performance of these experiments you are likely to suffer anxiety, which we have seen to be a self-regulating attempt to counteract faulty breathing during mounting excitement. Whether anxiety is present or not, practice the following respiratory experiment:

Exhale thoroughly, four or five times. Then breathe softly, making sure of the exhalation, but without forcing. Can you feel the stream of air in your throat, in your mouth, in your head? Allow the air to blow from your mouth and feel the stream of it with your hand. Do you keep your chest expanded even when no air is coming in? Do you hold in your stomach during inhalation? Can you feel the inhalation softly down to the pit of the stomach and the pelvis? Can you feel your ribs expand on your sides and back? Notice the tautness of your throat; of your jaws; the closure of the nose. Pay attention especially to the tightness of the midriff (diaphragm). Concentrate on these tensions and allow developments.

In your daily activity, especially in the moments of interest—in your work, when near someone sexually desirable, during an absorbing artistic experience, while confronted by an important problem—notice how you tend to hold your breath instead of breathing more deeply as the situation biologically requires. What are you restraining by holding back your breath? Crying out? Shrieking? Running away? Punching? Vomiting? Deflation? Weeping?

At the time of writing their reports on this experiment students varied tremendously in the amount of progress they had been able to make on this phase of the work—from virtually none to important unblockings of excitement. We repeat that there is no standard time-table for assimilation of the concepts introduced here, and it is certainly not to your discredit if at this stage the procedure is, so far as you are concerned, a "bust."

> "There is nothing that puts me to sleep more quickly than trying to do these exercises. This applies whether I intended to go to sleep or not."

If we say that this person "flees into sleep," it is without any moralistic implication that he ought not to. This is simply the way he functions at present. Structured as he is, he prefers to avoid his problems rather than to solve them. He can continue to exercise this preference so long as he subscribes to one or both of the following propositions: (1) the problems do not exist; (2) the problems are inevitable and cannot be solved.

> "In permitting one's attention to wander over the body noticing tensions, twitchings, pains, etc., I can report success, if success is to be measured in terms of finding that I do have these physical sensations. It is no great trick to focus attention on parts of the body and experience them. But may not the very focusing of attention, where the result has been foretold by the authors, be responsible for getting such results? How far would one have to go in getting uncomfortable physical sensations before either the help of a doctor was needed or the person worked himself into the position of the hypochondriac? I can't help but be dubious of the theory that every twinge in a tense muscle is associated with some long forgotten experience."

This man still insists on separating his "body" and "mind" so that "never the twain shall meet." For him the sensations are "physical sensations" which are natural to "parts of the body" and which anyone may have for the looking. But in the next breath they owe their existence to our having predicted that they will be found if looked for, that is, they are due to suggestion. At this point he apparently becomes quite able to resist "our influence," for he balks at the theory that the tensions have meanings as conflicts which can be discovered and worked through. Instead, he sees the more unfavorable outcome of having to get a doctor. To do what? Restore inattentiveness to the "body"? Unsuggest what was suggested? Prescribe aspirin in lieu of his previous pain-killer, inattentiveness? Tell him to forget it—or, as is actually the case, tell him that it is psychosomatic?

The last sentence quoted above may be an example of misstating an argument to make it easier to dispose of. Muscles may be painful for a number of reasons, including ordinary fatigue, inflammation, or various dietary deficiencies. We are concerned here not with such instances but with chronic contractions which one may, if attentive, notice time and time again in the absence of the usual explanatory factors. It is these which, if developed and analyzed, *may* lead to remembrance of situations in which they were learned as a means of squelching conflict. But such recapture of memories, if and when it occurs, is incidental, a mere by-product of discovering and expressing the conflict's component tensions.

"I did not have a headache to experiment on, so I had to use a 'barked shin' and its resulting pain."

While concentration on actually injured parts of the body does increase blood circulation and in this way promote recovery, this has no pertinence to the purpose of the experiment.

"I had no measure of success whatsoever. I followed through all the directions, but was unable to achieve anything more than a feeling of wasting my time and futility."

*   *   *

". . . This experiment has produced an interesting block. If, while lying down, I feel an ache or itch and concentrate on it, it disappears rather than comes to the foreground, and another in a totally different part of the body begins to distract my attention."

*   *   *

"I'm getting *awfully* tired of this whole over-rated rigmarole. I am not upset by any of my urges, and am completely aware of all of them. I have no desire to vomit, to go on a rape rampage, or to commit suicide. I am ashamed of nothing—absolutely nothing—about myself. I am not afraid of my desire to murder people. I am not afraid to holler good and loud, but out of consideration for the neighbors I try not to. I alienate no impulse on moral grounds. I am doubtless a psychopathic personality. I have stolen cars, taken dope, and lived with women. Try to prove it!"

*   *   *

"The tensions I feel around my shoulders, neck, and at times my legs, are due to the fact that I am worried and nervous of late. I feel all tightened up inside and this seems to manifest itself in the parts of my body just mentioned."

The next quotation is from a student who, at the time of writing her report, had permitted considerable development, but was still confused on what to express and how to express it:

"I have great resistance to putting my actual feelings on paper. Let me say that, whereas previously I regarded your statements as very confused, now they seem much clearer and I'm aware that it was I who was confused. Until now I've refused to face the responsibility of awareness—and I'm not really reconciled to it yet. But I realize that I must bring back many suppressed conflicts and either try to live with them or resolve them. I've gone back to the beginning experiments again and now, with reduced resistance so far as *they* are concerned, find them easy. However, when I attempt these present ones I'm afflicted with a nervous irritation which seems to start in my legs and spread slowly through my whole body, so that I scratch and seem to want to tear myself apart. In fact, even as I type this it begins again. I'm banging at the keys as if the aggression and irritation aroused by the experiments could be dissipated by the noise of the machine. Suddenly I have a pain in my left arm which seems to be in the bone. The whole lower part of my left arm is stiff. My right arm is unaffected. I've been trying to remember when the nervous reaction of scratching began.

"I can't keep thinking about the scratching, but start to think about crying instead. So I'll say something about that. I come from a family in which any display of emotion, especially of this sort, is frowned upon. At the moment I'm in conflict with my parents, and it is something that produces a guilt conflict, as I feel I'm in the wrong for making them suffer needlessly. I refuse to go home. When I'm there I feel materially very secure, but suffocated in every other direction by their only half-concealed distaste for my ideas and way of life. I have received a letter from them that makes me want to cry. When I got it and read it, or whenever I think about it, I get a lump in my throat, a tightening behind the eyeballs and a tenseness throughout my body. This is repeated now as I report it. But I won't allow myself the luxury of crying about it. What strikes me as peculiar is that I cry easily over a film, book, play, or work of art, but in my own personal relationships it is a privilege that so far I will not allow myself.

"Now I am aware that suddenly I feel very aggressive, as if I want to do something violent, and the way I'm pounding the typewriter is in keeping with this feeling. The pain has come back to my left arm.

"In regard to inner thinking I'm aware that the odd words and disjointed phrases 'in my head' have begun to crystallize. My thoughts seem to be about conflict, about compromise, and about the facades behind which I've hidden myself, a different one for every group I'm in. In one life one plays many roles. Which is the true one that represents the self? The awareness which has shaken me the most is the size of my resistances and their strength."

This person certainly has "unfinished business" with her parents. What, for example, does one owe to parents who will not accept one as he is? How can one make them "come to realize"? What life shall one live—what he chooses or what is chosen for him? Or something in between? This person will have to discover that, of the various roles she plays, there is not a "true one which represents the self." Instead, a part of her self is invested in and finds expression in each of the roles. The problem is to integrate them so that all of her self comes together and lives her life continuously.

The following excerpt is not very specific about the content of the conflict discovered and developed, but we include it because of the partial discharge attained and the consequent differentiation of the primitive impulse:

"While trying to be aware of my body certain feelings do arise; certain people are involved in the potential fulfillment of the aroused feeling; and certain embarrassments follow inevitably. I'm really seriously angry at the authors, for what has turned up was, to say the least, somewhat unorthodox and shocking with no chance whatsoever of fulfillment. All that has happened is that I've become aware of a certain function or desire and have become just as aware that its fulfillment is out of the question. I realize that the desire was there before, because I just lay on the bed and suddenly this thing popped into my mind, full-blown, completely developed in all its various details. The whole scenario was complete from beginning to end. I don't think it grew during the short course of the experiment. It probably was there latently all the time, but till now, at least, I was unaware of it. It has merely brought about a state of active, constant self-vituperative frustration. How can I release this by socking a pillow or screaming? There's only one way of getting rid of this. That's by doing it—and I can't!" (The report was interrupted at this point and not resumed until several days later.)

"Upon rereading the foregoing part of this I was tempted to destroy it and start all over. But I include it because of what I consider a rather curious aftermath. The sudden awareness of the cause of my bodily tension and the discovery of an unfulfillable need had actually made me so angry that I lost sight of what I now believe was important. Since starting on this report again a little while ago, I deliberately tried to imagine the whole sequence being acted out, although I knew it could never actually happen. I suddenly found myself blushing to the roots of my hair, not because it was the *forbidden act*, but because it was so silly! What a ridiculous way of trying to 'wreak vengeance.' I sincerely think that if the opportunity were now offered to do what I thought I couldn't, that now I wouldn't simply because it's so silly and ineffectual. There are other much more adequate ways of dealing with the situation. And now so many of my attitudes and poses in regard to X become meaningless."

What is important in the present context is that the primitive retroflected aggression and the act which it prevented did not for their relief require that the repressed wish be literally carried out against Person X. Once in awareness and fantasied with embarrassment, the primitive aggression underwent differentiation into "other much more adequate ways of dealing with the situation." *It was the repression itself which kept the aggression primitive and incapable of discharge.*

In the following example a symptom of the alimentary tract was subjected to concentration:

"For some months—in fact, on and off for a year— I have been suffering from diarrhoea, which, since there has been no physical basis found for it, was probably psychosomatic. During my awareness experiments I concentrated on the stomach and solar-plexus muscles to see if I could become aware of tensions there that might be causing this. I found many tensions in that region, and spent a good deal of time and several sessions isolating and testing them. Since then my diarrhoea has completely vanished. It is too soon to say whether it has gone for good, but, since I have changed neither my diet or anything else in my life-situation, it seems encouraging."

As a final example, we quote some effects obtained by a student which ordinarily require much more prolonged work with these techniques:

"I relaxed on the bed, getting the 'feel' of my body. After a short while I was in full contact with it, and felt around in first one part and then another. Then I breathed deeply, exhaling completely. Excitement kept starting forward. I'd feel a little surge of it, and then it would recede. That happened several times, and I realized that I was preventing my breath from coming faster. So I deliberately started *panting*—and there came the excitement! It *surged* all through me. It was as though my hands and feet were strapped down while tremendous bolts of electricity were being shot into me. My body strained upward, this way and that, twisting and turning with the force of the current— pelvis, shoulders, back, legs, head. *All of me* moved circularly and in every way. My body was as hot as fire; I actually *burned*, and my hands and feet felt as though they were blazing. The perspiration poured off me, tears streamed down my face, my breath came in huge gasps, and I was saying, 'Ohh . . . Ohh . . . Ohh . . .' I don't know just how long this lasted, but it was for at least several minutes. After it was over (that most intense part) I looked at my hands to see if they were scorched. I wouldn't have been surprised to find that they were. Little chills went through me for about another half hour, and *I felt very alive and strong!*

"There is a place in the back of my head that has to be relaxed before I can experience all the excitement. Work on that spot *and* the diaphragm resulted in my being able to have the above experience. By relaxing that little spot in the back of my head I can have little chills run up and down my spine any time.

"The word 'softly', whch appeared twice in the instructions, was of great importance to me in performing this experiment.

"Although I don't know what's around the next bend in the road so far as these experiments are concerned, I'm damn-well going to find out. So far it has just been the 'honeymoon phase' that you spoke of in the introduction. Maybe it will be over for me with the next experiment, but I shall continue to *try*."

EXPERIMENT 14: Executing the Re-reversed Act

This is the third and final experiment on retroflection, for which the preceding two were preparation.

In them, when you discovered and muscularly explored some retroflecting activity, we suggested merely that you reverse it in fantasy or imagination. The crucial stage, of course, is to reverse it in overt action directed outward upon the environment, for only in this way can your "inner conflicts" be changed back into strivings to obtain what you need in contact with people and objects in the "outer world."

You are not ready for this—and it would be premature to attempt it—unless you have, by concentrating on the muscular clinch, succeeded in loosening it somewhat and differentiating it into component parts. Assuming that you have, next comes the work of making approaches to overt reversal of the retroflected activity. As an example, suppose that you have been choking yourself to prevent screaming and that now, finally, you can feel in your throat the impulse to scream and in your fingers the impulse to choke. However bizarre this may sound if you have not yet become aware of this or a comparable conflict, we mean it literally—not just as a figurative way of speaking. If you do feel something of the sort, what to do about it?

Certainly it would be no solution to rush up to someone and, while screaming at the top of your voice, throttle him! The two parts of the conflict do have this meaning—the wish to scream and the wish to choke —but they are primitive and undifferentiated, and it is precisely their static clinch in your musculature that has kept them so. If you do not become paralyzed by the "silliness" of it, you can now give *some* overt expression to both sides in a way that is perfectly safe. You can choke a pillow! Dig your fingers into it as if it were a throat. Shake it as a mastiff shakes a rat. Show it no mercy! While doing this, fiercely absorbed in squeezing the life out of your enemy, you will also sooner or later find yourself vocalizing—grunting, growling, talking, shouting. This part will come sooner if you can perform the experiment beyond the earshot of others, but once you get into it fully, you are unlikely to care what the neighbors think.

Before such an occurrence you might feel that you

want to scream, to pound, to squeeze, but that you "couldn't possibly do it if you tried." The muscular ties holding the appropriate activity in confluence may be so subtle that even with the best concentration they are not loosened in their last details. Various approaches to expressing the impulse, such as the kind suggested above, may be made abortively without having the behavior come to life and be meaningful. It remains dead, a deliberate bit of play-acting. If you persist, however, extending the variations, going along with and falling into whatever absurdities, antics, posturings suggest themselves, eventually the deliberateness will change suddenly to spontaneity; you will become strongly excited, and the behavior will become a genuine expression of what was previously blocked. At this moment what was before impossible for you will now, paradoxically, become possible and be done.

Mere physical execution of what you are aware of wanting to do, be it yelling, punching, choking, or whatever, will be useless unless accompanied by a growing awareness of the meaning of the act, by recognition of its particular role in your own interpersonal situation—at whom you want to scream, whom or what you want to pound—and by the executive sense that *it is you* who are doing it and are responsible for it. Otherwise, the action is a bluff and a mere forcing. If you bully yourself into doing something on the ground that it is what you are "supposed" to do to fulfill the experiment, you will rasp your throat, strain your muscles, wrack yourself with new false excitements, but you will not achieve the integration you are seeking.

Here the truth of the unitary conception of the organism—unitary functioning of body, feeling, and environment—may dramatically be demonstrated. For if your orientation, your feeling, and your overt actions come together spontaneously and with the proper timing, you will suddenly find that you understand, feel and can act with an unexpected new self-awareness and clarity; you will spontaneously recover a lost memory, recognize what your true intention is in some present relationship, see clearly what is the next thing for you to do, and so on. It is because of the importance of parallel development of all factors involved that we have been reiterating: use an all-round approach—fantasy, analysis of the interpersonal situation, verbal or semantic analysis, emotional training, body-expression; do not prematurely relax and thus bypass some of the factors; do not force yourself or impose preconceptions, but allow for spontaneous developments.

When expression is overt, there normally is a release of pent-up energy—for instance, the seeming lethargy of depression will, if unblocked, be replaced by what it concealed and held in check: raging or the clonic movements of sobbing. When fears or social pressures remain so great that such expression cannot break through, the miniature and wholly inadequate motions of "thinking" are substituted for them—in this instance a kind of subvocal whining. The big movements which would suffice to discharge the energy are in a clinch with self-controlling tensions in the diaphragm, throat and head. Since the only way to release the energy is to express it and since the self-controlling "I" has no intention whatever of letting this particular impulse find appropriate outlet, the clinch does not change; without change it does not hold attention but becomes "forgotten"—an isolated, unaware conflict in the organism. If the cramped muscles give rise to psychosomatic pains, the "I" does not understand and accept these as consequences of its unrelenting self-control, but regards them as imposed upon it from "outside" and feels victimized. The energy of the organism cannot flow.

On the other hand, if you concentrate on a headache and permit development, you may sooner or later become aware that the headache is produced by muscular squeezing of your head. You may realize, further, that you are sad—in fact, that you want very much to cry. Unless you are alone, you may be unable to loosen the muscles and let go. To make it easier, retire to a place where you can have privacy. Even there, if you are a man, it may be difficult to let yourself weep, for you probably have been brought up on the fiction that "big boys don't cry." (Experiments to follow on "introjection" and "projection" will assist in overcoming this anti-biological prejudice.)

When you discover an impulse to do something which cannot reasonably in its primitive form find a direct expression, try above all not to turn it back against yourself; turn it, instead, against any kind of object that is convenient. Don't throttle yourself again, but throttle a pillow, meanwhile allowing the fantasy to develop of whom you really want to choke. Squeeze an orange instead of your own eyeballs. Punch a bag. Wrestle for sport. Kick a box. Allow your head to shake from side to side and shout "No!" At first you will do such things rather lamely, but after a while, if you are convinced that they are not "silly"—that they are, instead, safe first approaches to what you will later be able to do on a less primitive basis—you will permit yourself to express with full emotional force all the kicking, pounding and screaming of a child's tantrum. Despite conventional notions to the contrary, this is the healthy device by which the organism exteriorizes frustrated aggressions.

Symptoms may often be more deeply concealed than indicated in our discussion so far. If the pain of a particular conflict has been too much to bear, you may have desensitized its context, and so developed blindspots (scotomata). In that case, you may find during body-concentration, not aches and pains, but sensations of numbness, fogginess, nothingness. If so, then concentrate on these until you have them as a veil or blanket that you can lift, or as a fog that you can blow away.

In theory, male and female sexual frigidity are merely such blind spots and are curable by correct concentration. In practice, though, most cases of this sort have extremely complicated resistances. The chief muscular block in frigidity is the stifling of the pelvis, mainly in the small of the back and in the groin. This frequently is linked up with incorrect masturbation. And, since masturbation is a sexual kind of retroflection, normal or neurotic depending on the context, let us discuss it briefly.

Up to a generation ago masturbation was considered extremely sinful and harmful. Now it is approved of in many circles, even encouraged by "progressive parents," though often with great embarrassment on their part. Both attitudes—the condemnation and the approval—are over-simplifications. Whether masturbation is healthy or harmful depends on the urge which it expresses, the accompanying attitude, and the method employed.

It has been said that it is the guilt and remorse which constitute the damage that can be done by masturbation, and this is correct; without these feelings a person suffers no injury. But there is a general misconception on this point. The guilt does not so much concern the act itself as the fantasies which accompany it—for instance, sadism, watching for someone to surprise and punish one, ambitious self-glorification, etc. Since healthy masturbation expresses an outgoing drive—is a substitute for intercourse—the healthy masturbation fantasy would be that of approaching and having intercourse with a beloved person. Where masturbation gives rise to guilt, the problem is to notice the guilt-producing fantasy and to deal with it separately from the sexual act.

The second point of danger in masturbation is the lack of pelvic activity. The act becomes one in which the hands are the active, aggressive partner to intercourse, while the genitals are merely raped. A man, lying on his back, conceives a passive-feminine fantasy. Or, in the absence of spontaneously developing sexual excitement, the situation becomes a struggle, a striving for victory—the hands try to rape while the genitals resist and defy the rapist. The pelvis, meanwhile, does not move in orgastic waves and jerks, but is immobilized, tense and rigid. No satisfactory orgasm results, the artificially stimulated excitement is inadequately discharged, and there ensues fatigue and the need to try again.

Masturbation, furthermore, is often an attempt to live out tensions not sexual at all—for instance, non-sexual loneliness, depression, annoyance. Or, on the other hand, it is sometimes a non-sexual expression of general defiance and rebellion.

In healthy masturbation, as in healthy intercourse, the lead has to come from the pelvis or—what corresponds to this—genuine sexual need. If the small of the back is rigidly tensed and if the legs are pulled up into the trunk, no orgastic movements are possible. The sexual act, to give satisfaction, requires that one surrender to the sensations. If one "thinks" during intercourse, has fantasies which are not an integral part of what one is doing, avoids bestowing attention on one's partner, or omits to feel one's own pleasure, one cannot hope for the profound relief of consummated sexual expression.

Let us return now to the more general problem of the systematic undoing of retroflections. By concentrating on localized muscle-cramps or areas of numbness as you permit developments to occur, you will release a certain amount of energy that was previously bound up and unavailable. But after a time you will find that you cannot make further progress without giving attention to functional relationships among the larger divisions of the body. The felt-contact between one part and another must be reestablished before reintegration can be achieved. These parts are not detached from each other, of course, since they all go with you when you walk down the street; but still it is necessary to explore and feel vividly the structural and functional connection of upper with lower body, head with torso, torso with legs, right half with left half. As you do this work, you will be fascinated by the novel and yet obvious relationships that will assert themselves. You will comprehend at first hand what is meant by the Freudian notion of "displacement upward"—for instance, that repressed sexual and anal functions appear on an inadequate substitute basis in speech and thought, or the converse, that oral blocks repeat themselves in anal tensions. This presents no mystery, for, since the system is functioning as a whole, when one end of a large sub-system like the alimentary tract is disturbed, the other parts adjust progressively to compensate or at least to maintain a functioning, though less efficient, unity.

Detailed interrelatedness of various parts of the body vary with each personality. By now you should be able to discover and work out the special features of your own particular mode of functioning. For further discussion here, let us restrict ourselves to a few remarks on balance and on the relation that exists between left and right.

When muscular action is retroflected, it is obvious that posture must be deformed in every kind of way. For instance, if you hold your pelvis rigid, there can be no flexible base for any movement of the upper torso, arms and head. Attempts to recover correct posture and grace by "setting up exercises" will prove fruitless unless there is also a loosening of the rigidity. Mothers produce nothing but exasperation in their children by constant admonitions to "stand up straight," "throw back your shoulders," or "hold your head up." The "bad" posture feels "right" and will continue to as long as certain parts are held in a vise-like grip and not allowed spontaneous movement. For proper posture the head, unconstrained by taut neck muscles, must balance freely on the torso; and the upper torso, without any pushed-out chest or pulled-in back, must ride easily on the pelvis. These body-segments have been likened to three pyramids, each resting on its point, so that it can pivot readily in any direction.

Conflict between head and trunk often expresses itself elsewhere as a struggle between right and left hands. When the head, for instance, is moral and "right," the person is stiff-necked—afraid of losing his precarious balance. In this case the neck serves, not as a bridge between head and trunk, but as a barrier—literally, a muscular bottle-neck—between the "higher" and the "lower" functions of the personality. The shoulders, afraid to expand and work or fight, are held contracted. The lower body is well "under control." Ambidextrous cooperation is lacking. One hand tends to hold down and nullify the activity of the other, and the same is true for the legs. In sitting, balance is precarious; the upper carriage bears down on one buttock like a crushing piece of lead.

By concentrating on right/left differences you can regain much of the subtle balance required for adequate posture and locomotion. Lie on your back on the floor. Work first on the hollow small of the back and the arch of the neck. Although neither of these spots would remain up in the air as you lie there were your posture correct, do not try to relax or to force the vertebrae to flatten. Bring your knees up and spread them slightly apart, resting the bottoms of your feet on the floor. This will ease the tension along your spine, but you can still notice the rigidity of your back, and the short, pulled-in feeling of your legs. Allow any spontaneous adjustments that may occur in the direction of a more comfortable position. Compare every part of your anatomy on the right side with the left. You will observe many discrepancies in what should be bilateral symmetry. Your feeling that you are lying "all crooked" expresses, though in an exaggerated way, what is actually the case. Following the organism's own pressures as you notice them, softly correct your position—very, very slowly, without jerky movements. Compare your right and left eyes, shoulders, feet, arms, hands.

Throughout this work keep the knees somewhat apart, arms loose and uncrossed. Notice the tendency to bring them together. Consider what this tendency may mean. Do you want to protect your genitals? Do you feel too much exposed and defenseless to the world if you lie open in this manner? What will attack you? Do you want to hang on to yourself for fear that otherwise you will fall to pieces? Is your right/left discrepancy expressive of a wish to hang on to Person X with one hand and to push him away with the other? To go somewhere and not to go, at the same time? As you try to adjust your position, how are you doing it? Are you squirming, wriggling? Are you in a trap?

A highly important connection and discrepancy is between the front of the body and the back. For instance, while to all appearances your gaze is directed ahead, it may be that you are more concerned with what lies behind, in which case you can never see where you are. What unknown thing do you fear from behind? Or what are you hoping will overtake and assault you? If you tend to stumble and fall down easily, concentration on this discrepancy between front and back will prove useful.

As you allow muscular developments to take place, at times you may experience a vague, but fairly strong, urge to perform some particular type of movement. It may be, for instance, a kind of reaching out. If so, go along with it by experimentally reaching out. Should the feeling intensify, then reach out, not just with your hands, but with your arms, and, if it is the natural continuation of what you are doing, with your whole body. For whom are you reaching? Your mother? An absent beloved? At some stage does the reaching out begin to be a pushing away? If so, then push. Push against something solid like the wall. Do it with a force adjusted to the strength of your feeling.

Similarly, suppose you feel your lips tighten and your head draw away. Then let your head move from side to side and say, "No!" Can you say it firmly and loudly, or does your voice break? Do you plead? Or, quite the opposite, does your refusal develop into a general sense of defiance and rebelliousness, with pounding, kicking, and screaming? What does it mean?

In performing such mimetic movements, nothing is gained by forcing. It then becomes mere play-acting and throws you off the track. Your sense of what to express and act out must grow out of the exploration and development of feelings and their significance. If the movements are the right ones and properly timed, they will crystallize your feelings and clarify meanings in your interpersonal relations.

In quoting reactions to this experiment, we begin as usual with some of the more antagonistic ones.

"I'm a creature of habit and quite comfortable with my present posture. I'm not going to lie on the floor and do gyrations. I don't go reaching out for mother or an absent beloved, push things away, plead, kick, scream, or bellow 'No!' "

*   *   *

"I don't have aggressive drives. When younger I was temperamental, aggressive and self-righteous. It was quite a struggle learning to control these things during the past ten years, but *I did it!* It's really not that I now control my temper; the truth is that I don't have a temper any more. What I hoped to get out of these experiments and have completely failed to get is, not an invitation to develop a temper again, but rather to learn how to be self-assured. *That's* my problem! Where are the experiments that deal with that?"

*   *   *

"When I'm aware of an itch, I scratch it. If I'm uncomfortable, I change my position. Going around asking, 'Do I feel something?' isn't going to make me a happier or better-adjusted person."

*   *   *

"What's all this stuff about wanting to protect myself from things that *obviously aren't there?* This is all getting farther and farther out into left field."

*   *   *

"The frank discussion of sexual fornication and masturbation shocked me. At the risk of sounding like a prude, which I'm not, I may say that this shock has prevented me from doing this whole experiment."

*   *   *

"The assumptions in this experiment are utterly ridiculous. I fear nothing in back of me! After reading this kind of stuff, I begin wondering about the authors. The more I wonder, the more I think that the only benefit I'm getting out of these experiments is typing experience."

We now sample reports from those who describe more positive results:

"When I inhale, my stomach seems to move naturally, but my jaws are extremely tight, as is my throat and the rest of my face. I experience this as restrained shouting. I had a chance to make sure of this when my father was dressing me down over something where I felt positive I was right. I got this very same choked up feeling, but I couldn't let very much come out even when he demanded what was 'eating me.' The way it felt to me then was that *I mustn't hurt his feelings.* But that's precisely what I know I did do by sulking and moping around afterward. Next time I'm going to spare myself this pain—and spare him my sulking—by speaking my piece."

*   *   *

"Last week when I came home late from a party I had a terrific headache. Instead of taking aspirin, I tried, as you suggested, to take responsibility for it. I lay there quite a while, exploring my forehead from the inside, and gradually it seemed that the pain, which I had supposed was a general one, was actually centered in two, distinct points, one over each eye. It then became very clear that it wasn't just a pain, but very definitely a muscular ache. After concentrating for a while on the muscles around my eyes, without trying in any way to relax them, all of a sudden, with no effort on my part, they relaxed, and the pain was gone! It was a wonderful sensation of relief, and, naturally, I fell asleep almost immediately. It wasn't until next morning that I wondered what the meaning of the ache had been, but by that time I guess it was too late to do anything about becoming aware of that."

*   *   *

"The first tension I felt was this tenseness in the diaphragm, and in a heightened state of awareness I felt a subtle urge to vomit. As the awareness increased, I felt several convulsive heaves in the diaphragm region, but these, never too severe, stopped in a short while, and the whole area seemed relaxed. Throughout the whole period of nausea (actually it wasn't nausea in the usual sense) I tried to let my feelings come out, and almost spontaneously I felt my hands clench. The shaking of my head as if to say 'no' quite vehemently also came quite easily, and before I knew it I was saying the word 'no' out loud—and saying it quite loudly and with much emotion. I followed through with the experiment to the point of strangling a pillow, and it was while doing this that I saw some visual images which were exceedingly interesting and revealing to me. I don't feel that they should be described here, for they were of a rather intimate personal nature. The diaphragm tensions can't be found now, and I have hopes that they won't return with any degree of severity."

*　　　　*　　　　*

"There was no-one in the house for once and wouldn't be for a while, so I decided to do this experiment in the living room, since by pushing the table aside I would have considerable room for movement. At first, when I stretched out on the floor, I was completely dressed. This hampered me. It was the first time I really could go all out on a manipulation experiment and know I wouldn't be bothered, so I threw a blanket on the floor, drew the blinds, and stripped.

"I was more successful in body awareness than I had ever been. I was excited, and my breathing was rapid. I concentrated on it until, though it was still rapid, it was slow enough to permit full breathing. I tried to verbalize my various feelings—the throb of my chest, shoulders, and upper arms, and it was while I was working on these sensations I realized I was developing an erection. Involuntarily I tried to check this, and then I got an ache in my back. This was very interesting to me, because that particular ache is an old acquaintance, and now I'm beginning to put two and two together.

". . . My spine was extremely tight. Neither the small of my back nor the arch of my neck touched the floor. When I drew my legs up I felt somehow uncomfortable. The base of my spine pressed into the floor and it was quite an effort to put my feet down squarely. My legs felt very tense.

"When I began to compare the two sides of my body, I found the right side far more relaxed than the left. My right shoulder was slightly raised and most of my weight was on my left shoulder and left buttock. I had the distinct feeling that my pelvic arch was raised up. As I explored various muscle groups I suddenly had a terrific urge to stretch. I raised my arms high and stretched my shoulder muscles. I then spontaneously 'bridged,' as do wrestlers, raising my whole body and suspending myself on my feet and neck. When I lay back I felt relaxed and strangely relieved. My spine wasn't so tight and the small of my back was much closer to the floor, although both my neck and back were still 'held high'. . . . . Although the meanings of all this don't come through very clearly, I can feel that they are starting to emerge, and in a general sense I don't feel nearly so confused as I did."

*   *   *

"While lying on my bed and trying this experiment I became aware of feeling ashamed of my genitals. I wished to get up and cover myself, but continued to lie there to see what might develop. The desire to cover myself with my hand became very strong, and I remembered my mother telling me that 'nice girls never expose themselves.' I was brought up in a family which put tremendous weight on moral virtue. Emotions, particularly those related to sexual adjustment, were suppressed in strong verbal warnings and lectures.

"In doing this experiment I realized my natural desires and at the same time I felt the fears and warnings that had been implanted in me in childhood. I realize I have a great deal of reappraising and working out to do before I can finally come to terms with myself. There is a great deal of unfinished business in my life, but I'm getting clearer on ways and means of going about the job, and already I feel I've made a good start."

*   *   *

"Before doing this particular experiment I felt I had already gained some insight about the matter, but to discover how opposed forces act upon the body was something quite amazing to me. Until recently I was unable to experience anger, no matter what the circumstances. Instead, I felt hurt. I would become nervous and later develop a splitting headache.

"As I was lying on the floor with knees brought up and my feet flat, I became aware that my right arm was limp at my side and that my left arm was curved away from the body with fist tightly clenched. To me the right side represents the meek and non-aggressive tendencies in me, and the left side repressed aggressive tendencies. It is amazing to me, but not amusing, that although one might repress aggression, it inevitably comes to the surface in another form.

"I used to be very sarcastic, but eventually denied myself even this more or less subtle way of striking. I believe that when I gave this up I became unable to be aware of anger. This awareness has come back with the doing of these experiments, but I'm still unable to do much about it overtly. It somehow feels cruel and unjustified to attack anyone for any cause whatever. I know, though, that I actually want to do this and that in certain situations it is not only justified but necessary. I'm making some progress in that direction, but I've got an awful lot of retroflecting to undo and I'm trying to resign myself to its taking quite a while."

*   *   *

"I started shadow-boxing and allowed different people to wander in and out of my fantasies. Finally Sir X arrived. At this point I stopped throwing punches at my imaginary adversary and let go with my right foot. Immediately I felt a cramp in my shin. It surprised me considerably, not so much the cramp, as the thought of kicking someone. I had always abhorred such action and considered it impossible for me even to comprehend. Yet here I was attempting to stomp Mr. X's face! Since the experiment stopped at this point, naturally the cramp in my shin subsided. However, as I'm typing this I can feel tensions in my shin developing again!

"I now ask myself whether this is an example of retroflected behavior. Does it mean that I've been kicking myself all these years when I wanted to kick someone else? As yet there is no clear answer to these questions, but I shall pursue them again soon."

Because of its fine attention to detail we quote the following report at some length:

"As time went by I found that I could do the motor-muscular experiments for greater and greater stretches, and also that there was a quicker and more complete awareness of internal activities and tensions in each succeeding attempt. The first time I tried it, I got no results for some time. Then I became aware of my heart-beat, and then the results of my heart-beat, namely, circulation through my limbs, and the throbbing of the blood-vessels. Then I lost my gestalt and fell asleep.

"The second experiment started negatively. Suddenly I became aware that I was introspecting—doing nothing but stare internally in an attempt to force results. The moment I stopped this the results were instantaneous. I took no notes during the experiment, so I cannot report all the sensations I felt. I can only say, as I report those that I do recall, that they were multitudinous and came so fast that I could not have reported them without interfering fatally with the flow of awareness. First I felt the circulatory awareness I had felt the first time. On this occasion, however, I maintained the gestalt, and soon was rewarded with definite motor-muscular awareness. There were all sort of twinges, electric currents, and, especially, little internal jumps in the extremities. There seemed little or no anxiety, except a continued over-eagerness, which I noted as part of a compulsive drive toward premature success. At one time I almost fell asleep again, but as I reestablished the figure/ground, I felt a fine feeling of having overcome this resistance to awareness.

"Then I felt a severe pain in the stomach muscles, almost as if someone had kicked me in the solar-plexus. As I tried to concentrate on it, however, it disappeared. Then I felt a severe pain in my upper arm. This remained and intensified as I concentrated on it for about five minutes. It moved slightly, and alternately faded and increased in strength. I now tried to make free-associations with my life-situation to observe whether any connection could be made with this pain. I honestly do not remember what my train of thought was at this time, but something came to the surface which seemed to cause the pain to explode like an internal mushroom bomb. I can describe my feelings by saying that I felt as if I were about to have an orgasm in the area of the arm. This feeling mounted to almost unbearable tension and then faded without resolution, leaving me feeling very much as if an expected orgasm had not taken place. However, when I ceased the experiment I felt well, rather than having the typical unpleasant after-effect of an incomplete orgasm; I did, however, have the feeling that something terrific had almost occurred. I must now report further that, as I typed this report, memory of the experiment returned spontaneously in greater detail than I would have imagined possible, and suddenly I felt the same pain in the same region of the arm. It is there right now. This interests me, but also alarms me somewhat.

"I interrupted my report at this time to concentrate on the repeated pain in my arm. Internal awareness came at once, and the pain remained present. Suddenly it spread out over my entire body and I began to tremble with fear (literally), an emotion which both surprised and disgusted me. As I did this, I felt that I wanted to stretch my arms out to someone—my mother. Simultaneously an incident came to mind of when I had done just that. It occurred when I was four years old. I was traveling with my parents, and had taken an intense dislike to the manager of our hotel. I did something or other that was naughty, and my mother said that if I didn't behave she would go off and leave me behind with the hotel-manager, who was present at the time.

"I started to cry and ran to my mother with my arms outstretched. She consoled me, and assured me that she was joking, while the manager laughed at me and called me a 'mama's baby.' All this may be cooked up, and I wouldn't blame you for being sceptical. I am myself. However, to the best of my knowledge, I hadn't thought of this incident since the time it occurred, and now I remember it as clearly as if it had happened yesterday. The pain in my arm still persists, but it seems to be less acute and to cover a wider area.

"In my next muscle-tension experiment, awareness came a little more slowly than the previous time, possibly due to anxieties that had been aroused by the results of the previous one. It took about fifteen minutes for strong awareness to form, and this time it was in the area of the face. I first noticed a tendency of the muscles at the corner of my mouth to twitch upward in what I imagined was an attempt to smile. Ten minutes approximately passed before I realized that this upward twitch was not a smile, but actually part of the facial movement of a crying-spell. I thereupon proceeded to cry! This I hadn't indulged in since a small child. Embarrassment at my own behavior interfered with developments at this point. I could not associate my action with anything in my life-situation, except possibly the death of my mother two years ago, on which occasion I had been unable to cry although I wished to. I did become aware, however, that the pressure of my lower lip against my upper and the tension across my forehead—two tensions which I reported previously—existed to prevent my crying. After the experiment I felt fine and extremely happy to have made this outgoing action available to myself."

VII

INTROJECTION

EXPERIMENT 15: Introjecting and Eating

In dealing with introjects we again make use of the
same techniques of concentration and development
which were applied to retroflections, but there is a
crucial difference in procedure. In retroflections both
the retroflected act and the behavior which it holds in
check are parts of one's own personality, and what
must be done is, first, to accept and identify with both
parts, and, second, to find a new integration in which
both parts obtain overt expression. An introject, on the
other hand, consists of material—a way of acting, feeling, evaluating—which you have taken into your system of behavior, but which you have not assimilated
in such fashion as to make it a genuine part of your
organism. You took it in on the basis of a forced acceptance, a forced (and therefore pseudo) identification, so that, even though you will now resist its dis-
lodgment as if it were something precious, it is actually
a foreign body.

Both as an organism and as a personality one grows
by assimilating new material. To compare the acquisition of habits, attitudes, beliefs, or ideals to the process of taking physical food into the organism strikes
one at first as merely a crude analogy, but the more
one examines the detailed sequence of each, the more
one realizes their functional identity.

Physical food, properly digested and assimilated, becomes part of the organism; but food which "rests
heavy on the stomach" is an introject. You are aware
of it and want to throw it up. If you do so, you get it
"out of your system." Suppose, instead, you suppress

your discomfort, nausea and tendency to spew it forth. Then you "keep it down" and either succeed finally in painfully digesting it or else it poisons you.

When it is not physical food but concepts, "facts," or standards of behavior, the situation is the same. A theory which you have mastered—digested in detail so that you have made it yours—can be used flexibly and efficiently because it has become "second nature" to you. But some "lesson" which you have swallowed whole without comprehension—for example, "on authority"—and which you now use "as if" it were your own, is an introject. Though you have suppressed your initial bewilderment over what was forced into you, you cannot really use such foreign knowledge and, to the extent that you have cluttered your personality with gulped-down morsels of this and that, you have impaired your ability to think and act on your own.

On this point we differ with Freud. He held that some introjections are healthy; for instance, the models and imitations by which the developing personality of the child is formed—especially the introjection of the loving parents. But in this he was obviously failing to make the distinction between introjection and assimilation. What is assimilated is not taken in as a whole, but is first destroyed (de-structured) completely and transformed—and absorbed *selectively* according to the need of the organism. Whatever the child gets from his *loving* parents he assimilates, for it is fitting and appropriate to his own needs as he grows. It is the *hateful* parents who have to be introjected, taken down whole, although they are contrary to the needs of the organism. Accompanying this is the starving of the child's proper needs and his repressing of rebellion and disgust. The "I" which is composed of introjects does not function spontaneously, for it is made up of concepts about the self—duties, standards, and views of "human nature" imposed from the outside.

If you can realize the necessity for an aggressive, destructive, and reconstructive attitude toward any experience that you are really to make your own, you can then appreciate the need mentioned previously to evaluate aggressions highly and not to dub them glibly "anti-social"—on the basis of an introject. As commonly used, "social" often means being willing to introject norms, codes and institutions which are foreign to man's healthy interests and needs, and in the process to lose genuine community and the ability to experience joy.

To eliminate introjects from your personality the problem is not, as it was with retroflections, to accept and integrate dissociated parts of yourself. Rather, it is to become aware of what is not truly yours, to acquire a selective and critical attitude toward what is offered you, and, above all, to develop the ability to "bite off" and "chew" experience so as to extract its healthy nourishment.

To clarify further the process of introjection, let us review the earliest years of life. The foetus is in complete confluence with the mother, who provides oxygen, food, and environment. After birth the infant must get his own air and begin to differentiate the sensory environment, but his food, although now only intermittently available, still comes fully prepared for digestion. All that is required of him is to suck and swallow. Such fluid intake is equivalent to total introjection, for the material is swallowed whole. But this is *appropriate* to the pre-dental, suckling stage.

In the next stages of oral development, biting and chewing, the infant becomes more active with respect to his food. He selects and appropriates and changes in some degree what the environment offers. With the growth of incisors he is for a period in transition from suckling to "biteling." He makes the discrimination that the nipple is not to be bitten while he sucks from it, but for the rest of his diet he bites off bits of other still partially prepared food. With the eruption of molars, he reaches the chewing stage, which is of paramount importance because it allows for complete destroying of the food. Instead of accepting what is given and uncritically introjecting it, the "chewing" works over what is provided by the environment so as to insure his assimilation of it. It is on the basis of such competence, combined with almost complete development of sensory discrimination and perception of objects, that the child begins to speak and brings to a head the process of forming his "I."

The process of weaning—of "making" the child give up its suckling—is always regarded as difficult and traumatic. But it is very likely that, *if there has been no previous starvation and failure of affection* (that is, no accumulation thus far of interruptions, distortions, or unfinished aspects of the earlier stages), the child will be ready and eager to exercise his newly developed powers and to leave behind the introjective confluence. It was the tragic fact that this normal sequence almost never takes place in our society—that there is, therefore, imperfect biting off and chewing from the beginning—that led Freud and others to conceive as normal "partial introjection," the gulping down of poorly chewed morsels of one kind or another.

With biting, chewing, and the very important functions of locomotion and ability to approach, the child has the chief types of aggression available to him and under his control for his own growth. These, obviously, are not "anti-social," although they are the very antithesis of passive confluence. But if these biological activities are not used in the service of the growth-functions—as initiative, selection, overcoming of obstacles, seizing upon and destroying in order to assimilate— *then* the surplus energy finds discharge as displaced aggressions—domination, irritability, sadism, lust for power, suicide, murder, and their mass-equivalent, war! The organism does not develop in continuous creative adjustment with its environment—so that the "I" is a system of executive functions concerned with orientation and manipulation. Instead, it is saddled with an "I" which is a thrown-together collection of unassimilated introjects—traits and qualities taken over from "the authorities," which he cannot stomach, relations which he did not bite off and chew, knowledge he doesn't understand, sucking fixations he cannot dissolve, disgust he cannot release.

When, by reversing retroflections, an amount of aggressive energy is detached from the self as victim, it may be usefully reemployed for biting through and chewing physical food and its psychological counterpart: problems that must be faced, fixations that must be dissolved, concepts of the "I" which must be destroyed. That is what is attempted in the following experiments, but just as in working with muscular contractions, you must go slowly and not force yourself or you are sure to be disappointed and discouraged. The main resistances of which you will become aware will be impatience and greed, which are emotions perfectly normal to the gulping stage, but not to the more mature, differentiated stage of selection, biting off, and ruminating. Be content at first with the development of awareness. You will have accomplished much when, by concentrating on your mode of eating, you learn to distinguish between liquid food which may appropriately be drunk and solid food which *cannot* be handled adequately by drinking it down.

Concentrate on your eating without reading or "thinking." Simply address yourself to your food. Meals have for us become social occasions for the most part. The primitive goes off by himself to eat. Follow his example to this extent: set aside one meal a day to eat in solitude, and learn how to eat. This may take about two months, but, after that, you will have acquired a new taste, a new source of enjoyment, and you will not relapse. If you are impatient, this will seem too long. You will want magical effects, quick results without effort. For you to get rid of your introjects, you yourself must do the destroying and the reintegrating.

Notice your resistances to addressing the food. Do you taste the first few bites and then fall into a trance of "thinking," daydreaming, wanting to talk—meantime losing contact with the taste? Do you bite off your food by clean, efficient action of the front teeth? In other words, do you bite through on a meat sandwich held in your hands, or do you close your jaws part way and then tear off a hunk? Do you ever use your molars up to the point of complete destruction of the food, that is, liquefaction? Just notice whatever it is you do, without deliberately changing anything. Many changes will occur spontaneously if you keep in contact with your food.

As you eat with awareness, do you feel greed? Impatience? Disgust? Do you blame the hurry and bustle of modern life for your gulping of meals? Is it different when you have leisure? Do you avoid food that is flat and tasteless, or do you just down it without demurring? Do you experience a "symphony" of flavors and textures in your food, or have you so desensitized your palate that it all tastes pretty much alike?

When it is not a matter of physical but of "mental" food, how does the matter stand? Consider the same questions with regard, for instance, to your intake from the printed page. Do you skip over hard paragraphs or do you work them through? Is your taste for the sweet and easy alone—light fiction or "feature" stories—which you can gulp down without active response? Or do you compel yourself to partake only of "heavy" literature, though you get little pleasure for your effort?

What about your visual intake at the movies? Do you fall into a kind of trance and drink in the scenes? Study this as an instance of confluence.

In the same context let us consider alcoholism, which, although complicated and with many ramifications (including somatic changes), is muscularly anchored in oral under-development. No cure can have lasting effect or be more than a suppression unless the alcoholic ("adult" suckling) progresses to the stage of biting and chewing. Fundamentally, the drinker wants to drink his environment in—to get easy and total confluence without the excitement (which to him is a painful effort) of contacting, destroying and assimilating. He is a bottle-baby, a gulper, reluctant to take solid food and chew it. This applies to the steak on his platter and to the larger problems of his life-situation. He wants his solutions in liquid form, pre-prepared, so that he need but drink them down.

Socially, he wants to enter into immediate confluence without preparatory contact with the other person. His acquaintance of the moment becomes a pal to whom he will "pour out his heart." He by-passes those parts of his personality which would exercise discrimination; and then, on the basis of these supposedly deep and sincere but actually most superficial social contacts, he comes forth with impatient, extravagant demands.

Just as uncritically, he takes in social reproaches and accepts them as coming from himself, for he has a strong self-aggressive conscience. He may silence it by drowning it in alcohol, but when he awakes, its vindictiveness is redoubled. Since his aggression is not used in attacking his physical food or his problems, the surplus which is not invested in his conscience often turns outward in surly, irrelevant fights.

Drinking is the adequate way of appropriating fluids, and inebriation's easy sociability is warming and pleasurable. But these are only phases of experience, not the whole of it, and when they continually occupy the foreground as imperious needs, the possibility of other kinds and levels of experience is ruled out.

A similar mechanism manifests itself in sexual promiscuity. The demand here is for immediate terminal satisfaction, without preliminary contact and development of the relationship. Since he is cold and the victim of tactile starvation, the promiscuous person seeks crude tactile proximity of the skin-surface as his final sexual aim. While there are, of course, other complicating factors, what again is outstanding is impatience and greed.

For the most part, our views on introjection arouse nearly unanimous disagreement on first encounter. We cite a few comments from students:

"I cherish the illusion—which you will no doubt diagnose as neurotic—that being a human being implies more respect for the grandeur of the soul than to address myself to food."

*   *   *

"I don't see how changing your eating habits is supposed to aid your ability to reject introjected ideas.

I just don't see it. Even if early eating habits are connected with all this, simply changing your present habits isn't going to suddenly enable you to see that Freud's concept of introjection is wrong while this one may be partially correct. Why can't we work on something that will actually be of use rather than all this junk?"

*   *   *

"The whole business of the parallel between forcible intake of food and forcible intake of behavior is tenuous, especially when carried past just being a figurative way of speaking. The organism does not vomit out behavior, nor does it bite and chew experience. True, complex behavior may be introjected, but to me this has little to do with the eating functions, certainly when infancy is past. I have disregarded the eating experiments as I think they are useless, *a priori*, and I won't even give them the limited attention I've paid the other experiments—that is, doing them for the sake of curiosity. In the authors' own terms, I refuse to introject what they have to say about introjection."

*   *   *

"I'm no more impressed or moved to action by this drill than I have been by the others. Although much has been learned in the process of reading it, namely, an acute sense of awareness of one's thoughts, motives, habits, etc., with possible permanent benefits derived therefrom, I still fail to comprehend the essential thought behind this mass of verbal confusion. I assume that the dominating thought is to make the individual more cognizant of various processes within himself, and therefore expel many undesirable factors present in his thoughts and actions. As previously stated, though, I feel that the authors assume too much insight on the part of the student, and I feel further that the drills involve much too much preoccupation with self—a decidedly dangerous thing if devoid of trained guidance."

In all of the above excerpts there is the customary modern emphasis on verbal evidence and verbal proof. As a matter of fact, there are a number of "objective" experimental findings which could be brought to bear in this connection, perhaps sufficient to oblige the above-quoted students to give intellectual assent to the theory presented here; however, what we seek is not verbal agreement but the dynamic effects that you may obtain by directly discovering and proving the points in your own non-verbal functioning.

Several persons, apparently unable to reject the theory without more ado, rejected it temporarily by postponing its non-verbal testing:

> "I question this whole thing on the—Oh, how the hell *can* there be a functional identity of any such sort? I'm going to put this whole thing off until I go home this summer and work on it then."

Whatever doubts they had about the theory, most students took an experimental attitude toward the examination of their eating processes and reported various discoveries about their usual modes of ingestion:

> "After concentrating on my eating I found that I didn't know how to eat, but bolted my food gluttonously. I can't stop eating with a great rush even when there's no reason to hurry. I find that I use my molars scarcely at all."

The problem of keeping a presentable silhouette dominated many reports.

> "I would try on a dress that looked beautiful in Vogue or Harper's Bazaar. What I saw in the mirror didn't look like my long, willowy, blonde ideal. I would get sore and disgusted at myself and swear to go on a diet. Then I would get to feeling so sorry for myself that I would sit down and eat some candy or a piece of cake."

We quote in detail an account of attempting to chew some food to the point of liquefaction:

> "Since I'm quite well known in the family as a food-gulper and a 'reading-when-eating' type, I looked forward to the eating experiments with interest. They

have worked, but for fear they might work too well, I've stopped before going too far.

"First, I noted how I took the food, and wasn't too surprised to find that I'm a 'partial-biter, tear-the-rest-off' sort of operator. It was fairly easy to slow down enough to bite through my food as completely as I could before starting to chew. But since I rarely eat without reading, simply this concentration on biting off instead of tearing off sent me into daydreaming. I just sat there dumb, unaware of what I was doing and not thinking anything—so that literally before I knew it the food was down.

"As to whether I ever liquefy my food the answer emphatically is no (probably a reaction against my father who is an ardent Fletcherizer, although he doesn't actually count, and thus is the slowest eater I've ever seen). I tried to chew and chew until the food was about as liquid as I could stand it and noted two reactions:

"First, my tongue started to ache toward the back. What usually takes place is that after I have food in my mouth nothing happens until the food is on the way down the esophagus—that is, I'm not aware of swallowing, gulping, breathing or anything else. What happened, now that I tried to masticate completely, was that I found myself running out of air. My tongue started to ache uncomfortably. I seemed to be holding my breath. So I had to push the food to the sides of my mouth, make the gulping motions (although I wasn't swallowing anything), and then take a deep breath before going on. After these setting-up exercises I would have to bring back the food from wherever it had scattered in the sides of my mouth and then go to work on the messy left-overs of that last bite.

"This description is particularly detailed and, to me, nauseating, because that's how I felt after a couple of bites—nauseated. The food began to taste terrible and I now found myself deliberately avoiding trying to taste or even feel (in a sensory fashion) what was going on in my mouth. I usually don't taste or feel what's going on there anyhow, but this experiment did bring back a lot of taste, etc., so that now to get rid of the unpleasantness aroused by it I had to try to 'desensitize myself.'

"What I meant above when I wrote that I stopped the above experiment before going too far is that I was feeling so disgusted with what was going on in my mouth that I felt a very strong tendency to vomit. Immediately I switched over into daydream or stupor, telling myself, 'Now let's not spoil a whole meal by getting sick; after all, there's a limit.' So I stopped. Now this is obviously a resistance, but that's what I did twice."

A student who feels that he has good eating habits mentions the following:

"As a child these good eating habits were not present. I was an extremely poor eater and probably introjected most of what I ate, attempting to think or talk about anything to keep from becoming aware of what I was eating. The change occurred somewhere between my tenth and thirteenth year. The major event in my life during this period was when my father remarried and we finally moved away from my uncle's home where we had been living."

A number of students made comments such as the following:

"I am utterly amazed at how closely my ways of dealing with problems, with reading matter, with movies, etc., parallel my ways of dealing with food."

EXPERIMENT 16: Dislodging and Digesting Introjects

Introjection is characterized by a particular constellation of emotions and behavioral tendencies: impatience and greed; disgust and its negation through loss of taste and appetite; fixation, with its desperate hanging on and clinging to what has ceased to be nourishing. Let us examine these in detail.

Infants and children are said to be impatient and greedy. But these terms, appropriate as applied to adults who are under-developed, are *mis*applied to children. A baby, when hungry, wants the breast. If he does not get it right away, he squalls. Impatiently? No, for this is all that he *can* do in the direction of satisfying his need. This is not something to be corrected but rather to be *grown out of*. Impatience has no meaning apart from its opposite, patience. Adults have had a chance to differentiate these behaviors by acquiring the working-through techniques which, when applied, constitute patience. The child has not.

If he has a loving mother, his "hunger-cry" is to her an adequate and unresented signal. Given the breast, he eagerly and immediately swallows down the milk. Greedily? No, for liquid food requires no delay before ingestion. The behavior of the child is mistakenly called impatience and greed when obviously it is aggression that is fully adequate in the child's mother-confluent situation. Only when the primitive aggression does not, as the child gets older, differentiate into techniques for tackling and working through obstacles are we entitled to speak of impatience and greed. Although equipped with the apparatus and the opportunity for taking care of himself, such an "old child"—still wielding his aggression in its original, primitive form—insists that it be done *for* him and done at once!

If you investigate your own impatience, you will be able to confirm this. You will realize that it is a primitive aggression—a crude, angry reaction to frustration. To say, "I am impatient with you" is equivalent to, "I am annoyed with you because you do not come across with what I want right now, and I don't want to have to put out the additional effort (destruction of obstacles) to get you to come across."

In babies and cubs we can easily observe the further differentiation of aggression at the biting stage. They like to try out this new ability by sinking their teeth into whatever is bitable. The mouth, too, becomes an organ of manipulation. Subsequently, the hands take over the early exploratory function of the mouth and then its manipulating. As more and more discrimination and working over of food is required, the mouth specializes correspondingly in tasting and destroying.

Parental interference comes seriously into the picture at the biting stage. On the one hand, biting is punished as cruel and naughty, and, on the other, food that the child does not want or does not want *at the time* is forced into him. His tendency under these circumstances to make a barrier of his teeth to the unwanted food is forcibly vanquished. Denied adequate expression, the child's oral aggression must be displaced. Part of it is retroflected to suppress the punishable food-rejecting. Part of it turns against persons. This comprises the so-called "cannibalism" of those who want "to eat you up."

In order to get down and keep down the unwanted food the child has to repress his disgust. Furthermore, spontaneous use of his teeth has been denied him; he was punished for his "cruel and naughty" biting and also for clamping his teeth against the unwanted food. Only the behavior of the suckling—which he *was* in the process of outgrowing—is fully safe. His development out of this stage has been interfered with, and, because of the maiming of his "biteling" behavior, he retains in some degree or relapses into the "impatience and greed" of the suckling. Only liquid food still tastes good, but this is never enough to gratify hunger.

Because of "scheduled feedings" and other "scientific" practices applied to you as an infant, the blocking of oral aggression as described above is probably in some degree present in your own case. This condition is the basic prerequisite for tendencies to introject—to swallow down whole what does not belong in your organism. We shall, therefore, attack the problem at the source, namely, the process of eating. The solution involves remobilization of disgust, which is not pleasant and will rouse strong resistances. For once, therefore, in stating the following motor experiment, we do not propose it as something to try out in a spontaneous fashion to see what happens, but we appeal to your courage and charge you with it as a task.

During each and every meal, take one bite—remember, just one, single bite!—and liquefy the food completely by chewing. Do not let one morsel escape destruction, but seek it out with your tongue and bring it into position for further chewing. When you are satisfied that the food has been fully liquefied, drink it down.

In performing this task you will "forget yourself" in the middle of the operation and swallow. You will become inattentive. You will have no time. On occasion you will feel that you have "spoiled the taste" of something good. When you encounter disgust, you will be sorry you ever started the experiment. But sooner or later a welcome by-product of the experiment will be that you get much more taste and nourishment out of your mouthful than you would have imagined possible, and with this you will begin to have an increased feeling of yourself as an active agent.

The task is restricted to a single bite per meal, for this, no matter how simple it may sound, will be hard to do. It requires the remarshalling of an enormous amount of energy. The chewing as such is not what you are after but rather *the attitude of destroying and assimilating real material.* Avoid any obsessional practice such as counting your jaw-movements (Fletcherism), for this only distracts your attention.

As the functional counterpart of the task of chewing up a single bite of food, give yourself the same training in the intellectual sphere. For example, take a single difficult sentence in a book that is "tough meat," and analyze it, that is, take it apart thoroughly. Get the precise connotation of each word. For the sentence as a whole decide on its clarity or vagueness, its truth or falsity. Make it your own, or else make clear to yourself what part of it you don't understand. Perhaps you have not failed to comprehend, but instead the sentence is incomprehensible. Decide this for yourself.

Another profitable experiment, one which makes full use of the functional identity between eating physical food and "stomaching" some interpersonal situation is the following: When in an impatient mood— angry, upset, resentful—and thus inclined to gulp, apply the aggression in a deliberate attack on some physical food. Take an apple or a tough heel of bread and wreak your vengeance on it. In accordance with your mood, chew as impatiently, hastily, viciously, cruelly as you can. But bite and chew—do not gulp!

The neurotic's condemnation of aggression has two exceptions. The first is when the aggression is retroflected and he then drives or punishes himself, and the second is when the aggression is invested in conscience and moral judgment and is then directed against both himself and others. If he will use some of the aggression dentally—that is, in the biological aggression of the teeth—he will correspondingly let up in his attacks on himself and others, and, what is most important, he will learn to recognize aggressiveness as *a healthy function which prevents introjection.* He will learn to reject what is indigestible in his physical or psychological system and to bite off and chew what is potentially digestible and nourishing if adequately destroyed and assimilated. And, with respect to the introjects he now has, he will learn to bring them up and get rid of them or else, at last, to chew them properly as preparation for genuine digestion.

Disgust as a word comes from the prefix *dis-,* meaning "without," and *gustus,* meaning "relish." This understates what we experience as disgust. When disgusted we have nausea, the physical sensations that go with reverse peristalsis in the alimentary tract. This changed direction of the gastric and esophageal contractions is, of course, designed to regurgitate and thus make possible the elimination or the further chewing, as in ruminants like the cow, of indigestible or improperly masticated food.

The same process occurs in the organism when the environment presents objects or situations which could not possibly be mistaken for physical food but which can be termed instead "perceptual food." We retch even at the sight of a decomposed horse. You may "feel your gorge rise" slightly at mere reading of these words, and you certainly would if we elaborated further on the possibilities of taking the dead horse as food. In other words, the organism reacts to certain objects and situations—and we cannot impress this upon you too strongly—*as if they had been taken into the alimentary tract!*

Our language is full of expressions which reflect the psychosomatic identity of disgust produced by physical food and by what is indigestible only in the psychological sense. Consider, for instance, "You make me sick," "I gag over having to do this," "The sight was nauseating." It would be easy to think up another series of verbalisms about belching, that relatively milder but omnipresent indicator of bad digestion.

Disgust is the desire to bring up, to vomit forth, to reject material which is disagreeable to the organism. One "gets the stuff down" only by numbing and putting out of commission the healthy organism's natural means of discrimination, smelling, tasting, and so on. In such an event it is crucial at least that one feel the disgust later on, and thus be enabled to "get the stuff back up." Since introjects have been gulped down precisely in this manner, their elimination from your system requires that you remobilize disgust.

Neurotics talk much of being rejected. This is, for the most part, a projection onto others of their own rejecting (as we shall consider further in the next experiment). What they refuse to feel is their latent disgust with what they have incorporated in their own personalities. If they did, they would have to vomit up and reject many of their "loved" identifications—which were unpalatable and hateful at the time when swallowed down. Or else they would have to go through the laborious process of bringing them up, working them through, and then at last assimilating them.

Forced feeding, forced education, forced morality, forced identifications with parents and siblings, result in literally thousands of unassimilated odds and ends lodged in the psychosomatic organism as introjects. They are both undigested and, as they stand, indigestible. And men and women, long accustomed to be-

ing resigned to "the way things are," continue to
hold their noses, desensitize their palates, and swallow
down still more.

In psychoanalytical practice a patient may lie down
and bring up verbally all the undigested material accumulated since his last session. This furnishes relief,
for he has performed the psychological counterpart of
vomiting. But the therapeutic effect of this as such is
nil, for he will introject again. At the moment of taking
it in he does not feel disgust for what later he will
disgorge. If he did, he would reject it *then* and not save
it for his treatment hour. He has not learned to chew
up and work through what is nourishing and necessary.
He will drink down his analyst's words, too, as something new with which to identify, rather than mulling
them over and assimilating them. He expects his therapist to do the work of interpretation for him, and he
will later spew out these very interpretations to his
bored friends. Otherwise, "intellectually accepting"
the interpretation—without conflict, suffering, and disgust—he merely imposes on himself a new burden, a
further complication of his concept of himself.

Orthodox psychoanalysis makes the error of not regarding all introjects as "unfinished business" to be
worked through and assimilated; consequently, it accepts as normal much in the present-life attitude which
is not actually the patient's own and not spontaneous.
If, instead of limiting themselves to working through
merely the dreams and more spectacular symptoms,
analysts would concentrate on *every* aspect of behavior, they would find that the introjected "I" is not
the healthy "I." The latter is completely dynamic, consisting entirely of functions and shifting boundaries between what is accepted and what is rejected.

When one looks upon the introject as an item of
"unfinished business," its genesis is readily traced to a
situation of interrupted excitement. Every introject is
the precipitate of a conflict given up before it was resolved. One of the contestants—usually an impulse to
act in a given manner—has left the field; replacing it,

so as to constitute some kind of integration (though a false and inorganic one) is *the corresponding wish of the coercing authority*. The self has been conquered. In giving up, it settles for a secondary integrity—a means of surviving, though beaten—*by identifying with the conqueror and turning against itself*. It takes over the coercer's role by conquering itself, retroflecting the hostility previously directed outward against the coercer. This is the situation usually referred to by the conventional term "self-control." Here, although actually defeated, the victim is encouraged by the victorious coercer to perpetuate his defeat by forever rejoicing in the deluded notion that *he* was the victor!

Though admittedly unpleasant, there is no other way to discover what in you is not part of yourself except by remobilizing disgust and the accompanying urge to reject. If you wish to unburden yourself of those foreign bodies in your personality which are introjects, you must, in addition to the chewing experiments, intensify awareness of taste, find the spots where you are "taste-blind," and resensitize them. Become aware of changes in taste during mastication, differences in structure, consistency, temperature. In doing this, you are sure to revive disgust. Then, as with any other painful experience that is your own, you must confront this too, become aware of it, and accept it. When, finally, there comes the urge to vomit, do so. You will feel it as terrible and painful only because of your resistances to it. A small child vomits with perfect ease and in a strong orgastic stream; immediately afterward he is quite happy again, rid of the foreign matter that was bothering him.

"Fixations" form another most important part of the introjective constellation. They are the tendencies to static clinging and suckling when the situation has progressed to the point where active biting through and chewing are required. To be fixated is to be confluent with the situation of sucking, of skin-proximity, of holding on to, of dreamy recollection, etc. In our view a fixation does not result from a particular traumatic interpersonal or Oedipal experience, but is the work of a character-structure, a rigid pattern repeated continuously in the life of the neurotic. You may recognize the fixated, confluent type by his clenched jaw, his indistinct voice, and his laziness in chewing.

He hangs on "doggedly." He will not let go, but he cannot—and this is the decisive point—bite the piece off. He hangs on to exhausted relationships from which neither he nor his partner are any longer getting any profit. He hangs on to outworn customs, to memories, to grudges. He will not finish what is unfinished and try a new adventure. Where there is risk, he visualizes only the possible losses and never the compensating gains. His aggression, confined to holding his jaws locked—as if trying to bite himself—can be employed to destroy neither the object on which he is fixated nor such new obstacles as may present themselves. He is squeamish about hurting and—projecting his unacknowledged wish to hurt—fearful of being hurt.

Castration-fear has as a major component the clinging fear to hurt or be hurt, and the *vagina dentata,* a frequent fantasy of castration-anxiety, is the man's own unfinished bite projected into the woman. Little can be accomplished in working on castration-fantasies until dental aggression has been remobilized; but once this natural destructiveness has been reintegrated into the personality, not only the fear of damage to the penis but also the fear of other damages—to honor, property, eyesight, etc.—are reduced to proper size.

Here is a simple technique for starting to mobilize the fixed jaw. If you notice that your teeth are frequently clenched or that you are in a state of grim determination, instead of working with ease and interest, make your lower and upper teeth touch each other lightly. Keep them neither clamped nor apart. Concentrate and await developments. Sooner or later your teeth may begin to chatter, as if with cold. Allow this to spread, if it will, into a general shivering excitement all through your muscles. Try to let go until you are shivering and shaking all over.

If you succeed in this experiment, use the opportunity to try to increase the looseness and amplitude of your jaw. Touch your teeth together in various positions—incisors, front molars, back molars—and meantime press your fingers against the sides of your head where the jaws meet the ears. When you find painful spots of tension, use these as foci of concentration. Likewise, if you achieve general trembling in this or other experiments, use it to try to experience a complete giving up of all rigidity—to the point of dizziness or collapse of tension.

Try the alternative of clamping your teeth hard in any position—the situation of biting through. This will create a painful tension in the jaws that will spread to the gums, mouth, throat and eyes. Concentrate on the pattern of tension, and then, as suddenly as you can, let go with your jaws.

To mobilize your stiff mouth, open it wide in talking and bite through your words. Spit them out like bullets from a machine-gun.

The "hanging-on bite" is not restricted to the jaws, but spreads to throat and chest, impeding breathing and aggravating anxiety. It spreads also to the eyes, bringing about a fixed stare and preventing a "piercing" glance. If your states of anxiety tend to come when you are speaking—for example, in public, or even in a small group—you will benefit by considering the following: speaking is organized exhaling. Inhalation takes in oxygen for metabolism; exhalation produces the voice. (See how difficult it is to speak while inhaling.) When excited, you increase the speed of your speech (impatience and greed manifested not on the intake but this time on the output side) but do not inhale sufficiently, and breathing thus becomes difficult.

An experiment simple in structure yet exceedingly difficult to perform will remedy this, besides being an excellent means of making you feel your non-verbal existence in relation to your verbalizing. It coordinates breathing and thinking (subvocal speaking). You have already done it in part in your earlier work on internal silence. Talk in fantasy, silently and subvocally, but with a particular audience, perhaps a single person. Attend to your "talking" and your breathing. Try to have no words in your throat ("mind") during the inhalation; but let out your thoughts and your breath at the same time. Notice how often you hold your breath.

You will perceive, again, how much of your thinking is a one-sided interpersonal relationship, not a give and take; you are always lecturing, commenting, judging, or pleading, inquiring, etc. Seek for the rhythm of speaking and listening, give and take, exhaling and inhaling. (Though insufficient alone, this coordination of breathing and thinking is the chief basic therapy for stammering.)

The introjection experiments call forth more violent protests than any others in the series.

"The authors carry this chewing and food consciousness a little too far and insist upon it *ad nauseam.* That we eat the way we do is usually unrecognized by us, but surely there must be an easier way to point this out."

* * *

"Your statements are nothing but organized irrationality."

* * *

"If you are literally inviting us to chew a piece of food until it disgusts us so much that we throw up, then this is the most stupid business I've ever encountered. I do agree that we often do feel like throwing up for many causes, and perhaps we would feel better if we did throw up; however, like anything else it could get to be a habit and then we'd be in quite a fix."

* * *

"Eating is eating and that's all. Following your suggestion, I took a bite and chewed and chewed it until I was tired and couldn't chew any more. Then I swallowed. Okay, that's it. I didn't feel nauseous. I don't see how anyone can go into such detail about vomiting. What is there to vomit about? It's *food!* They eat it every day. And then, suddenly, after reading your experiment, they eat it again and vomit. They're certainly open to suggestion!"

The statement just above came from one of the very few students who expressed any astonishment that food, when chewed thoroughly, should arouse disgust in anyone. Most persons simply took it for granted that masticating to the point of liquefaction would produce nausea, and, furthermore, that *it would continue to do so permanently!* But why should it? As well stated above, "What is there to vomit about? It's *food!*"

If there is nothing intrinsically disgusting about *this particular bite of food*—in other words, if it is *good food* and *you are hungry*—then, if thorough chewing of it arouses nausea, *you must be making a mistake!* You must be tapping some *repressed disgust,* which was aroused but not expressed on past occasions. When obliged to down something unpalatable, your method was to inhibit chewing and desensitize yourself to the eating process. You behave now as if you *still* have to do this—and do it with respect to *all* food.

Actually, you are now in a position to be discriminating. You need no longer be, as one student put it, "the good child who eats everything." What disgusts you, you can reject; what you find nutritious and appetizing, you can consume with gusto. But *only after* you have remobilized and *e*xpressed the *r*epressed disgust!

Let us go over this again. Disgust is a *natural barrier* possessed by every healthy organism. It is a defense against taking into the organism what does not belong there—what is indigestible or foreign to its nature. However, by dint of great effort, parents and other authorities can get the child to *de*mobilize disgust— that is, attack and put out of commission its own defenses against what is unwholesome. The child's original ability—which has been experimentally demonstrated over and over again—to pick a balanced diet appropriate to its needs is overthrown by an arbitrary scheduling of officially designated "correct" foods in "correct" amounts at "correct" times. The child eventually "adjusts" to this by gulping down whatever is given with just as little contact with it as possible. Once the natural defenses of the organism have been breached, it is then comparatively easy to get the child to gulp down all sorts of unnatural and arbitrary "mental food" and thus "preserve society" for still another generation.

The healthy organism's way of eating—or, in its broader meaning, its way of selecting and assimilating from its environment what is needed for its own sustenance and growth—cannot, unfortunately, be restored over-night. Full remobilization of disgust for what *is* disgusting calls a halt to further introjecting, but it does not forthwith cause to be spewed forth what has already been introjected and now "lies heavy in the mental stomach." This takes time and a transitional period of more or less frequent or chronic nausea.

Persons differ widely in their attitude toward vomiting. For some it comes relatively easily and brings profound relief. Others have highly organized defenses against it.

"I have not been able to mobilize the feelings of disgust spoken of, probably because of tremendous fear of vomiting. I do not remember the origin of this fear, but I can remember that as a very young child I struggled for hours in order to prevent vomiting. Whether or not this was connected with forced feeding I don't know, but my mother still does talk about how, when I was little, she had to force food into me, mouthful after mouthful."

* * *

"In doing the experiment I did feel disgust and the desire to regurgitate. But that is as far as I went, for I have always been averse to vomiting. When I have known that it would be good for me and have tried it, the effort has almost always seemed too great. Attempts to force vomiting by the finger-in-the-throat technique always produce a pain in my chest, which is my reason for suppressing the desire to complete the act."

* * *

"I can vomit easily. As a child, when I had an upset stomach, my parents sent me to the bathroom with instructions on how to vomit. The result is that, for me, this is a perfectly natural and tremendously relieving process."

* * *

"When I gulp down my food, I have, pretty soon afterward, a pressure in my stomach or, more often, higher up in my esophagus. It feels as if something is stuck there and can't move forward or backward. This is the very same feeling I had when, as a child, I was late for school. On those occasions I often vomited on my way to school."

* * *

"Mealtime was the occasion, when I was a child, that my father chose to play the heavy-parent and lay down the law. Sometimes it took my appetite so that I couldn't eat a bite, and I remember several instances in which I had to excuse myself from the table and go vomit."

The remobilization of disgust in connection with eating may bring to the surface a number of past experiences for reconsideration.

"Perhaps it was just some kind of generalization, but the results I got in the eating experiments started me to thinking about a lot of things in my life. My father kept coming to mind. He is a very domineering man, one who wants to keep his children from growing up. I think that playing parent is for him his life-work to a much greater extent than his profession, and from *this* I don't think he ever intends to retire. Many of the ideas that he's crammed down my throat I think I'm starting to 'vomit up.' They flood into my mind, and I analyze them in terms of present-day social and moral views. It is perfectly amazing to see how many things I've taken for granted as being my views, when it's perfectly obvious now that they're his. They don't fit into my life, and already I feel a tremendous relief in sloughing off some of them. They have made my life so needlessly complicated."

One student reported in great detail the bringing up and freeing himself from "introjected blame" in connection with the accidental death, when he was a child, of a sibling. The process of ejecting the introject began with burning sensations in the stomach. These began after he had been performing the eating experiments for a short period.

Another student reported the onset of burning sensations in the stomach almost from the start of these experiments, but it was not until the work with introjects that the following events developed:

"In connection with wondering what introjects I might have lodged in me as foreign bodies, I went back to the work on confluence where we considered traits, speech, dress, etc., and from whom we had imitated them. I became aware of thinking about the problem of tolerance. Then came: 'How I hate her!' The words 'I' and 'her' were emphasized—really emphasized, with fists clenched, biceps contracted, lips compressed, teeth clamped together, eyebrows knit, temples pulsating, ears straining backward, and the entire body pressing hard against the ground and bench (this experiment was conducted in the park). Simultaneously—and this is what I considered important—the tension of the stomach and previously mild burning sensation increased to such an extent that I was sick. Then came the words 'Aunt Agnes!'—and all the tensions, burnings, pressures and pulsations vanished. The only symptom that lingered on—and then only for a few minutes—was the sour oral taste. 'Aunt Agnes' was a masculine, domineering, authoritarian woman who was temporarily put in charge of me when I was three.

"Prior to the start of the awareness experiments and throughout the span of my remembered life, I would fall asleep readily and rarely had dreams. Just before the confluence experiment, however, I began to have nightmares, and I had them every night. As soon as I spewed up this 'hateful introject,' the nightmares disappeared and my sleep has been untroubled since."

VIII

PROJECTIONS

aware of impulse
send out ward — to you

EXPERIMENT 17: Discovering Projections

A projection is a trait, attitude, feeling, or bit of behavior which actually belongs to your own personality but is not experienced as such; instead, it is attributed to objects or persons in the environment and then experienced as directed *toward* you by them instead of the other way around. The projector, unaware, for instance, that he is rejecting others, believes that they are rejecting him; or, unaware of his tendencies to approach others sexually, feels that they make sexual approaches to him.

This mechanism, like retroflection and introjection, functions to interrupt mounting excitement of a kind and degree with which the person cannot cope. It seems to require the following: (1) that you be aware of the nature of the impulse involved; but (2) that you interrupt the aggressive approach to the environment which would be necessary for its adequate expression; with the result (3) that you exclude it from the outgoing activities of your "I"; nevertheless, since you are aware that it *does* exist, then (4) it *must* come from outside—notably from a person or persons in your environment; and (5) it seems *forcibly* directed toward you because your "I", without realizing it, *is* forcibly interrupting your own outwardly directed impulse.

A transparent example of the projection mechanism is given by the inhibited woman who is forever complaining that men are making improper advances to her.

For projection to occur, retroflections and conflu-

248

ences also are necessary, just as they are in introjection; and, in general, as we have said before, the neurotic mechanisms are all functionally related to one another and interlocking. In retroflections both components of the conflict inhere in the personality, but, because of their clinch, the person in effect loses part of his environment, for before his outgoing impulse can come to grips with objects or persons, he intercepts it with his retroflecting behavior.

In projections one is aware of the impulse and of the environmental object, but he does not identify with and carry through his aggressive approach—and thereby loses the sense that *he* is feeling the impulse. Instead, he stands stock still and, without realizing it, waits for his problem to be solved for him from outside.

These mechanisms constitute neurosis only when inappropriate and chronic; all of them are useful and healthy when employed temporarily in particular circumstances. Retroflection is healthy behavior when it constitutes holding back for the sake of caution in a situation of genuine danger. Introjection of the dull and unimportant material of a required school course may be healthy when one has the chance to spew it forth and relieve himself of it on the final examination. Examples of healthy temporary projection are the activities of planning and anticipating. In them one "feels oneself" in a future situation—projects oneself into the environment—and then, when one follows through, in a practical way, *integrates oneself with the project*. Likewise, in certain kinds of sympathy one feels oneself into the other person and solves one's own problem by solving his. Imaginative artists alleviate their problems by projecting into their work. When a child at a very early age projects his teddy-bear out of the crib to the floor, this may mean that he himself wants to be there. What makes all these mechanisms unhealthy, of course, is the structural fixing on some impossible or non-existent object, the loss of awareness, the existence of isolated confluences, and the consequent blocking of integration.

The fear of rejection is crucial with every neurotic,

so we can profitably begin our experimentation with this. The picture of being rejected—first by his parents and now by his friends—is one that the neurotic goes to great lengths to establish and maintain. While such claims may have substance, the opposite is also certainly true—that the neurotic rejects others for not living up to some fantastic ideal or standard which he imposes on them. Once he has projected his rejecting onto the other person, he can, without feeling any responsibility for the situation, regard himself as the passive object of all kinds of unwarranted hardship, unkind treatment, or even victimization.

In your own case, by whom did you or do you feel rejected? Your mother, father, sister, brother? Do you bear them a grudge for it? On what grounds do you reject them? How do they fail to measure up?

Now call up in fantasy some acquaintance. Do you like or dislike this Person X? Do you like or dislike this or that trait or action? Visualize him or her and speak to him or her aloud. Tell him that you accept this mannerism or characteristic, won't have any more of that one, can't stand it when he does this, etc. Repeat the experiment many times. Do you talk stiltedly? Lamely? Self-consciously? Do you feel what you say? Does anxiety develop? Do you feel guilty, afraid that you might spoil the relationship irrevocably by your frankness? *Assure yourself of the difference between fantasy and material reality, for this is just what the projector confuses.* Now comes the decisive question: Do you feel that it is you who are rejecting on the very same grounds on which you believe yourself rejected? Do you feel that people "high hat" you? If so, can you be aware of instances in which you do or would like to "high hat" others? Do you reject in yourself the very things you think others reject you for? If you are skinny, fat, have buck teeth—or whatever it is about yourself that you don't like—do you feel that others are as scornful of these shortcomings as you are yourself? Also, can you notice yourself attributing things unwanted in yourself to others? If you take unfair advantage of someone, do you say, "He was just about ready to do it to me?"

It is not always easy to discriminate between what is genuinely observed and what is imagination. Error speedily dissolves when it produces a clear contradiction of some sort; projected behavior is then recognized as crazy, hallucinatory, and you say, "I don't know how I ever could have thought that." But, for the most part, the projector can find "proofs" that the imagined is the observed. Such rationalizations and justifications are always available to the person who wishes to find them. In the subtleties and many-sided aspects of most situations the projector (up to the stage of true paranoia) can fasten onto a true detail, perhaps some genuine but insignificant grievance, and then exaggerate and embroider it fantastically. Thus he does his damage—or, in his language, *is* damaged.

A person's unfelt need to reject Person X will lead to finding something in his own behavior which he thinks accounts for but does not justify X in rejecting him. If X were operating on the basis which the projector supposes and would actually reject him, then the projector's purpose would be accomplished—namely, it would bring about their separation, which is precisely what the projector wants without being aware of it.

Suppose one has an appointment with Person X and he is late in arriving. If, without further evidence, one jumps to the conclusion that this is a sign of contempt, then one is projecting one's own contemptuousness.

In everyday life the common case of paranoic projection is, of course, the jealous husband or wife. If you are prone to such jealousies and are continually suspecting and "providing" infidelity, see whether you yourself are not repressing the wish to be unfaithful in the very way that you attribute to your spouse. Apply the suspect details to yourself as clues—that is, *you* would go about it in just that way, make the clandestine phone-call, etc.

A second important source of paranoic jealousy is also a projection. The jealous partner represses his (or her) own homosexual impulse, and therefore imagines that the partner loves another man or another woman—and calls up images of them together. The epithets he then directs at the fancied lovers are the very ones that he would apply to his own taboo impulse.

In all these cases the degree of evidence or contradiction is unimportant. If one is a jealous husband or a touchy mother-in-law, it does no good to be proved wrong, for the same situation will repeat itself with other flimsy evidence. The projector clings to his passive-suffering role and avoids going outward.

An extremely important and dangerous class of projections is prejudice: race-prejudice, class-prejudice, snobbery, anti-semitism, misogyny, etc. In every such case, along with other factors, the following projection is operating: to the vilified groups are attributed traits which really belong to the prejudiced person, but which he represses from awareness. Hating and refusing to come to terms with his own "bestiality" (which is often, when it appears in proper context, nothing but a useful drive of the organism), he feels and "proves" that the despised race or group is "bestial."

Consult your own views on such matters as candidly as possible and see how many of them are prejudices. A useful sign is that particular salient "confirming" instances loom in your mind. These individual cases, of course, are quite irrelevant in issues which involve masses of people and which can be intelligently considered only in terms of cold statistics. When you notice such striking confirming instances of any pet idea of yours, look to see if you do not yourself possess the trait.

Contrary to the view that this attitude of the passive-suffering projector belongs only to masochistic and passive-feminine types, we believe it typical of modern dissociated man. It is imbedded in our language, our world-attitude, our institutions. The prevention of outgoing motion and initiative, the social derogation of aggressive drives, and the epidemic disease of self-control and self-conquest have led to a language in which the self seldom does or expresses anything; instead, "it" happens. These restrictive measures have also led to a view of the world as completely neutral and "objective" and unrelated to our concerns; and to institutions that take over our functions, that are to "blame" because they "control" us, and that wreak on us the hostility which we so carefully refrain from wielding ourselves—as if men did not themselves lend to institutions whatever force they have!

In such a world of projections a man, instead of raging, is "possessed" by a temper that he cannot "control." Instead of thinking, a thought "occurs" to him. He is "haunted by" a problem. His troubles "worry" him—when, indeed, he is worrying himself and anybody else he can.

Alienated from his own impulses, yet unable to obliterate the feelings and acts to which they give rise, man makes "things" out of his own behavior. Since he then does not experience it as himself-in-action, he can disclaim responsibility for it, try to forget or hide it, or project it and suffer it as coming from the outside. He does not dream or wish, but the dream "comes to him." He does not shine in glory, but abstract glory becomes a thing to die for. He does not progress and want to progress, but Progress, with a capital P, becomes his fetish.

When the early psychoanalysts introduced the concept of the Id or It as the source of drives and dreams, they were expressing this powerful truth: personality is not restricted to the narrow sphere of the "I" and its "sensible" self-controlled little thoughts and plans; these other drives and dreams are not idle shadows but real facts of the personality. But, having achieved this insight, orthodox analysis did not sufficiently insist on the next step—to loosen and enlarge the habits of the "I" and change it from a fixed form into a system of shifting processes, so that it can feel the Id-facts as its own facts, use its hallucinations (as a child does in play), and wield its drives for creative adjustment.

A careful criticism of our habitual language points the way to such loosening and adjustment. Let us reverse the process of alienation, self-conquest, and projection by reversing the "it" language. The aim is to come to realize again that you are creative in your environment and are responsible for your reality—not to blame, but responsible in the sense that it is you who lets it stand or changes it.

Examine your verbal expressions. Translate, as if they were in a foreign language, those sentences in which "it" is subject and you are object into sentences in which "I" is the subject. For instance, "It occurred to me that I had an appointment" translates into "I remembered that I had an appointment." Furthermore, setting yourself in the center of sentences that concern you, look for concealed indefinite expressions. Often, for instance, "I must do this" means either "I want to do this" or "I don't want to do it and won't, and meantime I am making excuses" or "I am keeping from doing something else." Also, recast sentences in which you are meaningfully an object into sentences expressing the fact that although you are object, you are experiencing something. For instance, change, "He hits me" into "He hits me and I am being hit"; "He tells me" into "He says something to me and I listen to it."

Attend to the detailed content of your "it" expressions; translate the verbal structure into visual fantasy. If you say, "A thought struck me," just where and how did it strike? Did it use a weapon? Whom did you want to strike at the time? If you say, "My heart aches," are you aching for something with all your heart? If you say, "I have a headache," are you contracting your muscles so that you hurt your head—or even in order to hurt your head?

Listen to and translate other people's language in the same way. This will reveal to you a good deal about their interpersonal relationships. Eventually you will understand that, as in art, although the content of what is said is important, it is much more the structure, the syntax, the style, that reveals character and underlying motivation.

Some reactions to this experiment are as follows:

". . . . You must think we have the intelligence of a child!"

*   *   *

"The last part of this experiment amounts to a gross dabbling in semantics. Translating 'it' phrases is about as constructive in psychological terms as doing a crossword puzzle."

*   *   *

"People have told me that I say 'I' too much, and in writing letters I've had to search around for substitutes so as not to seem egotistical."

*   *   *

"I don't believe that the amount of projecting that most people do is more than is healthy. From reading these instruction sheets I get the impression that the authors regard the whole world as filled with paranoids. It seems to me this indicates some projection on the part of the authors!"

*   *   *

"I was amazed to discover how often I used the impersonal form of speech. 'It occurs to me. . . . ,' 'It happened that. . . . ,' etc., all seem to be very common and I use them quite extensively. As I try consciously to change the syntax of my speech, I can feel a heightened awareness of the immediate environment and how I am responsible for it. I can make a great deal of sense out of this—I almost said, 'It makes a great deal of sense.' I shall keep this up, for I find it most important."

*   *   *

"I have a friend whom I tend to criticize because she spends so little time on her school work. Just before exams she crams, but the rest of the time she uses for going out and having fun. She does it quite openly, and doesn't seem ashamed. I, on the other hand, stay home with a book open in my hand. What I've just realized is that this is just a pretense of studying, and I might better spend my time doing what she does!"

*   *   *

"Changing 'it' into 'I' has been quite an eye-opener for me. When I've dropped something, I've caught myself explaining, 'It dropped out of my hand,' or when I've missed my train because I dawdled around,

I've complained, 'It went off and left me.' Just the same, some of these home-truths are pretty hard to take!"

* * *

"When I take unfair advantage of someone, I don't say, 'He was just about to do it to me.' Instead, I say, 'He was a fool not to do it first.' "

* * *

"I feel rejecting toward my sister because she treats my father like a bum. What I've just found out, though, is that I'm condemning her for expressing something that I hold back. Actually, I'm pretty sore that he hasn't done more for us. He's one of those persons with no other ambition than just to be able to scrape by."

* * *

"The other day I felt that my father was rejecting me by siding with my brother on an issue. Recalling this experiment, I examined my own attitude. Much to my surprise I found that I was the one who was really rejecting the help and advice they both were trying to give me."

EXPERIMENT 18: Assimilating Projections

In the moving picture theatre it is obvious to everyone except small children that the pictures do not emanate from the screen but are reflections of light-patterns cast upon it by the projector. What can appear on the screen, which is simply a blank surface, is strictly contingent on what is on the film in the machine. On the other hand, when a person projects parts of his personality, it ordinarily is not upon a blank surface but upon a screen—another person, object, situation— which *already possesses in its own right* some degree of what is projected upon it. We project onto persons who are "appropriate screens"—that is, who manifest enough of a particular trait or attitude to make it easy for us to justify loading them with our share of it as well.

Abstractions, concepts, theories can also serve as

projection-screens. A remarkable case of this occurs in the current terminology of psychotherapy. The system of muscular contractions by which the neurotic attacks and squeezes his spontaneous impulses is called (by Wilhelm Reich) his "character-armor." This gives it the status of an "objective" barrier that must somehow be attacked and broken through. Actually it is the person's own aggression turned against himself. Instead of regarding this armor as a dumb object, a shell or rigid crust to be crushed, surely the appropriate therapeutic technique is to interpret it as misdirected activities of the person himself. On such a basis he will become able to say, "I have a backache and a stiff stomach—that is, I contract my back till it hurts and I am cutting off indecent movements of the pelvis and suppressing evil desires." If this is pursued, he will then say, "I hate sex and my sexual desires," and *then* it will be possible to work on the person's false identification with the social taboo and try to dissolve what he has introjected. In other words, in such a case we must first undo the projection ("I am suffering from my armor"), then the retroflection ("I stifle my pelvis"), and then the introjection ("I hate sex").

No doubt the most important abstract projection-screen is conscience or moral law. It is abstract in the sense that the dictates of conscience are verbalized as "Society demands" or "Morality requires," when actually it is the person himself demanding or requiring *in the name of society or morality!* Conscience is always aggressive in its manifestations, for, like any screen, it reflects back to us what we project upon it. In this connection consider the following obvious facts: it is not those who live most "cleanly," with unbending rectitude, with continuous attention to the rules, who have the lightest consciences. Far from it! Their consciences are forever hounding and upbraiding them.

Is it their demanding consciences that make them restrict themselves and walk the tight-rope of propriety? In your own case consider some escapade in which you succeeded and had a good time. Under those circumstances your conscience gave you little trouble; but if you failed, got caught, or were disappointed, then you felt guilty and your conscience told you you should not have done it. Logically we must say that it is the person's anger against the frustrating obstacles —which anger, however, he cannot vent nor even feel *as such* because of his identification with (introjection of) the social standards—that now he projects into his conscience. Then he suffers under its lash.

It is not the introjected standard that gives strength to the conscience; it merely provides the nucleus—the appropriate screen upon which the person may project aggression. This is shown by the fact that conscience is always more demanding than the taboos and sometimes makes demands that are even unheard of socially. *The strength of conscience is the strength of one's own reactive anger!*

Perfectionism is another projection-screen. This is based on the so-called ego-ideal (as distinct from super-ego or conscience). While conscience serves, as we have said, as projection screen for aggressions and cruel demands that the person dissociates from himself, the ego-ideal receives by projection his dissociated love and admiration. Such dissociated love is often homosexual; and homosexual love can frequently be analyzed as a still earlier projection of a more primary self-love—which was a retroflection that one was punished for or "shamed out of."

To dissolve irrational conscience you must take two steps: First, translate from "My conscience or morality demands . . ." to "I demand from myself . . ."; that is, change the projection to a retroflection. Second, reverse this in both directions to "I demand from X" and "X (e.g., society) demands from me." You must differentiate the actual compulsion of society from both your private demands and your introjections. In your conscience are you nagging, threatening, blackmailing, casting sad, reproachful glances? If you concentrate on these fantasies you will find how much of your moral duty is your own masked attack, how much consists of particular introjected influences, and how much *is* rational.

Do not be afraid that by dissolving conscience you will become a criminal or an impulsive psychopath. You will be surprised, when you allow organic self-regulation to develop and your outgoing drives to contact other persons, how the principles that *you* ought to live by will seem to emerge from your very bones and will be *obviously appropriate* for living out regardless of the social situation you are in.

Delinquency is to a large extent a matter of inaccurate orientation, a misunderstanding of the person's role in society. As Socrates said long ago, evil is simply error. Pathological delinquency is frequently characterized by an over-stern conscience. As with self-control, so with conscience: too much self-control leads to nervous breakdowns; too much conscience to moral breakdowns. Submission to conscience is identification with rigid principles that do not work and are always lacking in charity. Organic function and self-awareness mean appreciation of concrete situations. Conscience imposes a duty and accomplishes very little work; aware function is interested, attracted, and gets the job done.

When you come to the second step of dissolving conscience, namely, reversing what you demand from yourself to a demand on X, you will experience the greatest reluctance, for accepting your conscience as part of yourself means admitting to powerful dictatorial desires and demands on other people—to be *their* conscience! You can, of course, become a moralist and try to make us all suffer; or let us hope you will restrict yourself to fantasy, and there work out your lust to be our ruler and our judge until you have developed a more integrated orientation and contact with the world. It will change your notions of conscience when you realize how the same intolerance that was invested in your conscience now shows up in your own cravings.

The projector throws outward his unwanted feelings, but he does not get rid of them. *The only way actually to get rid of an "unwanted feeling" is to accept it, express it and thus discharge it.* Projections are still bound to the person, just as repressed material is still "in" the person. The projector is connected with his projected omnipotence by awe, with his projected aggression by fear. Thus, it is not possible for the prejudiced person to rid himself of his "bestiality" simply by projecting it onto the vilified group; he must also become an anti-semite, an anti-vivisectionist, or what not, and ruin his life with such idiocies. The distinction between a prejudice and some simple, foolish notion that one is too lazy or unconcerned to correct can be made in terms of whether you can let the matter go. If you cannot—if it is an imminent, haunting danger—then you have a prejudice.

In dreams projection of aggression becomes nightmares. Dreams with projected dental aggression, where you are threatened by crocodiles, dogs, the *vagina dentata,* are typical for introjectors. In attempting to interpret a dream, at the beginning, at least, regard all persons in it and all the features of it as projections—that is, as parts of your own personality. After all, you are the maker of the dream, and whatever you put into it must be what is in you and therefore available for constructing the dream.

Just as with dreams, many "memories" are projections of the present situation. This frequently occurs in psychoanalysis with respect to childhood memories. The transference (emotional relation to the analyst) is construed as the reliving of the childhood events, when the simple facts of the analytic situation are sufficient to account for whatever happens, without reference to the past at all. For example, the patient, angry with his analyst in the present situation, does not express his anger openly, but brings up memories of the times when his father "mistreated" him in similar ways. To assimilate such projections it is not necessary to go roundabout through the long memories when the relevant events happen under one's nose. Whether the patient says, "You are bored," or "You think such and such of me," or "You want to be rid of me," the projection is obvious.

Your "reality" (what to you is the real world) is playing either of two functions: it is either the concernful environment of your needs and is known by sharp, interesting figures against empty grounds, or it is a screen for your projections. If the latter, you will attempt to make the projections conform with observation—you will always be seeking proofs, making mountains out of molehills, or otherwise distorting your perspective.

Instead, do the following: go through a period in which you say to everything, *Tat Twam Asi—that otherness is myself!* And do the same on any subsequent occasion when you feel a violent reaction, particularly of fear or passive helplessness. Be on the watch for projected initiative, rejection, admiration, aggression. Think yourself into the shoes of the aggressor, admirer, rejecter, foolhardy one. More often than not, the reversal will click.

Some reactions to this experiment are as follows:

"The instructions to 'think yourself into the shoes of the aggressor, admirer, et al. and more often than not the reversal will click' is the perfect final note for you to end on. It really caps the climax of absurdity!"

*   *   *

"I believe it will be a very long time before I can accept responsibility for all my projections, for I've scattered the parts of my personality pretty widely. But I am going to continue to put myself into all my various shoes, for, as nearly as I can judge at this time, all the shoes do fit!"

*   *   *

"I tried the Tat Twam Asi experiment and discovered that I have an over-stern conscience. In time I hope to reduce it substantially, but I can see that it's going to take time."

*   *   *

"Just as taking responsibility for one's behavior doesn't necessarily mean taking blame for it, I suppose it's just as unwarranted to take the credit for it. So long, though, as I continue to think in moralistic terms, I'm finding it exhilarating and releasing to take credit for what I do and to give credit to others for their actions. More and more I am noticing that when I or the people I know suffer a defeat, it almost always can be recognized to be, at least in part, an 'inside job.' "

*   *   *

"I 'dissolved' some irrational conscience that I've had as far back as I can remember. I've always felt that I must complete any job I start and, further than that, I must complete it in a given measure of time (in one day, for instance). In some specific instances I've recently stated it as 'My conscience demands that I finish this today.' Then I amplified it to, 'My conscience demands that I finish the job today even though I have plenty of time later.' My foolishness became perfectly clear, though, when I carried it on to, 'Society demands from me that I complete this job today,' for it was obvious that society was doing no such thing. Without any fireworks of an emotional sort this has made a radical change in my attitude toward my work. When I start a job now it's without the hopped-up melo-dramatics (the-die-is-cast-and-there's-no-turning-back sort of feeling) but instead I realize there's plenty of time and if anything more important should come up before I get this job finished, I can give it priority without the world's coming to an end. When I look back at the way I was operating, I wonder, 'How stupid can you get?' "

*   *   *

"You'll probably diagnose this with some fancy name, but I intend to get it off my chest just the same. In your attempt to induce a 'permissive' atmosphere, you bend too far the other way. With a casualness that can't be casual, you tell us how to masturbate, vomit, and choke pillows. You are moralistic all the way through, although not in the ordinary way. You are

trying to get us to introject your views in place of the
ones we now have. Do you go to sleep at night happy
in the thought that at this very minute countless people are vomiting up their insides for you?"

*   *   *

"I had trouble at first getting the hang of what was
involved in putting myself in the shoes of all these
other people who seemed so different from me. I
wasn't aware of projecting and the whole thing fell
flat. Then I figured that maybe I could sneak up on
it by trying first to notice when I thought other people
were projecting. Boy, what a revelation! I experienced
what away back you called the 'aha! phenomenon.'
The time when it hit me right between the eyes was at
a committee meeting to select candidates for election
to a club that I belong to. Whenever a particular name
came up and somebody wanted to give it a thumbs-
down, he had to state his reasons. Well, the reasons he
would give for disliking the candidate and not wanting
him in the club would amount to a listing of *his own
worst faults*! After seeing this sort of thing happen I
sure got the point about trying on the other fellow's
shoes and checking on whether they fit. Sad to say,
they do!"

NOVELTY, EXCITEMENT AND GROWTH

PART 1

Introduction

I

THE STRUCTURE OF GROWTH

1: The Contact-Boundary

Experience occurs at the boundary between the organism and its environment, primarily the skin surface and the other organs of sensory and motor response. Experience is the function of this boundary, and psychologically what is real are the "whole" configurations of this functioning, some meaning being achieved, some action completed. The wholes of experience do not include "everything," but they are definite unified structures; and psychologically everything else, including the very notions of an organism or an environment, is an abstraction or a possible construction or a potentiality occurring in this experience as a hint of some other experience. We speak of the organism contacting the environment, but it is the contact that is the simplest and first reality. You may feel this at once if, instead of merely looking at the objects before you, you also become aware of the fact that they are objects in your oval field of vision, and if you feel how this oval of vision is, so to speak, close up against your eyes—indeed, it *is* the seeing of your eyes. Notice, then, how in this oval field the objects begin to have esthetic relations, of space and color-value. And so you may experience it with the sounds "out there": their root of reality is at the boundary of contact, and at that boundary they are experienced in unified structures. And so motorically, if you are aware of throwing a ball, the distance comes close and your motor impulse has, so to speak, rushed to the surface to meet it. Now the purpose of all the practical experiments and theoretical discussions in this book is to analyze the

267

function of contacting and to heighten awareness of reality.

We use the word "contact"—"in touch with" objects —as underlying both sensory awareness and motor behavior. Presumably there are primitive organisms in which awareness and motoric response are the same act; and in organisms of higher grade, where there is good contact, one can always show the cooperation of sense and movement (and also feeling).

2: Interaction of Organism and Environment

Now in any biological, psychological, or sociological investigation whatever, we must start from the interacting of the organism and its environment. It makes no sense to speak, for instance, of an animal that breathes without considering air and oxygen as part of its definition, or to speak of eating without mentioning food, or of seeing without light, or locomotion without gravity and supporting ground, or of speech without communicants. There is no single function of any animal that completes itself without objects and environment, whether one thinks of vegetative functions like nourishment and sexuality, or perceptual functions, or motor functions, or feeling, or reasoning. The meaning of anger involves a frustrating obstacle; the meaning of reasoning involves problems of practice. Let us call this interacting of organism and environment in any function the "organism/environment field"; and let us remember that no matter how we theorize about impulses, drives, etc., it is always to such an interacting field that we are referring, and not to an isolated animal. Where the organism is mobile in a great field and has a complicated internal structure, like an animal, it seems plausible to speak of it by itself—as, for instance, the skin and what is contained in it—but this is simply an illusion due to the fact that the motion through space and the internal detail call attention to themselves against the relative stability and simplicity of the background.

The human organism/environment is, of course, not

only physical but social. So in any humane study, such as human physiology, psychology, or psychotherapy, we must speak of a field in which at least social-cultural, animal, and physical factors interact. Our approach in this book is "unitary" in the sense that we try in a detailed way to consider *every* problem as occurring in a social-animal-physical field. From this point of view, for instance, historical and cultural factors cannot be considered as complicating or modifying conditions of a simpler biophysical situation, but are intrinsic in the way any problem is presented to us.

3: What is the Subject-Matter of Psychology?

On reflection, the foregoing two sections must seem obvious and certainly not extraordinary. They assert (1) that experience is ultimately contact, the functioning of the boundary of the organism and its environment, and (2) that every human function is an interacting in an organism/environment field, socio-cultural, animal, and physical. But now let us attend to these two propositions in combination.

Among the biological and social sciences, all of which deal with interacting in the organism/environment field, *psychology studies the operation of the contact-boundary in the organism/environment field*. This is a peculiar subject-matter, and it is easy to understand why psychologists have always found it difficult to delimit their subject.* When we say "boundary" we think of a "boundary between"; but the contact-boundary, where experience occurs, does not *separate* the organism and its environment; rather it limits the organism, contains and protects it, and *at the same time* it touches the environment. That is, to put it in a way that must seem odd, the contact-boundary—for example, the sensitive skin—is not so much a part of the "organism" as it is essentially *the organ of a par-*

---

*Imitating Aristotle, modern psychologists (especially of the Nineteenth Century) start with the mere physics of the *objects* of perception, and then switch to the biology of the organs, etc. But they lack Aristotle's saving and accurate insight that "in act," in sensing, the object and the organ are identical.

ticular relation of the organism and the environment. Primarily, as we shall soon try to show, this particular relation is *growth.* What one is sensitive of is not the condition of the organ (which would be pain) but the interacting of the field. Contact is awareness of the field or motor response in the field. It is for this reason that contacting, the functioning of the mere boundary of the organism, can nevertheless pretend to tell reality, something more than the urge or passivity of the organism. Let us understand contacting, awareness and motor response, in the broadest sense, to include appetite and rejection, approaching and avoiding, sensing, feeling, manipulating, estimating, communicating, fighting, etc.—every kind of living relation that occurs at the boundary in the interaction of the organism and environment. All such contacting is the subject-matter of psychology. (What is called "consciousness" seems to be a special kind of awareness, a contact-function where there are difficulties and delays of adjustment.)

4: Contact and Novelty

Envisaging an animal freely roaming in a spacious and various environment, we see that the number and range of contact-functions must be vast, for fundamentally an organism lives in its environment by maintaining its difference and, more importantly, by assimilating the environment to its difference; and it is at the boundary that dangers are rejected, obstacles are overcome, and the assimilable is selected and appropriated. Now what is selected and assimilated is always novel; the organism persists by assimilating the novel, by change and growth. For instance, food, as Aristotle used to say, is what is "unlike" that can become "like"; and in the process of assimilation the organism is in turn changed. Primarily, contact is the awareness of, and behavior toward, the assimilable novelty; and the rejection of the unassimilable novelty. What is pervasive, always the same, or indifferent is not an object of contact. (Thus, in health, the organs themselves are not contacted, for they are conservative.)

5: Definition of Psychology and Abnormal Psychology

We must then conclude that all contact is creative and dynamic. It cannot be routine, stereotyped, or merely conservative because it must cope with the novel, for only the novel is nourishing. (But like the sense-organs themselves the internal non-contacting physiology of the organism is conservative.) On the other hand, contact cannot passively accept or *merely* adjust to the novelty, because the novelty must be assimilated. *All contact is creative adjustment of the organism and environment.* Aware response in the field (as both orientation and manipulation) is the agency of growth in the field. Growth is the function of the contact-boundary in the organism/environment field; it is by means of creative adjustment, change, and growth that the complicated organic unities live on in the larger unity of the field.

We may then define: *psychology is the study of creative adjustments.* Its theme is the ever-renewed transition between novelty and routine, resulting in assimilation and growth.

Correspondingly, *abnormal psychology is the study of the interruption, inhibition, or other accidents in the course of creative adjustment.* We shall, for instance, consider anxiety, the pervasive factor in neurosis, as the result of the interruption of the excitement of creative growth (with accompanying breathlessness); and we shall analyze the various neurotic "characters" as stereotyped patterns limiting the flexible process of creatively addressing the novel. Further, since the real is progressively given in contact, in the creative adjustment of organism and environment, when this is inhibited by the neurotic, his world is "out of touch" and therefore progressively hallucinatory, projected, blacked out, or otherwise unreal.

Creativity and adjustment are polar, they are mutually necessary. Spontaneity is the seizing on, and glowing and growing with, what is interesting and nourishing in the environment. (Unfortunately, the "adjustment" of much psychotherapy, the "conformity to the reality-principle," is the swallowing of a stereotype.)

6: The Figure of Contact against the Ground of the Organism/Environment Field

Let us return to the idea we began with, that the wholes of experience are definite unified structures. *Contact, the work that results in assimilation and growth, is the forming of a figure of interest against a ground or context of the organism/environment field.* The figure (gestalt) in awareness is a clear, vivid perception, image, or insight; in motor behavior, it is the graceful energetic movement that has rhythm, follows through, etc. In either case, the need and energy of the organism and the likely possibilities of the environment are incorporated and unified in the figure.

The process of figure/background formation is a dynamic one in which the urgencies and resources of the field progressively lend their powers to the interest, brightness and force of the dominant figure. It is pointless, therefore, to attempt to deal with any psychological behavior out of its socio-cultural, biological, and physical context. At the same time, the figure is specifically psychological: it has specific observable properties of brightness, clarity, unity, fascination, grace, vigor, release, etc., depending on whether we are considering primarily a perceptual, feelingful, or motor context. The fact that the gestalt has specific observable psychological properties is of capital importance in psychotherapy, for it gives *an autonomous criterion of the depth and reality* of the experience. It is not necessary to have theories of "normal behavior" or "adjustment to reality" except in order to explore. When the figure is dull, confused, graceless, lacking in energy (a "weak gestalt"), we may be sure that there is a lack of contact, something in the environment is blocked out, some vital organic need is not being expressed; the person is not "all there," that is, his whole field cannot lend its urgency and resources to the completion of the figure.

7: Therapy as Gestalt-Analysis

The therapy, then, consists in analyzing the internal structure of the actual experience, with whatever degree of contact it has; not so much *what* is being experienced, remembered, done, said, etc., as *how* what is being remembered is remembered, or how what is said is said, with what facial expression, what tone of voice, what syntax, what posture, what affect, what omission, what regard or disregard of the other person, etc. By working on the unity and disunity of this structure of the experience here and now, it is possible to remake the dynamic relations of the figure and ground until the contact is heightened, the awareness brightened and the behavior energized. Most important of all, *the achievement of a strong gestalt is itself the cure, for the figure of contact is not a sign of, but is itself the creative integration of experience.*

From the beginning of psychoanalysis, of course, a particular gestalt-property, the "Aha!" of recognition, has held a sovereign place. But it has always seemed a mystery why "mere" awareness, for instance recollection, should cure the neurosis. Note, however, that the awareness is not a thought about the problem but is itself a creative integration of the problem. We can see, too, why usually "awareness" does not help, for usually it is not an aware gestalt at all, a *structured* content, but mere content, verbalizing or reminiscing, and as such it does not draw on the energy of present organic need and a present environmental help.

8: Destroying as Part of Figure/Background Formation

The process of creative adjustment to new material and circumstances always involves a phase of aggression and destruction, for it is by approaching, laying hold of, and altering old structures that the unlike is made like. When a new configuration comes into being, both the old achieved habit of the contacting organism and the previous state of what is approached and contacted are destroyed in the interest of the new contact. Such destruction of the status quo may arouse fear, interruption, and anxiety, the greater in proportion as one is neurotically inflexible; but the process is accompanied by the security of the new invention experimentally coming into being. Here as everywhere the only solution of a human problem is experimental invention. The anxiety is "tolerated" not by Spartan fortitude—though courage is a beautiful and indispensable virtue—but because the disturbing energy flows into the new figure.

Without renewed aggression and destruction every achieved satisfaction soon becomes a matter of the past and is unfelt. What is ordinarily called "security" is clinging to the unfelt, declining the risk of the unknown involved in any absorbing satisfaction, and with a corresponding desensitizing and motor inhibition. It is a dread of aggression, destroying, and loss that results, of course, in unaware aggression and destroying, turned both inward and outward. A better meaning of "security" would be the confidence of a firm support, which comes from previous experience having been assimilated and growth achieved, without unfinished situations; but in such a case, all attention tends to flow from the ground of what one is into the figure of what one is becoming. The secure state is without interest, it is unnoticed; and the secure person never knows it but always feels that he is risking it and will be adequate.

9: Excitement is Evidence of Reality

Contact, figure/background formation, is a mounting excitement, feelingful and concernful; and conversely, what is not concernful, present to one, is not psychologically real. The different genera of feeling—e.g., pleasure or the various emotions—indicate altering organic involvement in the real situation, and this involvement is part of the real situation. There is no indifferent, neutral reality. The modern epidemic scientific conviction that most or even all of reality is neutral is a sign of the inhibition of spontaneous pleasure, playfulness, anger, indignation, and fear (an inhibition caused by such social and sexual conditioning as create the academic personality).

Emotions are unifications, or unifying tendencies, of certain physiological tensions with favorable or unfavorable environmental situations, and as such they give ultimate indispensable (though not adequate) knowledge of the objects appropriate to needs, just as esthetic feeling gives us ultimate (adequate) knowledge of our sensibilities and their objects. In general, *concern and the excitement of figure/background forming are immediate evidence of the organism/environment field*. A moment's reflection will show that this must be, for how otherwise would animals have motivations and strive according to their motivations, and yet be successful, for success comes by hitting the reality.

10: Contact is "Finding and Making" the Coming Solution

Concern is felt for a present problem, and the excitement mounts toward the coming but as yet unknown solution. The assimilating of novelty occurs in the present moment as it passes into the future. Its result is never merely a rearrangement of the unfinished situations of the organism but a configuration containing new material from the environment, and therefore different from what could be remembered (or guessed at), just as the work of an artist becomes unpredictably new to him as he handles the material medium.

So in psychotherapy we look for the urgency of unfinished situations in the present situation, and by present experimentation with new attitudes and new materials from the experience of the actual day to day, we aim at a better integration. The patient does not remember himself, merely reshuffling the cards, but "finds and makes" himself. (The importance of new conditions in the present was perfectly understood by Freud when he spoke of the inevitable transference of the childhood fixation to the person of the analyst; but the therapeutic meaning of it is not that it is the same old story, but precisely that it is now differently worked through as a present adventure: the analyst is not the same kind of parent. And nothing is more clear, unfortunately, than that certain tensions and blocks cannot be freed unless there is a real environmental change offering new possibilities. If the institutions and mores were altered, many a recalcitrant symptom would vanish very suddenly.)

11: The Self and its Identifications

Let us call the "self" the system of contacts at any moment. As such, the self is flexibly various, for it varies with the dominant organic needs and the pressing environmental stimuli; it is the system of responses; it diminishes in sleep when there is less need to respond. The self is the contact-boundary at work; its activity is forming figures and grounds.

We must contrast this conception of the self with the otiose "consciousness" of orthodox psychoanalysis which has as its function merely to look on and report to the analyst and cooperate by not interfering. And accordingly the revisionist para-Freudian schools, for instance, the Reichians or the Washington School tend to reduce the self altogether into the system of the organism or the interpersonal society: strictly speaking they are not psychologies at all, but biologies, sociologies, etc. But the self is precisely the integrator; it is the *synthetic* unity, as Kant said. It is the artist of life. It is only a small factor in the total organism/environment interaction, but it plays the crucial role of finding and making the meanings that we grow by.

The description of psychological health and disease is a simple one. It is a matter of the identifications and alienations of the self: If a man identifies with his forming self, does not inhibit his own creative excitement and reaching toward the coming solution; and conversely, if he alienates what is not organically his own and therefore cannot be vitally interesting, but rather disrupts the figure/background, then he is psychologically healthy, for he is exercising his best power and will do the best he can in the difficult circumstances of the world. But on the contrary, if he alienates himself and because of false identifications tries to conquer his own spontaneity, then he creates his life dull, confused, and painful. The system of identifications and alienations we shall call the "ego."

From this point of view, our method of therapy is as follows: to train the ego, the various identifications and alienations, by experiments of deliberate awareness of one's various functions, until the sense is spontaneously revived that "it is I who am thinking, perceiving, feeling, and doing this." At this point the patient can take over on his own.

I I

DIFFERENCES IN GENERAL OUTLOOK AND DIFFERENCES IN THERAPY

1: Gestalt-Therapy and the Trends of Psychoanalysis

The psychotherapy proposed in the previous chapters emphasizes: concentrating on the structure of the actual situation; preserving the integrity of the actuality by finding the intrinsic relation of socio-cultural, animal, and physical factors; experimenting; promoting the creative power of the patient to reintegrate the dissociated parts.

Now it may be helpful to the reader to point out that every element here is familiar in the history of psychoanalysis; and broadly speaking, the synthesis of these elements is the current trend. When Freud worked with the transference of repressed feelings onto the analyst, he was working through the actual situation; and in a more pervasive and systematic way those who speak of "inter-personality" practice by analyzing the structure of the actual interview. Most analysts now practice "character-analysis," first systematically developed by Reich, and this consists largely of unblocking by analyzing the structure of the observed behavior. And as for the structure of the thought and image, Freud taught it to us indelibly in *The Interpretation of Dreams,* for every symbolic interpretation concentrates on the structure of the content. Good physicians pay more than lip-service to the psychosomatic unity and the unity of society and individual. Again, in various ways from the primitive "acting out the scene" and Ferenczi's "active method" to recent "vegeto-therapy" and "psychodrama," experimental methods have been in use not only for cathartic release of tension but also for re-training.

And finally, Jung, Rank, progressive-educators, play-therapists and others have amply relied on creative expression as the means of reintegration; and especially Rank hit on the creative act as psychological health itself.

What we add is simply this: the insistence on the reintegration of normal and abnormal psychology, and with this the revaluation of what is taken for normal psychological functioning. To put it somewhat dramatically: from the beginning Freud pointed to the neurotic elements in everyday life, and he and others have increasingly uncovered the irrational bases of many institutions; now we come full circle and venture to assert that the experience of psychotherapy and the reintegration of neurotic structures often give better information of reality than the neurosis of normalcy.

Broadly speaking, we have said, the trend of psychotherapy is toward concentration on the structure of the actual situation. On the other hand, psychotherapy (and the history of psychotherapy) makes a difference in our seeing the actual situation. And the closer the therapy concentrates on the actual here and now, the more unsatisfactory appear the usual scientific, political, and personal preconceptions of what "reality" is, whether perceptual, social, or moral. Consider simply how a physician, aiming at "adjusting the patient to reality" might find, as treatment proceeds (and as it has proceeded for half a century), that the "reality" begins to look very different from his own or the accepted preconceptions; and then he must revise his goals and methods.

In what direction must he revise them? Must he propose a new norm of human nature and attempt to adjust his patients to it? This is in fact what some therapists have done. In this book we attempt something more modest: to regard the development of the actual experience as giving autonomous criteria; that is, to take the dynamic structure of experience not as a clue to some "unconscious" unknown or a symptom, but as the important thing itself. This is to psychologize without pre-judgment of normal or abnormal, and from this point of view psychotherapy is a method not of correction but of growth.

2: Gestalt-Therapy and Gestalt-Psychology

On the other hand, let us consider our relation to the psychology of the normal. We work with the chief insights of Gestalt-psychology: the relation of figure and background; the importance of interpreting the coherence or split of a figure in terms of the total context of the actual situation; the definite structured whole that is not too inclusive yet is not a mere atom; the active organizing force of meaningful wholes and the natural tendency toward simplicity of form; the tendency of unfinished situations to complete themselves. What do we add to this?

Consider, for instance, the unitary approach, to take seriously the irreducible unity of the socio-cultural, animal, and physical field in every concrete experience. This is, of course, the main thesis of the Gestalt-psychology: that phenomena which appear as unitary wholes must have their wholeness respected and can be analytically broken into bits only at the price of annihilating what one intended to study. Now applying this thesis mainly in laboratory situations of perception and learning, as the normal-psychologists have done, one discovers many beautiful truths, can demonstrate the inadequacy of the associationist and reflex psychologies, and so forth. But one is protected from a too sweeping rejection of the usual scientific assumptions, because the laboratory situation itself sets up a limitation as to how far one will think and what one will discover. *This* situation is the total context that determines the meaning of what emerges, and what emerges from the limitation is the peculiarly formal and static quality of most gestalt theory. Little is said about the dynamic relation of the figure and ground, or about the urgent sequence in which a figure rapidly transforms itself into the ground for the next emerging figure, until there is a climax of contact and satisfaction and the vital situation is *really* finished.

Yet how *could* much be said about these things? For a controlled laboratory situation is not in fact a vitally urgent situation. The only one vitally concerned is the experimenter, and his behavior is not the subject of the study. Rather, with a laudable zeal for objectivity, the Gestalists have shunned, sometimes with comical protestations of purity, all dealings with the passionate and interested; they have analyzed the solving of not exactly pressing human problems. They often seem to be saying, indeed, that everything is relevant in the field of the whole except the humanly interesting factors; these are "subjective" and irrelevant! Yet, on the other hand, only the interesting makes a strong structure. (With regard to animal experiments, however, such factors of urgency and interest are not irrelevant, especially since apes and chickens are not such docile laboratory subjects.)

The end result has been, of course, that Gestalt-psychology has itself remained irrelevant to and isolated from the on-going movement in psychology, psychoanalysis and the offshoots of psychoanalysis, for these have not been able to avoid urgent demands —of therapy, pedagogy, politics, criminology, and so on.

3: Psychology of the "Conscious" and the "Unconscious"

Yet the by-passing of Gestalt psychology by the psychoanalysts has been most unfortunate, for Gestalt psychology provides an adequate theory of awareness, and from the beginning psychoanalysis has been hampered by inadequate theories of awareness, despite the fact that to heighten awareness has always been the chief aim of psychotherapy. The different schools of psychotherapy have concentrated on different methods of heightening awareness, whether by words or mimetic muscular exercises or character-analysis or experimental social situations or via the royal road of dreams.

Almost from the start Freud hit on powerful truths

of the "unconscious" and these have proliferated into brilliant insights into the psychosomatic unity, the characters of men, the interpersonal relations of society. But somehow these do not cohere into a satisfactory theory of the self, and this, we believe, is because of a misunderstanding of so-called "conscious" life. Consciousness is still taken, in psychoanalysis and most of its offshoots (an exception was Rank), to be the passive receiver of impressions, or the additive associator of impressions, or the rationalizer, or the verbalizer. It is what is swayed, reflects, talks, and does nothing.

In this book then, as psychotherapists drawing on the Gestalt psychology, we investigate the theory and method of creative awareness, figure/background formation, as the coherent center of the powerful but scattered insights into the "unconscious" and the inadequate notion of the "conscious."

4: Reintegration of the Psychologies of the "Conscious" and the "Unconscious"

When, however, we insist on the unitary thesis, on the creativity of structured wholes, and so forth, not in the uninteresting situations of laboratories but in the urgent situations of psychotherapy, pedagogy, personal and social relations, then suddenly we find ourselves going very far—drawn very far and driven very far—in rejecting as fundamentally inadmissible, as "breaking into bits and annihilating the thing that it was intended to study," many commonly accepted assumptions and divisions and categories. Instead of truths stating the nature of the case, we find them to be precisely the expression of a neurotic splitting in the patient and in society. And to call attention to basic assumptions that are neurotic arouses anxiety (both in the authors and in the readers).

In a neurotic splitting, one part is kept in unawareness, or it is coldly recognized but alienated from concern, or both parts are carefully isolated from each other and made to seem irrelevant to each other, avoiding conflict and maintaining the status quo. But if in an urgent present situation, whether in the physician's office or in society, one concentrates awareness on the unaware part or on the "irrelevant" connections, then anxiety develops, the result of inhibiting the creative unification. The method of treatment is to come into closer and closer contact with the present crisis, until one identifies, risking the leap into the unknown, with the coming creative integration of the split.

5: The Plan of this Book

This book concentrates on and seeks to interpret a series of such basic neurotic dichotomies of theory, leading up to a theory of the self and its creative action. We proceed from problems of primary perception and reality through considerations of human development and speech to problems of society, morals, and personality. Successively, we draw attention to the following neurotic dichotomies, some of which are universally prevalent, some of which have been dissolved in the history of psychotherapy but are still otherwise assumed, and some of which (of course) are prejudices of psychotherapy itself.

"Body" and *"Mind":* this split is still popularly current, although among the best physicians the psychosomatic unity is taken for granted. We shall show that it is the exercise of a habitual and finally unaware deliberateness in the face of chronic emergency, especially the threat to organic functioning, that has made this crippling division inevitable and almost endemic, resulting in the joylessness and gracelessness of our culture. (Chapter 3)

"Self" and *"External World":* this division is an article of faith uniformly throughout modern western science. It goes along with the previous split, but perhaps with more emphasis on threats of a political and interpersonal nature. Unfortunately those who in the history of recent philosophy have shown the absurdity of this division have mostly themselves been infected with either a kind of mentalism or materialism. (Chapters 3 and 4)

③ *"Emotional"* (subjective) and *"Real"* (objective): this split is again a general scientific article of faith, unitarily involved with the preceding. It is the result of the avoidance of contact and involvement and the deliberate isolation of the sensoric and motoric functions from each other. (The recent history of statistical sociology is a study in these avoidances raised to a fine art.) We shall try to show that the real is intrinsically an involvement or "engagement." (Chapter 4)

④ *"Infantile"* and *"Mature"*: this split is an occupational disease of psychotherapy itself, springing from the personalities of the therapists and from the social role of the "cure": on the one hand a tantalizing preoccupation with the distant past, on the other the attempt to adjust to a standard of adult reality that is not worth adjusting to. Traits of childhood are disesteemed the very lack of which devitalizes the adults; and other traits are called infantile that are the introjections of adult neuroses. (Chapter 5)

⑤ *"Biological"* and *"Cultural"*: this dichotomy, which is the essential subject-matter of anthropology to eliminate, has in recent decades become entrenched precisely in anthropology; so that (not to mention the idiotic racialisms of one side) human nature becomes completely relative and nothing at all, as if it were indefinitely malleable. We shall try to show that this is the result of a neurotic fascination with artifacts and symbols, and the politics and culture of these, as if they moved themselves. (Chapter 6)

⑥ *"Poetry"* and *"Prose"*: this split, unitarily involved with all the preceding, is the result of neurotic verbalizing (and other vicarious experience) and the nausea of verbalizing as a reaction against it; and it leads some recent semanticists and inventors of languages of science and "basic" languages to disesteem human speech as though we had enough other media of communication. There are not, and there is a failure of communication. Universal terms, again, are taken as mechanical abstractions rather than expressions of insight. And correspondingly, poetry (and plastic art) becomes increasingly isolated and obscure. (Chapter 7)

7 *"Spontaneous"* and *"Deliberate"*: more generally, it is believed that the unsought and inspired belongs to special individuals in peculiar emotional states; or again to people at parties under the influence of alcohol or hasheesh; rather than being a quality of all experience. And correspondingly, calculated behavior aims at goods that are not uniquely appropriated according to one's fancy, but are in turn only good for something else (so that pleasure itself is endured as a means to health and efficiency). "Being oneself" means acting imprudently, as if desire could not make sense; and "acting sensibly" means holding back and being bored.

8 *"Personal"* and *"Social"*: this common separation continues to be the ruination of community life. It is both the effect and cause of the kind of technology and economy we have, with its division of "job" and "hobby," but no work or vocation; and of timid bureaucracies and vicarious "front" politics. It is to the credit of the therapists of interpersonal relations to try to heal this split, yet even this school, anxiously controlling the animal and sexual factors in the field, likewise usually comes to formal and symbolic rather than real communal satisfactions. (Chapters 8 and 9)

9 *"Love"* and *"Aggression"*: this split has always been the result of instinctual frustration and self-conquest, turning the hostility against the self and esteeming a reactive passionless mildness, when only a release of aggression and willingness to destroy the old situations can restore erotic contact. But in recent decades this condition has been complicated by a new high esteem given to sexual love at the same time as the various aggressive drives are especially disesteemed as antisocial. The quality of the sexual satisfaction may perhaps be measured by the fact that the wars we acquiesce in are continually more destructive and less angry. (Chapters 8 and 9)

10 *"Unconscious"* and *"Conscious"*: if taken absolutely, this remarkable division, perfected by psychoanalysis, would make all psychotherapy impossible in principle, for a patient cannot learn about himself what is unknowable to him. (He is aware, or can be made

aware, of the distortions in the structure of his actual experience.) This theoretical split goes with an underestimation of the reality of dream, hallucination, play, and art, and an overestimation of the reality of deliberate speech, thought, and introspection; and in general, with the Freudian absolute division between "primary" (very early) thought-processes and "secondary" processes. Correspondingly, the "id" and the "ego" are not seen as alternate structures of the self differing in degree —the one an extreme of relaxation and loose association, the other an extreme of deliberate organization for the purpose of identification—yet this picture is given at every moment of psychotherapy. (Chapters 10–14)

6: The Contextual Method of Argument

The foregoing are, in order, the chief neurotic dichotomies that we shall try to dissolve. With regard to these and other "false" distinctions we employ a method of argument that at first sight may seem unfair, but that is unavoidable and is itself an exercise of the gestalt approach. Let us call it the "contextual method," and call attention to it immediately so that the reader may recognize it as we use it.

Fundamental theoretical errors are invariably characterological, the result of a neurotic failure of perception, feeling, or action. (This is obvious, for in any basic issue the evidence is, so to speak, "everywhere" and will be noticed unless one will not or cannot notice it.) A fundamental theoretical error is in an important sense *given* in the experience of the observer; he must in good faith make the erroneous judgment; and a merely "scientific" refutation by adducing contrary evidence is pointless, for he does not *experience* that evidence with its proper weight—he does not see what you see, it slips his mind, it seems irrelevant, he explains it away, etc. Then the only useful method of argument is to bring into the picture the total context of the problem, including the conditions of experiencing it, the social milieu and the personal "defenses" of the observer. That is, to subject the opinion and his holding of it to a gestalt-analysis. A basic error is not refuted —indeed, a strong error, as St. Thomas said, is better than a weak truth—it can be altered only by changing the conditions of raw experience.

Then, our method is as follows: we show that in the observer's conditions of experience he *must* hold the opinion, and then, by the play of awareness on the limiting conditions, we allow for the emergence of a better judgment (in him and in ourselves). We are sensible that this is a development of the argument *ad hominem,* only much more offensive, for we not only call our opponent a rascal and therefore in error, but we also charitably assist him to mend his ways! Yet by this unfair method of argument, we believe, we often do more justice to an opponent than is common in scientific polemic, for we realize from the start that a strong error is already a creative act and must be *solving* an important problem for the one who holds it.

7: The Contextual Method Applied to Theories of Psychotherapy

But if we say, and intend to show, that psychotherapy makes a difference to the usual preconceptions, we must also say what we ourselves take psychotherapy to be, for it is only in the process of becoming something. So in the following chapters, as we proceed with our critique of many general ideas, at the same time we must keep referring to many specialist details of therapeutic practice, for the attainment of every new stage of general outlook makes a difference in the goals and methods of practice.

There is an integral relation of your theory, your procedure, and what you find. This is of course true in every field of research, but it is very much overlooked in the polemics among the schools of psychotherapy, so that there are foolish charges of bad faith or even insanity. The attitude and character of a therapist (including his own training) determine his theoretical orientation, and his method of clinical procedure springs from both his attitude and his theory; but also the confirmation that one gets for one's theory springs from the method employed, for the method (and the expectation of the therapist) partly creates the findings, just as the therapist was himself oriented as a trainee. And further, this relation must again be viewed in the social context of the selected run of patients that every school attracts for its observed material, and the varying standards of cure, and one's attitude with regard to the social evaluation of "acceptable" behavior and attainable happiness. All this is in the nature of the case, and it is profitable to accept it rather than to complain of it or condemn it.

In this book we candidly accept as powerful approaches a number of different theories and techniques: they are relevant in the total field and, however incompatible they may seem to their several proponents, they must nevertheless be compatible if one allows the synthesis among them to emerge by acceptance and free conflict—for we do not see that the best champions are either stupid or in bad faith, and since we work in the same world there must somewhere be a creative unity. The case is that as treatment progresses it is frequently necessary to change the emphasis of approach, from the character to the muscle-tension to the habit of language to the emotional rapport to the dream, and back again. We believe that it is possible to avoid circling aimlessly if, precisely by accepting all these to give a variety of contexts, one concentrates on the structure of the figure/background, and provides free occasions for the self progressively to integrate the self.

8: Creative Adjustment: the Structure of Art-Working and Children's Play

As examples of progressive integration, we shall frequently refer to creative artists and art-working and to children and child-play.

Now the references to artists and children in psychoanalytical literature are amusingly inconsistent. On the one hand, these groups are invariably singled out as "spontaneous," and spontaneity is recognized as central in health; in a successful therapeutic session the curative insight is marked by its spontaneity. On the other hand, the artists are considered exceptionally neurotic and the children are—infantile. Also, the psychology of art has always had an uneasy connection with the rest of psychoanalytic theory, seeming to be strangely relevant and yet mysterious: for why is the artist's dream different from any other dream? And why is the artist's conscious calculation more valuable than any other conscious calculation?

The solution of the mystery is fairly simple. The important part of the psychology of art is not in the dream or in the critical consciousness; it is (where the psychoanalysts do not look for it) in the concentrated sensation and in the playful manipulation of the material medium. With bright sensation and play in the medium as his central acts, the artist then accepts his dream and uses his critical deliberateness; and he spontaneously realizes an objective form. The artist is quite *aware* of what he is doing—after it is done, he can show you the steps in detail; he is not unconscious in his working, but neither is he mainly deliberately calculating. His awareness is in a kind of middle mode, neither active nor passive, but accepting the conditions, attending to the job, and *growing* toward the solution. And just so with children: it is their bright sensation and free, apparently aimless, play that allows the energy to flow spontaneously and come to such charming inventions.

In both cases it is the sensory-motor integration, the acceptance of the impulse, and the attentive contact with new environmental material that result in valuable work. Yet after all, these are rather special cases. Both art-works and children's play use up little social wealth and need have no damaging consequences. Can the same middle mode of acceptance and growth operate in adult life in more "serious" concerns? We believe so.

9: Creative Adjustment: in General

We believe that the free interplay of the faculties, concentrating on some present matter, comes not to chaos or mad fantasy but to a gestalt that solves a real problem. We think that this can be shown again and again with striking examples (and that, on careful analysis, nothing else can be shown). Yet it is this simple possibility that modern man and most modern psychotherapy refuse to entertain. Instead, there is a shaking of the head and a timid need to be deliberate and conform to the "principle of reality." The result of such habitual deliberateness is that we are more and more out of contact with our present situations, for the present is always novel; and timid deliberateness is not ready for novelty—it has counted on something else, something like the past. And then, if we are out of touch with reality, our abortive bursts of spontaneity are indeed likely to miss the mark (though not necessarily worse than our carefulness misses the mark); and this then becomes a disproof of the possibility of creative spontaneity, for it is "unrealistic."

But where one is in contact with the need and the circumstances, it is at once evident that the reality is not something inflexible and unchanging but is ready to be re-made; and the more spontaneously one exercises every power of orientation and manipulation, without holding back, the more viable the remaking proves to be. Let anyone think of his own *best* strokes, in work or play, love or friendship, and see if this has not been the case.

10: Creative Adjustment: "Organismic Self-Regulation"

With regard to the working of the organic body, there has recently been a salutary change in theory in this respect. Many therapists now speak of "organismic self-regulation," that is, that it is not necessary deliberately to schedule, to encourage or inhibit, the promptings of appetite, sexuality, and so forth, in the interests of health or morals. If these things are let be, they will spontaneously regulate themselves, and if they have been deranged, they will tend to right themselves. But the suggestion of the more total self-regulation, of all the functions of the soul, including its culture and learning, its aggression and doing the work that is attractive, along with the free play of hallucination, is opposed. The possibility that if these things are let be, in contact with the actuality, even their current derangements will tend to right themselves and come to something valuable, is met with anxiety and rejected as a kind of nihilism. (But we reiterate that the suggestion is a spectacularly conservative one, for it is nothing but the old advice of the Tao, "stand out of the way.")

Instead, every therapist knows—how?—what the "reality" is to which the patient ought to conform, or what the "health" or "human nature" is that the patient ought to realize. How does he know it? It is only too likely that by the "reality-principle" is meant the existing social arrangements introjected and reappearing as immutable laws of man and society. We say the social arrangements, for note that with regard to physical phenomena no such need to conform is felt at all, but physical scientists generally freely hypothesize, experiment, and fail or succeed, quite without guiltiness or fear of "nature," and thereby they make ingenious machines that can "ride the whirlwind," or foolishly stir it up.

11: Creative Adjustment: the Function of the "Self"

We speak of creative adjustment as the essential function of the self (or better, the self *is* the system of creative adjustments). But if once the creative functions of self-regulating, welcoming novelty, destroying and reintegrating experience—if once this work has been nullified, there is not much left to constitute a theory of the self. And so it has proved. In the literature of psychoanalysis, notoriously the weakest chapter is the theory of the self or the ego. In this book, proceeding by not nullifying but by affirming the powerful work of creative adjustment, we essay a new theory of the self and the ego. The reader will come to this in its place. Here let us continue to point out what difference it makes in therapeutic practice whether the self is an otiose "consciousness" plus an unconscious ego, or whether it is a creative contacting.

12: Some Differences in General Therapeutic Attitude

(a) The patient comes for help because he cannot help himself. Now if the self-awareness of the patient is otiose, a mere consciousness of what goes on that does not make any difference in his comfort—though to be sure it has already made the difference that *he* has come, moving his own feet—then the role of the patient is that something is done *to* him; he is asked only not to interfere. But on the contrary, if the self-awareness is an integrative force, then from the beginning the patient is an active partner in the work, a trainee in psychotherapy. And the emphasis is shifted from the rather comfortable sentiment that he is sick to the sentiment that he is learning something, for obviously psychotherapy is a humane discipline, a development of Socratic dialectic. And the term of treatment is not to dissolve most of the complexes or free certain reflexes, but to reach such a point in the technique of self-awareness that the patient can proceed without help—for here, as everywhere else in medicine, *natura sanat non medicus,* it is only oneself (in the environment) that can cure oneself.

(b) The self only finds and makes itself in the environment. If the patient is an active experimental partner in the session, he will carry this attitude abroad and make more rapid progress, for the environmental material is much more interesting and urgent. Nor is this more dangerous, but indeed less dangerous, than his going abroad passively subject to the moods that come up from below.

(c) If the self-awareness is powerless and only the reflex of the unconscious ego, then the very attempt of the patient to cooperate is obstructive; and so, in the usual character-analysis, the resistances are "attacked," the "defenses" are dissolved, and so forth. But on the contrary, if the awareness is creative, then these very resistances and defenses—they are really counter-attacks and aggressions against the self—are taken as active expressions of vitality, however neurotic they may be in the total picture.* Rather than being liquidated, they are accepted at face-value and met accordingly man to man: the therapist, according to his own self-awareness, declines to be bored, intimidated, cajoled, etc.; he meets anger with explanation of the misunderstanding, or sometimes apology, or even with anger, according to the truth of the situation; he meets obstruction with impatience in the framework of a larger patience. In this way the unaware can become foreground, so that its structure can be experienced. This is different from "attacking" the aggression when the patient does not feel it, and then, when it has a modicum of felt reality, explaining it away as "negative transference." Is the patient never to have a chance to *exercise* his wrath and stubbornness in the open? But in the sequel, if he now dares to exercise his aggressions in real circumstances and meeting a normal response without the roof's caving in, he will see what he is doing, remember who his real enemies are; and the integration proceeds. So again, we do not ask the patient not to censor, but to concentrate on *how* he censors, withdraws, falls silent, with what muscles, images, or blanks. Thus a bridge is made for him to begin to feel himself actively repressing, and then he can himself begin to relax the repression.

(d) An enormous amount of energy and previous creative decision is invested in the resistances and modes of repression. Then to by-pass the resistances, or "attack" them, means that the patient will end up by being less than he came, although freer in certain respects. But by realizing the resistances experimentally

---

*Rank's *Gegenwille*—negative will.

and letting them act and come to grips with what is being resisted in himself or in the therapy, there is a possibility for resolution rather than annihilation.

(c) If the self-awareness is otiose, the suffering of the patient is meaningless and had as well be relieved by aspirin while the therapeutic surgeon continues to do something to his passivity. And indeed it is partly on this theory that the resistances are quickly dissolved, in order to avoid the anguish of real conflict, lest the patient tear himself to pieces. But suffering and conflict are not meaningless or unnecessary: they indicate the destruction that occurs in all figure/background formation, in order that the new figure may emerge. This is not in the absence of the old problem but *solving* the old problem, enriched by its very difficulties, and incorporating new material—just as a great researcher does not shun the painful contradictory evidence to his theory but seeks it out to enlarge and deepen the theory. The patient is protected not by easing the difficulty, but because the difficulty comes to be felt just in the areas where the ability and creative élan are also being felt. If instead one attempts to dissolve the resistance, the symptom, the conflict, the perversion, the regression, rather than to increase the areas of awareness and risk and let the self live out its own creative synthesis—this means, it must be said, that the therapist in his superiority judges such and such human material as not worthy of regaining a whole life.

(f) Finally, no matter what the theory of the self, just as at the beginning the patient has come under his own steam, so at the end he must go under his own steam. This is true for any school. If in treatment the patient's past is recovered, he must finally take it as his own past. If he adjusts in his interpersonal behavior, he must himself be the actor in the social situation. If his body is brought to react in a lively way, the patient must feel that it is he and not his body that is doing it. But where does this new powerful self suddenly come from? Does it emerge waking as from a hypnotic trance? Or has it not been there all along, coming to the session, talking or falling silent, doing the exercise or lying rigid? Since *de facto* it exerts as much power as this in the proceedings, is it not plausible *de jure* to concentrate some attention on its proper actions of contact, awareness, manipulation, suffering, choice, etc., as well as on the body, the character, the history, the behavior? The latter are indispensable means for the therapist to find contexts of closer contact, but it is only the self that can concentrate on the structure of the contact.

We have tried to show what difference our approach makes in general outlook and in therapeutic attitude. This book is a theory and practice of gestalt-therapy, the science and technique of figure/background forming in the organism/environment field. We think that it will be of value in clinical practice. Even more, we trust that it will be helpful to many persons who can help themselves and one another on their own. But most of all, we hope that it might contain some useful insights for us all toward a creative change in our present urgent crisis.

For our present situation, in whatever sphere of life one looks, must be regarded as a field of creative possibility, or it is frankly intolerable. By desensitizing themselves and inhibiting their beautiful human powers, most persons seem to persuade themselves, or allow themselves to be persuaded, that it is tolerable, or even well enough. They seem, to judge by the kind of their concern, to conceive of a "reality" that is tolerable, to which they can adjust with a measure of happiness. But that standard of happiness is too low, it is contemptibly too low; one is ashamed of our humanity. But fortunately, what they conceive to be the reality is not the reality at all, but a comfortless illusion (and what the devil is the use of an illusion that does not at least give consolation!).

The case is that, by and large, we exist in a chronic emergency and that most of our forces of love and wit, anger and indignation, are repressed or dulled. Those who see more sharply, feel more intensely, and act more courageously, mainly waste themselves and are in pain, for it is impossible for anyone to be extremely happy until we are happy more generally. Yet if we get into contact with this terrible actuality, there exists in it also a creative possibility.

PART 2

Reality, Human Nature, and Society

I I I

"MIND," "BODY," AND "EXTERNAL WORLD"

1: The Situation in Good Contact

From the point of view of psychotherapy, when there is good contact—e.g., a clear bright figure freely energized from an empty background—then there is no peculiar problem concerning the relations of "mind" and "body" or "self" and "external world." There are, of course, any number of particular problems and observations concerning particular functioning, such as how flushing and tensing of the jaws and hands is functionally related to a certain feeling of anger, and this feeling and this behavior are functionally related to destroying a frustrating obstacle; but in such cases the total context is easily accepted and it is a question of clarifying the relations of the parts; and as the clarification proceeds in details, the bonds of relation are again felt and easily accepted.

The separation implying a peculiar "psychosomatic problem" or "problem of the external world" was not the rule in antiquity. Aristotle speaks of vegetative functions, sensation, and motivity as the chief classes of acts of the soul and goes on to relate them as "identical in act" with the nature of food, the objects of sensation, etc.* In modern psychology, Koehler says, "The whole-process is determined by intrinsic properties of a whole situation; meaningful behavior may be considered as a case of organization; and this applies also to certain perceptions. For the process consciousness is only of

*The ancient Platonic problem of the soul in the body and the world is not the modern problem, though not unrelated to it neurotically. The same may be said of the theological dilemmas of body and spirit, etc.

secondary importance.* Or, to quote another gestalt-psychologist, Wertheimer says, "Imagine a dance full of grace and joy. What is the situation in such a dance? Do we have a summation of *physical* limb movements and *psychical* consciousness? No. One finds many processes which in their dynamical form are identical regardless of variations in the material character of their elements."**

To a psychotherapist, however, the recognition that these peculiar problems are non-existent immediately raises another related question: how, for so long and among so many bona fide and intelligent persons, did it come about that such a non-existent problem was felt as an important problem? For, as we have said, basic splits of this kind are never simple errors that may be corrected by adducing new evidence, but they are themselves *given* in the evidence of experience.

2: Freud and these "Problems"

Freud's psychoanalytic theory stands midway between the earlier misconception of these problems as peculiarly thorny and the dissolution of these problems by various modern unitary psychologies.

Freud wrote in a long tradition—which he uneasily accepted by ignoring it—of the split between "mind" and "body," and "self" and "reality." The tradition produced various devices to unify the split, such as psycho-physical parallelism and pre-established harmony, or the reduction of consciousness to an epiphenomenon, or of matter to an illusion, or of constructing both from a neutral stuff, or (among the laboratory-psychologists) of refusing to consider introspection at all as either a method or an object of science.

To this discussion Freud made the famous addition that the mind, like an iceberg, is only a small part above

---

*We doubt that the "consciousness is only of secondary importance" in analyzing any such whole, but we give the quotation for its attitude.

**Quotations from Willis D. Ellis, *Source Book of Gestalt Psychology*, Kegan Paul, Trench, Trubner & Co., Ltd., London.

the surface and conscious, but is eight-ninths submerged or unconscious. This addition at first only increases the difficulty, for we now have to relate not two things but three, the conscious-mental, the unconscious-mental, and the body. If "mind" is defined in terms of introspection, then "unconscious-mental" is puzzling; but if, as Freud surely felt, the unconscious was logically independent of or prior to the conscious, then we have a third element incapable by its nature of any direct observation. Yet here, as is always the case, the introduction of further complexity because of practical urgency (the urgency of medicine in this case) has ultimately simplified the problem by bringing out the essential functional relationships.

Why did Freud insist on calling the unconscious mental at all, and not simply relegate the not-conscious to the physical, as was customary in previous psychiatry? (And indeed, to satisfy the neurologists he had to add the concept of "somatic compliance," a state of the body predisposing the mind to lose some of its contents into the unconscious—so that now instead of three elements he had four!) It was that the effects of the "unconscious" on mind and body both had all the properties usually assigned to the mental: they were purposive, meaningful, intentional, symbolic organizations of experience, they were everything but conscious. Even further, when the unconscious contents were recovered to consciousness, the conscious experience was altered quite as when ordinarily unnoticed but obviously mental contents were attended to, for instance, memory and habits. So Freud finally had *five* classes: conscious-mental, preconscious-mental (memories, etc.), unconscious-mental, somatic-compliant, and somatic. The conscious were intentions that could be introspected; the preconscious were intentions that were unattended to but could be conscious if attended to, and the turning of attention was a conscious power; the unconscious were intentions that could not become conscious by any conscious act of the self (this was where the psychotherapist came in, armed with the peculiar power of making known in fact what was unknowable in principle); the somatic-compliant and somatic were not intentions.

3: Contrast of Psychoanalysis and Gestalt-Psychology on these "Problems"

Yet throughout this illogically expanding series, psychoanalysis was able and has become increasingly able to produce a unitary functioning, good contact, and this provides a felt context in which the parts cohere.

From a formal point of view, Freud's calling the unconscious mental was not necessary. In the physical and psychological theory of the Gestaltists, we see that meaningful wholes exist throughout nature, in physical and conscious behavior both, in the body and the mind. They are meaningful in the sense that the whole explains the parts; they are purposive in that a tendency can be shown in the parts to complete the wholes. Quite apart from consciousness, such intentional wholes occur with formal similarity in perception and behavior in any event, and this is all that is required to speak of "symbols." (Fundamentally, Freud called the unconscious mental in order to combat the prejudice of the contemporary neurology that was associationist and mechanical.)

But the actual psychosomatic problem and the problem of the external world are not met by these formal considerations; they have to do with such given evidence as "I will to hold out my hand and I hold it out and there it is," or "I open my eyes and the scene either presses in on me, or it stands there," and so forth; these are questions not of what kind of wholes but of the relation of wholes of consciousness to other wholes. And these questions are avoided by the gestalt theorists who indeed—despite their continual recourse to the preeminently conscious function of "insight"—tend to regard consciousness, and mind in general, as an embarrassing epiphenomenon, "secondary" or insignificant. It is as if they are so embarrassed by their own attack on the mechanistic prejudice that they continually have to exculpate themselves from the charge of being "idealists" or "vitalists."

What makes the peculiarity of the problematic relations is the *given* feeling of disconnection and "not myself" in experiencing body and world. And it is just this matter that psychotherapy has attacked with great power. Let us explore the genesis of this feeling and show how it finally gives the erroneous conceptions.

4: Contact-Boundary and Consciousness

Every contacting act is a whole of awareness, motor response, and feeling—a cooperation of the sensory, muscular, and vegetative systems—and contacting occurs at the surface-boundary *in* the field of the organism/environment.

We say it in this odd way, rather than "at the boundary between the organism and the environment," because, as previously discussed, the definition of an animal involves its environment: it is meaningless to define a breather without air, a walker without gravity and ground, an irascible without obstacles, and so on for every animal function. The definition of an organism is the definition of an organism/environment field; and the contact-boundary is, so to speak, the specific organ of awareness of the novel situation of the field, as contrasted, for instance, with the more internal "organic" organs of metabolism or circulation that function conservatively without the need of awareness, deliberateness, selection or avoidance of novelty. In the case of a stationary plant, a field of organism/soil, air, etc., this *in*-ness of the contact-boundary is fairly simple to conceive: the osmotic membrane is the *organ of the interaction* of organism and environment, both parts being obviously active. In the case of a mobile complicated animal it is the same, but certain illusions of perception make it more difficult to conceive.*

---

*The illusions, to repeat them, are simply that the mobile wins attention against the stationary background, and the more tightly complicated wins attention against the relatively simpler. But at the boundary, the interaction is proceeding from both parts.

(The verbal embarrassments here are deep in our language. Consider the confusion of usual philosophic speech in this context, when we say "inner" and "outer." "Inner" means "inside the skin," "outer" means "outside the skin." Yet those who speak of the "external world" mean to include the body as part of the external world, and then "internal" means "inside the mind," inside the mind but not inside the body.)

Now again, as Freud and especially William James pointed out, consciousness is the result of a delaying of the interaction at the boundary. (James meant, of course, the interrupted reflex-arc, but let us here move in a gestalt theory.) And we can see at once that consciousness is functional. For if the interaction at the contact-boundary is relatively simple, there is little awareness, reflection, motor adjustment, and deliberateness; but where it is difficult and complicated, there is heightened consciousness. Increasing complexity of sensory organs means that there is need of more selectivity, as an animal becomes more mobile and adventures among more novelties. Thus, with increasing complexity we may conceive of the series: phototropism becomes conscious seeing, and this becomes deliberate attending; or osmosis becomes eating and this becomes deliberate food-taking.

5: Tendency toward Simplification of the Field

All this is, ultimately, to simplify the organization of the organism/environment field, to complete its unfinished situations. Let us now look closer at this interesting contact-boundary.

As a boundary of interaction, its sensitivity, motor response, and feeling are turned both toward the environment-part and the organism-part. Neurologically, it has receptors and proprioceptors. But in *act,* in contact, there is given a single whole of perception-initiating movement tinged with feeling. It is not that the self-feeling, for instance of being thirsty, serves as a signal that is noted, referred to the water-perception department, etc.; but that *in the same act* the water is given as bright-desirable-moved toward, or the absence of water is absent-irksome-problematic.

If you concentrate on a "close" perception such as tasting, it is evident that the taste of the food and your mouth tasting it are the same, and therefore this perception is never neutral in feeling, but always pleasant or unpleasant, dullness being a kind of unpleasantness. Or consider the genitals in copulation: awareness, motor response, and feeling are given as the same. But when we consider vision, where there is distance and the scene is uninteresting, the unity is less obvious; nevertheless, as soon as we concentrate on the oval field-of-vision in which the things are seen as "my vision," then the seeing becomes closely myself-seeing (often noticing that we have been staring), and the scene begins to have esthetic value.

Tending toward the simplest structure of the field is the interacting at the contact-boundary of the tensions of the organism and environment until a relative equilibrium is established. (Delay—consciousness—is the difficulty in finishing the process.) Note that in this process the so-called afferent nerves are far from being merely receptive; they reach out—the water is seen as bright and lively if one is thirsty; rather than merely responding to a stimulus, they respond, so to speak, even before the stimulus.

6: Possibilities at the Contact-Boundary

Let us consider various possibilities at the contact-boundary as the interaction variously works out:

(1) If the equilibrium is easily established, awareness, motor adjustment, and deliberateness are relaxed: the animal lives well and is as if asleep.

(2) If the tensions on both sides of the boundary have been difficult to equilibrate, and therefore there has been much deliberateness and adjustment, but now there is a relaxation: then there is the beautiful experience of esthetic-erotic absorption, when the spontaneous awareness and muscularity drinks in and dances in the environment as if self-oblivious, but in fact feel-

ing the deeper parts of the self responding to heightened meaning of the object. The beauty of the moment comes from relaxing deliberateness and expanding in an harmonious interaction. The moment is recreative and again ends in loss of interest and sleep.

(3) The situation of danger: if the boundary becomes intolerably overworked because of environmental forces that must be rejected by extraordinary selectivity and avoidance; and

(4) The situation of frustration, starvation, and illness: if the boundary becomes intolerably tense because of proprioceptive demands that cannot be equilibrated from the environment.*

In both these cases, of excess of danger and frustration, there are temporary functions that healthily meet the emergency *with the function of protecting the sensitive surface*. These reactions may be observed throughout the animal kingdom, and are of two kinds, subnormal or supernormal. On the one hand, panic "mindless" flight, shock, anesthesis, fainting, playing dead, blotting out a part, amnesia: these protect the boundary by temporarily desensitizing it or motorically paralyzing it, waiting for the emergency to pass. On the other hand, there are devices to cushion the tension by exhausting some of the energy of tension in the agitation of the boundary itself, e.g., hallucination and dream, lively imagination, obsessive thought, brooding, and with these motor restlessness. The subactive devices seem to be adapted to protecting the boundary from environmental excess, shutting out the danger; the superactive have to do rather with proprioceptive excess, exhausting the energy—except that when, in starvation or illness, the danger-point is reached, fainting occurs.

7: The Emergency-Function of Consciousness

We have thus come to another function of consciousness: to exhaust energy that cannot reach equilibrium.

---

*These two contrasting situations occasion the disagreement between the two most strongly opposed para-Freudian schools: those who trace the neurosis to insecurity and those who trace it to instinct-anxiety.

But note that this is again, as in the primary function, a kind of delaying: previously the delay consisted of heightened awareness, experimentation, and deliberateness in order to solve the problem; here it is delay for the sake of rest and withdrawal, when the problem cannot otherwise be solved.

The exhaustive function of consciousness is, in essence, Freud's theory of dreams; let us recapitulate the elements of that theory: In sleep, (a) the exploration and manipulation of the environment is in abeyance, and therefore there is frustration of any "physical" solution; (b) certain proprioceptive impulses continue to create tension—"the dream is the fulfillment of a wish"; this is the latent-dream; (c) but the apparent contents are largely the agitation of the sensory surface itself, the tag-ends of the day's events. This is very important to notice. Freud's beautiful distinction between the "manifest" and the "latent" dream means precisely that the dreaming consciousness is isolated from *both* the environment and the organism; the "self" that the dreamer is aware of is largely *merely* the surface-boundary. This is necessarily so, for if more than the mere boundary were admitted into the forming whole, it would involve practical adjustments, and therefore the motor muscles, and the animal would awake. Paradoxically, the dream is completely conscious; this is why it has its flat cinematic quality. The deeper the dream is, the more it lacks the obscure body-feeling of waking perception. The dreamer is spectacularly *un*aware of the proprioceptive contents whose meaning he is dreaming; when these begin to invade his dream, e.g., the thirst becoming very strong, the dreamer tends to awake; and finally (d) the function of the dream is to keep the animal asleep.

The same function of consciousness as an attempt to exhaust energy may be simply observed, as Wilhelm Reich has emphasized, in the bright sexual images that occur in temporary sexual frustration. Indeed, in this example we may see the entire picture of the simple functioning of the conscious-surface: at the organic need, the innervation brightens, reaching out to its goal;

with delay there is deliberate withholding and an increased tempo of seeking expedients; with satisfaction, the image at once becomes dull; but with frustration, it brightens still more trying to exhaust the energy.

There are thus at the boundary of contact these two processes to meet emergencies: blotting out and hallucination. They are, let us emphasize, healthy *temporary* functions in a complicated organism/environment field.

8: Scientific Adequacy of the Above Unitary Conception

Now at last we are in a position to explain the astonishing notion of "Mind" as against both "Body" and "External World," in place of the rather *prima facie* conception that we have been developing, of consciousness as a contact-function in a difficult organism/environment field.

This *prima facie* conception which, in modern but not greatly superior trappings, is like Aristotle's sensitive and rational soul, offers no peculiar scientific difficulties. There are definite observable and experimentable functional relations between this entity and others. There are, for example, criteria for "good contact," such as the singleness, clarity, and closure of the figure/background; grace and force of movement; spontaneity and intensity of feeling. Also the formal similarity of the observed structures of awareness, motion, and feeling in the whole; and the lack of contradiction of the several meanings or purposes. And variations from the norm of "good contact" can be shown, analytically and experimentally, to involve both effectual and causal relations with environmental and somatic abnormalities.

Nevertheless, we must now show that the motion of "mind" as a unique isolated entity *sui generis* is not only genetically explicable but is in a sense an unavoidable illusion, *empirically given in average experience*.

9: The Neurotic Possibility at the Contact-Boundary

For let us consider still another possibility at the contact-boundary. Conceive that (5) instead of either the reestablishment of equilibrium or blotting-out and hallucination in a temporary emergency excess of danger and frustration,* there exists a chronic low-tension disequilibrium, a continual irk of danger and frustration, interspersed with occasional acute crises, and never fully relaxed.

This is a dismal hypothesis, but it is unfortunately historical fact for most of us. Note that we speak of the double low-grade excess, of danger *and* frustration, creating a chronic overcharge of both receptor and proprioceptor. For it is extremely unlikely, though conceivable, that either chronic danger or chronic frustration would long continue separated from each other. Consider simply that danger diminishes the opportunity of satisfaction in a field rather finely adjusted to begin with; then frustration is heightened. But frustration increases the urgency of exploration and decreases the opportunity for scrupulous selection; it breeds illusions and overrides deliberateness, and thereby increases danger. (That is, whether one lays primary stress on insecurity or instinct-anxiety, all therapists would concur that these derangements mutually aggravate each other to a neurotic result.)

In the chronic low-grade emergency that we have been describing, what dispositions of the contact-boundary tend to the possible simplicity of the field? Both of the emergency functions, deliberate blotting-out and undeliberate hyperactivity are called into play, as follows: in a reaction which is different from that in the acute emergency, the attention is turned away from the proprioceptive demands and the sense of the body-as-part-of-the-self is diminished. The reason for this is that the proprioceptive excitations are the more controllable threat in the mutually aggravating troubles. Toward the more direct environmental threat, on the other hand, the attention is heightened to meet the danger, even

---

*A long emergency would destroy the structure, i.e., simplify it to a structure of a lower order. A medical example of simplifying on a lower level is lobotomy or any other excision. The question is whether the various "shock treatments" do not work similarly by creating a limited *fatal* emergency.

when there is no danger. But what is given by such attentiveness is "alien," it is irrelevant to any felt awareness of oneself, for the proprioceptive has been diminished. And in the attentiveness, the senses (receptors) do not reach out expansively, but rather shrink from the expected blow; so, if the process is long continued, the state of deliberate alertness to danger becomes rather a state of muscular readiness than of sensory acceptance: a man stares, but does not thereby see any better, indeed soon he sees worse. And with all this, again, goes a habitual readiness to take flight, but without actually taking flight and releasing the muscular tension.

To sum up, we have here the typical picture of neurosis: *under-aware proprioception and finally perception, and hypertonus of deliberateness and muscularity.* (Yet let us insist again that this condition is not unfunctional, in the given chronic low-grade emergency, for what is seen and felt *is* uninteresting because alien, and provocative of danger because a temptation to desire; and the danger *is* imminent.)

Meantime, however, the safe function of consciousness, to attempt to exhaust the inner tensions by activity of the boundary in isolation, increases to its possible maximum—there are dreams, futile wishes, illusions (projections, prejudices, obsessive thoughts, etc.). But note that the safety of this function depends precisely on keeping it in isolation from the rest of the system. Dreaming is spontaneous and undeliberate, but the safeguarding of day-dreaming from passing into movement is deliberate.

10: "Mind"

In the situation of chronic low-grade emergency that we have been describing, sense, the initiation of movement, and feeling are inevitably presented as "Mind," a unique isolated system. Let us review the situation from this point of view:

(1) Proprioception is diminished or selectively blotted out (for instance, by clenching the jaw, tight-

ening the chest or the belly, etc.). Thus the functional relation of the organs and consciousness is not immediately felt, but the excitations that come through must be "referred" (and then abstract theories, like this present one, are invented).

(2) The unity "desired-perceived" is split; the sensation does not reach out either beforehand or responsively, the figure loses liveliness. Thus the functional unity of organism and environment is not immediately aware and motoric. Then the "External World" is perceived as alien, "neutral" and therefore tinged with hostility, for "every stranger is an enemy." (This accounts for a certain obsessional and paranoid "sterilizing" behavior of positivist science.)

(3) The habitual deliberateness and unrelaxed self-constriction color the whole foreground of awareness and produce an exaggerated feeling of the exercise of "Will," and this is taken to be the pervasive property of the self. When "I will to move my hand," I feel the willing but I do not feel my hand; but the hand moves, therefore the willing is something somewhere, it is in the mind.

(4) The safe play of dream and speculation are maximized and play a disproportionate role in the self-awareness of the organism. Then the delaying, calculative, and restorative functions of the boundary are taken as the chief and final activities of mind.

What we are arguing, then, is not that these conceptions, Body, Mind, World, Will, Ideas are ordinary errors that may be corrected by rival hypotheses and verification; nor, again, that they are semantical misnomers. Rather, they are given in immediate experience of a certain kind and can lose their urgency and evidential weight only if the conditions of that experience are changed.

Let us stress the logical importance of the psychology. If a certain unrelaxed deliberateness is creating a discontinuity and thereby altering the kind of figure habitually presented in perception, it is from *these* perceptions as basic observations that one logically proceeds. Recourse to new "protocols" will not easily or quickly alter the picture, for these again are perceived with the same habit. Thus the socio-psychological character of the observer must, in matters of this kind, be considered as part of the context in which the observation is made. To say this is to espouse a form of the "genetic fallacy" and, what is worse, a particularly offensive form of the argument *ad hominem:* yet that is how it is.

(It will be evident from all this why psychotherapy is not the learning of a true *theory* about oneself—for how to learn this against the evidence of one's senses? But it is a process of experimental life-situations that are venturesome as explorations of the dark and disconnected, yet are at the same time safe, so that the deliberate attitude may be relaxed.)

11: Abstraction and Verbalizing as Acts of "Mind"

So far we have been speaking of a rudimentary consciousness, shared by us with the brute beasts of the field and forest. Let us brighten the scene a little and seek a loftier illustration, the process of abstracting and verbalizing (and even writing for the learned journals).

Psychologically, to abstract is to make relatively stationary certain activities for the sake of more efficiently mobilizing other activities. There can be sensory, postural, attitudinal, imaginative, verbal, ideal, institutional, and other kinds of abstraction. The abstractions are relatively fixed parts in a whole activity; the internal structure of such parts is unattended to and becomes habitual—the stationary is background for the moving —whereas the whole is more interesting and is larger than would otherwise be manageable; and of course it is the whole that selects, immobilizes, and organizes the parts. Consider, for example, the literally thousands of fixed forms that go into the process of a reader's gathering (we hope) meaning (we hope) from these sentences: the abstractions of childish verbalizing and attitudes of communication, of school-attendance, orthography, and homework; of typography and bookmaking; of genre of style and expectation of the audience; of the architecture and posture of reading-rooms; of the knowledge taken academically for granted and the assumptions taken for granted for this particular argument. All these are quite unattended to as we attend to the argument. One could attend to them but does not, unless there is a hitch, a bad typographical error or a purple passage or joke out of place, or a bad light, or a crick in the neck. All this is commonplace. (Abstraction is by definition efficient and "normal"; yet it cannot be denied that in fact the "literally thousands of abstractions"—the quantity makes a difference—invariably betoken a rigidity of training and functioning, a verbalizing-character that indeed *cannot* attend to the whole series, except in theory.)

Supposing now that well toward the bottom of the levels of verbal abstraction, in the early parts where symbolic speech is close to non-verbal imaging, feeling, and outcries—suppose that at that elementary level there has been and persists a blotting-out of awareness and paralysis of motion. Then there will be connections that one *cannot* attend to. For instance (to choose an example from the work of the Washington School of Psychiatry), a child learning to speak has an angry mother, finds that certain words or certain subjects, or even babbling itself, are dangerous; he distorts, conceals, or inhibits his expression; eventually he stammers and then, because this is too embarrassing, represses the stammering and learns to speak again with other emergency mouth parts. It is generally agreed that such a history of speech-habits importantly constitutes the split-personality of a person; but we here want to call attention not to the fate of the personality but to the fate of the speech. As his experience widens in society, the arts and sciences, our speaker makes wider and higher verbal abstractions. Must it not be the case that, since he is still blotting-out the awareness and paralyzing the expression of the lower preverbal connections, he will have defective contact with the actual functioning of the higher abstractions, both of their meaning to *himself* and also of what they really are? They do have a meaning, yet they do exist, ultimately, in a void. They are "mental."

A general proposition is offered; its importance to him, for instance the weight that makes certain evidence stand out in a field and be observed or overlooked by him, is never reducible to any behavior or observation that is noticeable by him. Other observers can notice things that he does not, but unfortunately they, as the case is, are engaged in a general conspiracy against him to pooh-pooh his "private" deliveries as not part of the system of nature. He is academically trained to agree with the consensus, yet he cannot grant that the *residue* of meaning is nothing at all; he *knows* that it is something. *Prima facie,* these literally baseless but not empty abstractions are felt to exist, then, in the "mind"— perhaps "private" mind. Along with Will, the baseless but not empty abstractions are proof of Mind par excellence.

Depending on his character he makes various adjustments of the abstractions to his other experience and the consensus. (Note that this Mind is necessarily very busy exhausting the energy of its tensions in speculation.) Noticing the incommensurability of his abstractions and the External World he may have recourse to different expedients: if he has the rather dry and affectless syndrome of the positivist-disease, he finds they are nonsense and despises himself still further. If he has the euphoric poetic mania, he considers the discrepancy a black mark against the External World and gives his Ideas a world by rhyming them. The man with Gestalt pachydermatitis flounders in a morass of sludgy terminology. And so on.

12: Psychosomatic Ailments

The "unavoidable misconception," in a chronic low-grade emergency, that there is such a thing as "Mind" becomes more frightening when one begins to suffer from psychosomatic ailments.

Firmly planted in his loved or despised mind, our man is unaware that he is deliberately controlling his body. It is his *body,* with which he has certain external contacts, but it is not *he;* he does not feel himself. Assume, now, that he has many things to cry about. Every time he is stirred to the point of tears, he nevertheless does not "feel like crying," and he does not cry: this is because he has long habituated himself not to be aware of how he is muscularly inhibiting this function and cutting off the feeling—for long ago it led to being shamed and even beaten. Instead, he now suffers headaches, shortness of breath, even sinusitis. (These are now more things to cry about.) The eye muscles, the throat, the diaphragm are immobilized to prevent the expression and awareness of the coming crying. But this self-twisting and self-choking in turn arouse excitations (of pain, irritation, or flight) that must in turn be blotted out, for a man has more important arts and sciences for his mind to be busy with than the art of life and the Delphic self-knowledge.

Finally, when he begins to be very ill, with severe headaches, asthma, and dizzy spells, the blows come to him from an absolutely alien world, his body. He suffers *from* headache, *from* asthma, and so forth; he does not say, "I am making my head ache and holding my breath, though I am unaware how I am doing it or why I am doing it."

Good. His body is hurting him so he goes to a doctor. And supposing the affection is as yet "merely functional," that is, there are not yet any gross anatomical or physiological ravages: the doctor decides there is nothing wrong with him and gives him aspirin. For the doctor too believes that the body is an affectless physiological system. Great institutions of learning are founded on the proposition that there are a body and a mind. It is estimated that more than 60% of visitors to medical offices have nothing the matter with them; but they obviously have *something* the matter with them.

Luckily, however, sickness rates high among the things that must be attended to, and our man now has a new lively interest. The rest of his personality be-comes more and more the background for a consuming interest in his body. The mind and body become at least acquaintances, and he speaks of "*my* headaches, *my* asthma, etc." Sickness is the unfinished situation par excellence, it can be finished only by death or cure.

13: Freud's Theory of Reality

To conclude this chapter, let us make a few further remarks about the genesis of the concept of the External World.

If we return to the psychoanalytic theory of Freud, we find that along with the body and the various kinds of the "mental," he spoke of Reality, and then of the "reality-principle," which he contrasted with the "plea-sure-principle" as the principle of painful self-adjust-ment to safe functioning.

It can be shown, we think, that he conceived of reality in two different ways (and did not understand the rela-tion between them). In one way, the mind *and* the body are parts of the pleasure-system, and reality is primarily the social "External World" of other minds and bodies painfully constraining one's pleasures by deprivation or punishment. In the other way, he meant the "External World" given in perception, including one's own body, and opposed to the imaginary elements of hallucination and dream.

The social External World he thought of especially in connection with the so-called helplessness and delu-sional omnipotence of the human infant. The infant lies there isolated, has ideas of its own omnipotence, and yet is dependent for everything except the satisfaction of its own body.

But let us consider this picture in its total social con-text and it will be seen to be the projection of an adult situation: the repressed feelings of the adult are at-tributed to the child. For how is the infant essentially helpless or isolated? It is part of a field in which the mother is another part. The child's anguished cry is an adequate communication; the mother *must* respond to it; the infant needs fondling, she needs to fondle; and so with other functions. The delusions of omnipotence (to the extent that they exist and are not adult projections), and the rages and tantrums of infinite abandonment, are useful exhaustions of the surface-tension in periods of delay, in order that inter-functioning can proceed without past unfinished situations. And ideally considered, the growing apart of the infant and the mother, the disruption of this field into separate persons, is *the same as* the increase of the child in size and strength, his growing teeth and learning to chew (and the drying up of the milk and the turning of the mother to other interests), and his learning to walk, talk, etc. That is, the child does not learn an alien reality, but discovers-and-invents his own increasing reality.

The bother, of course, is that the ideal condition does not obtain. But then we must say, not that the child is essentially isolated and helpless, but that he is soon made so, thrown into a chronic emergency, and eventually he conceives of an external social world. And what is the situation of the adult? In our societies that have no fraternal community, one exists in and grows deeper into this same isolation. Adults treat one another as enemies and their children as alternately slaves or tyrants. Then, by projection, the infant is inevitably seen to be isolated and helpless and omnipotent. The safest condition is then seen, truly, to be a breaking, a disconnection, from the continuity with the original unitary field.

(The passional attributes of the External World of science reveal the same projections. The world of "facts" is at least neutral: does this not reflect the sigh of relief at getting out of the family home and coming into contact with reasonable beings, even if they are only things? But of course, it is also indifferent; and try as one will, one cannot milk out of "naturalism" an ethics, except the stoic apathy. Natural resources are "exploited": that is, we do not participate with them in an ecology, rather *we* use *them,* a safe attitude that leads to much inefficient behavior. We "conquer" nature, we are the master of nature. And persistently, conversely, there is the strain that it is "Mother Nature.")

14: Freud's "External World" of Perception

When we scrutinize Freud's other way of regarding the External World, however, as that which is given in perception as opposed to dreams—and this is the way that sits easily with common and scientific preconceptions—we find suddenly that he is very uneasy. This is not the place to discuss his difficulties in detail (see Chapter 12 below). But let us sketch the problem by quoting some passages.

Exploring the world of dreams, Freud found that, in isolation from the motor-manipulation and the environment which were assumed to give the categories of meaning, nevertheless the dream-world made sense. It was a world not of fixed entities but of plastic handling, according to creative processes of getting beneath verbalizing to the image and the speech-act, of symbolizing, of destroying and distorting the given, condensing it, etc. This plastic handling Freud called the "primary process" and observed that it was the characteristic mental functioning of the early years of life.

> "The primary process strives for discharge of the excitation to establish with the quantity of excitation thus collected an *identity of perception*. The secondary process has abandoned this intention and has adopted instead the aim of an *identity of thought*."

> "The primary processes are present in the apparatus from the beginning, while the secondary processes take shape only gradually through the course of life, inhibiting and overlaying the primary, gaining complete control over them probably only in the prime of life."*

Now the question for Freud was whether the primary process, so considered, was merely subjective or gave

---

*Sigmund Freud, *The Interpretation of Dreams*, trans. by A. A. Brill, Macmillan Co., New York, 1933, pp. 553 and 555.

some delivery of reality. And from time to time he boldly affirmed that they give reality, e.g.:

> "The processes described as 'incorrect' are not really falsifications of our normal procedure, or defective thinking, but the *modes of operation of the psychic apparatus when freed from inhibition.*" (Italics ours)*

And the converse would be what we have here been saying, that the kind of world that seems real to ordinary conceptions is a delivery of chronic low-grade emergency, neurotic inhibition; it is *only* the infantile or dream-world that is real!

This is not very satisfactory either, and Freud understandably tended to shy away from it. From the formal point of view, however, the source of his troubles is simple. He is arrested not by his psychology of dreams (which he himself knew to be an immortal insight), but by the trivial psychology of "normal" waking consciousness that he shared with his contemporaries. For to a correct normal psychology it is clear that everywhere experience is given in plastic structures and the dreams are a special case. (It is touching to consider Freud's bafflement and abnegation when confronted with the psychology of art and invention.)

A more important clue to his difficulty, however, is given by juxtaposing his two theories of "reality": because he believed that the social "external world" into which the infant grows was inflexible, it was necessary for him to believe that the world of the "primary process," with its spontaneity, plasticity, polymorphous sexuality, etc., was repressed by maturation and put out of operation.

I V

REALITY, EMERGENCY, AND EVALUATION

Reality, we have been saying, is given in moments of "good contact," a unity of awareness, motor response, and feeling. Let us now begin to analyze this unity more closely and relate it to our method of psychotherapy. In the present chapter we shall argue that reality and value emerge as a result of self-regulation whether healthy or neurotic; and we shall discuss the problem of how, within the framework of the neurotic's self-regulation, to increase the area of contact. We shall answer this by defining psychotherapy as self-regulation in experimental safe emergencies.

1: Dominance and Self-Regulation

Let us call the tendency of a strong tension to stand out prominently and organize awareness and behavior, its *dominance*. When there is difficulty and delay in reaching equilibrium in the field, the dominance and its attempt to complete the organization are conscious (indeed they are what consciousness is).

Each most pressing unfinished situation assumes dominance and mobilizes all the available effort until the task is completed; then it becomes indifferent and loses consciousness, and the next pressing need claims attention. The need becomes pressing not deliberately but spontaneously. Deliberateness, selection, planning are involved in completing the unfinished situation, but conscious does not have to find the problem, rather it is identical with the problem. The spontaneous consciousness of the dominant need and its organization of the functions of contact is the psychological form of *organismic-self-regulation*.

Everywhere in the organism many processes of ordering, withholding, selection, and so forth are always going on without consciousness, for instance the ordered discharge of certain enzymes to digest certain foods. This non-conscious internal organization can be of the utmost qualitative subtlety and quantitative accuracy, but it always has to do with fairly conservative problems. But when these processes require for completion new material from the environment—and this is the case in turn with every organic process—then certain figures of consciousness brighten and become foreground; we have to do with contact. In a situation of danger, when the tension is initiated from outside, wariness and deliberateness are similarly spontaneous.

2: Dominance and Evaluation

Spontaneous dominances are judgments of what is important in the occasion. They are not adequate evaluations, but they are basic evidence of a kind of hierarchy of needs in a present situation. They are not "impulsive" and necessarily vague, but systematic and often quite specific, for they express the wisdom of the organism about its own needs and a selection from the environment of what meets those needs. They provide an immediate ethics, not infallible and yet in a privileged position.

The privilege comes simply from this: that what seems spontaneously important does *in fact* marshal the most energy of behavior; self-regulating action is brighter, stronger, and shrewder. Any other line of action that is presumed to be "better" must proceed with diminished power, less motivation, and more confused awareness; and must also involve devoting a certain amount of energy, and distracting a certain amount of attention, to keeping down the spontaneous self, which is seeking expression in self-regulation. This is the case even when self-regulation is inhibited in the obvious interests of the self: e.g., when a child is kept from running in front of automobiles, a situation in which his self-regulation is fallible—and the way we run our societies seems to consist largely of such situations. The inhibition then is necessary, but let us remember that to the extent to which we agree to situations in which self-regulation rarely operates, to that extent we must be content to live with diminished energy and brightness.

The question that most obviously strikes the average person is how far in our society and technology, and perhaps in the nature of things, organismic-self-regulation is possible, allowable, riskable. We believe immensely more than we now deliberately allow; people *can* be much brighter and more energetic than they are, and then they would also be shrewder. A great part of our troubles is self-inflicted. Many both "objective" and "subjective" conditions can and must be changed. And even when the "objective" situation cannot be changed, as when a loved one dies, there are regulating reactions of the organism itself, such as crying and mourning, that help restore equilibrium if only we allow them to. But let us defer this discussion for a later place. (Chapter 8)

3: Neurotic Self-Regulation

Now neurotic experience is also self-regulating. The structure of neurotic contact is characterized, we have said, by an excess of deliberateness, fixing attention and with the muscles set in readiness for a particular response. Then certain impulses and their objects are kept from becoming foreground (repression); the self cannot flexibly turn from one situation to another (rigidity and compulsion); energy is bound in an uncompletable (archaically conceived) task.

When extreme deliberateness is reasonable, in the face of chronic present dangers, we cannot speak of an "excess," but we might well speak of a "neurotic society" whose arrangements are out of human scale. But the neurotic has a hair-trigger sensitivity to the danger; he is spontaneously deliberate when he could safely relax. Let us put this more accurately. The neurotic cannot safely relax with regard to his actual situation, including his archaic estimation of it, for to that he spontaneously adjusts by *his* self-regulation, finds it dangerous, and becomes deliberate. But with help, *that* actual situation *can* be changed to his advantage. It is useful to express it in this complicated way rather than to say simply, "The neurotic is making a mistake," because the neurotic is self-regulating, and it is in order to complete a true unfinished situation that he comes to the therapist.

If the therapist regards the therapeutic situation in this light, as part of the on-going unfinished situation of the patient, which the patient is meeting with his own self-regulation, he is more likely to be helpful than if he regards the patient as mistaken, sick, "dead." For certainly it is not by the therapist's but by his own energy that the patient will ultimately complete the situation.

We are then led to the thorny question that we want to discuss in this chapter: *what is the relation between the neurotic patient's on-going self-regulation and the therapist's scientific conception of healthy organismic-self-regulation?* With respect to this question, we do well to pay careful attention to the following words of Kurt Lewin:

> "It is particularly necessary that one who proposes to study whole-phenomena should guard against the tendency to make the wholes as all-embracing as possible. The real task is to investigate the structural properties of a given whole, ascertain the relations of subsidiary wholes, and determine the boundaries of the system with which one is dealing. It is no more true in psychology than in physics that 'everything depends on everything else.' "*

4: Healthy Self-Regulation in an Emergency

Let us consider first a fairly healthy incident of dominance and organismic-self-regulation:**

---

*In Willis D. Ellis, *Source Book of Gestalt Psychology*, Kegan Paul, Trench, Trubner & Co., Ltd., London.

**We say "fairly healthy" because the military context of the incident is itself dubious; and *any* actual context that one chooses will be dubious in some way.

Corporal Jones goes on patrol in the desert. He loses his way but finally, exhausted, he arrives back in camp. His friend Jimmy is glad to see him and at once bursts out with the important news that during his absence Jones' promotion has come through. Jones stares at him with glazed eyes, muttering, "Water," and perceiving a dirty puddle that ordinarily one would not notice he drops to his knees beside it and tries to lap it up, but almost at once, choking, he gets up and staggers on to the well in the center of the camp. Later Jimmy brings him the sergeant's stripes and Jones asks, "What shall I do with these? I'm not a sergeant." "But I told you about your promotion when you came into camp." "No you didn't." "Don't be a fool, I did." "I didn't hear you."

In fact he didn't hear him; he was oblivious at that moment to everything but water. Yet while he was in the desert, just an hour before reaching camp, he had been attacked by an enemy plane. He was quick to take cover. Thus he did hear the plane; the water could not have claimed his whole attention.

We see that there was a hierarchy of dominances: the acute threat dominated the thirst, the thirst dominated the ambition. All immediate efforts were mobilized to the dominant unfinished situation until it was finished and the next task could assume dominance.

We have purposely chosen an example of *emergency,* because in such a case the underlying hierarchy appears very simply. First things come first and we commit ourselves to them without holding back. It is the common feeling that in emergencies we find out "what a man is."

This is the wisdom of the contemporary school of Existentialists, who insist on exploring "extreme situations" for the truth of reality: in extreme situations we *mean* what we do. But of course a man always means it, if we analyze his situation correctly. Paradoxically, it is just because our times are a chronic low-grade emergency that our philosophers declare that it is only in an acute emergency that the truth is revealed. Conversely, it is our general misfortune that we do not obviously act with more of the urgency and vividness that we sometimes show in emergencies.

5: The Hierarchy of Values Given by the Dominances of Self-Regulation

We have already seen that the evaluation given by self-regulation occupies a privileged position in ethics, because it alone marshals the brightest awareness and the most vigorous force; any other kind of evaluation must act with diminished energy. Now we may add to this that in fact, when the actuality is pressing, certain values oust other values, furnishing a hierarchy of what does in fact marshal brightness and vigor in its execution.

Sickness and somatic deficiencies and excesses rate high in the dominance hierarchy. So with environmental dangers. But so also do the need for love, someone to go out to, the avoidance of isolation and loneliness, and the need for self-esteem. Also maintaining oneself and developing oneself: independence. Acute intellectual confusion is attended to. And whatever relates closely to the way a man's life-career has been organized and habituated: so that sometimes heroism and bearing-witness dominate the fear of death. In an important sense, these values are not chosen; they simply loom. The alternative, even of saving one's life, is *practically* senseless, it does not organize behavior and it lacks spirit. Certainly one does not get the impression that heroism or creative sacrifice or creative achievement is much an act of will or deliberate self-constraint; if it were, it would not release such power and glory.

Any ordered collection of such dominances in actual situations is capital for ethics and politics. It is really nothing less than an inductive theory of human nature; the theory of human nature is the order of "healthy" self-regulation. Let us speculate about this for a paragraph. Considering the simple example of the thirsty corporal, we might conceive a rule, stated

negatively: "Whatever prevents *any* behavior of a kind
dominates a specific behavior of the kind, the genus
comes before the species"—e.g., avoiding sudden death
before quenching thirst, or preserving the creature-
comfort before the ego-comfort; or, to give a political
example, it is stupid for a society to inhibit any feeling
whatever and then to cultivate the arts. Or this rule
might be cast as an affirmative principle: "the basic
law of life is self-preservation and growth." Or again
we might conceive the rule that "the more vulnerable
and valuable is first defended"—as that a speck in the
sensitive eye is the most acute pain and claims attention; this is the "wisdom of the body."

6: Theories of Psychotherapy as Hierarchies of Value

However it may be, every theory of medicine, psychotherapy, or education is based on some conception
of organismic-self-regulation and its corresponding
hierarchy of values. The conception is the operation of
what the scientist considers *in fact* to be the chief
dynamic factor in life and society.

In the psychoanalytical theories, developed after the
work of Darwin, the dynamic factor is usually de-
ployed genetically as a history. For example, to Freud,
who attended closely to the libido and its somatic development, human nature is an order of the oral, anal,
phallic, and genital stages. (One does not have the
impression, in Freud, that women have a complete human nature—but to be sure they are therefore somewhat divine.) Other important behaviors are related
to these developments, such as sadistic-anal, oral-anal-
cannibalistic, phallic-narcissistic, etc. And the goal of
therapy is to re-establish the natural ordering in a
viable social whole, of fore-pleasure, sublimation, final
pleasure. Harry Stack Sullivan, to give a contrary example, finds the social whole to be the essentially human thing; it is interpersonality and communication
that release energy. So he deploys his infantile stages as
prototaxic, parataxic, and syntaxic, and defines the

Freudian erotic characters in these terms. The goal of therapy is to overcome loneliness, restore self-esteem, and achieve syntaxic communication. Horney and Fromm, along the same lines (after Adler), are impressed by the growing to independence of the infant; they find the neurosis in regressive power-relations in the individual and society, and they aim at the autonomy of the individual. And so we could go on.

Every school of psychotherapy has some conception of human nature, that in neurosis is repressed and regressed, and it aims to "recover" it or "bring it to maturity." According to the conception, there are certain drives or behaviors that *ought to be* dominant in healthy self-regulation, and the aim is to create an actuality in which they are dominant.

The point of detailing differences among the schools is not to choose among them, nor contrariwise to reject them one and all; nor certainly to discredit psychotherapy as sectarian. Indeed, by and large the various theories are not logically incompatible and often neatly supplement and indirectly prove one another. Further, as we have already indicated, it is not surprising that responsible scientists can reach such disparate theories if we bear in mind that for various reasons of personality and reputation different schools of therapists get different kinds of patients, and these prove to be empirical verification for their theories and the basis for further hypotheses along the same lines. Let us briefly illustrate this. As was natural in the beginning, Freud dealt with a range of chronic patients with spectacular symptoms: hysterias, obsessions, phobias, perversions. Both as a result of this and then as a cause of it, he used the interpretation of symbols as his method; and therefore he was bound to arrive at a certain theory of childhood and of human nature. But the Jungians came to treat on the one hand institutionalized psychotics and on the other hand middle-aged "nervous-breakdowns," and they accordingly developed artistic therapies and conceived a theory full of the ideas of high and primitive culture, with a di-

minished emphasis on sexuality. But Reich has dealt
mostly with younger people often not yet married;
and both his patients and his insights dictated a more
physiological method. Sullivan, again, dealt with am-
bulatory schizophrenics, and had little recourse except
to use conversational methods and to try to build up
the assurance of his patients. Moreno, dealing with
delinquents in a boarding-school, evolved a method
of group-therapy, a situation that in principle should
de-emphasize the phenomena of transference and make
for a more amenable sociality.

In every school, the bias, the range of patients, the
method, and the theory cohere. This is not scientifically
scandalous. One might wish that the theorists were less
ready to extrapolate from their own practice to "human nature"—and indeed for all medicos to be less
ready to extrapolate to "human nature," as if mankind
were by nature a patient; but contrariwise, one might
wish that lay critics and logicians would better inform
themselves about the empirical grounds of the theories
they belittle.

7: The Neurotic's Self-Regulation and the
Therapist's Conception

But any one who sympathetically surveys the various schools and methods of psychotherapy, as we have
been doing, however superficially, also thinks a new
thought: the basic human nature is in part given, as
they assume, but in part, adjusting to the various
therapies, it *creates itself;* and this creative adjustment
in favorable circumstances is itself an essential of the
basic human nature. It is the same essential power that
is *prima facie* evident in *any* worthwhile human experience. The problem of psychotherapy is to enlist the
patient's power of creative adjustment without forcing
it into the stereotype of the therapist's scientific conception.

So we come to our question of the relation between
the neurotic's on-going self-regulation and the thera-

pist's conception of what human nature to "recover." For the patient will largely truly create himself according to the therapist's conception; but he no doubt also has other possible directions. Therefore we can see the importance of the warning of Lewin that we quoted, not to analyze the structure of the actual situation in terms of too far-reaching a whole.

For consider it a moment in the following way: the common "human nature" (whatever the conception is) is a sharing of not only animal but cultural factors; and the cultural factors, especially in our society, are very divergent—the co-existence of divergences is perhaps the defining property of our culture. Besides, there are undoubtedly original eccentric dispositions of individuals and families. And more important still, the self-creation, the creative adjustment in various circumstances, has been going on from the beginning, not completely as an extrinsic "conditioning" that can be "de-conditioned," but also mainly as true growth. Given all these factors of variation and eccentricity in the patient, it is obviously desirable to have a therapy that establishes a norm as little as possible, and tries to get as much as possible from the structure of the actual situation, here and now.

Often, it must be said, the therapist tries to impose his standard of health on the patient, and when he cannot, he exclaims: "Be self-regulating, damn you! I am telling you what self-regulation is!" The patient tries hard and can't do it and then he does not escape the reproach, "You're dead," or "You don't want to," said partly as a therapeutic technique and partly in frank irritation. (Probably the irritation is better than the technique.)

The usual situation is as follows: the therapist is using his scientific conception as the general plan of treatment, adapting it to each patient. By this conception he chooses the task, notices what resistances there are, when to follow them up and when to let them pass; and according to his conception, he hopes or despairs at the progress. Now every such plan is of course an abstraction from the concrete situation, and the therapist necessarily puts faith in this abstraction. For instance, if his dynamic factor is vegetative-energy and his method is physiological, he hopes when he sees the muscular releases and the flowing of currents, and he despairs if the patient can't or won't do the exercise. The currents must, he believes, indicate a progress. Yet to an observer of another school, the situation might look like this: the patient is indeed changed in the context of lying submitting his body to manipulation by a therapist, or manipulating himself under command; but in the context of "being himself" outside the office, he has merely learned a new defense against the "threats from below," or worse, he has learned to bracket off "himself" and to act as if he were always in that office. The patient himself, of course, is generally soon convinced of the same abstraction as his therapist, whatever it is. In his capacity of observer of the goings-on, he sees that exciting events do occur. This gives an entirely new dimension to his life and is worth the money. And in the long run something works somewhat.

We are saying this satirically; yet everybody is in the same boat, perhaps inevitably. Even so, it is good to call a spade a spade.

8: "Following the Resistances" and "Interpreting What Comes Up"

Let us put it, again, in the context of the classical controversy between the archaic "interpreting whatever comes up" and the later "following the resistances" (ultimately "character-analysis"). But these are inextricably related.

One usually begins from "what comes up"—what the patient spontaneously brings as he walks in, either a nightmare, or a dishonest attitude, or spiritless speech, or a stiff jaw—whatever it happens to be that strikes one. Even here, though, it is the case (usually conveniently overlooked) that for him to walk in at all is partly a "defense" against his own creative adjustment, a resistance against his own growth, as well as a vital cry for help.* In any event, the therapist starts from what the patient brings in. Yet it is universally felt that if he long continues to follow what the patient brings, then the patient will evade and run circles. Therefore, as soon as one notices a crucial resistance (according to one's conception), one "hammers" at this. But while the hammering is going on, the patient is surely busily isolating the danger point and setting up another defense. Then comes the problem of attacking both defenses at once, in order that one cannot substitute for the other. But this amounts, does it not, to following what comes up, what the patient brings in? But of course the new situation has great advantages: the therapist now understands more, for he is involved in a situation that he himself has partly created; the reactions that occur either confirm his guesses or alter them in a certain direction; the therapist is himself growing into a real situation by giving in to what is brought in and defending himself against the neurotic elements in it. And the hope is that one day the structure of the neurotic elements, progressively enfeebled, will collapse.

What are we driving at in giving this curiously intricate picture of what goes on? We want to say that "interpreting what comes up" and "following resistances" are inextricably combined in the actual situation; and that, if there is any growth, both the patient's spontaneous deliveries and his neurotic resistances *and* the therapist's conception and his non-neurotic defenses against being taken in, manipulated, etc. are progressively destroyed in the developing situation. Then it is by concentrating on the *concrete* structure of the actual situation that one can best hope to dissolve the neurotic elements. And this means, certainly, a less rigid clinging to one's scientific conception than is commonly to be observed in this profession.

---

*And vice versa: in our society with its neurotic isolation and need "to do it by oneself," not to ask for help is a resistance.

9: The Double Nature of a Symptom

The structure of the situation is the internal coherence of its form and content; and we are trying to show that to concentrate on this gives the proper relation between the patient's on-going self-regulation and the therapist's conception.

One of Freud's grandest observations was the double nature of a neurotic symptom: the symptom is both an expression of vitality and a "defense" against vitality (we shall prefer to say a "self-conquering attack on one's vitality"). Now the common sentiment of the therapists is "to use the healthy elements to combat the neurosis." This sounds very pretty: it means the desire to cooperate, the innate honesty, the orgasm, the wish to be well and happy. But what if the most vital and creative elements are precisely the "neurotic" ones, the patient's characteristic neurotic self-regulation?

This matter is very important. The ordinary notion of using the healthy elements implies that the neurosis is merely a negation of vitality. But is it not the case that the self-regulating neurotic behavior has positive traits, often inventive, and sometimes of a high order of achievement? The neurotic drive is obviously not merely negative for it has indeed exerted a strong shaping effect in the patient, and one cannot explain a positive effect by a negative cause.

If the basic conception of healthy human nature (whatever it is) is correct, then all patients would be cured to be alike. Is this the case? Rather it is just in health and spontaneity that men appear most different, most unpredictable, most "eccentric." As classes of neurotics men are more alike: this is the deadening effect of sickness. So here again we can see that the symptom has a double aspect: as a rigidity it makes a man into just an example of a kind of "character," and there are half a dozen kinds. But as a work of his own creative self, the symptom expresses a man's uniqueness. And is there some scientific conception, perhaps, that presumes *a priori* to cover the range of human uniquenesses?

10: Curing the Symptom and Repressing the Patient

Lastly, let us consider our problem in the context of the patient's anxiety. In order to "recover" the human nature, the therapist hammers at the character, increases anxiety, and, in so far, diminishes self-esteem. Confronted with a standard of health that he cannot measure up to, the patient is guilty. He used to be guilty because he masturbated, now he is guilty because he doesn't enjoy it sufficiently when he masturbates (he used to enjoy it more when he felt guilty). More and more the physician is in the right and the patient is in the wrong.

Yet we know that underlying the "defensive" characteristic, indeed *in* the defensive characteristic, there is always a beautiful affirmative childlike feeling: indignation in the defiance, loyal admiration in the clinging, solitude in the loneliness, aggressiveness in the hostility, creativity in the confusion. Nor is this part at all irrelevant to the present situation, for even now and here there is plenty to be indignant about, and something to be loyal to and admire, and a teacher to be destroyed and assimilated, and a darkness where only the creator spirit has a glimmer of light. Of course no therapy can extirpate these native expressions. But we are saying that the native expressions and their neurotic employment now form a whole-figure, for they are the work of the patient's on-going self-regulation.

What must be the result of hammering at the resistances? Anxious and guilty, assailed by a frontal attack, the patient represses the entire whole. Supposing that in sum there has been a gain, bound energy is released. Yet the patient has importantly lost his own weapons and his orientation in the world; the new available energy cannot work and prove itself in experience. To a sympathetic and intelligent friend of the patient the result looks as follows: that the process of analysis has either been a levelling and "adjusting" one, or a narrow and fanatical one, depending on whether the basic scientific conception has laid more stress on interpersonal or personal releases. The patient has indeed approached the norm of the theory—and so the theory is again proved!

11: The Requirements of a Good Method

Let us collect and summarize what we have been saying on the relation of the neurotic's self-regulation and the therapist's conception of organismic self-regulation:

We found reason to believe that the power of creative adjustment to the therapy is present in every method. We saw that it was advisable to postulate normalcy as little as possible, in abstraction from the situation here and now. There is a danger that the patient will approach the abstract norm only in the context of the treatment. And we have tried to show that "what comes up" and the "resistances to treatment" are both present in the actuality, and that the involvement of the therapist is not simply as the object of the patient's transference, but is his own growing into the situation, putting his pre-conception at stake. Again, we called to mind that the neurotic symptom is an intrinsic structure of vital and deadening elements and that the patient's best self is invested in it. And lastly, that there is a danger that in dissolving the resistances, the patient will be left less than he was.

In all these considerations we saw reason to concentrate on the structure of the actual situation as the task of creative adjustment; to try for an altogether new synthesis and make this the chief point of the session.

Yet on the other hand, it is absurd to think even for a moment of not combating the resistances, of not rousing anxiety, of not showing that a neurotic response does not work, of not reviving the past, of withholding all interpretation and discarding one's science. For the results will be superficial, no bound energy will be released, etc.; and humanly speaking, what is the reality of an interview in which one of the partners, the therapist, inhibits his best power, what he knows and thereby evaluates?

The problem then comes down to the detailed one, of what is the structure of the interview: *how* to employ and deploy the conflict, the anxiety, the past, the conception and the interpretation, in order to reach the climax of creative adjustment?

12: Self-Awareness in Experimental Safe Emergencies

Now, going back to Corporal Jones and his hierarchy of healthy responses in an emergency, we propose as the structure of the interview: to excite a safe emergency by concentrating on the actual situation. This looks like an odd formulation, yet it is exactly what is done in moments of success by therapists of every school. Consider a situation somewhat as follows:

1. The patient, as an active partner in the experiment, concentrates on what he is actually feeling, thinking, doing, saying; he attempts to contact it more closely in image, body-feeling, motor response, verbal description, etc.

2. It is something of lively interest to himself, so he need not deliberately attend to it, but it attracts his attention. The context may be chosen by the therapist from what he knows of the patient and according to his scientific conception of where the resistance is.

3. It is something that the patient is vaguely aware of and he becomes more aware of it because of the exercise.

4. Doing the exercise, the patient is encouraged to follow his bent, to imagine and exaggerate freely, for it is safe play. He applies the attitude and the exaggerated attitude to his actual situation: his attitude toward himself, toward the therapist, his ordinary behavior (his ordinary behavior in family, sex, job).

5. Alternately he exaggeratedly inhibits the attitude and applies the inhibition in the same contexts.

6. As the contact becomes closer and the content be-

comes fuller, his anxiety is aroused. This constitutes a felt emergency, but the emergency is safe and controllable and known to be so by both partners.

7. The goal is that in the safe emergency, the underlying (repressed) intention—action, attitude, present-day object, memory—will become dominant and re-form the figure.

8. The patient accepts the new figure as his own, feeling that "it is I who am feeling, thinking, doing this."

This is surely not an unfamiliar therapeutic situation; and it does not prejudge the use of any method, whether anamnestic, interpersonal, or physiological; nor of any basic conception. What is new is the expectation of anxiety not as an inevitable by-product but as a functional advantage; and this is possible because the interested activity of the patient is kept central from the beginning to the end. Recognizing the emergency, he does not flee or freeze, but maintains his courage, becomes wary, and actively realizes the behavior that becomes dominant. It is he who is creating the emergency; it is not something that overwhelms him from elsewhere. And the toleration of anxiety is *the same as* the forming of a new figure.

If the neurotic state is the response to a non-existent chronic low-grade emergency, with medium tonus and dull and fixed alertness instead of either relaxation or galvanic tone and sharp flexible alertness: then the aim is to concentrate on an existing high-grade emergency with which the patient can actually cope and thereby grow. It is common to say to the patient, "You adopted this behavior when you were really in danger —for instance, when you were a child; but now you are safe, grown-up." This is true, so far as it goes. But the patient feels safe, indeed, just so far as the neurotic behavior is *not* involved, when he is lying talking to a friendly person, etc. Or conversely, the therapist attacks the resistance and the patient is overwhelmed by anxiety. *But the point is for the patient to feel the behavior in its very emergency use and at the same time to feel that he is safe because he can cope with the situation*. This is to heighten the chronic low-grade emergency to a safe high-grade emergency, attended by anxiety yet controllable by the active patient. The technical problems are (a) to increase the tension by the right leads, and (b) to keep the situation controllable yet not controlled: felt as safe because the patient is at a stage adequate to *invent* the required adjustment, and not deliberately ward it off.

The method is to employ every functioning part as functional, to bracket off or abstract from no functioning part in the actual situation. It is to find the context and experiment that will activate them all as a whole of the required kind. The functioning parts are: the patient's self-regulation, the therapist's knowledge, the released anxiety, and (not least) the courage and creative formative power in every person.

13: Evaluation

In the end the question of the right use of the therapist's conception comes down to the nature of evaluation.

There are two kinds of evaluation, the intrinsic and the comparative. Intrinsic evaluation is present in every on-going act; it is the end directedness of process, the unfinished situation moving toward the finished, the tension to the orgasm, etc. The standard of evaluation emerges in the act itself, and is, finally, the act itself as a whole.

In comparative evaluation, the standard is extrinsic to the act, the act is judged against something else. It is to this kind of evaluation that the neurotic (and the normal neurosis of society) is especially prone: every action is measured against an ego-ideal, need for praise, money, prestige. It is an illusion, as every creative artist or educator knows, that such comparative evaluation leads to any good achievement; the illusion in the cases where it seems to be a salutary spur is that the comparison stands for needed love, guiltlessness, etc., and these drives would be more useful (less harmful) if not concealed.

There is no use in the therapist's ever making comparative evaluations against his own conception of healthy nature. He must rather use his conception and other knowledge descriptively, for leads and suggestions, in subordination to the intrinsic evaluation emerging from the on-going self-regulation.

V

MATURING, AND THE
RECOLLECTION OF CHILDHOOD

1: Past and Future in the Present Actuality

When we emphasize self-awareness, experiment, felt emergency, and creative adjustment, we are laying less stress on the recovery of past memory ("childhood recollection") or anticipations and ambitions for the future ("life plan"). But memory and anticipation are acts in the present, and it is important for us to analyze their place in the structure of the actuality. You may experimentally get the context of this chapter if you say, *"Now, here* I am remembering so and so" and notice the difference from merely wandering off into memory; and so, *"Now here* I am planning or expecting so and so."

Memories and prospects are present imaginations. The warm play of imagination is in general not dissociative but integrative. Why is it that persons given to reminiscences or projects are so obviously in flight, and not refreshed afterward but empty and exhausted? It is that the events are not felt as their own, do not come home to them, are not re-created and assimilated; the telling always seems endless and becomes more and more dry and verbal. (Contrast for instance an artwork, where the memory becomes alive in the present handling of the medium.) Meantime the actuality is unsatisfactory, the past is lost, the future is not yet. What is the present sentiment of this garrulous person? It is not warm imagination, but regret, reproaches, self-reproach, or frustration, guilt of inadequacy, trying to exert the will; and these diminish self-esteem still further. For the sentiment of one's worthiness cannot be given by exculpating explanations nor by comparison with an extrinsic standard: "It wasn't my fault; I'm as good as anybody else. I'm not well, but soon I'll make my mark." The feeling of worthiness is given only by one's adequacy in an activity that is going on or in the relaxation after a completed situation (so that there is no remorse when the "guilty" sexual play has been satisfying, but only when it has been poor). To explain or to compare is always felt as a lie, either consoling or self-punishing. But to do something and be oneself is a proof; it is self-justifying for it completes the situation. So we lay stress on the patient's self-awareness in an experiment that he himself is carrying on, and expect that he will create a more advantageous kind of whole.

2: The Importance of Past and Future in Therapy

But the bother is that the "self" that is available, that is *there*, is pretty thin in content as well as split six ways. It is something but not enough to give the patient the "feel of himself" (Alexander); we must also reach the "underlying basis" that the self is unaware of, to increase the power of the self. The question is how this underlying basis is in the present.

Trying to answer this question, Freud repeated categorically in the last years of his life that no method could be called psychoanalysis that did not recover the infantile memory. From our point of view he meant by this that a large part of the self is still acting out old unfinished situations. And this must be true, for we live by assimilating the novelty to what we have become, in the way that we have become it.

Some para-Freudian schools, on the contrary, insist that the infantile memory is not necessary at all, that what is necessary is to reach a mature attitude. This could mean (what is certainly true) that many powers of growth in a person are frustrated; he has failed to become himself.

We shall try to show that the distinction "infantile/mature" is a false split and a misleading use of language. And without this division, the recovery of childhood and the need for maturing appear in a different light. In this chapter we treat mostly of memory. (Problems of prospect are a kind of aggression—Chapter 8.)

3: Past Effects as Fixed Forms in the Present

Freud seems to have believed that past times *do* exist psychologically otherwise than in their present-effects. In the famous illustration of the superimposed buried cities, he implies that the various pasts and the present interpenetrate one another, occupying the same space, and having additional relations to those of temporal succession. This is a powerful speculation.*

For the purposes of therapy, however, only the present structure of sensation, introspection, behavior is available; and our question must be what role remembering plays in this structure. Formally considered, memories are one of the kinds of more fixed (unchangeable) forms in the on-going present process.

(We have already spoken of "abstractions" as such fixed forms, made relatively stationary in order that something else may move more efficiently. Abstractions draw away from the more sensory and material particularity of the experience; memories, rather, are fixed imaginations of especially the sensory and material particulars, but they abstract from the motor response—then the past is unchangeable; it is what is experienced as unchangeable.** Habits, for instance, techniques or knowledge, are other fixed forms: they are assimilations to the more conservative organic structure.)

Many such fixed forms are healthy, mobilizable for the on-going process, for instance a useful habit, an art, a particular memory that now serves for comparison with another particular to yield an abstraction. Some

---

*Indeed, the Freudian dream-theory, the non-Euclidian geometries, and the relativity physics are similar attempts to refute the Kantian conception of space and time. Their effect is to limit Kant's transcendental aesthetic to the sensory and introspective actual experience: but this was no doubt what he intended.

**Of course we are not here discussing the metaphysical question: what is the past? that is, whether or not what is given in the experience of memory has existence, and what kind of existence.

fixed forms are neurotic, such as "character," compulsive repetition. But whether healthy or neurotic, *the past and every other fixity persist by their present functioning:* an abstraction persists when it proves itself in present speech, a technique when it is practiced, a neurotic characteristic when it reacts against a "dangerous" recurring urge.

As soon as they are no longer of present use, the organism by its self-regulation sloughs off the fixed effects of the past; useless knowledge is forgotten, character dissolves. The rule works both ways: *it is not by inertia but by function that a form persists, and it is not by lapse of time but by lack of function that a form is forgotten.*

4: The Compulsion to Repeat

The neurotic compulsion to repeat is a sign that a situation unfinished in the past is still unfinished in the present. Every time enough tension accumulates in the organism to make the task dominant, there is another try at a solution. From this point of view, the neurotic repetition is no different from any other repeated accumulated tension, such as hunger or sexual pulsation; and needless to say it is by these other repeated accumulations that the neurotic repetition is energized. The difference from what obtains in health is that each time the healthy repetition occurs the task is completed, equilibrium is restored, and the organism has maintained itself or grown by assimilating something new. The circumstances are always changing, the organism meets them unencumbered with fixed sensations of other particular circumstances (but only with the flexible tools of useful abstractions and conservative habits); and it is the novelty of the new circumstance that is interesting—not that this steak is like the one I ate last week (which would rouse disgust), but that it is steak (something I know I like in general, and that is giving off *its own,* novel, smell).

But the neurotic tension is not completed; yet it is dominant, it *must* be completed before anything else is attended to; so the organism that has not grown by success and assimilation assumes the same attitude to make the same effort again. Unfortunately, the fixed attitude, which failed before, has become necessarily more inept in the changed circumstances; so that the completion is less and less likely. There is here a miserable circularity: it is only by assimilation, completion, that one learns anything and is prepared for a new situation; but what has failed of completion is ignorant and out-of-touch and therefore becomes more and more incomplete.

Thus it is that a *present* need for a *present* satisfaction comes to seem "infantile." It is not the instinct or the desire that is infantile, no longer relevant to the adult, but that the fixed attitude, its abstract conceptions and images, are old-fashioned, unlikely, ineffectual. To give the classical example: the desire to be fondled *knows* only the image of mother as its language and guide—this image brightens as the desire is further frustrated—but mother is not to be seen anywhere—and any other possible fondler is *a priori* disappointing, or at least one does not look in that direction. *Neither* the desire *nor* the image is past because the situation is unfinished, but the image is inept and old-fashioned. Finally, when the prospect is hopeless and the pain is too intense, the attempt is made to inhibit and desensitize the whole complex.

5: The Structure of a Forgotten Scene and its Recall

Consider now a memory that is apparently forgotten—not simply forgotten (like useless knowledge), nor subject to recall because it is a mobile part of the background of the present (like useful knowledge)—but repressed.

In structure, this is best regarded as a bad habit, an ineffectual effort to annihilate, with the forgotten unannihilable complex as its center. The bad habit is the present deliberate constraint—a constraint that is always unitarily muscular, sensory, and feelingful (for instance, the eye-muscles keep one looking ahead and prevent free play of seeing; the withdrawal of desire prevents certain visions from brightening; and what is actually seen distracts feeling and behavior in a contrary direction). And what is constrained, the complex at the center, contains a particular scene that, being particular, cannot recur or be useful in that form—to be useful in the present it would have to be not annihilated, but destroyed (taken apart) and brought up to date. Obviously this is a very durable fixity: a forgetting continually renewed with present strength and safeguarded from recollection by the irrelevance of its contents.

How has it occurred? Suppose there was once a present-situation in which one was aware of a strong desire, in a scene with objects. (For simplicity's sake let us think of a single dramatic moment, a "trauma.") The desire was frustrated: there was a danger in satisfaction: and the tension of frustration was unbearable. One then deliberately inhibited the desire and awareness of the desire, in order not to suffer and to keep out of danger. The whole complex of feeling, expression, gesture, and the sensory impression that is especially deep because importantly unfinished, is now out of use; and considerable energy is continually expended to *keep* it out of use in every present. (Considerable energy because the traumatic scene is importantly unfinished and must be strongly countered.)

Now how does the recall occur? Suppose that the *present* deliberate inhibition is relaxed, e.g., by exercising the eye-muscles and letting the vision play, by imagining desirable objects, by becoming dissatisfied with the distractions, etc. At once the *ever-present* underlying feeling and gesture express themselves, and with them comes the image of the *old* scene. It is not the old image that has released the feeling, but the relaxation of the present inhibition. *The old scene is revived because that happened to be the last free exercise of the feeling and gesture in the sensory environment, trying to complete the unfinished situation.* The old scene is, so to speak, the last symbol in which one had learned to express the feeling.

For if, contrariwise, the image occurs first, by chance, as when a man is struck by a passing face, or even at the end of a series of free-associations, then one may suddenly feel an "alien" emotion, a strange attraction, nameless grief. But it is meaningless, evanescent, at once stopped by the continuing *present* inhibition.

Thus in classical psychoanalysis, the forgotten scene must be "interpreted" in order to effectuate release, that is it must be related to the present attitude and experience. But the interpretation will work successfully only if it goes so far as to alter the structure of the present attitude, the bad habit.

6. The "Trauma" as Unfinished Situation

Probably there is never such a single traumatic moment as we have been describing, but rather a traumatic series of more or less like frustrated and dangerous moments, during which the tension of the feeling and the dangerous explosiveness of the response gradually heighten, and the inhibition of these habitually strengthens until, in the interest of economy, feeling and response are blotted out. Any one of this series may stand, as the later remembered scene, for what is inhibited. ("I remember papa beating me on a particular occasion.") Note that this traumatic scene does not express the habitual inhibition, the character or self-conquest, which is in the present continually renewed, but precisely the free not-yet-inhibited feeling, more organic and ever-present, e.g., my desire to be close to papa or my hatred of him, or both.

The trauma does not *attract* the repetition, as Freud thought. It is the organism's repeated effort to satisfy its need that brings on the repetition, but this effort is repeatedly inhibited by a present deliberate act. To the degree that the need gains expression, it uses old-fashioned techniques ("the return of the repressed"). If the feeling is released, it may or may not momentarily revive an old scene; but in any case it will at once seek a present satisfaction. Thus, the early scene is an expected by-product of the change of the bad habit and the release of feeling, but it is neither a sufficient nor a necessary cause of it.

Obviously the repressed trauma will tend to return, for it is in a way the most vital part of the organism, it draws on more organic power. To draw a strict analogy, a dream is obviously a "wish," no matter how nightmarish, for with waking deliberateness in abeyance the underlying more organic situation asserts itself—and evaluation is nothing but the motion of the unfinished toward completion.

7: The Therapeutic Use of the Recovered Scene

The recovered scene does not produce the release, yet when it accompanies the renewed flooding of feeling it is very important in the self-awareness. Just as it stands for the last time that the inhibited excitement was active, so now it is the first exercise of the excitement renewed. It at once provides a kind of "explanation" as to what the unaccustomed, long disused, feeling "means," the kind of object it applies to; but of course the feeling does not, in the present, *mean* the archaic objects at all. It is at this point that interpretation is valuable, to explain the patient's new feeling of himself to himself. He must learn to distinguish between the present need expressed in the feeling and this object that is *merely* a particular memory, and as particular lost and unchangeable. Such interpretation as this is not arcane; it is simply pointing out the obvious, though that may be hard to swallow.

8: The Erroneous Conception of "Infantile" versus "Mature"

The usual opinion, however, is that the need, the feeling, is "infantile," a thing of the past. Freud, we have seen (and as we shall discuss in detail in Chapter 13), goes so far as to say that not only certain needs but a whole mode of thought, the "primary process," is infantile and necessarily repressed. Most theorists regard certain sexual needs and certain interpersonal attitudes as childish and immature.

Our view is that *no* persisting desire can be regarded as infantile or illusory. Suppose, for instance, it is the "childish" need to be taken care of by a "self-sacrificing" nurse. It is pointless to say that this desire is a clinging to mother. Rather we must say that the desire affirms itself; it is the image and name of "mother" that is impossible, and indeed not meant.* On the contrary the desire is now fairly safe and probably in some way fulfillable. (Perhaps, "Take care of yourself for a change; stop trying to help everybody else.") It is not the goal of therapy to talk a man out of certain desires. Indeed, we must say further: that if, in the present, the need is not fulfillable, and actually not fulfilled, the whole process of tension and frustration will recommence, and the man will either again blot out the awareness and succumb to the neurosis or, as is now likely, he will know himself and suffer until he can make an environmental change.

We can now return to our question, the importance of childhood recovery, and sketch out a more rounded answer. We have said that the recollection of the old scene is unnecessary; it is at most an important clue to the meaning of the feeling, but even in that way it is dispensable. Does it follow that, as Horney, for instance, maintains, the recovery of child-life does not occupy a privileged position in psychotherapy? No. For our thought is that the content of the recovered scene is rather unimportant, but that the childish feeling and attitude that lived that scene are of the utmost importance. *The childish feelings are important not as a past that must be undone but as some of the most beautiful powers of adult life that must be recovered:* spontaneity, imagination, directness *of awareness and*

---

*The language for the emotional needs is extremely crude, except in poetry and the other arts. Psychoanalysis has vastly enriched the language by showing in adult life the analogies of early years. Unfortunately the contempt of childhood is such that if a term applies also to an infant it is a denigration. Thus "motherly" is regarded as a good attribute, but "sucking" as a ridiculous one.

manipulation. What is required, as Schachtel has said, is to recover the child's way of experiencing the world; it is to free not the factual biography but the "primary process of thought."

Nothing is more unfortunate than the current indiscriminate use of the words "infantile" and "mature." Even when the "infantile attitude" is not considered evil in children themselves, its traits are frowned on in "maturity" simply en bloc, without discriminating what is naturally outgrown, what makes no difference either way, and what should be persistent but is blotted out of almost all adults. "Maturity," precisely among those who claim to be concerned with "free personality," is conceived in the interest of an unnecessarily tight adjustment to a dubiously valuable workaday society, regimented to pay its debts and duties.

9: Discrimination Among Child Attitudes and their Objects

We saw that if we considered the infant as an integral part of a field in which grown-ups were another part, the infant could not be called isolated or helpless. Now as he grows in strength, communication, knowledge and technique, certain functions belonging to the previous whole are altered in another kind of whole: e.g., more free-standing, there is a more locomotory self that could be called his own self, so that the function of fostering care in the previous whole can become, in many ways, self-fostering care. But let us look at the correlated feeling and motivation. It would be tragic if even in the altered whole, the previous sense of "dependency as a part in a social whole" would be simply blotted out and have to be "introduced" as part of a mature attitude, when it is really the warm continuation of an infantile attitude. Again, such typically infantile behavior as body-exploration and fascination with pre-genital pleasures naturally becomes less interesting when they *have* been explored and the dominance of genital desire establishes itself; but it would be tragic if body-satisfaction and the impulse to body-exploration were blotted out—certainly it makes an inept lover. When the so-called infantile traits of clinging or sucking recur after repression they answer a mature need, but their language and proportion are often comically archaic. But this is largely because of unfinished situations caused by the projections of adults who enforced premature growing-up. Or again, infants experiment with nonsense-syllables and play with the sounds and the vocal organs; and so, in continuation, do great poets, not because this is "infantile" but because it is part of the fullness of human speech. It is not exactly a sign of maturity when a patient is so embarrassed that he can make only "correct" sentences in a flat tone.

10: How Freud Discriminated Between "Infantile" and "Mature"; Childish Sexuality, Dependency

We can distinguish four main contexts in which Freud spoke of maturing: (1) the libidinous zones, (2) relation to the parents, (3) adaptation to "reality," (4) assumption of parental responsibility. In all of these Freud made the split too absolute, each functionally reinforcing the split of the others; yet by and large Freud was not prone to use the distinction between "infantile" and "mature," or even between "primary" and "secondary" process, to the child's disadvantage.

(1) The "primacy" of the genitals over the pre-genital erotic stages. This work of organismic-self-regulation is accomplished in the earliest years. But the continuation of the childish practices is much too coldly regarded by most therapists. Sexual foreplay is not discouraged, but is not spoken of joyously. Art aimed at arousing sexual excitement is frowned on, against the evidence of primitive and the most vital high cultures; yet if one is not to be merry about this, about what is one supposed to be merry? Erotic curiosity is abhorred, yet it is near the heart of all novel writing and reading and of theater of every kind. And in manners in general there is not nearly enough kiss-

ing and petting among friends, and friendly exploration of strangers, against the evidence of other gregarious animals. And so again a kind of primary homosexuality, based on narcissistic exploration, is rather discouraged than encouraged, resulting, as Ferenczi has pointed out, in an obsessive heterosexuality that makes true community life impossible, for every man is jealously hostile to every other.

(2) The transcending of personal dependency on the parents. We can regard this work of organismic-self-regulation as the alteration and complication of the organism/social field by increasing the number of members involved and each member's mobility and choices and ability to abstract to higher levels. Thus a child, learning to walk, talk, chew, and exert more strength, spontaneously ceases to cling as a suckling and make exclusive demands. Yet with other objects there persist the out-going filial attitudes of trust, docility, the sense of one's dependency in a community, the claim to get nourishment and caresses as an undenied right and as a free-born heir of nature, to feel at home in the world. If the world and the communities we create in the world are not such as to be frankly embraced with trust and confidence of support, a man will find this out for himself without a physician's telling him that his attitude is infantile. Likewise in education: it is very beautiful to "accept nothing that you do not find out for yourself," yet a part of this process is a faith in benevolent teachers and classic authorities, whose point of view we tentatively embrace beforehand, then test, chew up, make our own or reject. When there are no more individual teachers in this sense, we transfer the same attitude toward the natural world as a whole. The exclusive admiration of therapists for independence is a reflex (both by imitation and reaction) to our present societies that are so lonely and coerced. And what is remarkable is to see how their therapeutic procedure—instead of being that of a teacher who, accepting the authority that is freely given, trains the student to help himself—is that of first a bad and then a too good parent, to whom a

neurotic attachment is transferred: and then he breaks it off and sends the child out to fend for himself.

11: Childish Emotions and Unreality:
Impatience, Hallucination, Aggressiveness

(3) Freud spoke also of maturing as the adaptation to "reality" and the inhibition of the "pleasure-principle." These, he felt, are accomplished by biding one's time and making various resignations, and by finding "sublimations,"* socially acceptable releases of tension. It is fairly clear that Freud, who under a thick hide of paternalism often betrayed a childish heart, regarded this kind of maturation with a dim eye; he thought it made for the advance of society and civilization at the expense of every person's growth and happiness; and he often urged that this kind of growing-up had already gone too far for safety. And looked at coldly, in the terms he stated it, the adaptation to "reality" is precisely neurosis: it is deliberate interference with organismic-self-regulation and the turning of spontaneous discharges into symptoms. Civilization so conceived is a disease. To the degree that all this *is* necessary, surely the reasonable attitude is not to praise maturity but for both therapist and patient to learn to cry stinking fish, as Bradley said, "This is the best of all possible worlds and the duty of every honest man is to cry stinking fish." This would also have the virtue of letting out aggression in a justified gripe.

But we think the problem is wrongly posed. In the first place Freud was notoriously timid about entertaining the possibility of radical changes in the social reality that would make it more nearly conform to a (continuing) child-heart's desire, for instance the possibility of a little more disorder, dirt, affection, absence of government, and so forth.** He seems to have vacillated between the brazenness of his theory and

---

* "Sublimation" we take to be something that does not exist; what may be meant by it we discuss below (Chapter 12).

** One has the impression that once Freud had talked himself into the necessity of the prohibition of incest, "the most maiming wound ever inflicted on mankind," he thought that nothing else made much difference.

the excruciating embarrassment of his feelings. But also he misinterpreted the behavior of children themselves by considering it out of context, from the point of view of a very deliberate adult.

Consider, for example, "biding one's time." The advocates of maturity agree that children cannot wait; they are impatient. What is the evidence of this? When temporarily frustrated of what he "knows" he will get, a small child screams and pounds. But then we see that when he gets the thing—or soon after—he is at once bafflingly sunny. There is no indication that the previous dramatic scene meant anything beyond itself, but it meant itself. What did it mean? Partly the scene was a calculated persuasion; partly it was a lurking fear of real deprivation due to not really knowing the circumstances that proved the thing must be given after all. Both these are simple ignorance and vanish with knowledge; they do not spring from an "infantile attitude." But it is the residue that is interesting: the scene carried on for its own sake as a letting off of a petty tension. Is that bad? Far from proving that a child can't wait, it proves precisely that he *can* wait, namely, by jumping with impatience: he has an organic equilibrating technique for the tension; and afterwards, *therefore,* his satisfaction is pure, full, unclouded. It is the adult who cannot wait—he has lost the technique; we do not make a scene, so our resentment and fear mount, and then we enjoy soured and insecure. What is the harm in the childish drama? It offends the adult audience because of their repression of the similar tantrum, not because of the sound and fury but because of the unconscious distraction. What is here called maturity is likely neurosis. But if we think of the adults of Greek epic or tragedy or of Biblical Genesis and Kings, we notice that they—not undistinguished for their intellect or sense of responsibility—do indeed carry on in a most infantile manner.

Consider, again, a child's astonishing ability to hallucinate in his play, to treat the sticks as if they were ships, the sand as if it were food, the stones as if they were playmates. The "mature" adult faces up to the realities—when he breaks down he flees into reminiscing and planning, but never into frank hallucination unless he is far gone. Is that good? The question is, what *is* the important reality? So long as the *felt activity* is carried on well enough, the child will accept any props; the core of the real is the action in any case. The "mature" person is comparatively enslaved, not to the reality but to a neurotically fixed abstraction of it, namely "knowledge" that has lost its subservient relation to use, action, and happiness. (We do not mean pure knowledge, which is a difficult form of play.) When the fixity to the abstraction becomes acute, imagination is stifled, and with it all initiative, experiment, and perspective, and openness to anything new; all invention, trying out the actuality as if it were otherwise—and therefore all increased efficiency in the long run. Yet all adults except great artists and scientists are somewhat neurotic in this way. Their maturity is a fearful deliberateness with regard to the actuality; it is not a frank acceptance of it for what it is worth. And of course, at the same time as he is sticking close to the actuality, the adult is projecting into it the worst madness and making the silliest rationalizations.

A child perfectly well distinguishes the dream and the actuality. Indeed he distinguishes four things, the actuality, the as-if, the make-believe, and let's pretend (weakest at the last, for he has a poor sense of humor). He can be a real Indian using a stick as if it were a gun, yet dodge the actual automobile. We do not observe that children's curiosity or ability to learn is injured by their free fantasy. On the contrary, the fantasy functions as an essential medium between the pleasure-principle and the reality-principle: on the one hand, it is a drama to try out and become expert, on the other, a therapy to become friendly with the strange and bitter actuality (e.g., playing school). In brief, when a therapist bids his patient to grow up and face the reality, he often does not mean the concrete actuality in which a creative adjustment is possible, but some daily situation that is often better dealt with by not directly facing it.

Another infantile trait that is supposed to give way to maturity is the child's free aggressiveness. We shall devote a chapter (Chapter 8) to the inhibition of aggression in our adult mores. Here we need only point out that a small child's indiscriminate blows are dealt precisely when his strength is weakest—the inference that he means to annihilate is likely an adult projection. A boy's hard punches are thrown only at enemies. So a dog in play bites, and yet he does not bite.

Finally, with regard to the adjustment of the mature person to reality, must we not ask—one is ashamed to have to mention it—whether the "reality" is not rather closely pictured after, and in the interests of, western urban industrial society, capitalist or state-socialist? Is it the case that other cultures, gaudier in dress, greedier in physical pleasures, dirtier in manners, more disorderly in governance, more brawling and adventurous in behavior, were or are thereby less mature?

12: Childish Irresponsibility

(4) Lastly, Freud considered maturing as becoming a responsible parent (father) instead of an irresponsible child. In Freud's scheme this would occur after a normal evolution of object-choices, from the auto-erotic through the narcissistic-homosexual (ego-ideal and gang) to the heterosexual. He conceives of a healthy early introjection of (identification with) the father; and then maturity is to accept this introject as oneself and assume the parental role. (We shall later take exception to his language here, but he was evidently reading off his own character.)

Later para-Freudians have learned to be suspicious of paternal and other authority, and they lay stress rather on the contrast between the "irresponsible child" and the "responsible adult," answerable for his actions and their consequences. Responsibility in this sense seems to mean a kind of contractual relation with other adults.

We can interpret this growth to responsibility again as organismic-self-regulation in a changing field. A child's irresponsibility follows from his dependency; to the extent that he is closely part of the parental field, he is not answerable to himself for his behavior. Given more mobility, meaningful speech, personal relationships, and choices, he begins to require of himself, to *mean*, a closer accounting between promise and performance, intention and commitment, choice and consequences. And the relationship of contract is not so much taken on as a duty, as a development of the feeling for symmetry that is very strong in the youngest. With the stage of becoming an authority, a teacher, a parent, the field has altered again: for the independent person is now less on his own, since others spontaneously attach themselves to or depend on him simply because he has ability, and they give him in turn occasions for new out-going acts. It is a rare person who grows as mature as this: to advise, guide, and care for without embarrassment, domination, etc., but simply *noblesse oblige,* giving up his "independent" interests as really less interesting.

In these ways a child is not responsible. But there is an underlying basis of responsibility in which any child is superior to most adults. This is *earnestness,* entering into the task seriously, even if the task is play. A child leaves off capriciously, but while he is engaged he gives himself. The adult, partly because he is so preoccupied with being responsible for himself, gives himself less earnestly. Again it is only the gifted person who retains this ability of childhood; the average adult finds himself caught in responsibility toward things in which he is not deeply interested. In our times it is not the case that the average man is irresponsible, does not hold himself together; rather he is too responsible, keeps meeting the time-clock, will not give in to sickness or fatigue, pays his bills before he is sure he has food, too narrowly minds his own business, does not take a risk. Would it not be wiser, then, to bring to the fore, instead of responsibility and its mere negation, the childhood opposition of earnest and caprice, both positively valuable?

Earnest is the activity to which one is committed

and cannot leave off, because the self as a closer whole
is involved in completing a situation that involves the
actuality; play is more capricious, because the actuality
is hallucinated and one can leave off. If one says to a
person, "This is irresponsible behavior," the other person both feels guilty and, seeking to amend, constrains
himself. But if one says, "You are not in earnest about
this," he may or may not decide that he means to be
in earnest; he can admit that he is playing, or even that
it is a mere caprice. If he means to be in earnest, then
he attends to the actuality of the object and his relation
to it, and this is a motion of growth. An irresponsible
person is one who is not in earnest about what is necessary. A dilettante plays capriciously with an art, he is
pleasing himself but has no responsibility for the results; an amateur plays earnestly with the art, he is
responsible to the art (for instance, to its medium and
structure) but he need not engage in it; an artist is
earnest with the art, he is committed to it.

13: Conclusion

We conclude that it is a poor use of words to speak
of a "childish attitude" as something to be transcended,
and a "mature attitude" as a *contrasting* goal to be
achieved.

With growth, the organism/environment field
changes: this makes for changes in kinds of feeling
and also for changes in the *meaning,* the relevant objects, of persistent feelings. Many traits and attitudes of
children cease to be important; and there are adult
traits that are new, for the increase in strength, knowledge, fertility, and technical ability does constitute progressively a new whole. At the same time, often it is
only the relevant objects that are altered; we must not
overlook the continuity of feeling, as is customary in a
neurotic society that both projects a false estimation of
childhood and considers many of the most beautiful
and useful powers of adulthood, manifested in the most
creative persons, to be merely childish.

Especially in psychotherapy: habitual deliberateness, factuality, non-commitment, and excessive responsibility, traits of most adults, are neurotic; whereas spontaneity, imagination, earnestness and playfulness, and direct expression of feeling, traits of children, are healthy.

14: Unblocking the Future

This is the "past" that is lost and must be recovered.

At the beginning of this chapter, however, we spoke of the past *and* the future, of those who reminisce and those who make projects, of the early scene and the life-plan. Why have we devoted all our space to the former? It is that the neurotic difficulties of those who reminisce and try with mere words to live out the unfinished situations of the past require the recovery of lost feelings and attitudes. With those who make projects and try with mere words to live out their frustrated powers, the trouble is better located not in what is lost but in what is falsely present, the introjections, false ideals, enforced identifications that block the way and must be destroyed if the person is to find himself. Therefore we prefer to discuss it in the chapter on Aggressions.

Verbal reminiscing tends to be dry and lifeless, for the past consists of unchangeable particulars. It becomes alive only when it is related to present needs that have some possibility of change.

Verbal anticipation, on the other hand, tends to be fatuous and empty, for the future consists of particulars that could change in every conceivable way, unless it is limited by some present felt need and existing power to make it be. In neurotic anticipations, there is a fixed form in the indefinite futures, that given by some introjected ideal or concept of the ego, a life-plan. The verbal anticipator is pathetically boring, because it is not *he* who is talking; he is like a ventriloquist's dummy, and nothing one can say will make any difference.

In these terms, again, we can make a provisional

definition of the present actuality. The present is the experience of the particular that one has become dissolving into several meaningful possibilities, and the reforming of these possibilities toward a single concrete new particular.

V I

HUMAN NATURE AND THE
ANTHROPOLOGY OF NEUROSIS

1: The Subject-Matter of Anthropology

In the previous chapter we discussed the importance of the recovery of "lost," that is inhibited, childhood powers in the mature individual. Now let us broaden the view and talk a little about what is "lost" in our grown-up culture and in the present use of the powers of man, for here too, in the altering fields given by new powers and new objects, many feelings and attitudes are by-passed or inhibited that should healthily be continuous and employed.

This is a chapter in abnormal anthropology. The subject-matter of anthropology is the relationship between man's anatomy, physiology, and faculties and his activity and culture. In the Seventeenth and Eighteenth Centuries, anthropology was always so studied (climaxing, probably, in Kant's *Anthropology*): for instance, what is laughter? how does it culturally manifest itself for man's well-being? More recently, anthropologists lost sight of the relationship as their special study and their books display a quite astonishing split into two unrelated sections: Physical Anthropology, the evolution and races of man; and Cultural Anthropology, a kind of historical sociology. For instance, it is an important proposition of Cultural Anthropology that technical innovations (e.g., a new plow) diffuse rapidly to neighboring areas, but moral innovations diffuse slowly and with difficulty. But this proposition is left groundless, as if it were part of the nature of these cultural objects, rather than shown to be part of the nature or conditioning of the animals involved, the men carrying the culture, these men, in turn, being shaped by the culture they carry. Most recently, however, owing mainly to the impact of psychoanalysis, the classical animal/cultural interrelationship is again being studied, in terms of early child-training, sexual practices, and so forth. And from the point of view of abnormal psychology, we here offer some biological/cultural speculations.

2: The Importance of This Subject for Psychotherapy

We can see the importance of the anthropological question: "What is Man?" if we consider that medical psychology owes a difficult double allegiance. As a branch of medicine it aims at "merely" biological health. This includes not only healthy functioning and absence of pain, but feeling and pleasure; not only sensation, but sharp awareness; not only absence of paralysis, but grace and vigor. Dealing with a psycho-somatic unity, if psychotherapy could achieve this kind of health, its existence would be justified. And in medicine the criteria of health are fairly definite and scientifically established; we know when an organ is functioning well. This aspect of "human nature" is unambiguous.

But there is no such thing as "merely" biological functioning (for instance, there is no such drive as "mere" sex, without either love or the avoidance of love). So medical means are insufficient.

Once beyond medicine, however, the very aim of therapy, the norm of health and "nature," becomes a matter of opinion. The patient is a sick man and man is not finally known for he is always changing himself and his conditions. His nature is surprisingly malleable. Yet at the same time it is not so completely malleable that the nature can be disregarded, as some democratic sociologists and fascist politicians seem to assume; it is also surprisingly resistant, so that suddenly there are neurotic reactions of individuals and a stupidity, torpor, and rigidity of the average.

In psychotherapy, moreover, these changes of condition are all-important, for they are what engage a patient's interest; they involve his fears and guilts and his hope of what he will make of himself. They rouse his excitement—they are the only things that rouse excitement—they organize awareness and behavior. Without these peculiarly "human" interests there is no biological health and no way of achieving it by psychotherapy.

3: "Human Nature" and the Average

So the doctor beats about for models and theories of what is humanly enlivening. (In Chapter 4 we discussed several such theories.) This is why Freud insisted that not medical men, but, with medical collaboration, literary men, teachers, lawyers, social-workers make the best therapists, for they understand human nature, they mix with ideas and people and have not been content to waste their youth acquiring a specialty.

The task would, of course, be immensely easier if we enjoyed good social institutions, conventions that gave satisfaction and fostered growth, for then these could be taken as a rough norm of what it means to be a full man in the specific culture; the question would not then be one of principles but of casuistical application to each case. But if we had reasonable institutions, there would not be any neurotics either. As it is, our institutions are not even "merely" biologically healthy, and the forms of individual symptoms are reactions to rigid social errors. So, far from being able to take fitness to social institutions as a rough norm, a doctor has more hope of bringing about the self-developing integration of a patient if the patient learns to adjust his environment to himself than if he tries to learn to maladjust himself to society.

Instead of a dynamic unity of need and social convention, in which men discover themselves and one another and invent themselves and one another, we are forced to think of three warring *abstractions:* the mere animal, the harried individual self, and the social pressures. The normal person either keeps himself unaware of this raging war within his personality, does not notice its manifestations in his behavior, and keeps it fairly dormant, or he is aware of it and has concluded an uneasy truce, snatching at safe opportunities. In either case there is much energy spent in pacification and valuable human powers are sacrificed. In the neurotic person, the conflicts rage to the point of exhaustion, contradictions, and breakdown—nor can it be concluded that he was therefore in some way weaker than the normal, for often precisely stronger gifts are socially disastrous. There is an important difference between the normal and neurotic, but it is not such that when a neurotic comes as a patient and poses an earnest *practical* problem for the doctor, the doctor can set as his goal a normal adjustment, any more than he could give an arrested tuberculosis a clean bill of health, though he might have to discharge the patient. Rather he must hope that, as the patient begins to reintegrate himself, he will turn out to be more "human" than is expected, or than the doctor is.

(Further, we must remember that in the present run of patients of psychotherapy, the distinction between normal and neurotic has become less than irrelevant; it is positively misleading. For more and more of the patients are not "sick" at all; they make "adequate" adjustments; they have come because they want something more out of life and out of themselves and they believe that psychotherapy can help them. Perhaps this betrays an over-sanguine disposition on their part, but it is also evidence that they are better than the average, rather than the reverse.*)

---

*We have mentioned above that the selected run of patients is an intrinsic factor in the various psychoanalytical theories, for they are both the observed material and the confirmatory evidence of response to the method. Obviously the trend of patients toward the "well enough" or even "better than well enough" is an important factor in the trend of recent theories toward those like the one in this book. In this way psychotherapy is taking over the functions of education, but that is because the customary education, in home, school, university, and church, is increasingly inept. What we would hope for, of course, is that education would take over the functions of psychotherapy.

4: Neurotic Mechanisms as Healthy Functions

Neurosis, too, is part of human nature and has its anthropology.

The split of personality—breakdown as a form of equilibrium—is probably a recently acquired power of human nature, only a few thousand years old. But it is one in a long line of evolutionary developments that are worth briefly reviewing in order to recognize where we are.

If we consider organismic-self-regulation, the process by which the dominant needs come to the forefront of awareness as they arise, we are struck not only by the wonderful system of specific adjustment, signals, co-ordination, and subtle judgment, that go to maintain the general equilibrium, but also by the devices that serve as cushioners and safety-valves to protect the contact-boundary. We have mentioned blotting-out and hallucinating and dreaming, and regarding as-if, and accepting instead-of; and there are also immobilizing (playing dead), isolating, mechanical trial and error (obsessive re-doing), panic flight, and so forth. Man is an organism of great power and efficiency, but also one that can take rough treatment and bad times. The two sides go together: ability leads to adventure and adventure to trouble. Man *has* to be malleable. These safety-functions all, of course, play a chief role in mental disorders, but they are themselves healthy.

Indeed, without being paradoxical one could say that in the neuroses just these safety-functions—of blotting out, distorting, isolating, repeating—that seem so spectacularly "crazy," are working fairly healthily. It is the more respectable functions of orientation and manipulation in the world, especially the social world, that are out of kilter and cannot work. In a finely-adjusted whole, the safety-devices are made for trouble and continue working while the more usual functions rest for repairs. Or to put it another way, when the orientation is lost and the manipulation is failing, the excitement, the vitality of the organism, expresses itself especially in autism and immobilizing. And so again, if we speak, as we must, of a social or epidemic neurosis, it is not the symptomatic social eccentricities (dictators, wars, incomprehensible art, and the like) that are pathologically important, but the normal knowledge and technique, the average way of life.

The problem of abnormal anthropology is to show how the average way of a culture, or even of the human state, is neurotic and has become so. It is to show what of human nature has been "lost" and, practically, to devise experiments for its recovery. (The therapeutic part of anthropology and sociology is politics; but we see that politics—perhaps fortunately—does not devote itself to this at all.)

In reviewing the steps of evolution leading to modern man and our civilization, therefore, we lay the stress contrary to where it is usually laid: not on the increased power and achievement gained by each step of human development, but on the dangers incurred and the vulnerable points exposed, that then have become pathological in the débacle. The new powers require more complicated integrations, and these have often broken down.

5: Erect Posture, Freedom of Hands and Head

(1) Erect posture developed along with differentiation of the limbs and ultimately the fingers. This had great advantages for both orientation and manipulation. A large upright animal gets a long view. Established on broad feet, it can use its hands to get food and tear it, while the head is free; and to handle objects and its own body.

But on the other hand, the head is removed from close-perception, and the "close" senses, smell and taste, atrophy somewhat. The mouth and teeth become less useful for manipulation; as such, in an intensely manipulating animal, they tend to pass from felt awareness and response (e.g., there can be a gap between disgust and spontaneous rejection). The jaws and muzzle degenerate—and later will become one of the chief places of rigidity.

In brief, the entire field of the organism and its environment is immensely increased, both in largeness and in minute intricacy; but the closeness of contact is more problematic. And with erect posture comes the need to balance and the danger, so momentous in later psychology, of falling. The back is less flexible, and the head is more isolated from the rest of the body and from the ground.

(2) When the head is freer and less engaged, a sharper stereoscopic vision develops, able to appreciate perspective. The eyes and fingers cooperate in drawing outlines, so that the animal learns to see more shapes and to differentiate objects in his field. By outlining one differentiates experience into objects. Perspective, discrimination of objects, ability to handle: these greatly increase the number of connections among impressions and the deliberate selectivity among them. The cerebrum grows larger and likely the brightness of consciousness increases. The ability to isolate objects from their situations improves memory and is the beginning of abstracting.

But conversely, there is now likely to be occasional loss of immediacy, of the sense of ready flow with the environment. Images of objects and abstractions about them intervene: the man pauses, with heightened consciousness, for a more deliberate discrimination, but then may forget or be distracted from the goal, and the situation is unfinished. A certain pastness that may or may not be relevant increasingly colors the present.

Finally, one's own body too becomes an object—although later, for this is perceived very "closely."

6. Tools, Language, Sexual Differentiation, and Society

(3) When things and other persons have once become outlined and abstracted objects, they can enter into useful deliberate fixed and habitual relations with the self. Permanent tools are developed, along with the

ad hoc objects that were spontaneous extensions of the limbs; and denotative language is developed along with instinctive situational outcries. Objects are controlled, tools applied to them, and the tools too are objects and may be improved and their use learned and taught. Language too is learned. Spontaneous imitation is deliberately intensified, and the social bond tightens.

But of course the social bond pre-existed; there was communication and the manipulation of the physical and social environment. It is not the use of tools and language that brings persons together or workmen and objects together; they have already been in felt organized contact—the tools and language are convenient differentiations of the contact that exists. The danger that is incurred is this: that if the original felt unity weakens, these high-order abstractions—object, person, tool, word—will begin to be taken as the original ground of contact, as if it required some deliberate high-order mental activity in order to get in touch. Thus interpersonal relations become primarily verbal; or without a suitable tool a workman feels helpless. The differentiation that existed "along with" the underlying organization now exists *instead* of it. Then contact diminishes, speech loses feeling, and behavior loses grace.

(4) Language and tools combine with the earlier pre-verbal bonds of sex, nourishment, and imitation, to broaden the scope of society. But such new intricacies may upset the delicately balanced activities that are crucial to the animal's welfare. Consider, for example, how from remote phylogenetic antiquity we have inherited a sexual apparatus exquisitely complicated, involving the senses as excitants, and the motor responses of tumescence, embracing, and intromission, all nicely adjusted toward a mounting climax. (The so-called "adolescent sterility" [Ashley Montagu], the time between the first menstruation and fertility, seems to indicate a period of play and practice.) Besides its advantages of sexual selection and cross-breeding, all this complexity requires at least temporary partnerships: no animal is complete in its own skin. And the strong

emotional bonds of lactation, suckling, and fostering care tighten the sociality. Also, in higher phyla, the young animal acquires much of its behavior from imitative learning. Then consider how much depends on what delicate adjustments! Consider that the function of the orgasm (Reich), the essential periodic release of tensions, is bound with the workings of the finely-adjusted genital apparatus. It is clear both how important is the social manner of reproduction, and how vulnerable it makes the well-being of the animal.

7: Differentiations of Sensory, Motoric, and Vegatative

(5) Another critical development of fairly remote antiquity has been the separation of the motoric-muscular and sensoric-thought nerve centers. In animals like the dog sensation and motion cannot be much disengaged; this was long ago pointed out by Aristotle when he said that a dog can reason but it makes only practical syllogisms. The advantages of the looser connection in man are, of course, enormous: the ability to survey, hold back, cogitate, in brief to be deliberate and muscularly hold back the body while letting the senses and thoughts play, along with immediately spontaneously moving in smaller motions of the eyes, hands, vocal cords, etc.

But in neurosis this same division is fateful, for it is seized on in order to prevent spontaneity; and the ultimate practical unity of sense and motion is lost. The deliberation occurs "instead of" rather than "along with": the neurotic loses awareness that the smaller motions are taking place and preparing the larger motions.

(6) Primitively, the ties of sex, nourishment, and imitation are social but pre-personal: that is, they likely do not require a sense of the partners as objects or persons, but merely as what is contacted. But at the stage of tool-making, language, and other acts of abstraction, the social functions constitute society in our special human sense: a bond among persons. The per-

sons are formed by the social contacts they have, and they identify themselves with the social unity as a whole for their further activity. There is abstracted from the undifferentiated felt-self a notion, image, behavior, and feeling of the "self" that reflects the other persons. This is the society of the division of labor, in which persons deliberately use one another as tools. It is in this society that taboos and laws develop, bridling the organism in the interest of the super-organism, or better: keeping the persons as persons in interpersonal relationship as well as animals in contact. And this society is, of course, the bearer of what most anthropologists would consider the defining property of mankind, culture, the social inheritance surviving the generations.

The advantages of all this are obvious, and so are the disadvantages. (Here we can begin to speak not of "potential dangers" but of actual surviving troubles.) Controlled by taboos, the imitations become unassimilated introjections, society contained inside the self and ultimately invading the organism; the persons become merely persons *instead* of also animals in contact. The internalized authority lays open the way for institutional exploitation of man by man and of the many by the whole. The division of labor can be pursued in such a way that the work is senseless to the workers and is drudgery. The inherited culture can become a dead weight that one painfully learns, is forced to learn by the duteous elders, yet may never individually use.

8: Verbal Difficulties in this Exposition

It is instructive to notice how, in discussing this subject, verbal difficulties begin to arise: "man," "person," "self," "individual," "human animal," "organism" are sometimes interchangeable, sometimes necessary to distinguish. For example, it is deceptive to think of the "individuals" as primitive and combined in social relations, for there is no doubt that the existence of "individuals" comes about as the result of a very complicated society. Again, since it is meaningful to say that it is by organismic-self-regulation that one imitates, sympathizes, becomes "independent," and can learn arts and sciences, the expression "animal" contact cannot mean "merely" animal contact. Again, "persons" are reflections of an interpersonal whole, and "personality" is best taken as a formation of the self by a shared social attitude. Yet in an important sense the self, as the system of excitement, orientation, manipulation, and various identifications and alienations, is always original and creative.

These difficulties can, of course, be partly avoided by careful definition and consistent usage—and we try to be as consistent as we can. Yet partly they are inherent in the subject-matter, "Man," making himself in different ways. For instance, the early philosophic anthropologists of modern times, in the Seventeenth and Eighteenth Centuries, spoke usually of individuals compacting society; after Rousseau, the Nineteenth Century sociologists returned to society as primary; and it has been a great merit of psychoanalysis to restore these distinct concepts to a dynamic interaction. If the theory is often confusing and ambiguous, it may be that the nature too is confusing and ambiguous.

9: Symbols

We have now brought our history down to the last several thousand years, since the invention of writing and reading. Adapting himself to the vast accumulation of culture, both knowledge and technique, man is educated in very high abstractions. Abstractions of orientation, distant from concernful felt perception: sciences and systems of science. Abstractions of manipulation distant from muscular participation: systems of production and exchange and government. He lives in a world of symbols. He symbolically orients himself as a symbol to other symbols, and he symbolically manipulates other symbols. Where there were methods, now there is also methodology: everything is made the object of hypothesis and experiment, with a certain distance from engagement. This includes society, the taboos, the super-sensory, the religious hallucinations, and science and methodology itself, and Man himself. All this has given an enormous increase in scope and power, for the ability symbolically to fix what one used to be fully engaged in allows for a certain creative indifference.

The dangers in it are, unfortunately, not potential but realized. Symbolic structures—e.g., money or prestige, or the King's peace, or the advancement of learning—become the exclusive end of all activity, in which there is no animal satisfaction and may not even be personal satisfaction; yet apart from animal or at least personal interest there can be no stable intrinsic measure, but only bewilderment and standards that one can never achieve. Thus, economically, a vast mechanism is in operation that does not necessarily produce enough subsistence goods and could indeed, as Percival and Paul Goodman have pointed out in *Communitas,* proceed in almost as high gear without producing any subsistence at all, except that the producers and consumers would all be dead. A worker is crudely or skillfully fitted into a place in this mechanical symbol of plenty, but his work in it does not spring from any pleasure of workmanship or vocation. He may not understand what he is making, nor how, nor for whom. Endless energy is exhausted in the manipulation of marks on paper; rewards are given in kinds of paper, and prestige follows the possession of papers. Politically, in symbolic constitutional structures symbolic representatives indicate the will of the people as expressed in symbolic votes; almost no-one, any more, understands what it means to exert political initiative or come to a communal agreement. Emotionally, a few artists catch from real experience symbols of passion and sensory excitement; these symbols are abstracted and stereotyped by commercial imitators; and people make love or adventure according to these norms of glamour. Medical scientists and social-workers provide other symbols of emotion and security, and people make love, enjoy recreation, and so forth according to prescription. In engineering, control over space, time, and power is symbolically achieved by making it easier to go to less interesting places and easier to get less desirable goods. In pure science, awareness is focussed on every detail except the psychosomatic fear and self-conquest of the activity itself, so that, for instance, when there is a question of making certain lethal weapons, the issue debated is whether the need of a country to get superiority over the enemy outweighs the duty of a scientist to publicize his findings; but the simpler reactions of compassion, flight, defiance are not operative at all.

In these conditions it is not surprising that persons toy with the sadomasochism of dictatorships and wars, where there is at least control of man by man instead of by symbols, and where there is suffering in the flesh.

10: Neurotic Split

So finally we come to a very recent acquisition of mankind, the neurotically split personality as a means of achieving equilibrium. Faced with a chronic threat to any functioning at all, the organism falls back on its safety-devices of blotting-out, hallucination, displacement, isolation, flight, regression; and man essays to make "living on his nerves" a new evolutionary achievement.

In the early stages there were developments that the healthy organism could each time merge into a new integrated whole. But now it is as if neurotics went back and singled out the vulnerable points of the past development of the race: the task is not to integrate erect posture into animal life, but to act on the one hand as if the head stood in the air by itself and on the other hand as if there were no erect posture or no head at all; and so with the other developments. The potential "dangers" have become factual symptoms: contactlessness, isolation, fear of falling, impotence, inferiority, verbalizing, and affectlessness.

It remains to be seen whether or not this neurotic turn is a viable destiny for our species.

11: Golden Age, Civilization, and Introjections

We have been generally defining the neurotic adjustments here as those which employ the new power "instead of" the previous nature, which is repressed, rather than "along with" it, in a new integration. The repressed unused natures then tend to return as Images of the Golden Age, or Paradise; or as theories of the Happy Primitive. We can see how great poets, like Homer and Shakespeare, devoted themselves to glorifying precisely the virtues of the previous era, as if it were their chief function to keep people from forgetting what it used to be to be a man.

And at best, indeed, the conditions of advancing civilized life seem to make important powers of human nature not only neurotically unused but rationally unusable. Civil security and technical plenty, for instance, are not very appropriate to an animal that hunts and perhaps needs the excitement of hunting to enliven its full powers. It is not surprising if such an animal should often complicate quite irrelevant needs—e.g., sexuality—with danger and hunting, in order to rouse excitement.

Further, it is likely that there is at present an irreconcilable conflict between quite desirable social harmony and quite desirable individual expression. If we are in such a transitional stage toward a tighter sociality, then there will in individuals be many social traits that must appear as unassimilable introjections, neurotic and inferior to the rival individual claims. Our heroic ethical standards (that come from the inspiriting dreams of creative artists) certainly tend to look backward to the more animal, sexual, personal, valorous, honorable, etc.; our behavior is quite otherwise and lacks excitement.

On the other hand, it is also likely (even if the different likelihoods are contradictory) that these "irreconcilable" conflicts have always been, not only at present, the human condition; and that the attendant suffering and motion toward an unknown solution are the grounds of human excitement.

12: Conclusion

However it is, "human nature" is a potentiality. It can be known only as it has been actualized in achievement and history, and as it makes itself today.

The question may quite seriously be asked, by what criterion does one prefer to regard "human nature" as what is actual in the spontaneity of children, in the works of heroes, the culture of classic eras, the community of simple folk, the feeling of lovers, the sharp awareness and miraculous skill of some people in emergencies? Neurosis is also a response of human nature and is now epidemic and normal, and perhaps has a viable social future.

We cannot answer the question. But a medical psychologist proceeds according to three criteria: (1) the health of the body, known by a definite standard, (2) the progress of the patient toward helping himself, and (3) the elasticity of the figure/background formation.

VII

VERBALIZING AND POETRY

Among the evolutionary developments of mankind, speech is of especial importance and deserves a separate chapter. As with the other developments, the neurotic abuse consists in using a form of speech that is "instead of" rather than "along with" the underlying powers. This is the isolation of the verbal personality.

1: Social, Interpersonal, and Personal

People ordinarily notice their emotional conflicts with regard to ethical demands and responsibilities: they find confronted within themselves their "personal" wishes and their societal roles. The conflict, with its subsequent inhibition or guilt, is considered to be between the "individual" and "society." The chapters following this one will be devoted to the structure of such incorporated alien standards: conforming and anti-social, aggression and self-conquest.

But as we have already pointed out, the differentiation of the individual in the organism/environment field is already a late development. Social relations, like dependency, communication, imitation, object-love, are original in any human field, long prior to one's recognizing oneself as an idiosyncratic person or identifying the others as constituting society. Personality is a structure created out of such early interpersonal relationships; and in its formation there has usually already been the incorporation of an enormous amount of alien, unassimilated or even unassimilable material (and this, of course, makes the later conflicts between individual and society so much the more insoluble).

From one angle, it is useful to define "personality" as a structure of speech habits and consider it as a creative act of the second and third years; most thinking is subvocal speaking; basic beliefs are importantly habits of syntax and style; and almost all evaluation that does not spring directly from organic appetites is likely to be a set of rhetorical attitudes. To define in this way is not to belittle or explain away personality, for speech is itself a profound spontaneous activity. A child forming his personality by learning to speak is making a spectacular achievement, and from antiquity philosophers have felt that education is primarily learning humane speech and letters, e.g., "grammar, rhetoric, and dialectic" or "classics and scientific method."

That is, we may think of the sequence (a) preverbal social relations of the organism, (b) the formation of a verbal personality in the organism/environment field, (c) the subsequent relations of this personality with the others. Clearly the right cultivation of speech is one that keeps this sequence flexibly open and creative throughout: habits that allow what is pre-verbal to flow freely and that can learn from the others and be altered.

But just as in our culture as a whole there has grown up a symbolic culture devoid of contact or affect, isolated from animal satisfaction and spontaneous social invention, so in each self, when the growth of the original interpersonal relations has been disturbed and the conflicts not fought through but pacified in a premature truce incorporating alien standards, there is formed a "verbalizing" personality, a speech that is insensitive, prosy, affectless, monotonous, stereotyped in content, inflexible in rhetorical attitude, mechanical in syntax, meaningless. This is the reaction to or identification with an accepted alien and unassimilated speech. And if we concentrate awareness on these "mere" habits of speech, we meet extraordinary evasions, making of alibis, and finally acute anxiety—much more than the protestations and apologies accompanying the revealing of important "moral" lapses. For to call attention to speech (or to clothes) is indeed a *personal* affront.

But the difficulty is that, disgusted with the customary empty symbolizing and verbalizing, recent philosophers of language set up astringent norms of speech that are even more stereotyped and affectless; and some psychotherapists give up in despair and try to by-pass speaking altogether, as if only inner silence and non-verbal behavior were potentially healthy. But the contrary of neurotic verbalizing is various and creative speech; it is neither scientific semantics nor silence; it is poetry.

2: Contactful Speech and Poetry

Speech is good contact when it draws energy from and makes a structure of the three grammatical persons, I, Thou, and It; the speaker, the one spoken to, and the matter spoken about; when there is a need—to communicate—something. As properties of the flow of speech these three persons are (1) the style and especially the rhythm, animation, and climax, expressing the organic need of the speaker; (2) the rhetorical attitude effective in the interpersonal situation (e.g., wooing, denouncing, teaching, bullying); (3) the content, or truth to the impersonal objects spoken about.

Again, especially as the contact of organism and environment becomes closer, the following powers interact:

1. The sounding speech—the physical exercise of uttering and hearing.
2. Thought—the filling out with content of various skeletal organizations.
3. Subvocal speech—repeated unfinished verbal situations.
4. Pre-personal social communication (e.g., outcries) and silent awareness (images, body-feeling, etc.).

In speech of good contact, these levels cohere in the present actuality. The thought is directed to efficient orientation and manipulation; the present situation is taken as an adequate possible field for solving an unfinished situation; the social animal is expressing itself; the physical exercise initiates the flow as a forepleasure and makes the whole an environmental reality.

Bearing in mind these psychological levels of speaking, thought, subvocal speech, and outcries and silent awareness, let us now consider poetry as a fine art as distinguished from ordinary contactful speech, and then contrast both of these with neurotic verbalizing.

A poem is a special case of good speech. In a poem, as with other good speech, the three persons, the content, the attitude and character, and the tone and rhythm, mutually express one another, and this makes the structural unity of the poem. For example, character is largely choice of vocabulary and syntax, but these rise and fall with the subject and are rhythmically distorted from the expected by feeling; or again, the rhythm gathers climactic urgency, the attitude becomes more direct, and the proposition is proved; and so forth. But the speaking activity of the poet is, as the philosophers say, "an end in itself"; that is, just by the behavior of the overt speech, just by handling the medium, he solves his problem. Unlike ordinary good speech, the activity is not instrumental in a further social situation, as to persuade the listener, to entertain him, to inform of something, in order to manipulate him for the solution of the problem.

Essentially, the poet's is the special case where the problem is to solve an "inner conflict" (as Freud said, the art-work replaces the symptom): the poet is concentrating on some unfinished subvocal speech and its subsequent thoughts; by freely playing with his present words he at last finishes an unfinished verbal scene, he in fact utters the complaint, the denunciation, the declaration of love, the self-reproach, that he should have uttered; now at last he freely draws on the underlying organic need and he finds the words. We must therefore notice accurately what the poet's I, Thou, and It are in his present actuality. His Thou, his audience, is not some visible person nor the general public, but an "ideal audience": that is, it is nothing but assuming the appropriate attitude and character (choosing a genre and diction) that let the unfinished speech flow with precision and force. His content is not a present truth of experience to be conveyed, but he finds in experience or memory or fancy a symbol that in fact excites him without his (or our) needing to know its latent content. His I is his style in its present use, it is not his biography.

At the same time as the overt words are forming, the poet can maintain the silent awareness of image, feeling, memory, etc., and also the pure attitudes of social communication, clarity and verbal responsibility. Thus instead of being verbal stereotypes, the words are plastically destroyed and combined toward a more vital figure. Poetry is therefore the exact contrary of neurotic verbalizing, for it is speech as an organic problem-solving activity, it is a form of concentration; whereas verbalizing is speech that attempts to dissipate energy in the speaking, suppressing the organic need and repeating, rather than concentrating on, an unfinished subvocal scene.

On the other hand, poetry is distinguished from ordinary contactful speech—e.g., good conversational prose—simply as one species of a class: a poem solves a problem that can be solved by verbal invention alone, whereas most speech occurs in situations where the solution requires also other kinds of behavior, the response of the listener, and so forth. It follows that in poetry—where the entire actuality must be carried by the speaking—the vitality of the speech is accentuated: it is more rhythmic, more precise, more feelingful, more imagistic, etc.; and most important of all, a poem has a beginning, a middle, and an end; it finishes the situation. Other contactful speech can be rougher and more approximate; it can rely on non-verbal means such as gesture; it need barely mention what is pressing for expression; and it breaks off into non-verbal behavior.

3. Verbalizing and Poetry

When divorced from its use as an instrument in a further social situation, or again from its own rules as a vital poetic activity, speech easily mirrors any and all experience. It is easy for a person to be deceived that he is feeling or even doing something if he speaks or "thinks" of feeling and doing it. So verbalizing easily serves as a substitute for life; it is a ready means by which an introjected alien personality, with its beliefs and attitudes, can live instead of oneself. (The only inconvenience is that the verbalized meal, encounter, etc., does not give nourishment, sexual pleasure, etc.) Thus, to revert to a previous discussion, most apparent reminiscing and planning is not really memory or anticipation at all, which are forms of the imagination, but it is something that one's concept of oneself is telling to oneself; and most indignation and judgment have little to do with felt anger or rational measure but are an exercise of mama's and papa's voices.

It is not *that* the verbalizer talks, but *how* he talks. With regard to the three grammatical persons, I, Thou, and It, he manifests a rigidity, fixation, or stereotype that abstracts only a meager part of the possibilities of the actual situation, enough to maintain a social face and avoid the anxiety and embarrassment of silence, revelation, or self-assertion; and also enough to exhaust the speech-energy so that one does not hear the unfinished subvocal scenes that might otherwise become clamorous. That is, instead of being a means of communication or expression, verbalizing protects one's isolation from both the environment and the organism.

The lack of contact with the I is often spectacularly observable in the division of the body into a sounding mouth with rigid rapid lips and tongue and an unresonant vocalism, with all the rest of the body kept at bay uninvolved; or sometimes the eyes and a few gestures from the wrists or the elbows join the verbalizing mouth; or sometimes one eye, while the other is glassy, wandering, or disapproving the chatter; or the face is divided into two halves. The words come in bursts irrelevant to the breathing, and the tone is monotonous. In poetic speech, on the other hand, the rhythm is given by pulses of breathing (verses), by the gaits of locomotion and dance (meters), by syllogism, antithesis, or other beats of thought (stanzas and paragraphs), and by the orgastic intensification of feeling (climax), then diminishing into silence. Variety of tone and richness of overtone are the potentiality of ringing in the primitive outcries as occasion arises. The verbalizer rarely hears his own voice, when he listens to it he is surprised; but the poet attends to the subvocal murmurs and whispers, he makes them audible, criticizes the sound and goes back over it. (There is an in-between character, a kind of interpretative actor without a poet, who notices nothing but the sound of his voice, modulates the tone and tastes the words; presumably he is getting a real oral satisfaction out of it, holding the center of the floor while the audience steals away.)

The rhetorical attitude, the Thou, of the verbalizer is irrelevant to the actual social scene, but the tone that sounds shows that he is fixedly acting out some unfinished subvocal situation. No matter what the occasion, the voice is complaining or reproaching or condemning, or contrariwise wrangling or making an alibi or vindicating itself. In the repetition of this scene —perhaps alternately playing both roles—the rest of the organism is rigidly immobilized. The poet, we have said, capitalizes on the subvocal situation: concentrating on it, he finds the right audience, the ideal audience of literature; he plastically molds the language to express the relevant organic need and come to an insight, a solution. The subvocal alien is thus assimilated again to his own personality. It is often asserted that the art-work does not *solve* any problem or solves it only temporarily, because the artist does not know the latent content of his symbol; and if this were so, poetry would again be an obsessive exhaustion of energy in a repeating situation, like verbalizing. This is both true and false: the problem that the artist does not solve is the one that makes him only an artist, free only in the vital activity of speaking but unable to use the words also instrumentally in further free acts; and many poets feel the obsessiveness of their art in this respect—finishing a work they are exhausted, and still have not regained a lost paradise. (It is not to be seen, by the way, that many other activities—even psychotherapy—win us that lost paradise.) But as for the particular subvocal problems, they *are* really solved, one by one; the proof is that the successive art-works are fundamentally different, there is a deepening of the art-problem; and indeed, this activity sometimes proceeds so far that the poet is finally forced to confront life-problems that he cannot solve by artistic means alone.

In the content, the It, of his speech, the verbalizer is in a dilemma: he must stick to the facts of actuality in order not to seem demented or be ridiculous, yet they are not his real concern nor can he allow himself to notice them too closely, with sense and feeling, for then they would, since any reality is dynamic, disrupt his truce, destroy his projections and rationalizations, and arouse anxiety; the actual life would invade the substitute life. The verbalizer bores because he means to bore, to be let alone. The compromise is to speak in stereotypes, vague abstractions or superficial particularity, or other ways of saying the truth and not saying anything at all. (Meantime, of course, the content is energized by projections of his unfelt needs.) The poet again makes just the contrary choice of content: the actual truth is freely distorted and made a symbol for the underlying concern; he does not hesitate to lie or be irrational; and he richly develops the symbols with a lively use of his senses, keenly noticing sights, scents, and sounds, and empathizing with, projecting *himself* into, emotional situations, rather than alienating his own feelings and projecting *them*.

Finally, the verbalizer is embarrassed by the activity of speaking itself. He uses meaningless expressions to gain assurance, "Don't you think?" "You know," "In my opinion," or he fills out the silence with grunts; he is self-conscious of the syntax; and he hedges his speech with a literary frame before he ventures his own remarks, such as they are, like "It may be far-fetched, but it seems to me that . . ." But for the poet the handling of the words is the activity itself; the form, e.g., the sonnet, is not a frame but integral to the plot; he is responsible to the function of syntax but free with the forms; and as he progresses in the art, his vocabulary becomes more and more his own—more idiosyncratic if his subvocal problems are obscure and hard for him to catch, more classical if they are the problems he recognizes in others.

4: Critique of Free-Association as a Technique of Therapy

Let us now consider a special case of verbalizing: the experiment of free-association as practiced by orthodox psychoanalysis. What we want to call attention to is the difference between the patient's behavior in this technique and the therapist's; and from this critique we shall again come to conclusions about the nature of good speech similar to those we have been advancing.

In free-association the patient is given some content A to begin with, usually the detail of a dream he has had; he associates to it another word B—whatever comes to his tongue—and to this another word C, and so on. He "freely" associates, that is he does not try to organize the series to make sense or whole-meanings, or to solve a problem. Also he must not censor (decline to make the association because of his criticism of the words as they flow). Such a behavior can be called the limiting or ideal case of verbalizing.

According to the older association-theory, the sequence of words would follow the law: If A has frequently occurred with B, or has a similarity to it, or at furthest a similarity to what has frequently occurred, then there is a tendency for it to call up B, and so likewise B calls up C, and so on. The whole chain would be analyzed and "explained" piecemeal in this way. It was the genius of psychoanalysis to show that the free-associations did not in fact follow merely by this law of piecemeal association; rather they had a tendency to organize themselves in meaningful wholes or clusters, and to proceed in a certain direction, and that these clusters and directions had an important meaningful relation to the original stimulus, the dream detail, and to the underlying problem of the patient. The patient was not in fact "mechanically" producing the stream but was, though unaware of it, expressing certain tendencies, circling back to certain emotional needs, and trying to fill out an unfinished figure. This was, of course, a capital proof of the existence of the unconscious; the question is whether it is useful for psychotherapy.

Note that the *therapist* is concentrating on the stream and creating whole figures in it (finding and making them): he attends to the clusters, times the associations that lag and indicate resistance, notices the tone and facial expression. In this way he becomes aware of something about the patient, namely the patient's behavior in unawareness.

But the goal of psychotherapy is not for the therapist to become aware of something about the patient, but for the patient to become aware of himself. Therefore there must then begin the process by which the therapist *explains* to the patient what he (the T) now knows about him (the P). In this way the patient acquires much interesting knowledge about himself, there is no doubt of it; but it is a question whether or not he thereby increases his awareness of himself. For the knowledge-about has a certain abstractness, it is not concernful; and it occurs again in his customary context of introjecting the wisdom of an authority. If he could come to recognize the object of knowledge as *himself*, then this kind of knowledge—that one knew and did not know one knew—would be close and terribly concernful. The goal of therapy is to make him recognize this, but this is just where we started in the first place.

The problem is that in the activity that *he* was engaged in, he had been verbalizing a stream of meaningless words. That activity did not especially add to his experience at all—on the contrary, it was a fair facsimile of a usual experience: he knows himself in that role. The rule Do Not Censor, relieved him from responsibility for the words—also not an unusual attitude for many people. But the knowledge that is now explained to him is quite alien to *that* activity; it belongs to quite a different usual activity: namely taking the unpleasant truth and swallowing it whole; and again the old man is saying terrible things about him. (But perhaps it is a nicer man, so he may think, as Stekel used to say, "I'll get well just to please the old fool." This is a method of cure, but it is not as such free-association.)

The danger of the technique would be that, bracketing off the self that is responsible, feels concern, and makes decisions, the patient might relate his new knowledge strictly to his verbalizing, pleasantly tinged with the euphoria of a warm atmosphere and a friendly paternal audience. Then, instead of healing the split, the technique would confuse it further.

5: Free-Association as an Experiment in Language

But let us consider the useful and beautiful aspects of free-association: taking it for what it is in itself, as a mode of language.

To begin with, the associations circle round a dream detail. Let us assume that the patient accepts the dream as his own, remembers and can say that he dreamt it rather than that a dream came to him. If now he can connect new words and thoughts with that act, there is a great enrichment of language. The dream speaks in the image-language of childhood; the advantage is not to recollect the infantile content, but to learn again something of the feeling and attitude of child speech, to recapture the mood of eidetic vision, and connect the verbal and pre-verbal. But from this point of view, the best exercise would perhaps be not free-association *from* the image and application of cold knowledge *to* the image, but just the contrary: careful literary and pictorial representation of it (surrealism).

Yet something can be said for the free-associating itself. It is salutary for a patient who is too scrupulous and prosy in his speech to babble and find the heavens do not fall. This is the playful matrix of poetry: to let the speech apparently develop itself, from image to thought to rhyme to exclamation to image to rhyme, however it comes, but at the same time to feel that it is *oneself* who is speaking, it is not automatic speech. But here again the best exercise would perhaps be a more direct one: to concentrate on the speech act while free-associating or uttering nonsense syllables or snatches of song.

There is a more essential virtue in free-association, closer to the use classically made of it in psychoanalysis. The reason the patient is asked to free-associate rather than to tell his story and answer questions is, of course, that his habitual discourse is neurotically rigid, it is a false integration of his experience. The figure he is aware of is confused, dark, and uninteresting because the background contains other repressed figures of which he is unaware but that distract his attention, absorb energy, and prevent creative development. The free-association disrupts this frozen relation of figure and ground, and allows other things to become foreground. The therapist notes them down, but what is the advantage to the patient? It is not, we have seen, that the new figures can be made to cohere with his habitual figure of his experience, for the attitude of free-associating is dissociated from that experience. But it is this: he learns that something, not known as his, comes from his darkness and yet is meaningful; thereby perhaps *he* is encouraged to explore, to regard his unawareness as terra incognita but not chaos. From this point of view, he must of course be made a partner in the interpreting. The thought here is that the maxim,

Know Thyself, is a humane ethics: it is not something done to one in trouble, but something one does for oneself as a human. The therapist's arcane attitude toward the interpretation, withholding it or doling it out at the right moment, is contrary to this. It does not follow for the analyst to reveal all his interpretations; rather, to interpret very little, but to give the patient the *tools* of the analyst. It should be obvious that the appalling incuriosity of people is an epidemic and neurotic symptom. Socrates knew that this was due to fear of self-knowledge (Freud emphasized the particular fear of the sexual knowledge kept from children). Then it is unwise to conduct a course of healing in a context that confirms the split: the therapist, the grownup, knows everything; and oneself can never know the secret unless told. But it is the possession of tools that overcomes the sense of being excluded.

Finally, let us contrast the three modes of speech used in the free-association experiment: the patient free-associating, the therapist learning something and telling it to himself, and the therapist explaining what he knows to the patient. Here we have three different sets of words relating to an existing case. To the patient, his associations are the equivalent of nonsense-syllables: they are pure verbalizing. From these words, however, the therapist becomes aware of the patient, and this awareness, formulated in sentences that he tells to himself, state an existing case, they are truth. Yet in this context, the same sentences, told to the patient, are no longer true—neither true to the patient nor now to the therapist: they are not true because they do not work, they have no value as proof, they are *mere* abstractions. To a logician this factor, of the therapist's concern or the patient's unconcern, of accepting the propositions into one's reality or not accepting them, might seem irrelevant; he would say it is a merely "psychological" question, therapeutically momentous but logically insignificant, whether or not the patient grasps the truth of the interpretation, or on what level he grasps it. But we should rather put it as follows: the "existing case" here is as yet potential, it is an abstraction; and whether there is one actuality or quite a different actuality to have a "truth" of, depends on the words of the formulation, the concern, and the attitude with which it is learned.

To a logician trained in physics, the "right" use of words, the speech that is most meaningful about "reality," has a meager vocabulary of thing-symbols, an analytic syntax expressing the complex by additions, and an absence of passional tone; and he would reform language in this direction (e.g., toward Basic English). But to a psychologist concerned with the affectlessness of our times, right speech has just the opposite traits: it is full of the passional tones of childhood speech, its words are complex functional structures like the words of primitives, and its syntax is poetry.

6: Philosophies of Language-Reform

Given the modern epidemics of symbolic social institutions instead of communities, and verbalizing instead of experience, there have been numerous attempts to reform language, by rhetorical analysis and logical analysis. The underlying rhetorical motives of the speaker are brought to light; and by empirical criticism, empty stereotypes and abstractions are measured and deflated against the standard of concrete things and behavior. For our purposes we may summarize these philosophies of good language as "empirical," "operational," and "instrumental."

Empirical language reduces the good use of words to signs for either percepts or observable phenomena or easily manipulable objects and simple behaviors. (The highest degree of concreteness is generally assigned to inanimate "physical" objects, but this is a metaphysical prejudice; Auguste Comte, for instance, considered social relations and institutions to give the most concrete protocols.) The thing-words are then synthesized by a simple logic of combination.

Operational languages lay the primary emphasis on the manipulation-of-the-things, rather than the things themselves. This provides at least a sensory-motor unity as basic.

Instrumental languages require that the basic unities include also the ends-in-view, therefore the motives and rhetorical attitudes of the speech.

There is thus a series more and more inclusive of the factors of contact; yet no such analytic language can reach contactful speech itself, for contactful speech is partly creative of the actuality, and the creative use of words plastically destroys and remolds the words: no list of basic words can be given only from the things, the non-verbal behavior, or the ends-in-view. Contact involves orientation, manipulation, and feeling—and feeling is verbally given especially in rhythm, tone, and the choice and distortion of the words and syntax. The norms and protocols of good speech cannot be analyzed to simple concrete things and drives—these are not concrete enough; they are given in concrete and often very complicated whole-structures. To put it bluntly, linguistic reform—the cure of empty symbols and verbalizing—is possible only by learning the structure of poetry and humane letters, and finally by making poetry and making the common speech poetic.

The matter has a philosophical importance far beyond linguistic reform. There is a continual search, precisely among empiricists and instrumentalists, for a "naturalistic ethics," one that will involve no norms outside the on-going processes. But if the criteria of correct language are so chosen that the feelingful and creative aspects of speech do not lend to the "meaning," are "merely subjective," then no such ethics is possible in principle, for no evaluation invites assent on logical grounds. On the other hand, if it is once understood—as should be obvious—that feelings are not isolated impulses but structured evidence of reality, namely of the interaction of the organism/environment field, for which there is no other direct evidence except feeling; and further, that a complicated creative achieving is even stronger evidence of reality; then the rules of the language can be made so that every contactful speech is meaningful, and then evaluation can be logically grounded.

VIII

THE ANTI-SOCIAL AND
AGGRESSION

1: Social and Anti-Social

We have been at pains to show that in the organism before it can be called a personality at all, and in the formation of personality, the social factors are essential. Let us now for a couple of chapters consider "Society" in the more usual sense, the relations and institutions of the persons. It is in this sense that we can speak of a conflict between the individual and society and call certain behavior "anti-social." In this sense, too, we must certainly call certain mores and institutions of society "anti-personal."

The underlying social nature of the organism and the forming personality—fostering and dependency, communication, imitation and learning, love-choices and companionship, passions of sympathy and antipathy, mutual aid and certain rivalries—all this is extremely conservative, repressible but ineradicable. And it is meaningless to think of an organism possessing drives which are "anti-social" in this sense, opposed to his social nature, for this would be a conserved inner contradiction; it would not be conserved. But there are, rather, difficulties of individual development, of growing-up, of realizing all of one's nature.

The society of persons, however, is largely an artifact, like the verbal personalities themselves. It is continually being changed in every detail; indeed, to initiate social changes, to create institutional artifacts, is probably part of the underlying conservative social nature, repressed in any society one chooses to consider. In this sense, a personal behavior is meaningfully "anti-social" if it tends to destroy something of the mores, institutions, or personality current at the time and place. In therapy we must assume that a delinquent behavior that contradicts a person's social nature is alterable, and the delinquent aspects of it will vanish with further integration. But with a delinquent behavior that is merely anti-social, contradicts the social artifact, it is always a question whether with further integration it may not become more pronounced and the person try harder not to adjust himself to society but to adjust society to himself.

2: Changes in the Anti-Social

In considering the anti-social, let us first distinguish what the neurotic considers anti-social from what is anti-social.

Any drive or aim that we have but will not accept as our own, that we keep unaware or project onto others, we fear to be anti-social. Obviously, for we inhibited it and drove it from awareness because it did not cohere with an acceptable picture of ourselves, and this picture of ourselves was an identification with, an imitation of, those authoritative persons who constituted our first society. But of course when the drive is released and accepted as part of ourselves, it turns out to be much less anti-social; we suddenly see that it is not unusual, is more or less accepted, in our adult society—and the destructive intensity that we attributed to it is less than we feared. An impulse that was vaguely felt to be hellish or murderous turns out to be a simple desire to avoid or reject something, and no-one cares whether we do or not. But it was the repression itself that (a) made the idea a persistent threat, (b) obscured its limited intent and made us not see the social actuality, (c) painted on the lurid colors of the forbidden, and (d) itself created the idea of destructiveness, for the repression is an aggression against the self and this aggression was attributed to the drive. (To cite the classic instance: in 1895 Freud thought that masturbation caused neurasthenia; later he found that it was guilty masturbation, the attempt to repress masturbation and the inhibition of the orgastic pleasure, that caused neurasthenia. Thus it was the very fear of the damage, mistaken medicine abetting the sexual taboo, that caused the damage.) Since Freud first wrote, the "contents of the id" have become less hellish, more tractable. Likely he would not now have felt called on to use that vaunting motto,

Flectere si nequeo superos, Acheronta movebo

—which would have been a pity.

Yet the neurotic estimate is also in the right. Theorists have gone too far in showing that the underlying drives are "good" and "social"; they have tried too hard to be on the side of the angels. What has in fact happened is that in the past fifty years there has been an extraordinary revolution in social mores and evaluation, so that much that was considered wicked is not now considered wicked. It is not that certain behavior is now acceptable because it is seen to be good or social or harmless, but that it is considered good, etc. because it is now an accepted part of the picture of humanity. Man does not strive to be good; the good is what it is human to strive for. To put this another way, certain "contents of the id" were hellish not only because the repression made them so in the four ways mentioned above, but because also (e) they contained a residue that was really destructive of the then social norms, it was real temptation or vice—and it was real social pressure, passed through the early authorities, that led to the neurotic repression.

Where the repressed temptation was fairly universally present, however, when once it was revealed as common and somewhat accepted, it made its way in the open with astonishing rapidity; becoming public and more or less satisfied, it lost its hellish aspects; and in a generation the social norm has changed. Indeed it is remarkable with what unanimity society comes to a new picture of itself as a whole; one would have expected parts of the moral code to be more tenaciously conservative (but of course there has been the cooperation of every kind of social factor: changed economy, urbanism, international communication, increased standard of living, etc.). It is only by visiting a very provincial community, or by picking up an 1890 manual of child-care or an essay on "Christianity and the Theater," that one realizes the sharpness of the change. And what is capital is this: the older attitude is not necessarily lurid, exaggerated, nor especially ignorant; rather it is often a sober well-considered judgment that something is inadvisable or destructive that we now hold to be useful or salutary. For instance, it used to be seen with perfect clarity that strict toilet-training is useful to form ruly character; this is by no means ignorant, it is probably true. But they said, therefore *do* it; and we say, therefore *don't* do it. One reason for the change, for example, is that in our present economy and technology, the old standard of closeness, laboriousness, and duty would be socially injurious.

Freud took seriously this hostile residue, that which was in fact socially destructive. He kept warning of the social resistance to psychoanalysis. If our modern mental-hygienists find that what they release is invariably good and not anti-social, and that therefore they need not encounter resistance among the liberal and tolerant, it is simply that they are fighting battles already mainly won and are engaging in, no doubt necessary, mopping up. But aggressive psychotherapy is inevitably a social risk. This ought to be obvious, for social pressures do not deform organismic-self-regulation that is "good" and "not anti-social" when it is properly understood and said with the acceptable words; society forbids what is destructive of society. There is not a semantical mistake but a genuine conflict.

3: Unequal Progress and Social Reaction

Let us consider two quite spectacular recent changes in mores in which psychoanalysis has played a leading role: the affirmative attitude toward sexual pleasure and the permissive attitude in child-care. These changes are now so widespread that they should be cumulative; that is, there should be enough actual satisfaction and self-regulation (in certain spheres) quite generally to diminish public resentment and that projection of bogey-men; therefore the taboos should become still less enforced, and there should be still more satisfaction and self-regulation, and so forth. Especially in the case of children, the permission of thumbsucking, the more self-regulating standards of nourishment, the permission of masturbation, the relaxation of toilet-training, the recognition of the need for body-contact and suckling, the omission of corporal punishment, all these ought to show fruit in the happiness of the rising generation. But let us scrutinize the case more closely.

We have here an interesting example of unequal development, the advance in some respects toward self-regulation while maintaining, and even increasing, a neurotic deliberateness in other respects. How does society adjust itself to attain a new equilibrium in the unequal development, to prevent the revolutionary dynamism latent in any new freedom—for any freedom would be expected to release energy and lead to a heightened struggle. The effort of society is to isolate, compartment, and draw the teeth of the "threat from below."

Thus, the increase in the quantity of fairly unrestrained sexuality has been accompanied by a decrease in the excitement and depth of the pleasure. What does this mean? It has been argued that deprivation as such is necessary for the accumulation of tension; but organismic-self-regulation ought to suffice to measure the times of appetite and discharge without external interventions. It is said that faddish imitation and "overindulgence" cheapen sexual pleasure; this is true, but if there were more satisfactions, more contact and love, there would be less compulsive and automatic indulgence; and the question we are asking is, *why* is there less satisfaction, etc.? It is wiser to consider this particular de-sensitizing as similar in kind to the rest of the desensitizing, contactlessness, and affectlessness now epidemic. They are the result of anxiety and shock. In the unequal development, the release of sexuality has come up against a block of what is not released; anxiety is aroused; the acts are performed, but the meaning and the feeling is withdrawn. Not fully completed, the acts are repeated. Guiltiness is generated by anxiety and lack of satisfaction. And so forth.

A chief block, we are shortly going to argue, is the inhibition of aggression. And this is obvious anyway from the fact that the commercial exploitation of sexuality, in the movies, novels, comic-strips, etc. (as Legman-Keith has demonstrated), concentrates on sadism and murder. (The style of this kind of commercialized dream is always an unerring index of what goes on, for it has no other criterion but to meet the demand and sell.)

A chief social device for isolating sexuality is, paradoxically, the healthful, sane, scientific attitude of sex-education on the part of educators and progressive parents. This attitude sterilizes sexuality and makes official, authoritative, and almost mandatory what by its nature is capricious, non-rational, and psychologically explosive (though organically self-limiting). Sexuality is organically periodical, no doubt, but it is not by prescription that one loves. It was against this isolation that Rank warned when he said that the place to learn the facts of life was in the gutter, where their mystery was respected, and blasphemed—as only true believers blaspheme. It is now taught that sexuality is beautiful and ecstatic and not "dirty"; but of course it is, literally, dirty, *inter urinas et faeces;* and to *teach* that it is ecstatic (rather than to let this be the surprise of an occasion) must, in the vast majority of persons whose aggressions are blocked and who therefore cannot give in themselves nor destroy resistance in others, only cause disappointment and make them ask, "What, is it only this?" It is far better, permitting everything, to say nothing at all. But the so-called wholesome attitude, that turns an act of life into a practice of hygiene, is a means of control and compartmenting.

Of course the pioneer sex-educators were revolutionaries; they were bent on undoing the contemporary repression and unmasking the hypocrisy; therefore, they shrewdly seized on all the good and angelic words. But these same words are now a new taboo—"sex is beautiful, keep it clean"—they are a social defense-in-depth. This is why deprivation and the forbidden seem to lead to more intense sexual excitement; it is not that the organism needs these extrinsic aids, but that, in the blocked organism, they prevent compartmenting, they keep open the connections to resentment and rage and the unaware aggression against authority and, at a very deep level, to the desperate risking of the self. For at the moment that one is defying the taboo and running the fatal danger, one is likely to have a flash of spontaneous joy.

The permissive attitude in child-care, again, is a delicious study in unequal development and the social counter-defenses; only a comic genius like Aristophanes could really do it justice. Consider simply that, on the one hand, our generation has learned to unblock much of the noisy savagery of children; and on the other we have tightened the regimental order of all our physical and social environment. We have minimum housing in big cities—and neat playgrounds that no self-respecting boy would be seen dead in. Naturally the parents are flattened in-between. The astonishing overestimation of children in our culture, that would have baffled the Greeks or the gentry of the Renaissance, is nothing but the reaction to the repression of the spontaneity of the adults (including the spontaneous urge to slaughter their children). Also, we are overcome with our own inferiority, and identify with the children and try to protect their native vigor. Then as the children grow up, they have to make a more and more deliberate and complicated adjustment to the civilization of science, technique, and super-government. Thus the period of dependency is necessarily longer and longer. The children are allowed every freedom except the essential one of being allowed to grow up and exercise economic and domestic initiative. They do not finish going to school.

The contradictory compartments are apparent: in progressive homes and schools we encourage self-regulation, lively curiosity, learning by doing, democratic freedom. And all this is carefully impossible in the city-plan, in making a living, in having a family, in running the state. By the time the lengthy adjustment has been made, there has been no sharp frustration that could rouse a deep-seated rebelliousness, but only a steady molding pressure that forms good healthy citizens, who have early nervous breakdowns and complain that "life has passed me by." Or another outcome, as we shall see, is to wage a good, well-behaved, orderly, and infinitely destructive war.

The history of psychoanalysis itself is a study of how teeth are drawn by respectability. It is a perfect illustration of Max Weber's law of the Bureaucratization of the Prophetic. But this law is not inevitable; it is a consequence of unequal development and consequent anxiety, the need of the whole to adjust itself to the new force and to adjust the new force to itself. What must psychotherapy do to prevent this bureaucratizing respectability? Simply, *press on to the next resistance.*

4: The Anti-Social is presently the Aggressive

The most salient passional characteristics of our epoch are violence and tameness. There are public enemies and public wars unbelievable in scope, intensity, and atmosphere of terror; and at the same time, unexampled civil peace and the almost total suppression of personal outbreaks, with the corresponding neurotic loss of contact, hostility turned against the self, and the somatic symptoms of repressed anger (ulcers, tooth-decay, etc.). In Freud's time and place the passional climate seems to have been much more marked by deprivation and resentment as regards both pleasure and sustenance. At present in America, there is a general high standard of living and the sexuality is not so much frustrated as it is unsatisfactory. On a more superficial level, the neurosis has to do with isolation and inferiority; but these are generally felt and therefore less serious; the mores are increasingly emulative and eager for sociability. Underlying is the inhibited hatred and self-hatred. The deep-going neurosis, which appears masked in such dreams as comic-books and foreign-policy, is retroflected and projected aggression.

The cluster of drives and perversions that are called aggressive—annihilating, destroying, killing, combativeness, initiative, hunting, sado-masochism, conquest and domination—these are now felt to be the anti-social *par excellence*. "But!" one can hear the spluttering objection, "these are *obviously* anti-social, destructive of the order of society!" The fact of the immediate unquestioning social rejection of various aggressions can be taken as *prima facie* evidence that it is in the analysis and release of aggressions that we must look for the next progress of society toward happier norms.*

5: Annihilating and Destroying

The attitude and acts called "aggressive" comprise a cluster of essentially different contact-functions that are usually dynamically interconnected in action and thereby get a common name. We shall try to show that at least annihilating, destroying, initiative, and anger are essential to growth in the organism/environment field; given rational objects, they are always "healthy," and in any case they are irreducible without loss of valuable parts of the personality, especially self-confidence, feeling, and creativity. Other aggressions, like sado-masochism, conquest and domination, and sui-

---

*The change in the anti-social since Freud's time is also indicated by the change in the method of psychotherapy from symptom-analysis to character-analysis and further. This is partly an improvement in technique, but partly it meets a different run of cases. The symptoms were originally "neurasthenic"; they were, as Freud said (circa 1895), the direct result of sexual frustration; the psychogenic symptoms were transparently sexual acts. (Medical men mention the disappearance of cases of grand hysteria.) Now, it seems, this direct sexual poisoning is less common; for instance, there is obviously much more masturbation without overwhelming guilt. In the character-neuroses the sexual block is related not to the discharge, but somewhat to the act, and largely to the contact and feeling. The therapeutic attitude is likewise altered: the older orthodoxy was a kind of seduction (with disapproval), and the character-analysis is combative.

cide, we shall interpret as neurotic derivatives. Most often, however, the total mixture is not accurately analyzed and is "reduced" too much *en bloc*. (The ineradicable factors are in turn repressed.)

Let us begin by distinguishing annihilating from destroying. Annihilating is making into nothing, rejecting the object and blotting it from existence. The gestalt completes itself without that object. Destroying (destructuring) is the demolition of a whole into fragments in order to assimilate them as parts in a new whole. Primarily, annihilation is a defensive response to pain, bodily invasion, or danger. In avoidance and flight, the animal takes himself out of the painful field; in killing, he "coldly" removes the offending object from the field. Behaviorally, shutting the mouth tight and averting the head, and smashing and kicking. The defensive response is "cold" because no appetite is involved (the threat is external). The existence of the object is painful, but its non-existence is not enjoyed, it is not felt in completing the field; the enjoyment sometimes apparent is the flooding back at relaxing one's shrinking: sigh of relief, beads of sweat, etc.

When neither flight nor removal is possible, the organism has recourse to blotting out its own awareness, shrinking from contact, averting the eyes, clamping the teeth. These mechanisms become very important when circumstances require opposite responses to the "same" object (really to different properties bound together in one thing): especially when need or desire makes necessary the presence of an object that is also painful and dangerous. One then is obliged to possess without spontaneously enjoying, to hold without contact. This is the usual inevitable plight of children and often the inevitable plight of adults. The analysis must make clear just what property in the object is needed and what is rejected, so the conflict may come into the open and be decided or suffered.

Destroying, on the contrary, is a function of appetite. Every organism in a field grows by incorporating, digesting, and assimilating new matter, and this requires destroying the existing form to its assimilable elements, whether it be food, a lecture, a father's influence, the difference between a mate's domestic habits and one's own. The new matter must be accepted only according to its place in a new spontaneous functioning. If the previous form is not totally destroyed and digested, there occurs, instead of assimilation, either introjection or areas of no contact. The introject may have two fates: either it is painful foreign matter in the body and it is vomited forth (a kind of annihilation); or the self partially identifies with the introject, represses the pain, seeks to annihilate part of the self—but since the rejection is ineradicable, there is a permanent clinch, a neurotic splitting.

The destructive appetite is warm and pleasurable. It approaches, reaching out to seize, with teeth bared, and it slavers in chewing. Such an attitude, especially if literally or figuratively there is killing, is of course deemed ruthless. Declining to commit the destruction, the self can either introject, or else inhibit the appetite altogether (renounce certain areas of experience). The first is the response especially to the inheritance of the family and social past; forcibly fed, not at one's own time and need, the self introjects parents and culture and can neither destroy nor assimilate them. There are multiple partial-identifications; these destroy self-confidence, and in the end the past destroys the present. If the appetite is inhibited, through nausea or fear of biting and chewing, there is loss of affect.

On the other hand, the warm pleasurable (and angry) destroying of existing forms in personal relations often leads to mutual advantage and love, as in the seduction and defloration of a shy virgin, or in the breaking down of prejudices between friends. For consider that if the association of two persons will in fact be deeply profitable to them, then the destruction of the incompatible existing forms they have come with is a motion toward their more intrinsic selves—that will be actualized in the coming new figure; in this release of the more intrinsic, bound energy is liberated and this will transfer to the liberating agent as love. The process of mutual destruction is probably the chief

proving ground of profound compatibility. Our unwillingness to risk it is obviously a fear that if we lose this
we shall have nothing; we prefer poor food to none; we
have become habituated to scarcity and starvation.

6: Initiative and Anger

Aggression is the "step toward" the object of appetite or hostility. The passing of the impulse into the
step is initiative: accepting the impulse as one's own
and accepting the motor execution as one's own. Obviously initiative can be stifled by the repression of the
appetite altogether, as described above. But more common in modern times, it is likely, is the dissociation
of the appetite from the motor behavior, so that it
becomes manifest only as garrulous planning or dreamy
prospects. One has the impression that with the giving
up of hunting and fighting, people cease to move altogether; the motions of athletic games are not related
to organic needs, the motions of industry are not one's
own motions.

A child's statement, "When I grow up, I'll do so
and so," indicates his initiative, the imitative assumption of behavior that will realize the desire still obscure
in him till it is acted. When it is repeated by the adult,
the unfinished desire persists but the initiative is gone.
What has occurred in between? It is that, in our economy, politics, and education, the so-called goals are
too alien and the ways of reaching them therefore too
complicated, not enough to hand. Everything is preparation, nothing realization and satisfaction. The result
is that the problems cannot be worked through and
assimilated. The system of education results in a number of unassimilated introjects. After a while the self
loses confidence in its own appetites. There is a lack of
faith, for faith is knowing, beyond awareness, that if
one takes a step there will be ground underfoot: one
gives oneself unhesitatingly to the act, one has faith that
the background will produce the means. Finally, the
attempt to assimilate is given up and there is bafflement and nausea.

At the same time as the initiative is being lost in bewilderment, in pursuing too difficult ends, it is being directly discouraged in the pursuit of simple ends, as a child is slapped for being "forward." Fear results in giving up the appetite. On the whole, there is the reduction to a simpler order of appetite and non-initiative or dependency: to be fed and cared for, not understanding how, and this leads to a persistent insecurity and inferiority.

Let us suppose, however, that an appetite is strong and is under way toward its goal, and it then meets an obstacle and the appetite is frustrated: the tension flares and this is hot anger.

Anger contains the three aggressive components, destroying and annihilating and initiative. The warmth of anger is that of the appetite and initiative themselves. At first the obstacle is regarded simply as part of the existing form to be destroyed, and it is itself attacked with pleasurable heat. But as the frustrating nature of the obstacle becomes manifest, the on-going tension of the engaged self becomes painful, and there is added to the warm destructive appetite the cold need of annihilating. In extreme cases the appetite (the motion toward the goal) is quite transcended and there is fierce white fury. The difference of white fury (murderousness) from simple annihilating (need for the thing not to exist in the field) is the outgoing engagement of the self; one is already committed to the situation, is not just brushing it off; murderousness is not simply a defense, for oneself is engaged and therefore cannot merely avoid. Thus a man who is slapped becomes furious.

In general, anger is a sympathetic passion; it unites persons because it is admixed with desire. (So hatred is notoriously ambivalent with love. When the transcendence of desire toward "pure" anger is based on a repression of desire, then the self is wholly engaged in the hostile attack, and if the repression suddenly dissolves—for instance by finding that one is stronger and is safe—the desire has suddenly crystallized into love.)

It will be seen that the usual formula, "Frustration

leads to hostility," is true but too simple, for it omits mentioning the warm appetite in the angry aggression. Then it becomes difficult to understand why anger, an angry disposition, persists when annihilation of the obstacle has been effectively achieved by death or distance (e.g., the parents are dead, yet the child is still angry with them), or again, why in revenge and hatred the annihilation of the enemy gives satisfaction, his non-existence is *not* indifferent but is fed on: he is not only annihilated but destroyed and assimilated. But this is because the frustrating obstacle is first taken as part of the desired goal; the child is angry with dead parents because they are still part of the unfinished need—it is not enough for him to understand that, as obstacles, they are out of the way. And the victim of revenge and hatred is part of oneself, is loved, unaware.

On the other hand, it is the admixture of annihilating within anger that rouses such intense guilt with regard to difficult loved objects; for we cannot afford to annihilate, make nothing of, what we need, even when it frustrates us. Thus it is that persistent anger, uniting appetite and annihilating, leads to the inhibition of appetite altogether and is a common cause of impotence, inversion, etc.

In red anger, awareness is somewhat confused. In white fury it is often very sharp, when, stifling all bodily appetite, it yet draws on the vividness of imagery that belongs to delayed appetite, as the self confronts its object to annihilate it. In purple or congested rage the self is bursting with its frustrated impulses and is confused indeed. In black wrath, or hatred, the self has begun to destroy itself in the interests of its hostile aim; it no longer sees the reality but only its own idea.

7: Fixations of the Above, and Sado-Masochism

Annihilating, destroying, initiative, and anger are functions of good contact, necessary for the livelihood, pleasure, and protection of any organism in a difficult field. We have seen that they occur in various combinations and are likely to be pleasurable. Acting the aggressions, the organism fills out its skin, so to speak, and touches the environment, without damage to the self; inhibiting the aggressions does not eradicate them but turns them against the self (as we shall discuss in the next chapter). Without aggression, love stagnates and becomes contactless, for destroying is the means of renewal. Further, a hostile aggression is often rational precisely where it is considered neurotic: e.g., hostility may be turned toward a therapist not because he is "father" but because he is again some one who is forcing unassimilable interpretations and putting one in the wrong.

The fixations of these functions, however—hatred, vengeance, and premeditated murder, ambitiousness and compulsive love-hunting, habitual combativeness —these are not so amiable. To these settled passions other functions of the self are sacrificed; they are self-destructive. To hate a thing involves binding energy to what is by definition painful or frustrating, and usually with diminished contact with the changing actual situations. One clings to the hateful and holds it close. In revenge and premeditated murder, there is a burning settled need to annihilate a "person" whose existence insults one's concept of oneself; but if this concept is analyzed, it is found that the drama is internal. So most righteous indignation is directed against one's own temptation. The cold killer, again, is trying systematically to annihilate his environment, which is tantamount to committing suicide: "I don't care for them" means "I don't care for myself," and this is an identification with the terrible judgment, "We don't care for you." The combative man strikes one as a man with appetite who initiates an approach and then suddenly frustrates himself, because he feels inadequate, disapproved, or so; his anger flares against the frustrator; and he projects the "obstacle" into any likely or unlikely object; such a man clearly wants to be beaten.

In general (we shall consider it more in detail in the next chapter) when an appetite is repressed, habitually kept unaware, the self is exercising a fixed hostility against itself. To the extent that this aggression is kept inward, there is a well-behaved masochism; to the extent that it finds some environmental image of itself, there is a fixed sadism. The pleasure in the sadism is the increment of appetite released by letting up on the self; to strike, stab, etc. is the form in which the sadist desiringly touches the object. And the object is loved because it is like one's own dominated self.

In primary masochism (Wilhelm Reich) it is not the pain that is wanted but the release of the dammed-up instincts. The pain is a "fore-pain," a sensation in one habitually desensitized, that then allows much more feeling to be recovered.* The more the instinctual excitement is increased without a corresponding increase of awareness that it is one's own excitement and also one's own deliberateness in restricting it, the more the masochistic longing. (It would seem, by the way, that this situation would be experimentally induced by a physiological therapy like Reich's). In masochism, the appetites become more expansive and increase the tension, and the restriction is correspondingly tightened; the longing for release is neurotically interpreted as the wish to have it done to one, to be forced, broken, punctured, to let loose the inward pressures. The masochist loves the brutal lover who both gives the underlying release and yet is identified with his own self-punishing self.

8: Modern War is Mass-Suicide without Guiltiness

Let us now return to the more broadly social context and say something further about the kind of violence that characterizes our epoch.

We have at present in America a combination of unexampled general wealth and unexampled civil

---

*We should like to substitute the concept of "fore-feeling," as the small element releasing a large flow of feeling, for the Freudian concept of "fore-pleasure." For obviously fore-pain operates in the same way: a man stubs his toe and his cosmic rage and grief well forth. Or a fore-pleasure may bring on a deep feeling that would not be called pleasure: as a lover touches one with a consoling hand and, as D. W. Griffith said, "all the tears of the world wash over our hearts."

peace. Economically and sociologically these are benefi-
cent causes of each other: the more civil order the
more productivity, and the more wealth the less in-
centive to destroy the civil order. By civil order we
mean not the absence of crimes of violence, but the
pervasive safety of both city and country. Compared
with all other ages and places, travel is without danger
anywhere by day or night. There are almost no brawls,
riots, or armed bands. Madmen do not roam the streets;
there is no plague. Disease is quickly isolated in hospitals; death is never seen, childbirth rarely. Meat is
eaten, but no urban person ever sees an animal slaughtered. Never before has there existed such a state of
non-violence, safety, and sterility. Concerning our
wealth, again, we need only point out that none of the
debated economic issues has to do with subsistence.
Unions demand not bread but better wages and hours
and more security; capitalists demand fewer controls
and better conditions for reinvestment. A single case of
starvation is a scandal in the press. Less than ten per
cent of the economy is devoted to elementary subsistence. More than ever in history there are comforts,
luxuries, entertainments.

Psychologically the picture is more dubious. There
is little physical survival frustration but little satisfaction, and there are signs of acute anxiety. The general
bewilderment and insecurity of isolated individuals in
a too-big society destroy self-confidence and initiative,
and without these there cannot be active enjoyment.
Sports and entertainments are passive and symbolic;
the choices on the market are passive and symbolic;
people make and do nothing for themselves, except
symbolically. The quantity of sexuality is great, the desensitizing is extreme. It used to be felt that science,
technology, and the new mores would bring on an age
of happiness. This hope has been disappointed. Everywhere people are disappointed.

Even on the surface, then, there is reason to smash
things up, to destroy not this or that part of the system
(e.g., the upper class), but the whole system *en bloc*,
for it has no further promise, it has proved unassimila-

ble in its existing form. This sentiment is even in awareness with varying degrees of clarity.

But considering more deeply, in the terms we have
been developing, we see that these conditions are almost specific for the excitement of primary masochism.
There is continual stimulation and only partial release
of tension, an unbearable heightening of the unaware
tensions—unaware because people do not know what
they want, nor how to get it, and the available means
are too big and unmanageable. The desire for final
satisfaction, for orgasm, is interpreted as the wish for
total self-destruction. It is inevitable, then, that there
should be a public dream of universal disaster, with
vast explosions, fires, and electric shocks; and people
pool their efforts to bring this apocalypse to an actuality.

At the same time, however, all overt expression of
destructiveness, annihilation, anger, combativeness, is
suppressed in the interests of the civil order. Also the
feeling of anger is inhibited and even repressed. People
are sensible, tolerant, polite, and cooperative in being
pushed around. But the occasions of anger are by no
means minimized. On the contrary, when the larger
movements of initiative are circumscribed in the com-
petitive routines of offices, bureaucracies, and factories,
there is petty friction, hurt feelings, being crossed.
Small anger is continually generated, never discharged;
big anger, that goes with big initiative, is repressed.

Therefore the angry situation is projected afar. People must find big distant causes adequate to explain
the pressure of anger that is certainly not explicable
by petty frustrations. It is necessary to have something
worthy of the hatred that is unaware felt for oneself.
In brief, one is angry with the Enemy.

This Enemy is, needless to say, cruel and hardly
human; there is no use in treating with him as if he
were human. For we must remember, as is shown by
the content of all popular cinema and literature, that
the dream of American love is sado-masochistic, but
the behavior of love-making is not sado-masochistic,
for that would be anti-social and indecent. It is "some-

one else" that is sadistic; and surely "someone else" that is masochistic.

Now in civil life, we have been saying, the cluster of aggressions is anti-social. But fortunately in war it is good and social. So people, longing for universal explosion and disaster, wage war against enemies who indeed enrage and fascinate them by their cruelty and subhuman strength.

The mass-democratic army is excellently apt for the popular needs. It gives the personal security that is lacking in civil life; it imposes a personal authority without making any demand on the secret self, for after all one is only a unit in the mass. It takes one from jobs and homes where one is inadequate and gets no great pleasure; and it organizes one's efforts much more effectively toward sadistic practices and a masochistic débacle.

People observe the débacle approach. They listen to rational warnings and make all kinds of sensible policies. But the energy to flee or resist is paralyzed, or the danger is fascinating. People are eager to finish the unfinished situation. They are bent on mass-suicide, an outcome that solves all problems without personal guiltiness. The counter-propaganda of pacifists is worse than useless, for it solves no problems and it increases personal guiltiness.

9: Critique of Freud's Thanatos

It was in similar circumstances that Freud dreamed up his theory of the death-instinct. But the circumstances were less extreme than now, for he could still at that time, in the flush of the theory of the libido, speak of a conflict between Thanatos and Eros and look to Eros for a counter-weight to Thanatos. The new mores had not yet had a trial.

Freud seems to have based his theory on three evidences. (a) The kind of social violence we have been describing: the World War I that went apparently counter to any principle of vitality and culture. (b) The neurotic compulsion to repeat or fixate, that he attributed to the attraction of the trauma. We have seen, however, that the repetition-compulsion is more simply explicable as the effort of the organism to complete with archaic means its *present* unfinished situation, each time enough organic tension accumulates to make the difficult attempt. Yet in an important sense this repetition and circling round the trauma may correctly be called a death-wish; but it is precisely the death of the more deliberate inhibiting self that is wished for (with its apparent present needs and means), in the interests of the more vital underlying situation. What is necessarily neurotically interpreted as a wish for death is a wish for a fuller life. (c) But Freud's most important evidence was probably the apparent irreducibility of primary masochism. For he found that, far from being reduced, precisely as patients began to function more, their dreams (and no doubt Freud's own dreams) became more catastrophic; the theorist was then forced by the evidence to extrapolate to a condition of perfect functioning and total masochism: i.e., to die is an instinctual craving. But on the theory of masochism we have been advancing, this evidence is better explained as follows: the more the instinctual release without the corresponding strengthening of the self's ability to create something with the new energy, the more disruptive and violent the tensions in the field. And just as the physiological method of Reich experimentally induces this condition, so the anamnestic free association of Freud: there is release without integration. But Reich's better control of the situation enabled him to find a simpler explanation.

Yet as a biological speculation, Freud's theory is by no means negligible, and must itself be met speculatively. Let us cast it in the following schematic form: every organism, says the theory, seeks to diminish tension and reach equilibrium; but by reverting to a lower order of structure it can reach a still more stable equilibrium; so ultimately every organism seeks to be inanimate. This is its death-instinct and is a case of the universal tendency toward entropy. Opposed to it are the appetites (eros) that tend to the ever more complex structures of evolution.

This is a powerful speculation. If we accept the presuppositions and mystique of Nineteenth Century science, it is hard to refute. Its rejection by most theorists, including many of the orthodox, is largely, one feels, because it is offensive, anti-social, rather than because it is seen to be erroneous.

But to think, as Freud does, of a *chain* of causes, consisting of connected elementary links back to the beginning, is a misreading of the history of evolution; it is to make actual and concrete what is an abstraction, namely some line of evidence (e.g., the fossils in the strata of rocks) by which we learn the history. He speaks as if the successive complexities were "added on" to a single operating force, of "life," isolatable from its concrete situations; as if onto a protozoon were added the soul of a metazoon, etc.; or conversely, as if within a vertebrate were introjected an annelid, etc.—so that falling asleep as a vertebrate, the animal then addresses itself to falling asleep as an annelid, then as a platyhelminth, and finally to becoming inanimate. But in fact every successive stage is a new whole, operating as a whole, with its own mode of life; it is *its* mode of life, as a concrete whole, that it wants to complete; it is not concerned with seeking "equilibrium in general." The condition of a molecule or of an amoeba is not an unfinished situation for a mammal because the existing organic parts tending to completeness are quite different in the separate cases. Nothing would be solved for an organism by solving the problem of some other kinds of parts.

(It is useful to consider Freud's theory as a psychological symptom: if a man resigns the possibility of present solutions, he must blot out the present needs; and thereby he brings to the fore some other needs of a lower order of structure. The lower order of structure is then given a kind of existence by the act of present resignation.)

Freud seems to misunderstand the nature of a

"cause." A "cause" is not itself an existing thing but a principle of explanation for some present problem. Therefore a *chain* of causes—proceeding in either direction, as a final teleological goal or as a primitive genetic origin—the longer such a chain gets, the more it becomes nothing at all, for we seek a cause in order to orient ourselves in a specific individual problem, for the purpose of changing the situation or accepting it. A good cause solves the problem (of specific orientation) and then ceases to occupy us. We set down the causes in a chain, as in a textbook, not when we are handling the actual material, but when we are teaching it.

Lastly, Freud's theory systematically isolates the organism from the on-going organism/environment field; and he isolates an abstract "time" as another factor. But this field is existing; its presentness, its on-going time, with the continual event of novelties, is essential to its definition and to the definition of "organism." It is as part of this ever-novel field that one must think of an organism as growing, and of the species as changing. The passage of time, the change in time, is not something that is added onto a primal animal that has an internal principle of growth isolated from the time of the field, and that somehow adjusts to ever-new situations. But it is the adjustment of ever-new situations, changing both the organism and the environment, that is growth and the kind of time that organisms have— for every scientific subject has its own kind of time. To a history novelty and irreversibility are essential. An animal trying to complete its life is necessarily seeking its growth. Eventually the animal fails and dies, not because *it* is seeking a lower order of structure, but because the field as a whole can no longer organize itself with that part in that form. We are destroyed just as, growing, we destroy.

The aggressive drives are not essentially distinct from the erotic drives; they are different stages of growth, either as selecting, destroying, and assimilating, or as enjoying, absorbing, and reaching equilibrium. And thus, to return to our starting point, when the aggressive drives are anti-social, it is that the society is opposed to life and change (and love); then it will either be destroyed by life or it will involve life in a common ruin, make human life destroy society and itself.

I X

CONFLICT AND SELF-CONQUEST

1: Conflict and Creative Disinterestedness

We must now say something about the finales of the aggressions: victory (or defeat), conquest, and domination. For in the neuroses, the need for victory is central; and given this need, there is a readily available victim, the self. Neurosis may be regarded as self-conquest.

But the neurotic need for victory is not a need for the object fought for, exercising aggression in open conflict; it is a need to *have* won, to be a victor as such. The meaning of it is that one has already importantly lost and been humiliated and has not assimilated the loss, but repeatedly tries to save face with petty triumphs. So every interpersonal relation, and indeed every experience, is turned into a little battle with a chance to win and prove prowess.

Important conflict, however, struggling for an object that will make a difference and risking oneself in an initiative that may change the status quo—this is precisely avoided. Small symbolic conflicts and large false and therefore unending conflicts like "Mind versus Body," "Love versus Aggression," "Pleasure versus Reality," are means of avoiding the exciting conflicts that would have a solution. Instead people cling to security, here recognized as the fixation of the background, the underlying organic need and the past habit; the background must be kept background.

The opposite of the need for victory is "creative disinterest." We shall later attempt to describe this peculiar attitude of the spontaneous self (Chapter 10).

Accepting his concern and the object, and exercising the aggression, the creatively impartial man is excited by the conflict and grows by means of it, win or lose; he is not attached to what might be lost, for he knows he is changing and already identifies with what he will become. With this attitude goes an emotion that is the opposite of the sense of security, namely faith: absorbed in the actual activity he does not protect the background but draws energy from it, he has faith that it will prove adequate.

2: Critique of the Theory of the "Removal of Inner Conflict": Meaning of "Inner"

Psychoanalysis has classically devoted itself to the uncovering of "inner conflicts" and their "removal." Roughly speaking this is a fine conception (like the other conception: "re-education of the emotions"); but it is now time to scrutinize it more closely.

"Inner" here presumably means either inside the skin of the organism or within the psyche or in the unconscious; examples would be the conflict between sexual tension and pain, or between instinct and conscience, or between introjected father and mother. Opposed to these, and non-neurotic, would presumably be conscious conflicts with the environment or with other persons. But put this way, the distinction between "inner conflicts" and other conflicts is not valuable, for clearly there are non-"inner" conflicts that may well be considered as neurotic. For example, to the extent that a child has not yet grown free-standing from the child/parent field—he is still suckling, learning to talk, economically dependent, etc.—it is pointless to speak of the neurotic disturbances (unaware starvation, hostility, deprivation of contact) as within any individual's skin or psyche. The disturbances are in the field; true, they spring from the "inner conflicts" of the parents, and they will later result in introjected conflicts in the offspring as he becomes free-standing; but their essence in the disturbed felt-relation is irreducible to the parts. Thus child and parents must be treated together. Or again, the lapse of community in political societies is not reducible to the neuroses of individuals, who indeed have become "individuals" because of the lapse of community; nor is it reducible to the bad institutions, for these are maintained by the citizens; it is a disease of the field, and only a kind of group-therapy would help. As we have already said frequently, the distinction of "intra-personal" and "interpersonal" is a poor one, for all individual personality and all organized society develop from functions of coherence that are essential to both person and society (love, learning, communication, identification, etc.); and indeed, the contrary functions of division are also essential to both: rejection, hate, alienation, etc. The concept of contact/boundary is more fundamental than intra or inter, or than inner and outer. And further, again, there are disturbances that may be called neurotic that occur in the organism/natural-environment field, for instance the magic rituals of primitives that develop, quite without personal neurosis, from starvation and thunder-fear; or our contemporary disease of "mastering" nature rather than living symbiotically, for quite apart from the personal and social neuroses (that are, to be sure, here working overtime), there is a dislocation in the interaction of sheer material quantities and dearths, caused by unaware abuses. The primitive says, "The earth is starving, therefore we are starving"; and we say, "We are starving, therefore let us wrest something more from the earth": symbiotically both attitudes are bad dreams.

The classical wording "inner conflict" contains, however, a very important truth, stated characteristically upside-down. It is that the inner conflicts—those inside the skin, inside the psyche (the opposed tensions and checks and balances of the physiological system, the play, dreams, art, etc.)—all these are for the most part reliable and *not* neurotic; they can be trusted to be self-regulating; they have proved themselves for thousands of years and have not much changed. The inner conflicts in this sense are not the subject of psychotherapy; when they are unaware they can be left unaware. It is, on the contrary, the meddling inward of outside-the-skin social forces that deliberately upsets the spontaneous inner-system and calls for psychotherapy. These forces are new-comers and often ill-conceived. A large part of psychotherapy is a process of disengaging these properly outside-the-skin forces from meddling inside-the-skin and disturbing the organismic-self-regulation. And by the same token, it is a process of disengaging such more distant unreliable economic and political forces as competition, money, prestige, power, from meddling inside the primary personal system of love, grief, anger, community, parenthood, dependence and independence.

3: Meaning of "Conflict"

Obviously in the classical formula, "conflicts" are not the opposed internal tensions and checks and balances, the wisdom of the body; they are meant as bad conflicts, and hence the inner conflicts must be dissolved. Why is this necessary?

The badness of conflicts seems to mean one or all of the following: (1) All conflicts are bad because they waste energy and cause suffering. (2) All conflicts excite aggression and destruction, which are bad. (3) Some conflicts are bad because one of the contestants is unhealthy or anti-social, and rather than being allowed to conflict, it should be eliminated or sublimated, e.g., pre-genital sexuality or various aggressions. (4) Mistaken conflicts are bad, and the contents of the unconscious are mostly archaic and mistaken (displaced).

The point of view we are here developing, however (it is largely but not mainly a proposal for a better use of language), is that, fundamentally, *no* conflict should be dissolved by psychotherapy. Especially the "inner" conflicts are strongly energized and concernful and are the means of growth; the task of psychotherapy is to make them aware so that they may feed on new environmental material and come to a crisis. The least desirable conflicts are the aware petty battles and unending clinches based on semantical mistakes of which we spoke at the beginning of this chapter; we interpret these not in order to avoid conflict but precisely in order to bring forth the important conflicts for which they are signs.

Let us then consider conflict itself, aware and attended by suffering. The notion that conflict, whether social, interpersonal, or intra-psychic, is wasteful of energy, is plausible but superficial. Its plausibility is based on the assumption that the work to be done could be got at directly; then it would be wasteful for the contestant that will have to do the work to have to fight off or overcome the friction of an opponent; and perhaps both contestants can harmoniously join in the work. But this is superficial, for it assumes that one knows beforehand what the work is that is to be done, where and how the energy is to be expended. The assumption is that we know—and a part of the patient knows—just what good is to be aimed at; in that case the opposition is deceived or perverse. But where a conflict is deeply concernful, *what* to do, what belongs to oneself rather than to a stereotyped norm, is just what is being tested. Even more, the true work to be done, perhaps even the true vocation, is first being discovered in the conflict; it has not hitherto been known to anybody, and is certainly not adequately expressed in the contesting claims. The conflict is a collaboration going beyond what is intended, toward a new figure altogether.

Surely this is true of any creative collaboration among persons. The best efficiency is attained not by establishing an *a priori* harmony among their interests, or by compromising their individual interests to a preconceived goal. Rather (so long as they remain in contact and are earnestly aiming at the best creative achievement), the more sharply they differ and have it out, the more likely they are to produce collectively an idea better than any of them had individually. So in games it is the competition that makes the players surpass themselves. (The bother with neurotic competitiveness is not the competition but the fact that the competitor is not interested in the game.) Now also in the creative act of a single person, for instance in a work of art or theory, it is the warring of disparate, irreconcilable elements that suddenly leaps to a creative solution. A poet does not reject an image that stubbornly but "accidentally" appears and mars his plan; he respects the intruder and suddenly discovers what "his" plan is, he discovers and creates himself. And so a scientist seeks out the disproving evidence.

The question is whether the same must not be true of intrapsychic emotional conflict. In ordinary unblocked situations there is no problem: by organismic-self-regulation an instinct-dominance flexibly establishes itself, e.g., a strong thirst puts other drives in abeyance until it is satisfied. And longer range orderings flexibly occur in the same way: through conflict, biting-chewing-drinking establish themselves over suckling, and the genitals establish themselves as the final aim in sexuality: genital orgasm becomes the terminus of sexual excitement. In the development of these orders there were conflicting tensions, but the conflicts worked themselves out—with disruption of habits, destruction, assimilation, and a new configuration. Now suppose the situation has been a blocked one: e.g., suppose the genital primacy was not strongly established because of oral unfinished situations, genital fears, so-called "regressions," and so forth. And suppose that all the contestants are brought into the open, into open contact and open conflict, with regard to object-choices, social behavior, moral guilt on the one hand and affirmation of pleasure on the other. Must not this conflict and its attendant suffering and hardship be the means of coming to a self-creative solution? Such a conflict is severe because there is much to be destroyed; but is the destructiveness to be inhibited? If the solution—the normal primacy—is pre-conceived and forwarded by the therapist (just as it has long been skilfully pre-conceived by the social self of the patient), much suffering and danger may be avoided; but the solution will be so much the more alien and therefore less energetic. That is, it is unwise to allay the conflict or suppress or interpret away any strong contestants, for the result must then be to prevent a thorough destruction and assimilation, and therefore to condemn the patient to a weak and never perfectly self-regulating system.

Above all we must remember that where the contestants are natural drives—aggressions, special gifts, sexual practices that in fact give pleasure, etc.—they cannot be reduced, but their manifestations only deliberately suppressed, bullied or shamed out. When all the contestants are in awareness and in contact, a man may make his own hard decisions; he is not a patient. The hope is that in such a case a difficult drive will spontaneously find its measure in a new configuration, by creative adjustment and convalescent organismic-self-regulation.

4: Suffering

Let us also consider the meaning of the suffering. The creative solution, we have said, is not known to the warring contestants; it first arises from the conflict. In the conflict, the contestants, their habits and interests, are in part destroyed; they lose and suffer. Thus, in the social collaboration, the partners quarrel and destroy one another, they hate the conflict. In making a poem, the poet is annoyed by the intruding image or the idea that goes off at a tangent; he gives himself a headache, he clings to his plan, becomes confused and sweats. Yet engaged in the conflict, these cannot avoid the pain, because to suppress it now would not give pleasure but un-pleasure, dullness, and uneasiness and nagging doubt. Besides, the conflict itself is painfully exciting. How in fact do they finally lessen the pain?

By finally "standing out of the way," to quote the great formula of Tao. They disengage themselves from their preconceptions of how it "ought" to turn out. And into the "fertile void" thus formed, the solution comes flooding. That is, they engage themselves, put forward their interests and skills and let them clash, in order to sharpen the conflict, and in order to be destroyed and changed into the coming idea; and finally they do not cling to the interests as "theirs." In the excitement of the creative process they come to a creative impartiality among the warring parts; and then, with great recklessness and gleeful savagery, each contestant is likely to exercise all his aggression both for and against his own part. But the self is no longer being destroyed, for it is first finding out what it is.

The question again is whether this same interpretation of the use and means of lessening pain and suffering applies to somatic and emotional pain and suffering. Let us speculate a moment on the function of pain.

Pain is primarily a signal; it calls attention to an immediate present danger, for instance the threat to an organ. The spontaneous response to it is to get out of the way or, failing that, to annihilate the threatener. Animal life does not dwell on pain and suffering; when injury persists and nothing deliberately can be done to help, the animal becomes numb to the pain or even faints. (The neurotic reaction of touching the injured part to elicit the pain is a desire for sensation in the de-sensitized; and this too is probably a useful signal, though it is difficult to interpret.)

What, then, is the function of prolonged suffering common among human beings? We hazard the guess that it is to get us to attend to the immediate present problem and then to stand out of the way, to give the threat all our powers, and then to stand out of the way, to relax useless deliberateness, to let the conflict rage and destroy what must be destroyed. Consider two simple illustrations: a man is ill, he tries to go about his business and he suffers; forced to realize he has quite other business, he attends to his illness, lies down and waits; the suffering lessens and he falls asleep. Or, a loved one dies; there is a sad conflict between intellectual acceptance on the one hand and desires and memories on the other; the average man tries to distract himself, but the superior man obeys the signal and engages himself in the suffering, calls up the past, sees his present hopelessly frustrated; he cannot imagine what to do now that the bottom has fallen out of everything; the grief, confusion, and suffering are prolonged, for there is much to be destroyed and annihilated and much to be assimilated, and during this time he must not go about his unimportant business, deliberately suppressing the conflict. Finally the mourning-labor is complete and the person is changed, he assumes a creative disinterest; at once new interests become dominant.

Emotional suffering is a means of preventing the isolation of the problem, in order that, working through the conflict, the self may grow in the field of the existent. The sooner one is willing to relax struggling against the destructive conflict, to relax to the pain and confusion, the sooner the suffering is over. (This interpretation of the suffering of mourning, as a means of letting go the old self to change, explains why mourning is attended by self-destructive behavior like scratching the skin, beating the breast, tearing the hair.)

To the physician, of course, the danger in emotional conflict and suffering is that its raging may destroy the patient, tear him to pieces. This is a true danger. But it is to be met not necessarily by weakening the conflict but by strengthening the self and the self-awareness. When one realizes that it is one's own conflict, and that one is tearing oneself to pieces, there is a new dynamic factor in the situation, namely oneself. Then, as the conflict is attended to and sharpens, one sooner reaches the attitude of creative impartiality and identifies with the coming solution.

5: Self-Conquest: Premature Pacification

We are saying, then, that neurosis does not consist in any active conflict, inner or outer, of one desire against another, or of social standards against animal needs, or of personal needs (e.g., ambition) against both social standards and animal needs. All such conflicts are compatible with the integration of the self, and indeed are means of the integrating of the self. But neurosis is the premature pacification of conflicts; it is a clinch or truce or numbness to avoid further conflict; and it secondarily manifests itself as a need for victory in petty battles, as if to unmake the underlying humiliation. It is, briefly, *self*-conquest. Let us here distinguish two stages of satisfaction: (1) the satisfaction of the cessation of conflict and (2) the satisfaction of conquest.

Suppose that instead of being able to identify with a coming solution, the self despairs of a solution and has no prospect but continued suffering and a too crushing defeat. In our families and society this must often be the case, for a creative solution is often impossible. An adult, understanding the situation, may suffer on, but a child necessarily gives up. Let us consider the meaning of resignation.

At the moment of extreme conflict and despair, the organism responds by blotting out, spectacularly by fainting, more usually by numb feeling, paralysis, or some other method of temporary repression. But when the immediate crisis is passed, if the circumstances are no more promising for a solution, the further conflict is avoided, the self no longer aggresses, and the more bearable situation of the repression is stabilized; one is resigned. But there is then an empty space in the figure, for the general context of need, opportunity, difficulty, etc. is the same; but the self-assertion that occupied the central place in the conflict is missing. This empty space is now filled by identifying with another person, namely the person who made the conflict unbearable and who made one resign. This person is usually one who is feared and loved—the conflict is resigned both out of fear and in order not to risk disapproval—and now that person becomes "oneself." That is, instead of pressing on to the new self one would become in the unknown solution of the conflict, one introjects this other self. Identifying with it, one

lends it the force of one's own aggressions now disengaged from the advancement of one's own needs.
These aggressions are now retroflectively turned against
those needs, averting attention from them, tensing the
muscles against their excitations, calling such needs
silly or vicious, punishing them, and so forth. According to the norms of the introjected person, one alienates
and aggresses against the conflicting self. This is easy
to do, for the more filial and social part of oneself,
which was one of the contestants, can ally with the
introjected authority; useful aggressive and repressive
attitudes are close at hand and easy to learn. It is easy
to avoid occasions of temptation once one has agreed
to be good; it is easy to consider a drive vicious and
alien to oneself when one has identified with those who
consider it so.

The opposite of the excitement of the conflict is the
numbness of resignation. The opposite of the "fertile
void" when one has attained a level of disinterest (and
that void is the creativity of the self) is the empty
space of resignation, where the self used to be. And
the opposite of identification with the coming new self
is the introjection of an alien personality. There is
thus a premature pacification. In the sequel, of course,
the unfinished conflict is still unfinished, but it manifests
itself as a need for victory in small battles instead of a
willingness to consider difficult opposition with a certain disinterestedness; and it is a clinging to security
instead of having faith.

The emotional conflict was hard to solve because another person, for example, the parent, was both loved
and feared; yet unfortunately when the conflict, the
self's own complicated needs and struggling confusion,
is resigned and the parent is introjected and the self's
aggression turned against the self, then this love also is
lost: for there is no contact with what is clung to and
no renewed love with outgoing aggression.

6: Self-Conquest: Satisfactions of Conquest

Let us now look at the peace that has been achieved.
We must distinguish positive and negative peace. When

the conflict has raged itself out and come to a creative solution with the change and assimilation of the warring factors, there is a relief of suffering and the completed excitement of the new created whole. This is positive. There is no sense of conquest and no object to dominate, for indeed the victims have vanished, they are destroyed and assimilated. In positive peace, paradoxically, there is the flush of victory without the sentiment of conquest; the chief sentiment is the liveliness of new possibilities, for there is a new configuration. So Victory is portrayed as winged, on her toes, facing onward.

There is a positive peace also in crushing defeat, if one has gone to one's limits, exhausted every resource and not withheld the maximum of rage. For by tantrum and the labor of mourning the need for the impossible is annihilated. The new self is sombre but whole; that is, its animation is restricted in the new conditions but it has not internalized and identified with the conqueror. So Péguy, for instance, has beautifully described how the suppliants in Greek tragedies have more strength than the arrogant victors.

The peace of conquest, however, where the victim is still in existence and must be dominated, is, as peace, a negation: the suffering of the conflict has ceased but the figure of awareness is not alive with new possibilities, for nothing has been solved; victor and victim and their relations continue to fill the news. The victor is watchful, the victim resentful. In social wars we see that such negative peace is not stable; there are too many unfinished situations. How is it that, in self-conquest, the pacification proves to be stable at all and the conquering self can continue for decades to dominate the alienated part of itself? For indeed the vitality of any natural drive is strong; it can be alienated but not annihilated. We should expect it to be too strong to be long subdued by fear or the need for affection. Why does the conflict not recommence as soon as there is a favorable change in the situation?

It is that the self now gets an enormous *positive* satisfaction from its identification with the strong authority. As a whole the self has been defeated, for its conflict has not been allowed to mature and become some new positive thing; but the identifying self can now say "*I* am the victor." This powerful satisfaction is arrogance. What are the elements?

First, added to the relief of the cessation of suffering the conflict, is the expansive relief from the pressures of threatened defeat, shame, humiliation; by assuming another role, arrogance is expansive, brash, confident. Second, there is the blushing satisfaction of gloating, a species of vanity; in Freudian terms, the super-ego is smiling on the ego. Third, the proud self arrogates to itself the fancied virtues of the authorities, strength, rights, wisdom, guiltlessness. Last and most important, and by no means an illusion, the arrogant self can now wield its aggression and *continually prove* that it is a conqueror, for the victim is always available for domination. The stability of the resigned character does not come from having given up "once and for all," but from the fact that the aggression is continually exercised. Unfortunately the chief victim of the aggression is just oneself, always available to be beaten, squelched, squeezed, bitten, and so forth. Thus the apparent increase of strength and aggressiveness is a crippling weakness. (At first there may often be a real bloom in health, one has made an adjustment; but the toll comes later.) Energy is bound in keeping down the alien drive. If the inner tension becomes too great, the threat from below is projected and one finds scapegoats: these are other persons who have, or to whom can be attributed, one's own offensive and alien drive. They add to the roster of the victims and heighten the arrogance and pride.

Let us be careful to see just what is unfortunate in this process. The elements of expansiveness, ego-ideal, and the arrogation of virtues do not, as such, constitute an unattractive childlike attitude: this is blushing pride, basking in self-approval and social approval, and saying, "See what a big boy am I!" It is a species of exhibition, offensive probably only to those who are disappointed and envious. When the fourth element, the unrestrained aggression, is added, the portrait becomes darker, terrible yet still not ugly. Where there is absolute pride in the self and unbridled outward aggression, we have the true conqueror, a mad spectacle like a torrent or other irrational force, destroying all and soon destroying itself; this is the combination of self-love, self-assurance, and power, without the self-regulation or interpersonal regulation of organic need or social purpose. Such dark madness is not without grandeur; we *both* wonder at it and try to annihilate it.

It is this grand image, of course, that the weak self-conqueror dreams of; his concept of himself is illusory through and through; it does not draw on his energy. The true conqueror is a distraught creator who appoints himself to the role and acts it out. The self-conqueror has resigned himself and been appointed to another role by someone else.

7: Self-Control and "Character"

Beneath the surface need for victory and clinging to security, then, is a remarkable arrogance and conceit; it is only underneath that one comes to the resignation. The conceit proves itself by being able to show that it can in fact produce the goods, be strong, for its victim is always available. The typical remark is: "I'm strong, I'm independent, I can take it or leave it (sex)." Every exercise of self-control, as it is called, is a proof of one's superiority.

Again a difficulty arises, especially in our mores; the social grounds of self-esteem are ambiguous. It is necessary to prove not only that one is strong but that one is "potent," sexually excitable. This contradictory requirement can be met only if the act of love can be made sado-masochistic enough to be able to use aggression as a releasing fore-feeling for sexuality, and sexuality in turn as a means of being punished, to allay anxiety.

Self-conquest is socially esteemed as "character." A man of character does not succumb to "weakness" (this "weakness" actually is the spontaneous eros that accomplishes all creation). He can marshal his aggression to put over his "ideals" (ideals are the norms that one is resigned to). The anti-sexual society that bases its ethics on character—perhaps somewhat more in the immediately previous centuries than nowadays—attributes all achievement to repression and self-control. And certain aspects of our civilization are probably due to character: namely the vast empty façade, the mere quantity, the imposing front; for these constitute the ever-needed proofs of dominating men and nature, they are proofs of potency. But grace, warmth, strength, good sense, gayety, tragedy: these are impossible to persons of character.

Even so, given such major satisfactions of the self, and the freedom to wield aggression, and the highest social prestige, self-conquest is a viable partial integration: it results merely in diminished happiness, personal illness, the domination and misery of others, and the waste of social energy. All these can be put up with. But suddenly the repressions begin to fail because of the general spread of luxuries and temptations; the self-esteem is weakened by social insecurity and insignificance; character is not rewarded; and out-going aggression in civil enterprise is hampered, so that aggression is wielded only against the self; in this present-day situation self-conquest looms in the foreground as the center of neurosis.

8: Relation of Theory and Method

What the theorist sees as the "center of neurosis" depends partly on such social conditions as we have been describing. But partly, of course, it depends on the method of therapy employed (and the method in turn depends on such social factors as the run of patients, the criterion of health, etc.).

In the method explained in this book, where the attempt is made to help the self integrate itself, extending the areas of vitality to include wider areas, the chief resistance is found in the self's unwillingness to grow. The self maintains a grip against its own on-going development.

In the early orthodox technique, where the patient passively, unthinkingly and irresponsibly, produced his id-contents, naturally what struck the therapist was the clash between these and the social norms; the task of integration was a more viable readjustment. Later this concept was felt to be insufficient; the resignation and character-deformation of the patient loomed in the center. But we must point out a remarkable and almost ridiculous contradiction in the usual terminology of theories of character-analysis.

We have seen that, identifying with the authority, the self wields its aggression against its alienated drives, e.g., its sexuality. It is the self that is the aggressor; it conquers and dominates. Yet strangely, when the character-analysts come to speak of the boundary between the self and the alien, they suddenly mention not the "weapons of the self" but the "defenses of the self," its "defensive armor" (Wilhelm Reich). The self, controlling the motoric system and deliberately averting the attention and throttling the excitations, is thought of as defending itself against the threats from below. What is the reason for this odd blunder? It is that the self is not taken seriously by the therapist. He can speak of it in any way that suits his convenience, because *practically* it is nothing. To him only two forces exist, the authority and the instincts; and first the therapist, not the patient, assigns power to the first, and then rebelliously he assigns power to the second.

But there is another existing thing, the self of the patient, and this must be taken seriously by the therapist, for, to repeat, it is only the self that is really available for help. The social norms cannot be altered in psychotherapy, and the instincts cannot be altered at all.

9: What is Inhibited in Self-Conquest

The genesis, in reverse order, of the self-conquest is as follows:

Need for victory
Clinging to security
Conceit of the arrogated personality
Introjection
Resignation
Withdrawal of the self

Now what is primarily inhibited in self-conquest, what is the fundamental loss inflicted on itself by the self? It is the "coming solution" of the conflict that is inhibited. It is the excitement of growing that is driven underground. Sexual excitation, aggression, and grief may to a degree be released in a compartmented way; but unless one feels that he is risking himself in them, the fundamental dullness, boredom, and resignation must persist; the out-going acts are meaningless. Meaningfulness is the same as the excitement of the coming solution. The premature interruption of the conflict, through despair, fear of loss, or avoidance of suffering, inhibits the creativity of the self, its power to assimilate the conflict and form a new whole.

The therapy, conversely, must free the aggression from its fixed target, the organism; make the introjects aware in order that they may be destroyed; bring the compartmented interests, the sexual, the social, etc., back into contact and conflict; and rely on the integrative power of the self, its peculiar style, as expressed precisely in the vitality of the neurosis.

Many questions at once arise. Is not a "coming solution" something future and non-existent? How can the non-existent be importantly inhibited and do much damage? How does the self create itself anew: from what material? with what energy? in what form? Is not "relying on the integrative power" an attitude of therapeutic laissez-faire? And if the conflict is further stirred up and further disintegrates the self, how will the self maintain itself at all, much less grow? What is the "Self"? We shall try to answer these questions in the next chapters. Here let us mention only the chief point.

The self is the system of contacts in the organism/ environment field; and these contacts are the structured experience of the actual present situation. It is not the self of the organism as such, nor is it the passive recipient of the environment. Creativity is inventing a new solution; inventing it both as finding it and as devising it; but this new way could not rise in the organism or its "unconscious," for there are only conservative ways; nor could it be in the novel environment as such, for even if one hit on it there, one would not recognize it as one's own. Yet the existing field passing into the next moment is rich with potential novelty, and contact is the actualization. Invention is original; it is the organism growing, assimilating new matter and drawing on new sources of energy. The self does not know beforehand what it will invent, for knowledge is the form of what has already occurred; certainly a therapist does not know it, for he cannot grow somebody else's growth—he is simply part of the field. But growing, the self risks—risks it with suffering if it has long avoided risking it and therefore must destroy many prejudices, introjects, attachments to the fixed past, securities, plans and ambitions; risks it with excitement if it can accept living in the present.

PART 3

Theory of the Self

X

SELF, EGO, ID, AND PERSONALITY

1: Plan of the Following Chapters

In what has preceded we have discussed some problems of the fundamental perception of reality, of human animal nature and maturation, of language and the formation of personality and society. In all of these, we have tried to show the self performing its function of creative adjustment, often in situations of emergency and enforced resignation where the new created whole is "neurotic" and does not seem to be a work of creative adjustment at all. Indeed, we have chosen to discuss mainly those problems and situations —e.g., the idea of the external world, or the infantile, or the anti-social—the misunderstanding of which tends to obscure the true nature of the self, as we consider it.

Let us now make a new beginning and develop more systematically our notion of the self and its neurotic inhibition. First, drawing on material of the introductory chapter, "The Structure of Growth" (which we suggest be re-read at this point), we consider the self as the function of contacting the actual transient present; we ask what its properties and activity are; and we discuss the three chief partial systems, ego, id, and personality, that in special circumstances seem to be the self. Next, in a critique of various psychological theories, we try to show why our notion has been overlooked and why other incomplete or erroneous views have seemed plausible. Then, deploying the activity of the self as a *temporal process,* we discuss the stages of fore-contact, contacting, final contact, and post-contact; and this is an account of the nature of creative-adjustment growth. Finally, after first clarifying and trying to make coherent the customary Freudian analysis of repression and the genesis of neurosis, we explain the various neurotic configurations as various inhibitions of the process of contacting the present.

2: Self is the System of Present Contacts and the Agent of Growth

We have seen that in any biological or socio-psychological investigation, the concrete subject-matter is always an organism/environment field. There is *no* function of any animal that is definable except as a function of such a field.* Organic physiology, thoughts and emotions, objects and persons, are abstractions that are meaningful only when referred back to interactions of the field.

---

*This should be obvious, but the abstractions have become so ingrained that it is useful to insist on the obvious and point out the common classes of error.

(a) Standing, walking, lying down are interactions with gravity and supports. Breathing is of air. Having an external or internal skin or envelope is an interaction with temperature, weather, fluid, gaseous and solid pressures and osmotic densities. Nutrition and growth are assimilations of selected novel materials that are bitten, chewed, sucked, digested. In such cases, however, there is a common tendency to abstract the "organism," as a man "eats for his health," without addressing himself to the food; or he tries to "relax," without resting on the earth; or he tries to "breathe," without exhaling as well as inhaling.

(b) All perception and thinking are more than a mere response and go out to as well as come from the field. The visible (oval of vision) is touched by the eyes, it is sight; the sounding (audible spheres) touches the ears in hearing and is touched by them. "Objects" of sight and hearing exist by interest, confrontation, discrimination, practical concern. The causes of change and the forms of permanence are solutions of orientation and manipulation. In such cases, however, there is a tendency to abstract the "environment" or the "reality" and consider it prior to the "organism"—the stimulus and the facts are thought of as prior to the response and the need.

(c) Communication, imitation, caring-for, dependency, etc. are the organic social nature of certain animals. Personality is formed of interpersonal relations, rhetorical attitudes; and society, contrariwise, is bound together by intra-personal needs. The symbiosis of organisms and inanimate forces is an interaction of the field. Emotions, concern, and so forth are contact-functions, definable only as relations of needs and objects. Both identification and alienation are ways of functioning in a field. In these cases, however, the common tendency is to abstract both "organism" and "environment" in isolation, and to recombine them secondarily.

The field as a whole tends to complete itself, to reach the simplest equilibrium possible for that level of field. But since the conditions are always changing, the partial equilibrium achieved is always novel; it must be grown to. An organism preserves itself only by growing. Self-preserving and growing are polar, for it is only what preserves itself that can grow by assimilation, and it is only what continually assimilates novelty that can preserve itself and not degenerate. So the materials and energy of growth are: the conservative attempt of the organism to remain as it has been, the novel environment, the destruction of previous partial equilibria, and the assimilation of something new.

Contacting is, in general, the growing of the organism. By contacting we mean food-getting and eating, loving and making love, aggressing, conflicting, communicating, perceiving, learning, locomotion, technique, and in general every function that must be primarily considered as occurring at the boundary in an organism/environment field.

The complex system of contacts necessary for adjustment in the difficult field, we call "self." Self may be regarded as at the boundary of the organism, but the boundary is not itself isolated from the environment; it contacts the environment; it belongs to both, environment and organism. Contact is touch touching something. The self is not to be thought of as a fixed institution; it exists wherever and whenever there is in fact a boundary interaction. To paraphrase Aristotle, "When the thumb is pinched, the self exists in the painful thumb."

(Thus, supposing that, concentrating on one's face, one feels that the face is a mask, and then wonders what one's "real" face is. But this question is absurd, for one's real face is a response to some present situation: if there is danger, one's real face is fright; if there is something interesting, it is an interested face, etc. The real face underlying a face felt as a mask would be the response to a situation kept in unawareness; and it is this actuality, of the keeping something in unawareness, that is expressed by the mask: for the mask is then the real face.* So the advice "Be Yourself" that is often given by therapists, is somewhat absurd; what is meant is "contact the actuality," for the self is only that contact.)

Self, the system of contacts, always integrates perceptive-proprioceptive functions, motor-muscular functions, and organic needs. It is aware and orients, aggresses and manipulates, and feels emotionally the appropriateness of environment and organism. There is no good perception without involving muscularity and organic need; a perceived figure is not bright and sharp unless one is interested in it and focusses on it and scans it. Likewise there is no grace or skill of movement without interest and proprioception of the muscles and perception of the environment. And organic excitation expresses itself, becomes meaningful, precisely by imparting rhythm and motion to percepts, as is obvious in music. To put this another way: it is the sensory organ that perceives, it is the muscle that moves, it is the vegetative organ that suffers an excess or deficit; but it is the organism-as-a-whole in contact with the environment that is aware, manipulates, feels.

This integration is not otiose; it is creative adjustment. In contact situations the self is the power that forms the gestalt in the field; or better, the self *is* the figure/background process in contact-situations. The sense of this formative process, the dynamic relation of ground and figure, is excitement: excitement is the feeling of the forming of the figure-background in contact-situations, as the unfinished situation tends to its completion. Conversely, since self exists not as a fixed institution but especially as adjusting to more intense and difficult problems, when these situations are quiescent or approach equilibrium, the self is diminished. So it is in sleep or in any growth as it approaches assimilation. In food-getting, the hunger, imagination, motion, selection, and eating are full of

*It expresses: "I am one who does not want to feel," or "I want to conceal what I feel."

self; the swallowing, digestion, and assimilation occur with less or no self. Or so in the contact by proximity of charged surfaces, as in love: the desire, approach, touching, and total release of energies are full of self, the subsequent flowing occurs with diminished self. So again in conflicts: the destruction and annihilation are full of self, the identification and alienation occur with diminished self. In brief, where there is most conflict, contact, and figure/background, there is most self; where there is "confluence" (flowing together), isolation, or equilibrium, there is diminished self.

Self exists where there are the shifting boundaries of contact. The areas of contact may be restricted, as in the neuroses, but wherever there is a boundary and contact occurs, it is, in so far, creative self.

3: Self as Actualization of the Potential

The present is a passage out of the past toward the future, and these are the stages of an act of self as it contacts the actuality. (It is likely that the metaphysical experience of time is primarily a reading off of the functioning of self.) What is important to notice is that the actuality contacted is not an unchanging "objective" state of affairs that is appropriated, but a potentiality that in contact becomes actual.

The past is what is unchanging and essentially unchangeable.* In concentrating awareness on the actual situation, this pastness of the situation is given as the state of the organism and the environment; but at once, at the very instant of concentration, the unchanging given is dissolving into many possibilities and is seen to be a potentiality. As concentration proceeds, these possibilities are reformed into a new figure emerging from the ground of the potentiality: the self experiences itself as identifying with some of the possibilities and alienating others. The future, the coming,

---

*So abstractions and unchanging abstract "reality" are constructs of fixed past experience. Essentially "eternal" real conditions are experienced not as unchanging, but as continually renewed the same.

is the directedness of this process out of the many possibilities toward a new single figure.

(We must point out that there is a contactful experience of an "unchanging" objective state, of an "object." This is the experience of concentrated observation of something, in which one takes up an attitude
of confronting and scanning the thing, but refraining
from intervening or adjusting *it* in any way. Obviously
the ability to assume this attitude with lively eros is
what makes a great naturalist, like Darwin, who used
to look for hours, fascinated, at the flower.)

The inhibition of self, in neurosis, is said to be an
inability to conceive of the situation as changing or
otherwise; neurosis is a fixation on the unchanging
past. This is true, but the function of self is more
than the accepting of the possibilities; it is also their
identification and alienation, the creative coming to a
new figure; it is to differentiate between "obsolete responses" and the unique new behavior called for.

We can see here again how the usual advice, "Be
Yourself," is misleading, for the self can be felt only
as a potentiality; anything more definite must emerge
in actual behavior. The anxiety roused by this advice is
fear of the void and confusion of so indefinite a role;
the neurotic feels he is then worthless in comparison
with some conceited concept of his ego; and underlying is the dread of the repressed behavior that might
emerge from the void.

4: Properties of Self

Self is spontaneous, middle in mode (as the ground
of action and passion), and engaged with its situation
(as I, You, and It). Let us consider these properties
in turn, though they involve one another.

Spontaneity is the feeling of acting the organism/
environment that is going on, being not merely its
artisan nor its artifact, but growing in it. Spontaneity is
not directive nor self-directive, nor is it being carried
along though essentially disengaged, but it is a dis-

covering-and-inventing as one goes along, engaged and accepting.

The spontaneous is both active and passive, both willing and done to; or better, it is middle in mode, a creative impartiality; a disinterest not in the sense of being not excited or not creative, for spontaneity is eminently these, but as the unity prior (and posterior) to activity and passivity, containing both.* (It is curious that this feeling of impartiality or disinterest, testified to by creative persons, is analytically interpreted precisely as *loss* of self, rather than as the proper feeling of self, but we shall shortly attempt to show how this comes about.) The extremes of spontaneity are on the one hand deliberateness and on the other relaxation.**

Of the chief classes of contact-functions, feelings are most often considered the underlying self or "soul"; this is because feelings are always spontaneous and middle; one can neither will nor be compelled to feel something. Muscular movement is often predominantly active, and perception is sometimes predominantly passive. But of course both motion and perception may be spontaneous and middle—as in animated dancing or in esthetic perception; and deliberateness itself can be spontaneous, e.g., the uncanny deliberateness of inspired heroic action; and so can relaxation, as when basking in the sun or in the favor of a beloved.

"All things that admit of combination must be capable of reciprocal contact: and the same is true of any two things of which one acts and the other suffers action in the proper sense of the terms." (Aristotle, *De Gene. et Corrupt.*, I, 6)

**In speaking of the middle mode, there is again an important difficulty of language. In English we have mostly only active or passive verbs; our intransitives, "walking," "talking," have lost their middle mode and are merely activities without object. This is a disease of language. Greek has a regular middle mode with, plausibly, the disinterested meaning we here require: e.g., *dunamai*, have power to, or *boulomai*, want. So it is with some French reflexives, *s'amuser*, have a good time, or *se promener*, to take a walk. But we must make a careful distinction: just what the middle is not is action *on* the self—this we shall later call "retroflection," often a neurotic mechanism. The middle mode means, rather, that whether the self does or is done to, it refers the process to itself as a totality, it feels it as its own and is engaged in it. So perhaps in the English, "address oneself to."

By "engaged with the situation," we mean that there is no sense of oneself or of other things other than one's experience of the situation. The feeling is immediate, concrete, and present and integrally involves perception, muscularity, and excitation. Let us contrast two attitudes: when our perceptions and proprioceptions give us orientation in the field, this orientation may be abstractedly regarded, and so felt, as indicating a locomotion and then arriving at a goal where we shall be satisfied, or it may be concretely felt as being on the way and in a sense having arrived and now getting one's bearings. In contact with a task, again, the plan is lit up with fragmentary flashes of the finished product, and contrariwise the finished product is not what is abstractly thought but what clarifies itself in the planning and the working up of the material. Further, there are no mere means and ends; with regard to every part of the process there is a well-rounded but on-going satisfaction: getting one's bearing is itself a manipulation and a fore-feeling. If this were not so, nothing could ever be done spontaneously, for one would spontaneously break off and pursue what does excite feeling. To give a dramatic example (after Gide), the warrior engaged in a death-struggle passionately feels and takes pleasure in the fight.

Finally, spontaneously engaged in a present concern and accepting it as it develops, the self is not aware of itself abstractly, but is aware of itself as contacting something. Its "I" is polar with a "You" and an "It." The It is the sense of the materials, urges, and background; the You is the directedness of interest; the I is taking the steps and making the progressive identifications and alienations.

5: Ego, Id, and Personality as Aspects of Self

The activity we have been discussing—actualizing the potential—and the properties—spontaneity, middle mode, etc.—belong to self engaged in a kind of generalized present; but of course there is no such moment (though to persons of strong feeling and subtle skill moments of intense creativity are not infrequent, if the persons also have luck). For the most part the self creates special structures for special purposes, by bracketing-off or fixing certain of its powers while it freely exercises the rest; so we have mentioned numerous neurotic structures, have just previously alluded to the structure in natural observations, and so forth. The subject-matter of a formal psychology would be the exhaustive classification, description, and analysis of the possible structures of the self. (This is the subject-matter of Phenomenology.)

For our purposes, let us briefly discuss three such structures of the self, the Ego, the Id, and the Personality, because, for various reasons of the run of patients and the methods of therapy, these separate partial structures have been taken, in theories of abnormal psychology, for the whole function of the self.

As aspects of the self in a simple spontaneous act, Id, Ego, and Personality are the major stages of creative adjustment: the Id is the given background dissolving into its possibilities, including organic excitations and past unfinished situations becoming aware, and the environment vaguely perceived, and the inchoate feelings connecting organism and environment. The Ego is the progressive identification with and alienation of the possibilities, the limiting and heightening of the on-going contact, including motor behavior, aggressing, orientation, and manipulation. The Personality is the created figure that the self becomes and assimilates to the organism, uniting it with the results of previous growth. Obviously all this is just the figure/background process itself, and in such a simple case there is no need to dignify the stages with special names.

6: The Ego

A more common healthy experience, however, is the following: One is relaxed, there are many possible concerns, all accepted and all fairly vague—the self is a "weak gestalt." Then an interest assumes dominance and the forces spontaneously mobilize themselves, certain images brighten and motor responses are initiated. At this point, most often, there are also required certain deliberate exclusions and choices (as well as the spontaneous dominances where possible rival concerns subsided of themselves). It is necessary to *pay* attention as well as to be attentive, to budget one's time and resources, to mobilize means not in themselves interesting, and so forth. That is, deliberate limitations are imposed in the total functioning of the self, and the identification and alienation proceed according to these limits. Nevertheless, of course, during this intervening period of deliberate concentration the spontaneity is pervasive, in the background and in the creative act of deliberateness and in the mounting excitement in the foreground. And finally, at the climax of excitement, the deliberateness is relaxed and the satisfaction is again spontaneous.

In this common experience, what is the self-awareness of the ego, the system of identifications? It is deliberate, active in mode, sensorily alert and motorically aggressive, and conscious of itself as isolated from its situation.

Healthy deliberateness is aware restricting of certain interests, perceptions, and motions in order to concentrate with a simpler unity elsewhere. Perception and proprioception are restricted by "not noticing," e.g., the attention may be motorically averted, or if an organic excitation is inhibited, the percept loses brightness. Motor impulses may be checked by rival motor impulses. Excitations may be inhibited by isolating them, not giving them objects to sharpen and arouse them, nor muscular initiative to gather impetus. (Meantime, of course, the chosen interest *is* developing and gathering excitement.)

Now these mechanisms necessarily produce a sense of being "active," of *doing* the experiencing, for the self is identified with the lively chosen interest, and seems from this center to be an extrinsic agent in the field. The approach in the environment is felt as an active aggression rather than as a growing into, for here again the reality is not met according to its spontaneous brightness but is selected or excluded according to the interest identified with. One has the sense of making the situation. Means are selected purely as means, according to previous knowledge of similar situations: one then has the sense of using and mastering rather than of discovering-and-inventing. The senses are on the alert, on the lookout for, rather than "finding" or "responding."

There is a high degree of abstraction from the perceptive-motoric-affective unity and from the total field. (Abstraction, as we have said, is a fixing of certain parts in order that other parts may move and be foreground.) Plan, means, and goal are separated from one another. These abstractions cohere in a tighter, simpler unity.

Finally, an important abstraction that is felt as real in the situation of deliberateness is the ego itself: for organic need is restricted to the goal, perception is controlled, and the environment is not contacted as the pole of one's existence but is held at a distance as "external world," to which oneself is an extrinsic agent. What is felt as close is the unity of goal, orientation, means, control, etc., and this is precisely the actor itself, the ego. Now all theorizing, and especially introspecting, is deliberate, restrictive, and abstractive; so in theorizing about the self, especially from introspections, it is the Ego that looms as the central structure of the self. One is aware of oneself in a certain isolation, not always in contact with something else. The exertion of will and the exercise of one's technique impress by their apparent energy. Besides there is the following important neurotic factor: acts of deliberateness continually recur in quieting unfinished situations, so that this habit of the self impresses itself on the memory as the pervasive feeling of self, whereas spontaneous contacts tend to finish the situation and be forgotten. However it may be, the fact is that in the orthodox psychoanalytic theories of consciousness, it is the ego and not the self that is made central (as we shall discuss at length in the next chapter).

That is, in a paradisal world of spontaneous identifications and alienations without deliberate restriction, the ego would be merely a stage of the function of the self. And' if only behavior is observed, the ego still does not loom, even when there is much deliberateness. But in any introspective theory it necessarily looms large; and where the subject is neurotic, nothing else exists in consciousness but the deliberate ego.

7: The Id

To the orthodox Freudian theorist, however, the conscious deliveries of the neurotic patient count for very little; his deliberate efforts are seen to be lacking in energy. Instead, the theorist goes to the opposite and finds that the important, energetic part of the "mental" apparatus is the Id; but the Id is mainly "unconscious"; introspection tells us nothing about it; it is observable in behavior, including verbal behavior, to which only a rudimentary consciousness attaches. This notion of the properties of the Id is, of course, a consequence of the method of therapy: the relaxed patient and the free-association, and the meanings created by the concentration not of the patient but of the therapist. (Ch. 7, 4ff.)

But let us consider, rather, the structure of the self in common aware relaxation. The situation is that, in order to rest, the self suspends sensory readiness and loosens the muscles from the middle tone. The Id then appears as passive, scattered and irrational; its contents are hallucinatory and the body looms large.

The sense of passivity comes from the act of accepting without engagement. Desirous of resting, the self is not going to rally and act out the impulse; motor initiation is completely inhibited. One after another momentary signals assume dominance and lapse, for they are not further contacted. To the small center of introspective activity, these possibilities seem to be "impressions"; they are given and done to one.

The images that occur tend to be hallucinatory, real objects and whole dramatic incidents contacted with a minimum of expenditure of effort, e.g., hypnagogic images or fantasies of masturbation. Their energy comes from unfinished situations of such a kind as to be satisfied by the agitation of the contact-boundary itself (Ch. 3, 7). For if the organic unfinished situations are urgent, then rest is impossible: the attempt to enforce it results in insomnia, restlessness, etc.; but if they are feeble (relative to the day's fatigue), they can be more or less gratified by hallucination. The passive sexuality of masturbation combines these passive fantasies with an active self-aggression that quiets the need for motoric response.

The self seems scattered, and it is indeed disintegrating and vanishing into mere potentiality, for it exists, is actualized, by contacting. Since both sensory orientation and motor manipulation are inhibited, nothing makes any "sense" and the contents seem mysterious. To contrast ego, self, and id: the deliberate ego has the tight abstract unity of aiming at a goal and excluding distractions; spontaneity has the flexible concrete unity of growing, of engagement and accepting the distractions as possible attractions; and relaxation is disintegrating, unified only by the looming sense of the body.

The body looms large because, sense and motion suspended, the proprioceptions usurp the field. These have been deliberately suppressed; now released, they flood into awareness. If they do not provide an urgent center of concentration, one falls asleep.

8: The Personality

The personality as a structure of the self is again largely discovered-and-invented in the analytic procedure itself, especially when the method is the interpretation and correction of the interpersonal relations. The Personality is the system of attitudes assumed in interpersonal relations; is the assumption of what one is, serving as the ground on which one could explain one's behavior, if the explanation were asked for. When the interpersonal behavior is neurotic, the personality consists of a number of mistaken concepts of

oneself, introjects, ego-ideals, masks, etc. But when the
therapy is concluded (and the same holds for any
method of therapy), the Personality is a kind of framework of attitudes, understood by oneself, that can be
used for every kind of interpersonal behavior. In the
nature of the case, this is the ultimate achievement of
a psychoanalytic interview; and the result is that the
"free" structure thus achieved is taken by the theorists
to be the self. But the Personality is essentially a verbal
replica of the self; it is that which answers a question or
a self-question. It is characteristic of the interpersonal
theorists that they have little to say of organic functioning, sexuality, obscure fantasy, or again of the
technical working up of physical materials, for all these
are not primarily matter for explanation.

What is the self-awareness of the Personality, as we
have spoken of the self-awareness of the Ego and the
Id? It is autonomous, responsible, and self-known
through and through as playing a definite role in the
actual situation.

Autonomy must not be confused with spontaneity.
It is free choosing, and has always a sense of primary
disengagement followed by commitment. The freedom
is given by the fact that the ground of the activity has
already been achieved: one commits oneself according
to what one *is,* that is, has become. But the middle
mode of spontaneity does not have the luxury of this
freedom, nor the feeling of security that comes from
knowing what and where one is and being able to engage or not; one *is* engaged and carried along, not in
spite of oneself, but beyond oneself. Autonomy is less
extrinsically active than deliberateness and of course
less extrinsically passive than relaxation—for it is one's
own situation that one engages in according to one's
role; one is not working on nor worked on by something
other; therefore, free personality is thought to be spontaneous and middle in mode. But in spontaneous behavior, everything is novel and progressively made
one's own; in autonomy the behavior is one's own because in principle it has already been achieved and
assimilated. The "actual situation" is really not novel,

but a mirror image of the Personality—thus it is known to be one's own and one is secure.

The Personality is "transparent," it is known through and through, because it is the system of what has been recognized (in therapy, it is the structure of all the "aha" insights). The Self is not at all transparent in this sense—though it is aware and can orient itself—for its consciousness of self is in terms of the other in the actual situation.

Likewise, Personality is responsible and can hold itself responsible in a sense that the creative self is not responsible. For responsibility is the filling out of a contract; a contract is made according to what one is, and responsibility is the further consistency of behavior in this framework. But pure creativity cannot contract in this sense; its consistency comes to be as it goes along. Thus Personality is the responsible structure of the self. To give what is not so much an analogy as an example: a poet, recognizing the kind of situation and the kind of attitude of communication required, may contract to write a sonnet, and he responsibly fills out this metric form; but he creates the imagery, the emotional rhythm, the meaning as he more and more closely contacts the speech.

X I

CRITIQUE OF PSYCHOANALYTIC THEORIES OF THE SELF

1: Critique of a Theory that Makes the Self Otiose

The self-function is the figure/background process in boundary-contacts in the organism/environment field. This conception is so available in both ordinary and clinical experience and is also so useful for therapy that we are confronted with the problem of why it is disregarded or overlooked altogether in the current theories. In this chapter, then, let us discuss the shortcomings of these theories of consciousness (generally advanced as Theory of the Ego). Later (Chapter 13) we shall see that the self-function is more adequately treated by Freud himself, except that, because of a faulty theory of repression, he assigns its creative work mostly to the unconscious.

The difficulties of the orthodox theories begin when they distinguish between the healthy consciousness and the diseased consciousness; for the healthy consciousness is regarded as *otiose*—dynamically otiose in the theory and, therefore, practically otiose in the therapy—it does nothing. It is only the diseased consciousness that is effective and attended to in order to put it out of the way.

Consider the following passage from Anna Freud's *The Ego and the Mechanisms of Defense:*

"When the relations between the two neighboring powers—ego and id—are peaceful, the former fulfills to admiration its role of observing the latter. Different instinctual impulses are perpetually forcing their way from the id into the ego, where they gain access to the motor system by means of which they attain gratification. In favorable cases the ego does not object to

448

the intruder but puts its own energies at the other's disposal, and confines itself to perceiving. . . . The ego, if it assents to the impulse, does not enter into the picture at all."*

In this passage, first, of course, there is an important truth: the impulse assumes dominance by organismic-self-regulation, without deliberate effort; there is an identification with what is given. (In our terms, the ego is a progressing stage of the self-function.) But what a peculiar use of words to say the impulse "forces its way" as an "intruder," and the ego does "not object," as if in favorable circumstances there were not a unitary process of the self as the ground. And so everywhere in the passage the cart is put before the horse: instead of beginning from a pre-differentiated contact of perception-motion-feeling which then develops as the obstacles and problems become more definite, it is necessary for the ego to "put its energies at the other's disposal," etc.; but in fact one could not show an "impulse" that was not also a perception and a muscular motion.

One is at a loss to conceive the relation of organism and environment that is implied by "the ego confines itself to perceiving," to being aware, and "otherwise does not enter into the picture." Awareness is not otiose; it is orientation, appreciating and approaching, choosing a technique; and it is everywhere in functional interplay with manipulation and the mounting excitement of closer contact. The perceptions are not mere perceptions; they brighten and sharpen, and attract. Throughout the process there is discovery and invention, not looking on; for although the need of the organism is conservative, the gratification of the need can only come from the novelty in the environment: the id-function more and more becomes ego-function up to the point of final contact and release, just the opposite of what Miss Freud asserts. It is precisely in favorable circumstances, when the id and the ego are in

*Anna Freud, *The Ego and the Mechanisms of Defense,* International Universities Press, Inc., New York, 1946.

harmony, that the creative work of awareness is most manifest, not "out of the picture." For suppose that this were not the case: why, functionally, should the awareness be necessary at all? Why could not the gratification occur and the tension be released while the animal is vegetating in a dreamless sleep? But it is because contacting the novel present requires a unified functioning of the powers.

Let us cite another passage to show how this theoretical error of the otiose awareness-system is baneful for therapy. The context of Anna Freud's book—a book, by the way, that is a valuable contribution—is as follows: consciousness is what is most available for treatment; it is the fixed "ego-defenses" that constitute the neurosis. With these theses we of course agree (though we should speak of ego-aggressions rather than ego-defenses). And the problem, as she sees it, is how to catch the ego at work. This cannot be a healthy situation, she argues, for then the ego is otiose. Nor can it be when the ego is successfully "defensive," for then its mechanism is hidden, the impulse is repressed. But, e.g.,

> "Reaction-formation—a neurotic ego-mechanism—can best be studied when such formations are in process of disintegration. . . . For a time instinctual impulse and reaction-formation are visible within the ego side by side. Owing to another function of the ego —its tendency to synthesis—this condition of affairs which is particularly favorable for analytic observation, lasts only for a few moments at a time."*

Notice, here, that the "tendency to synthesis" is called "another" function of the available ego, mentioned in parentheses at the end of the chapter; but this tendency is what Kant, for instance, judged to be the essence of the empirical ego, the synthetic unity of apperception, and it is what we have been considering to be the chief work of the self, gestalt-formation. In this

---

*Anna Freud, *The Ego and the Mechanisms of Defense,* International Universities Press, Inc., New York, 1946.

passage, however, this synthetic tendency is regarded as an unfortunate obstacle to the observation of— what? of the Ego! Clearly by ego, here, Miss Freud means not the awareness-system at all, but the neurotic unaware deliberateness; yet this is not the consciousness that is most available for treatment, enlisting the cooperation of the patient. The alternative is what we have been suggesting all along, to analyze precisely the structure of the syntheses: for the patient to concentrate on how his figures are incomplete, distorted, awkward, feeble, obscure, and to let them develop to more completeness not by circumventing the synthetic tendency but by mobilizing more of it; in this process anxiety is aroused and conflicts emerge, and at the same time the patient is progressively in a position to cope with the anxiety, so it again becomes breathing excitement. Thus the theory of the self develops directly with the therapy of the self. But in the orthodox conception, the opposite is the case: by not concentrating on the patient's integrative power, but tricking it out of the way as much as possible, the analyst learns something about what the patient would be like if he were completely disoriented and paralyzed. What then? Will the analyst then put together the patient from the disparate parts? But this must be done by the patient's integrative power. But not only has the analyst not called this into exercise at all, and has weakened it as much as he can, but he still knows nothing about it.

A theory that makes the awareness-system practically otiose and even an obstacle gives a false picture of the healthy situation and does not help in the neurotic situation.

2: Critique of a Theory that Isolates the Self in Fixed Boundaries

Most of the orthodox theories of awareness are on the previous pattern. Less typical is Paul Federn's theory of the ego and its boundaries. (The following quotations are from a paper on *The Mental Hygiene of the Psychotic Ego.*) In this theory the ego is not otiose, it acts and is felt as an existent synthetic unity.

Personality

> "The ego consists in the feeling of unity, contiguity, and continuity of the individual's body and mind in the proprioception of one's individuality . . . The ego is a functional cathexis unit, changing with every actual thought and perception, but retaining the same feeling of its existence in distinct boundaries."*

And again, Dr. Federn warns of the error of the otiose:

> "The temptation to believe that one presents ego psychology by using the word 'ego' instead of 'personality' or 'individual' . . . Any tautological terminology easily serves self-deception. We must bear in mind that the ego is a specific psychosomatic unit cathected with mental energy."**

And Dr. Federn shows how to use this energetic unit in therapy. For instance, specific operating awareness-functions, such as abstraction or conceptual thinking, may be weakened (in schizophrenia); and the therapy consists in strengthening them by exercises of the ego.

So far so good. But the difficulty with this conception is this: if the contact-system is essentially (rather than sometimes and as a special structure) the proprioception of one's individuality within distinct boundaries, then how possibly does one get into contact with a reality outside the boundaries? The difficulty confronts us squarely in the following formulation of Dr. Federn's:

> "Whatsoever is mere thought is due to a mental process lying *inside* the mental and physical boundary; whatsoever has the connotation of being real lies *outside* the mental and physical ego-boundary."

---

*This is a fair description of what above (10, 8) we have called the Personality. The self as such does not so much feel its own existence as the unity of its contacting.

**Paul Federn, "Mental Hygiene of the Psychotic Ego," *American Journal of Psychotherapy,* July, 1949, pp. 356–371.

In the present state of philosophy, this kind of formulation seems perfectly reasonable, but it is absurd. For how does one become aware of the distinction between the inside and the outside, the "thought" and the "real"? Is it not by awareness? Therefore in some way the system of awareness must directly contact the "external" real; the self-sense must go beyond the proprioception of one's individuality. (We have been arguing, of course, that the essence of contact is being in touch with the situation; the self-function is a function of the field.) The problem is an ancient one: how, awake, do you know that you were dreaming and are not now dreaming? And the answer must still be the classical one: it is not by a special "connotation" of "reality," as if reality were a detachable quality, but by integrating more awareness into the actual situation, more consistency, more body-feeling, and especially in this case more deliberate muscularity. (You pinch yourself to see if you are awake; not that you may not be dreaming also of pinching yourself, but that this is more evidence, and if all the available evidence of this kind coheres, it makes no difference whether you are awake or dreaming anyway.) If the doctor were also to speak of motor-behavior as part of the ego-sense, as well as of perception and proprioception, the absurdity would become patent, for then the "body" of the individual could not be bounded from the other things of the environment.

Let us see how, dynamically, one comes to Dr. Federn's plausible picture. Consider the following propositions:

"The mental and the bodily ego are felt separately, but in the wake state always in such a way that the mental ego is experienced to be inside the body ego."

Certainly *not* always. A situation of strong interest looms in awareness much larger than the felt body, the body is felt as part of *it*, or it is not the "body" that is felt at all, but the object-in-its situation qualified by the bodily appetite. At such a moment the body is felt

as small and turned outward toward the interest. But
what the author is likely thinking of is the moment of
introspection; and it is true that in this act the "mind"
is inside the "body"—especially if the body resists being background and looms bored, restive, itching.

We can now appreciate the formulation:

> "The ego as subject is known by the pronoun 'I' and
> as object it is called 'the self.' "

This is reasonable language if the observational technique is introspection, for then the "mental" ego is
active and the "mental" and "bodily" self is passive;
and since the body-awareness is not controllable—unless the introspection turns into a lively fantasy—the
object body-feeling is larger than the introspective subject. But let us consider the logic of such language for
general usage: The body-awareness is not active, in
introspection; what then, is it "I" or not? If the body-
awareness is "I," then the self is not mere object, and
the "I" is in part not subject. If the body-awareness is
not "I," then there is a system of awareness beyond the
ego's scrutiny (namely the awareness that is not introspection), and what then becomes of the unity? Both
the conclusions happen to be true and both are incompatible with Federn's theory. Fortunately, the true underlying unity can be demonstrated by a simple experiment: introspecting, try to include as objects of the
acting "I" more and more pieces of the larger passive
body-self; gradually, then all at once, the mind and
body will coalesce, "I" and self will merge, the distinction of subject and object will disappear, and the
aware self will touch the reality as perception or interest in some "external" problem, without the intervention of "mere" thoughts.

That is, the self, aware in middle mode, bursts the
compartmenting of mind, body, and external world.
Must we not conclude that for the theory of the self
and its relation to the "I," introspection is a poor *primary* method of observation, for it creates a peculiar
condition? We must begin by exploring a wide range

of concernful situations and behaviors. Then if we resume the introspection, the true situation is apparent: that the introspecting ego is a deliberate restrictive attitude of the psycho-somatic awareness, temporarily excluding the environmental awareness and making the body-awareness a passive object.

When this deliberate restricting is *unaware* (when the ego-function of alienation is neurotic), then there is the sense of a fixed boundary of the self, and of an isolated active center. But this existence is created by the attitude. And then, too, we have "mere" thoughts emptied of "reality." But in the context of aware introspection, the thoughts *are* reality: they are the actual situation when excluding the environment; and then the bounded self and its active center are a good gestalt.

But in general, the aware self does not have fixed boundaries; it exists in each case by contacting some actual situation and is limited by the context of concern, by the dominant interest and the consequent identifications and alienations.

3: Comparison of the Above Theories

The discussion of the above theories brings to light the opposite dilemmas in the usual modern psychologies:

(a) Like Anna Freud, one saves the functional field, the interplay of organism and environment (instinct and gratification), but one makes otiose the synthetic power of the self.

Or (b) like Federn, one saves the synthetic power of the self by cutting off the self (thoughts) from the environment (reality).

But these dilemmas are soluble if we bear in mind that what is primarily given is a unified ground of perceptive, motoric, and feeling functions and that the self-function is a creative adjustment in the organism/environment field.

We can now tackle the question proposed in the beginning of this chapter: how is it that the self-function is so grossly misconceived and that, as is notorious, the theory of the ego is the least developed part of psychoanalysis? Let us mention four interrelated causes:

(1) The philosophic climate compartmenting mind, body, external world.

(2) The social fear of creative spontaneity.

(3) The history of the division between depth and general psychology.

(4) The active and passive techniques of psychotherapy. These causes have conspired to produce the customary dilemmas of the ego-theory.

4: Philosophic Compartments

The method of psychology has been, classically, to proceed from the objects of experience to the acts to the powers, the last being the proper subject-matter—e.g., from the nature of the visible to the actuality of sight to the power of seeing as part of the organic soul. This is a reasonable sequence, from the observable to the inferred. But if the experiencing happens to be neurotic, a curious difficulty rises: abnormal powers give distorted acts and these give defective objects, and then if we proceed from this defectively-experienced world we shall mistakenly infer the powers of experience, and the mistakes reinforce one another, in a vicious circle.

We saw in Chapter 3 how the reaction to epidemic chronic low-grade emergency is to perceive a world of compartmented Mind, Body, and External World. Now the objects of such an external world are such as require to be pushed about by an aggressive will (rather than interacted with in a process of growth), and cognitively they are alien, fragmented, etc., such as to be known only by an elaborate abstract ratiocination. The self inferred as experiencing such objects would be the deliberate ego we have been describing. But this inference is reinforced by the fact that the chronic hypertonus of unaware muscularity, the over-alert perception, and the diminished proprioception produce a sense of willing and exaggerated consciousness: the essential self as the isolated deliberate ego. Likewise in the relation of Mind and Body: the self-conquering aggression keeps down the appetites and anxieties; medical observation and theory exfoliate in the direction of invasion by external poisons and microbes; and medical practice consists of sterile hygiene, chemical cures, vitamins, and analgesics. The factors of depression, tension, and susceptibility are overlooked. So in general, behavior that does not count on the unity of the field prevents the emergence of evidence against the current theory. There is little apparent creativity, contact is lacking, and energy seems to come from "within," and the parts of the gestalt seem to be "in the mind."

Then, given this theory (and feeling) of the isolated active ego, consider the problem that confronts a physician. If the synthetic power of the ego is taken seriously with regard to the physiological functioning, there is an end to organismic-self-regulation, for the ego will intervene rather than accept and develop; but interference with self-regulation produces psychosomatic disease; therefore, theoretically and practically, in comparative health the ego is treated as otiose, an onlooker. And this is proved by the fact that the isolated ego indeed lacks energy, does not count for much. Likewise, if the synthetic power of the ego is taken seriously with regard to the reality, we have the world of the psychotic, a world of projections, rationalizations, and dreams; therefore, in comparative health a final distinction is made between "mere" thoughts and the "real"; the ego is fixed in its bounds.

It is interesting to notice what occurs when one part of the philosophic compartmenting is dissolved, but not the other part. Both in theory and therapy, Wilhelm Reich has completely reestablished the psychosomatic unity; but despite certain concessions to the plain evidence, he fundamentally still regards the animal as functioning inside its skin—e.g., the orgasm is compared with the pulsation in a bladder; the "organism" is not taken as an abstraction from the existing field. What then occurs in his theory? At the boundary, contact-situations are seen as contradictory drives, and to find their unity one cannot look to the creative synthesis of the self but must leave the socio-biological surface and explore in the biological depths; all human energy comes "from inside." The possibility of a creative solution of the surface contradictions, e.g., in culture or politics, is more and more despaired of (but of course this despair has been one of the causes of the theoretical retreat from the surface). In therapy, the method comes in the end merely to trying to awaken the oracles of the body. The creative power of the self is assigned completely to the non-conscious organismic-self-regulation, against all the evidence of the humane sciences, art, history, etc. But then, secondarily, overleaping the boundary of contact, the repressed unity of the field is abstractly projected into the heavens and everywhere, as a bio-*physical* power, directly energizing (and directly attacking) the organism from "without." And this abstraction and projection—the "orgone theory"—is accompanied by the usual obsessional scientific positivism. (This is not to say that Reich's biophysical force is necessarily an illusion, for much projection in fact hits the mark; but what is an illusion is the notion that such a force, if it exists, can be directly effective without going through the channels of ordinary human assimilation and growth.)

On the other hand, suppose the compartmenting of the social environment is dissolved but the psychosomatic unity is not grasped but is paid only lip-service. We then come to the view of the interpersonal theorists (the Washington school, Fromm, Horney, etc.). These reduce the self to what we have above called the Personality, and then—astonishingly but inevitably—they tell us that much of the biological nature is neurotic and "infantile." But their construction lacks vitality and originality; and just where one would hope they would be at their best, as inventive and revolutionary social initiators, we find their social philosophy to be a peculiarly tasteless hall of mirrors of the free but empty Personalities.

5: Social Fear of Creativity

So much for the splittings in the field, the ground of contact. Let us now turn to the gestalt-forming in the field, the spontaneity of the self.

As we tried to show in Chapter 6, there is an epidemic fear of spontaneity; it is the "infantile" par excellence, for it does not take into account the so-called "reality"; it is irresponsible. But let us consider the social behavior in a usual political issue, and see what these terms mean. There is an issue, a problem; and there are opposing parties: the terms in which the problem is stated are taken from the policies, vested interests, and history of these parties, and these are considered to be the only possible approaches to the problem. The parties are not constituted from the reality of the problem (except in great revolutionary moments), but the problem is thought to be "real" only if stated in the accepted framework. But in fact neither of the opposing policies spontaneously recommends itself as a real solution of the real problem; and one is therefore continually confronted with a choice of the "lesser of two evils." Naturally such a choice does not excite enthusiasm or initiative. This is what is called being "realistic."

The creative approach to a difficulty is just the opposite: it tries to advance the problem to a different level by discovering or inventing some new third approach that is essential to the issue and that spontaneously recommends itself. (This then would be the policy and the party.) Whenever the choice is merely and exclusively the "lesser evil," without envisaging the truly satisfactory, it is likely that there is not a real conflict but the mask of a real conflict that no-one wants to envisage. Our social problems are usually posed to conceal the real conflicts and prevent the real solutions—for these might require grave risks and changes. If a man, however, spontaneously expresses his *real* irk, or simple common sense, and aims at a creative adjustment of the issue, he is called escapist, impractical, utopian, unrealistic. It is the accepted way of posing the problem, and not the problem, that is taken for the "reality." We may observe this behavior in families, in politics, in the universities, in the professions. (So, afterwards, we notice how past eras, whose social forms we have outgrown, seem to have been so stupid in some respects. We now see that there was no reason why a spontaneous approach, or a little more common sense, could not easily have solved their problems, prevented a disastrous war, etc., etc. Except that, as history shows, whatever fresh approach was at that time suggested, was simply not "real.")

Most of the reality of the Reality-principle consists of these social illusions, and it is maintained by self-conquest. This is obvious if we consider that in the natural sciences and in technology, where they are at their best, every kind of guess, wish, hope, and project is entertained without the least guilt or anxiety; the *real* subject-matter is not "conformed to" but is observed with fascination and experimented on with temerity. But in other affairs (where face must be saved) we have the following circle: the Reality-principle makes creative spontaneity otiose, dangerous, or psychotic; the repressed excitement is turned more aggressively against the creative self; and the "reality" of the norm then is experienced as real indeed.

The most dismal timidity is not the fear of instinct nor of doing injury, but the fear of doing something in a new way of one's own; or to omit doing it if one is not really interested. But people consult manuals, authorities, newspaper-columnists, informed opinion. What picture of the self will one then draw? It is not even assimilative, no less creative; it is introjective, additive, and regurgitating.

6: The Fine Arts in Analytic Theory

A beautiful example of the blotting out of spontaneity from analytic theory may be observed in the treatment of the fine arts and poetry, just where one

would expect to find creative spontaneity in the foreground.

Long ago Freud declared that psychoanalysis could
deal with the themes that artists chose and with the
blocks to their creativity (these are the topics of his
Leonardo), but not with the creative inspiration, which
was mysterious, nor with the technique, which was the
domain of art-history and art-criticism. This dictum
has since for the most part been adhered to (not always
with the humanistic grace with which Freud made it);
and when it has not been adhered to, the result has
been to make of art a peculiarly virulent neurotic
symptom.* Yet what an extraordinary conception it is!
For theme and inhibition belong to every activity
whatever; it is just the creative force and the technique that make the artist and poet; so that the so-
called psychology of art is the psychology of everything
but particularly not art.

But let us consider just these two forbidden subjects
and especially the technique. To the artist, of course,
technique, style, is everything: he feels creativity as his
natural excitement and his interest in the theme
(which he gets from "outside," that is, from the unfinished situations of the past and from the day's
events); but the technique is *his* way of forming the
real to be more real; it occupies the foreground of his
awareness, perception, manipulation. The style is himself, it is what he exhibits and communicates: style
and not banal repressed wishes nor the news of the
day. (That the formal technique is primarily what
communicates is, of course, obvious from the Ror-
schach or other projective tests. Surely it is not Cé-
zanne's apples that are interesting—though they are by
no means irrelevant—but his handling and what he
makes of, precisely, apples.)

The working up of the real surface, the transformation of the apparent or inchoate theme in the material
medium, is the creativity. In this process there is no

---

*The outstanding exception was Rank, whose *Art and the Artist* is
beyond praise.

mystery at all, except the merely verbal mystery that it is not something one knows beforehand, but something one does and then knows and can talk about. But this is true of every perception and manipulation that confronts any novelty and forms a gestalt. To the extent that, as in psychological experiments, we can isolate a task and repeat similar parts, we can predict the whole that will be spontaneously perceived or performed; but in all important concerns in art and the rest of life, the problem and the parts are always somewhat new; the whole is explicable but not predictable. Even so, the whole comes into being by a very ordinary (everyday) experience.

The "mystery" of the creative for psychoanalysts comes from their not looking for it in the obvious place, in the ordinary health of contact. But where could one expect to find it in the classical concepts of psychoanalysis? Not in the super-ego, for that inhibits creative expression; it destroys. Not in the ego, for that originates nothing, but either observes or executes, or suppresses and defends itself. It cannot be the ego that is creative, for the artist cannot explain himself; he says, "I don't know where it comes from, but if you're interested in how I do it, this is what I do—" and he then begins a boring technical explanation that is the subject-matter of art-criticism and art-history but not of psychology. Therefore psychoanalysts guess that the creative must be in the id—and there it is well hidden. Yet indeed, an artist is not *un*aware of what he does; he is quite aware; he does not verbalize it nor theorize it, except *a posteriori;* but he makes something by handling the material medium and solving a rough new problem that refines itself as he goes along.

Theorizing from the self-conquering ego, psychoanalysis can make no sense of a kind of contact that is exciting and changes the reality. And the disgrace of our generation is that this kind of ego is so epidemic that what the artist does seems *extra*ordinary. Instead of theorizing the ego from the most lively cases of creativity, which are (in this respect) the normal ones, the theory has sprung from the average, and the

lively cases are considered mysterious or else virulent-
ly neurotic.

Yet the right theory could also be gleaned from the
spontaneity of children who, with perfect aplomb, hallucinate reality and still recognize reality, and who
play with reality and alter reality, without being in the
least psychotic. But they, of course, are infantile.

7: The Split between Depth and General Psychology

Historically, psychoanalysis developed in the hey-
day of association-psychology, and in the first flush of
the reflex-arc and conditioned-reflex grounding of the
associations. The functional and dynamic theory of
Freud was so at variance with these conceptions that it
seemed to belong to a different world; and this was in
fact the truce arrived at, a division of worlds. The world
of the conscious Freud conceded to the associationists
(and the biologists); the world of dreams he took for
himself and correctly mapped with functional signals.
At the boundary of the two worlds, where the dreams
emerged into waking, occurred what Freud in a brilliant flash (of contempt?) called the "secondary elabo-
ration"; it certainly was not primary and energetic, but
was an attempt to make sense by conforming to the
"laws of reality," namely the associations. (We shall
return to Freud's primary process and secondary process in Chapter 13.) Meantime, the psychologists
more and more proved that these were indeed the laws
of reality by constructing experimental situations that
were less and less vitally interesting, and in which the
response tended to be in fact reflex: mazes and shocks,
the reactions to which were not secondary but tertiary
and quaternary, up to the point of nervous breakdown.
(If psychology is the study of creative adjustments,
reflex-psychology is the penological branch of physics.)

Occasionally, to be sure, Freud indicated that the
dream-laws might be the laws of reality—but he did
not see how to reconcile the discrepancies. Yet indeed,
just on logical grounds, given the two worlds, the world
of dreams with its laws of pleasure and fantastic dis-

tortions, and the world of conscious-reality with its no-pleasure and additive associations, it is hard to avoid the recurring epistemological question: with what unitary awareness does one distinguish these two worlds, and what are the laws of that unitary system?

In general psychology occurred the Gestalt revolution—that was mainly a return to ancient conceptions. (For the working of thought and behavior is not a bashful or recondite subject-matter and the ancients, though no keen experimenters, could not help experimenting it.) Perception, abstraction, problem-solving came to be conceived as formed and forming wholes, the completion of unfinished needful tasks. Now one would have expected an immediate rapprochement between gestalt-psychology and psychoanalysis, a synthesis of contact and depth-psychology, and therefore, again, a functional theory of the self, id, ego, and personality. This failed to occur. The lack of daring to do it must be attributed to the gestaltists, for the psychoanalysts have not lacked daring. First, for years, in order to refute the associationists, the Gestalt-psychologists devoted themselves to proving that the perceived wholes were "objective" and essentially physical, not "subjective" nor the result of emotional tendencies. Yet what an astonishing victory to win! for throughout physical nature the gestaltists keenly sought out whole tendencies, insisted on the context and the interrelation of all the parts, in order to bolster their psychology; but it was only in this one case of human feelings that the gestalt-principle did not apply! An emotion was not a real part of the perception it accompanied; it did not enter the figure!

Secondly, ambitious for this victory, they carefully sterilized (controlled) the experimental situations, making them less and less possibly interesting to any subject; and nevertheless, by wonderful ingenuity, they were able to demonstrate the gestalt. Yet their very success should have alarmed them and served as disproving evidence, for it was against their basic principle of the context: that it is where all the functions are mobilized by a real need that the gestalt is most evident. What they ought to have experimented was just the reverse: to show the *weakening* of the formative tendency when the task becomes a mere laboratory task, abstract, isolated, unconcernful. (And this was from the beginning the tack with the animal experiments.) Thirdly, from the beginning they have clung to the scientific method of the formal laboratory. But consider the following difficulty: what if the very thing that offers the essential explanation, the creative power of lively excitement, will either withdraw from this situation or intervene in the experiment, upset the controls, unsterilize the situation, perhaps decline to be experimented on at all, and insist on the existing problem, not the abstract problem? In such a case, in the interests of science, one must turn away from the fetishism of the accepted "scientific method." The experiment must be real and *meant,* in the sense of making a personal difference, of being a sophisticated effort for happiness, and therefore a partnership in which the "experimenter" and the "subject" are both men. Such studies are by no means out of the question. Politically they occur in cooperative communities; socially and medically they occur in such projects as the Peckham Health Centre; and they exist in every session of psychotherapy.

Be that as it may, we have now had for two generations the anomalous situation of the two most dynamic schools of psychology advancing parallel with little interaction. And inevitably it is just their meeting ground, the theory of the self, that has suffered and is the least developed.

8: Conclusion

Lastly, the methods used in psychotherapy itself have obscured true theories of the self and of growth, and have tended to confirm theories of the ego as either otiose or merely resistant, of the id as unaware, of the personality as merely formal, etc. They have produced situations of observation—and employed criteria of cure—in which the evidence is *prima facie* confirmatory of such theories. Throughout this book we have been showing examples of how this comes about.

Nevertheless, it would be unjust to conclude this unfriendly chapter without saying the following:

With all its defects, no other discipline in modern times has conveyed the unity of the organism/environment field so much as psychoanalysis. If we look at the grand lines rather than the details, we can see that in medicine, psychology, sociology, law, politics, biology, biophysics, anthropology, culture-history, community-planning, pedagogy, and other specialties, psychoanalysis has discovered and invented a unity. In each case the specialist scientists have rightly rejected the simplifications and the reductions; yet we see that in their very replying to the errors of psychoanalysis they begin to use the terms of psychoanalysis, and the evidence marshalled to refute psychoanalysis as irrelevant was quite overlooked before the advent of psychoanalysis.

XII

CREATIVE ADJUSTMENT: I.
FORE-CONTACT AND CONTACTING

1: Physiology and Psychology

Although there is no function of the organism that is not essentially an interacting in the organism/environment field, yet at any time the greater part of the great majority of animal functions are tending to complete themselves inside the skin, protected and unaware; they are not contact-functions. Contacts are at the "boundary" (but of course the boundary is shifting and may even, in pains, be deep "inside" the animal), and essentially they contact the novel. Organic adjustments are conservative; they have been built into the organism during long phylogenetic history. Presumably at some time every inside function was also a contact-function, adventuring in and suffering the environment (e.g., peristalsis-locomotion, osmotic digestion-touch, mitosis-sexuality, etc.); but now, even in emergencies, regulation occurs with little contact of the novel.

The system of conservative inherited adjustments is the physiology. It is, of course, integrated and regulates itself as a whole, it is not a collection of elementary reflexes: this wholeness of the physiology the ancients used to call the "soul," and "psychology" (science of the soul) included also the discussion of the physiology. But we prefer to make the subject of psychology the special set of the physiological adjustments that are also in relation with what is not physiological: namely the contacts at the boundary in the organism/environment field. The defining difference between the physiology and the psychology is the self-regulating,

467

relatively self-contained conservatism of the "soul" and the confronting and assimilation of novelty by the "self." It will be seen from this that presentness in a situation and creative adjustment constitute the self-function.

In a certain sense, the self is nothing but a function of the physiology; but in another sense it is not part of the organism at all, but is a function of the field, it is the way the field includes the organism. Let us consider these interactions of the physiology and the self.

2: Fore-Contact: Periodic and Aperiodic

A physiological function completes itself internally, but ultimately no function can continue to do so (the organism cannot "preserve itself") without assimilating something from the environment, without growing (or discharging something into the environment, and dying). Thus unfinished physiological situations periodically excite the contact-boundary because of some deficit or surfeit, and this periodicity applies to every function, whether metabolism, need for orgasm, need to divide, need to exercise or rest, etc.; and all these occur in the self as urges or appetites, hunger, urge to excrete, sexuality, fatigue, etc.

We may see from this why breathing plays such an interesting role in psychology and therapy. ("Psyche" or "animus" is breath.) Breathing is a physiological function, yet its period of requiring the environment is so frequent, and indeed continuous, that it is always on the verge of becoming aware, a kind of contact. And in breathing one sees par excellence that the animal is a field, the environment is "inside" or essentially pervading at every moment. And so anxiety, the disturbance of breathing, accompanies any disturbance of the self-function; thus the first step in therapy is contacting the breathing.

The conservative functions become contact, also, when a novel situation occurs because of aware malfunction. These are the aperiodic pains. Let us contrast the periodic urges and the aperiodic pains. In the urges and appetites, the figure of contact develops—for instance, thirst and possible water—and the body (disequilibrium) is background and more and more recedes. (This is true also with the urge to excrete, which healthily is an urge to "let go of.") In pain the body is more and more attended to as the foreground figure. So the classic therapeutic maxim is: "The healthy man feels his emotions, the neurotic feels his body"—which is not to deny, of course, but rather to imply that in therapy one tries to extend the area of body-awareness, for it is because some areas *cannot* be felt that others are unduly tensed during excitement and are felt as painful.

Other novelties occur in the conservative physiology because of environmental stimuli, perceptions, poisons, etc. These are aperiodic. Either they meet with and are responded to by, some urge or appetite, in which case they become centers of the developing figure of contact, with the body more and more as background; or they are annoyances, irrelevant, and so forth, in which case they will become pains, with the body as foreground and the attempt to annihilate the novelty from the figure, in order again to become unaware.

Lastly, there are the novelties in the physiology that are especially fateful for neurosis: the disturbances of the conservative organismic-self-regulation. Suppose, for instance, that an urge or appetite is not satisfied from the environment and the emergency-functions (tantrum, dream, blacking out, etc.) cannot operate or are exhausted, then there will be a readjustment of the physiology, an attempt to establish a new unaware conservatism in the new conditions. The same will happen if there are chronic painful environmental demands or persistent foreign bodies in the body. Obviously all these *ad hoc* physiological adjustments cannot easily cohere with the conservative inherited system; they malfunction, produce diseases and pains. Yet it is clear that they are a secondary physiology; for the novelty does not lead to awareness and creative adjustment, but itself becomes unaware and (poorly) organically-self-regulating. Deformed posture is an example. Being no longer novelties, these structures do not appear in the self, in contact, but they are evident, as we shall see, precisely in the defects and fixations of the self-functioning. The poor adjustment between the inherited and the new physiology occurs in the self, again, in periodic pain-tinged urges or symptoms.

It is with the occurrence of novelty, then, that the physiology becomes contactful. We have distinguished the following classes:

1. Periodic urges and appetites, the contact developing toward the environment.

2. Aperiodic pains, the contact developing toward the body.

3. Stimulations, either developing as appetites (emotions), or as pains.

4. Readjustments of physiology because of environmental conditions, appearing as deficiencies in the structure of contact, or periodically as symptoms.

These excitations or fore-contacts initiate the excitement of the figure/background process.

3: First Stages of Contact

The excitations at the contact-boundary lend their energy to the formation of a sharper and simpler object-figure, approaching it, appreciating it, overcoming obstacles, manipulating and altering the reality, until the unfinished situation is complete and the novelty is assimilated. This process of contacting—touching the loved, interesting, or appetizing object; or expelling from the field, by avoidance or annihilation, the dangerous or painful object—is in general a continuous sequence of grounds and figures, each ground emptying out and lending its energy to the forming figure that in turn becomes ground for a sharper figure; the whole process is an aware mounting excitement. Note that the energy for the figure-formation comes from both poles of the field, both the organism and the environment. (In learning something, for instance, the energy comes from the need to learn it, and from the social milieu and the teaching, and also from the intrinsic power of the subject-matter: it is common, but we think misleading, to think of the "interest" of the subject-matter as being completely cathected to it from the learner and his social role.)

The process of contact is a single whole, but we may conveniently divide the sequence of grounds and figures as follows:

1. Fore-contact: the body is the ground, the appetite or environmental stimulus is the figure. This is what is aware as the "given" or Id of the situation, dissolving into its possibilities.
2. Contacting: (a) the excitement of appetite becomes the ground and some "object" or set of possibilities is the figure. The body diminishes. (Or contrariwise, in pain, the body becomes figure.) There is an emotion.
   (b) there is choosing and rejecting of possibilities, aggression in approaching and in overcoming obstacles, and deliberate orientation and manipulation. These are the identifications and alienations of the Ego.
3. Final Contact: against a background of unconcernful environment and body, the lively goal is the figure and is in touch. All deliberateness is relaxed and there is a spontaneous unitary action of perception, motion, and feeling. The awareness is at its brightest, in the figure of the You.
4. Post-Contact: There is a flowing organism/environment interaction that is not a figure/background: the self diminishes.

In this chapter we discuss the first two of these, in the next chapter the remaining two.

Appetite seems either to be stimulated by something in the environment or to rise spontaneously from the organism. But of course the environment would not excite, it would not be a stimulus, unless the organism were set to respond; and further, it can often be shown that it was a dimly aware appetite that put one in the way of the stimulus at the appropriate time. The response reaches out to the stimulus.

The appetite is, however, usually vague until it finds some object to work on; it is the work of creative adjustment that heightens awareness of what one wants. But in cases of extreme need, extreme physiological deficit or surfeit, the spontaneous appetite may make itself definite, bright, and sharply delineated to the point of hallucination. In the defect of an object it makes an object, largely out of fragments of memory. (This occurs, of course, in the neurotic "repetition," when the need is so overpowering in its influence and the means of approach are so archaic and irrelevant that an ordinary creative adjustment, assimilating a real novelty, is impossible.) Hallucination to the point of blacking out the environment is an emergency-function, but it calls our attention to what occurs in the ordinary case.

For in the more hopeful case of strong but vague appetite with possibilities in the environment, the self functions as follows: the tendency to hallucination, to make the object, enlivens something that is actually perceived: it spontaneously focusses, remembers, and anticipates it. What is confronted is not what a moment before was, but an object made of perception *and* imagination, against a background of mounting excitement. Such a figure is already a created reality. Meantime, motor behavior is adding other novelties to the rapidly altering whole: paying attention and approaching. There is aggressive initiation of new possibilities; if there are obstacles, anger and annihilating alter the reality. And in general, one's technique or style, the learned possibilities of manipulation, add to and determine what is perceived as an "object."

That is, from the beginning and throughout, on being excited by a novelty, the self dissolves the given (of both the environment and the body and its habits) into possibilities and from them creates a reality. The reality is a passage from past to future: this is what exists, and this is what the self is aware of, discovers and invents.

4: Gratuitous Creativity

Often, indeed, the self seems hardly responsive at all to organic excitations and environmental stimuli, but acts as if, hallucinating a goal and flexing its technique, it were spontaneously making a problem for itself in order to force growth. This kind of "gratuitous act" is extremely interesting. *Prima facie* it appears to be neurotic because it lays so heavy a stress on the creative and so little on the adjusting; it seems to be a flight *from* the reality, a mere hallucination. Nevertheless, it is probably a normal function: for given a field so complicated and subtle as human beings have, it is plausible that spectacular success requires the ability to make occasional quite uncalled-for projects, to "make trouble for oneself," and also to suspend utility and play. Certainly, although most wisdom is the fruit of solving obvious needs, the most characteristically human wisdom and folly have always seemed at first gratuitous. Further, in neurotic gratuitous action, flight from reality, we must distinguish two aspects: first is the safe expression of unaware unfinished situations—these are the garrulous plans, busy-making enterprises, substitute activities, etc.; but also there is the expression of dissatisfaction with one's circumscribed self, the desire to change without "knowing" how, and thence the reckless adventure, which in fact is often perfectly reasonable and integrative, but felt as reckless only by the neurotic. And besides, as Yeats used to say, without a touch of recklessness there is no courtliness and poetry.

Consider again the enormous expenditure of human effort in creating a more desirable surface reality, either out of perceptions and images in the arts or out of essences and explanations in the speculative sciences. In one aspect this effort is entirely gratuitous; it is work of the contact-boundary alone. (The non-gratui-

grace — gratuity

tous aspect of the arts is, of course, cathartic abreaction, the beauty serving as fore-feeling to release a
repressed unfinished situation; and the speculative
sciences have the utility of pragmatic application.) Yet
the naive judgment of beauty and truth—a usual judgment in antiquity and analyzed once and for all by
Kant—has to do with the surface itself: it is not an
adjustment of the organism to the environment, nor a
satisfactory completion of an organic drive in the environment, but it is an adjustment of the whole field
to the self, to the surface of contact: as Kant well said
it, there is a sense of purpose, without a purpose. And
the act is pure self, for the pleasure is disinterested and
spontaneous; the organism is in abeyance. Is there
perhaps a function for it? In a difficult and conflictful
field, where almost nothing can exist without deliberateness and caution and effort, beauty is suddenly a symbol of Paradise, where all is spontaneous—"beasts
without fangs, and without thorn the rose"; yes, or
beasts with fangs, and heroes who can win or lose
grandly; and where, as Kant said, happiness is the reward of good intentions. Then this gratuitous creativity
of awareness is truly re-creative for an animal that
requires recreation; it helps to relax our habitual prudence, in order that we may breathe.

5: Creativity/Adjustment

For the most part, however, we may consider the
self's creativity and the organism/environment adjustment as polar: one cannot exist without the other.
Given the novelty and indefinite variety of the environment, no adjustment would be possible by the
conservative inherited self-regulation alone; contact
must be a creative transformation. On the other hand,
creativity that is not continually destroying and assimilating an environment given in perception and resisting
manipulation is useless to the organism and remains
superficial and lacking in energy; it does not become
deeply exciting, and it soon languishes. It is useless to
the organism because there is no completion of unfin-

ished physiological situations without, ultimately, new environment material for assimilation.

This last point is obvious with regard, for instance, to metabolic deficit, hunger, and feeding, and so with the other appetites; but it is sometimes overlooked with regard to the (secondarily physiological) unfinished situations of neurosis. It is the truth in the orthodox insistence on "transference" in the cure, for the relation to the therapist is a real social situation. And the change of attitude of a patient, when he turns his aggression from himself toward his introjects in order to assimilate them or regurgitate them, is a change in the reality. Yet we must go even further and say the following: that relaxing deliberateness, learning correctly to interpret one's case, and even feeling one's body and one's emotions: these do not, in the end, solve any problems. They make a solution again possible; they transform the unaware secondary physiology again into a problem of creative contact; but then the solution must be lived out. If the social environment is still refractory to creative adjustment, if the patient cannot adjust it to himself, then he must again adjust himself to it and keep his neurosis.

Creativity without outgoing adjustment remains superficial, then, first because the excitement of the unfinished situation is not drawn on, and the mere interest in contact lapses. Secondly, it is in manipulating the resistant that the self becomes involved and engaged; knowledge and technique, more and more of the achieved past, are called into play and into question; and soon the "irrelevant" difficulties (the irrationality of reality) prove to be the means of exploring oneself and finding out what it is that one really intends. Frustrations, anger, partial satisfactions, feed the excitement—it is fed partly from the organism, partly from the resistant and destroyed and suggestive environment. To make the comparison again with the fine arts: the Crocean notion of the creative moment being the intuition of the whole, and the rest being mere execution, is true and yet profoundly false. The intuition does adumbrate the final product: it is projected from the beginning as a hallucination; but the artist does not understand the dream, he does not know what he intends; it is the handling of the medium that practically reveals his intention and forces him to realize it.

6: Emotions

To illustrate the transition from the excitations and stimuli of fore-contact to the creative figure-formation of contacting, let us consider the emotions.

An emotion is the integrative awareness of a relation between the organism and the environment. (It is the foreground figure of various combinations of proprioceptions and perceptions.) As such, it is a function of the field. In psychotherapy this can be shown experimentally: by concentration and muscular exercises, it is possible to mobilize particular combinations of body-behavior, and these rouse a kind of restless excitation—e.g., tightening and loosening the jaw, clenching the fists, beginning to gasp, and so forth, and the feeling of a frustrated anger. Now if to this proprioception is added the environmental awareness, either fantasy or perception of some thing or person that one can be angry with, at once the emotion flares in full force and clarity. Conversely, in an emotional situation, the emotion is not felt until one accepts the corresponding bodily-behavior—it is when one clenches one's fist that one begins to feel the anger.

(Thus the James-Lange theory of the emotions—that the emotion is a condition of the body, it is in running away that one becomes afraid—is partly true; what must be added to it is that the bodily condition be also a relevant orientation and potential manipulation of the environment; that is, it is not running, but running *away, away from something,* that is fearful.)

If we think of the functioning of an organism in its environment, the need for such integrative combinations is evident. The animal must know immediately and truly what the relations of the field are; and he must be impelled by the knowledge. Emotions are such motivating knowledge as allow the animal to experience the environment as his own, to grow, protect himself, and so forth. For instance, longing is the heightening of appetite confronted with a distant object, in order to overcome distance or other obstacles; grief is the tension of loss or lack in accepting the absence of the object from the field, in order to withdraw and recuperate; anger is the destroying of obstacles to appetite; spite is an attack on an unavoidable overpowering enemy in order not altogether to capitulate; compassion is the avoidance or undoing of one's own loss by helping another; and so forth.

In the sequence of grounds and figures, the emotions take over the motivational force of the urges and appetites; but the motivation, made definite by its objective reference, is thereby stronger. But the emotions in turn, except in very simple adjustments, give up their motivational force to the still stronger and more definite feelings, the actualized virtues and vices (e.g., courageousness, sullenness, determination, etc.) that impel more complicated orientations and manipulations, especially when they are deliberate. In this transition, again, we can see that both more of the organism (the virtues and vices are habits) and more of the environment are drawn on.

Let us say a few more words about the emotions. It is clear that emotions are not confused or rudimentary impulses, but sharply differentiated functional structures. If a person has crude emotions, it is that his experience as a whole is crude. But of course the dictionary words for the emotions are crude and few; to express the emotions that are felt in sensitive experience requires nuance and reticence, and much objective reference. Works of plastic and musical art are pure language of the emotions, elaborated to statements of conviction.

The emotions are means of cognition. Far from being obstacles to thought, they are unique deliveries of the state of the organism/environment field and have no substitute; they are the way we become aware of the appropriateness of our concerns: the way the world is for us. As cognitions they are fallible, but are corrigible not by putting them out of court but by trying out whether they can develop into the more settled feelings accompanying deliberate orientation—e.g., to proceed from the enthusiasm of discovery to conviction, or lust to love.

Finally, in psychotherapy, the "training of the emotions," we see that only a combined unitary method is of any avail: we must concentrate both on the world of "objects"—interpersonal relations, fantasy, memory, etc.—and on releasing bodily mobility and appetite, and also on the structure of the third thing, the emotion of the self.

7: Excitement and Anxiety

Excitement persists and increases through the sequence of creative adjustment, and is strongest at the final contact. This is so even if obstacles and lost conflicts prevent the finale; but in such a case the excitement becomes spectacularly disruptive of the organizing self itself. Rage turns into tantrum, there is grief and exhaustion, and perhaps hallucination (day-dream of victory, revenge, and gratification). These are emergency functions to release tension and enable one to start afresh the next time, for of course the physiological need and its excitation are still unfinished. This process, of total frustration and unlimited explosion, is not unhealthy but it is not, needless to say—despite the opinion of many parents—useful for learning anything, for the self is disrupted and there is nothing left to assimilate.

But suppose now that the excitement is interrupted. Let us attend to the stronger breathing that is a factor in all excitements: the excitement is interrupted, the breath is held. This is anxiety.

The most clear-cut case of healthy anxiety is fright, the choking off of the feeling and movement in which one is fully engaged in order to meet a sudden danger. This situation is especially likely to be traumatic, as can be seen by contrasting it with ordinary fear. In fear, the dangerous object is foreseen; one is deliberate and defensive with regard to it; therefore, when it is necessary to withdraw because the danger is too great, the approach to the environment is still open; and later, with increase of knowledge and power, it will be possible to confront the danger again and avoid or annihilate it. In fright the threatened pain and punishment loom suddenly and overwhelmingly large, and the response is to cut off the environment, that is, to play dead and withdraw within one's skin. The anxiety, the excitement which was suddenly muscularly dammed up, continues to shake for a long time, till one can breathe freely again.

An anti-sexual society is designed to produce this traumatic situation with maximum frequency and efficiency among its children. Because the sexuality is secretive (and they want, of course, to exhibit it), the children engage themselves where there is the most likelihood of being surprised; and when they are surprised, the punishment has no relation to anything in their experience of causes and effects, therefore it might well be capital. Such a society is a neatly calculated trap.

Breathing may, of course, be interrupted and cause anxiety, in other ways than by fright; generally fright and the other ways cooperate. Freud singled out coitus interruptus, interrupting the climax of contact, as a special cause of primary anxiety (actual-neurosis) with neurasthenic symptoms. Interruption by punishing the aggressive excitement of the stage of conflict or tantrum seems to be a likely cause of resignation and self-conquest, the avoidance of the previous struggle as "not worth the trouble." Or the excitement may be cut off still earlier, at the state of noticing an object in the environment, and this would lead to *projections*. We shall discuss the various kinds of interruptions in Chapter 15.

At whatever stage of contacting the interruption, fright and anxiety occur, the effect is to become cautious about the original appetite itself, and to control it by averting the attention, distracting the interest with other things, holding the breath, gritting the teeth, tightening the abdominal muscles, retracting the pelvis, tightening the rectum, etc. The urge or appetite recurs anyway but now, muscularly restricted, it is painful —for urges and appetites tend to be expansive, outgoing. That is, there is now a change from the sequence in which the body served as the diminishing ground for the developing self; now the body is the figure; and the self, in its structure of the motorically active and deliberate ego, is the ground. This process is still fully aware; it is an attempt at a creative adjustment, working on the body instead of on the environment.

But if this deliberate suppression is persisted in, there is likely to be repression, unaware deliberateness. The nature of repression will be the subject of Chapter 14.

8: Identifying and Alienating
I: Conflict

In the work of contacting, we may now define the function of the ego, identifying and alienating and determining the boundaries or context. "Accepting an impulse as one's own" means, in the sequence, to have it as part of the ground in which the next figure will develop. (This is what Freud meant to say by "the ego is part of the id.") Such identifying is often deliberate; and the ego will function well—in its orientations and manipulations—if it is identified with grounds that in fact will develop good figures, provided the grounds have energy and likelihood. (So Freud says, "The ego as part of the id is strong, the ego cut off from the id is weak.")

Let us run through the process again. In process, background and figure are polar. A figure can be experienced only against its ground, and without its figure a ground is simply part of a larger vague figure. But the relation between ground and figure, in creativity, is a dynamic and shifting one. The mounting excitement flows from the ground toward the more and more sharply defined figure. (This, to repeat it, does not mean merely "cathecting" the figure, for some of the energy comes from the environmental ground, as must be, since it is only new energy that can complete an unfinished situation.) Energy is released for figure-formation when the chaotic environmental parts "meet" an instinctual excitation, define and transform it, and are themselves destroyed and transformed. Mounting excitement is the progressive leaving behind of the ground. At the stage of emotion, the body-ground diminishes and the environmental possibilities loom; next the environment is delimited and deliberately appropriated as one's own; finally the deliberateness is relaxed, the active ego-feeling vanishes, and there is, momentarily, only the figure and the feeling of spontaneity, with the ground empty.

But we speak of accepting something only when there is a tendency to reject it. When the identifying with an impulse, an object, or a means is spontaneous and obvious—as in fascination or in using an expert skill—and when everything else is out of the question, there is no point in distinguishing self, id, and ego. What is accepted by the ego is an aware conflict and the exercise of aggression.

Conflict is a disturbance of the homogeneity of the ground and prevents the emergence of a sharp and lively next figure. The conflicting excitements bring alternative figures into dominance. The attempt to unify a single figure when the ground is busy, in order to get on and come to an easy solution (that is, to choose one of the contestants and exclude the rest, or to choose a facile compromise, and make this choice the ground of the on-going activity)—such an attempt must result in a weak gestalt, lacking in energy. But on the contrary, if what is chosen is the conflict itself, then the figure will be exciting and energetic, but it will be full of destruction and suffering.

Every conflict is fundamentally a conflict in the grounds of action, a conflict of needs, desires, fascinations, pictures of oneself, goals hallucinated; and the function of the self is to live it through, to suffer loss and change and alter the given. When the grounds are harmonious, there is rarely a true conflict in the choice of foreground objects, expedients, or policies; rather, something is at once found or invented better than any of the alternatives. The case of Buridan's ass who with a single appetite starved between two likely objects, is not much to be observed. (When there *is* a genuine indifference of objects—a number of similar cookies on a platter—appetite at once forms the gestalt of choosing a "sample of a class," the very indifference being made a positive quality.) A strong conflict in the foreground is a sign that the true conflict in the background is alienated and concealed, as in obsessive doubt. (Concealed might be a desire not to get anything at all, or to be torn in two.)

From this point of view, let us consider again the meaning of the proposition, "To excite the conflict weakens the self," and the therapeutic method of meeting such a danger. The source of the danger is that a large part of the self is already apparently invested in some weak figure, a facile choice having been previously made. If a new excitation is accepted from the alienated background, the conflict will destroy this weak "self"—the self will lose such organization as it has; therefore, it is said, play down the new excitation. But in fact the self is only apparently invested in the weak figure, for *the self is not the figure it creates but the creating of the figure:* that is, self is the dynamic relation of ground and figure. Therefore, the therapeutic method, which can only strengthen the self, is to insist on relating the foreground weak-figure (e.g., a man's concept of himself) to its ground, to bring the ground more fully into awareness. Suppose, for instance, the foreground is a verbal rationalization that is clung to. The therapeutic question must be, not whether the proposition is true or false (thus setting up a conflict of objects), but what is the motive for this use of words? does one really care whether or not it is true? or is it a manipulation? of whom? is it an attack? against whom? is it an appeasement? a concealment, of what, from whom?

The necessity of this method is obvious if we consider that many rationalizations, especially of intelligent people, happen to be true propositions and yet are rationalizations. To attack any proposition leads to endless wrangling; and patients are like as not to be as generally informed as therapists.

But when the figure is related to its motive, new excitations suddenly appear, both from the organism and the past and from new things noticed in the environment. The weak figures lose interest and become confused, the self loses its "security" and suffers. Yet this suffering is not a weakening of the self, but a painful transitional excitement of creativity. It is the reverse of anxiety. This suffering is painful and involves the deeper breathing of labor. Anxiety is unpleasurable, static, breathless. A conflict of grounds is attended by destruction and suffering; a false conflict of objects, expedients, or ideas freezes in a dilemma attended by anxiety. The purpose of false conflict is to interrupt the excitement; anxiety as an emotion is the dread of one's own daring.

9: Identifying and Alienating
II: "Security"

Timidity to be creative has two sources: the pain of the mounting excitement itself (originally, the "fear of instinct"), and the fear of rejecting or being rejected, destroying, making changes; these two mutually aggravate each other, and are at bottom the same. A sense of "security," on the contrary, is given by clinging to the status quo, one's past achieved adjustments. The new excitement threatens to shake this security to pieces.

What we must understand is that there is no such thing as a true security, for then the self would be a fixity. When there is no irrational fear, the problem does not arise whether or not one is secure, but one attends to the problem confronting. Sense of security is a sign of weakness: the person who feels it is always waiting for its disproof.

The energy of clinging with death-grip to the status quo comes from the unfinished situations still tending to complete themselves opposed by aggression turned against oneself by the alien identifications introjected after previous defeats: this clinch gives something of a feeling of solidity, stability, power, self-control, and "security." Meantime, in fact, the self has little out-going power to draw on.

The secure person is using his powers in a safe and unsurprising struggle with his unassimilated identifications. The struggle continues and rouses feeling because the situation is unfinished and recurs; but it is a "safe" feeling, because nothing new will turn up, and one has already suffered the defeat. Such a struggle is also reliable; it cannot be terminated, for the organism keeps producing the need, but the aggression will not turn toward the environment where a solution might be found. Also—if it is a good "social" identification —it is often possible to find many speciously similar real problems that can be solved on the same pattern as the former defeat; one can apparently cope quite easily with the reality without learning anything, suffering anything new, or making any change: all that is necessary is to avoid any real situation that is interesting or venturesome, to avert attention from anything in one's affairs that makes today different from yesterday; and this can be conveniently accomplished by calling the new the "unrealistic." So by a beautiful economy, precisely an accepted defeat serves to give a sense of power and adequacy. In popular language this is called "making a good adjustment." The only things lacking are excitement and growth and the sense of being alive.

But where the self has power to draw on, it has precisely no sense of security. It has perhaps a sense of readiness: the acceptance of excitement, a certain foolish optimism about the alterability of reality, and an habitual memory that the organism regulates itself and does not in the end wear out or explode. (This readiness is perhaps what the theologians call faith.) The answer to the question "Can you do it?" can be only,

"It's interesting." A sense of adequacy and power grows as the particular problem is met and generates its own structure, and new possibilities are found in it, and things surprisingly fall into place.

XIII

CREATIVE ADJUSTMENT: II.
FINAL CONTACT AND POST-CONTACT

1: Unity of Figure and Ground

Final contact is the goal of contacting (but not its functional "end," which is assimilation and growth). In final contact the self is immediately and fully engaged in the *figure* it has discovered-and-invented; momentarily, there is practically no background. The figure embodies all the concern of the self, and the self is nothing but its present concern, so the self *is* the figure. The powers of the self are now actualized, so the self becomes something (but in so doing it ceases to be self).

Clearly such a point can be reached only under the following conditions: (1) The self has been selecting the reality toward its own reality—that is, it has been identifying with what activates or mobilizes the background, and alienating the rest. (2) It has been addressing the environmental reality and changing it, so that no relevant concern remains unchanged in the environment. (3) And it has accepted and completed the dominant unfinished situations of the organism, so that no appetite remains in the body-awareness. (4) And during this process, it has been not merely an active-artificer of the solution, nor a passive-artifact of it (for these are extrinsic), but it has more and more been assuming a middle mode and growing into the solution.

Let us consider the nature of an awareness that has no environmental or body background, for awareness is a figure against a ground. Such awareness is possible only of a whole-and-parts, where each part is immediately experienced as involving all the other parts and

486

the whole, and the whole is just of these parts. The whole figure could be said to be the background for the parts, but it is more than ground for it; it is at the same time the figure *of* the parts, and they are ground. To put this another way: the experience does not allow for any more possibilities because it is necessary and actual; the actual is necessary; these parts at this moment cannot mean anything else. Let us give some examples: in a moment of insight, there are no more hypotheses, for one sees how the parts work together (one has grasped the "middle term"); and thus, as a problem approaches the insightful moment, everything begins to fall into place; and after the insight, the application to further cases is immediate and habitual —the problem has been contacted once and for all. Likewise, when one loves there are no alternatives: one cannot oneself withdraw, look elsewhere, etc., and one feels that any further traits that might appear in the beloved will either be lovable or will be completely irrelevant and unimportant. Or more darkly, in a moment of final despair, there are no more resources; the figure in such a case is nothing but the empty ground with nothing to relieve it, and it is felt as necessary, for the impossible is a kind of necessary.

In such a whole-of-parts the figure provides its own boundary. Therefore there are no ego-functions: no boundaries are chosen, there are no identifications and alienations, and no further deliberateness. The experience is entirely intrinsic, one is in no way acting on it. The relaxation of deliberateness and the vanishing of boundaries is the reason for the extra brightness and vigor—e.g., the "flash of insight" or the "shock of recognition"—for the energy that went into withholding oneself or aggressively putting connections into the environment is now suddenly added to the final spontaneous experience. The spontaneity is most easily noticed in behaviors where there has been deliberate muscular movement—e.g., the spontaneous pelvic movement before orgasm, and the spasm, or the spontaneous swallowing of food that has been well liquefied and tasted.

In all contacting, there is an underlying unity of perceptual, motor, and feelingful functions: there is no grace, vigor, dexterity of movement without orientation and interest; no keen sight without focusing; no feeling of attraction without reaching, etc. But it is only in final contact, perhaps, with its spontaneity and absorption, that these functions are all foreground, they are the figure: one is aware of the unity. That is, the self (which is nothing but contact) comes to feel itself. What it is feeling is the interacting of the organism and environment.

2: Concern and its Object

Let us try to analyze the absorption of final contact as a feeling (though one must apologize for one's poverty of language). In analyzing the sequence of contacting, we mentioned a sequence of motivations: first, urges, appetites, and responses to stimuli that set the organism to going out toward the environment (e.g., hunger, pinprick); secondly, emotions or the feeling of relationship between appetite, pain, etc. and some environmental situation (e.g., lust, anger), these eliciting aggressive approach; thirdly, the more settled activation of virtues or vices (e.g., determination, sullenness) that see one through complicated orientations, manipulations, and conflicts. It is clear that in the process of creative adjustment there must be such drives or motivations relating the organism's sense of itself as an "I" (accepted ground) and the environmental novelty sensed as an "It," an "object" to work on.

During the spontaneous absorption* of final contact, however, there is no need for such motivation, for there are no other possibilities; one cannot choose otherwise. The feeling of absorption is "self-forgetful"; it attends completely to its object; and since this object

---

*The point here is not the spontaneity, for all feelings are spontaneous, acts of self (see 10,4); but in the motivations there is a sense of one-self developing. Thus in "fascination" one is spontaneously attracted despite oneself, but in "absorption" one is wholly "in" the object.

fills the entire field—anything else is experienced as to the interest of the object—the object becomes a "Thou," it is what is addressed. The "I" lapses altogether into its attentive feeling: we speak of being "all ears, all eyes," for instance in hearing the great music one "forgets himself and is all ears"; and any possible "It" becomes simply an interest of the "Thou." Let us use the word "concern" for this kind of selfless feeling. Compared with the appetites or emotions, the concerns have a certain static or final quality, for they are not motivations. On the brighter side, compassion,* love, joy, serenity, esthetic appreciation, insight, etc. are such states rather than motions of feeling. (Triumph or Victory are interesting examples, because the "Thou" in these cases is likely to be just the Ego-ideal.) More darkly, despair, mourning, etc., and we can now see how terrible these are, for if there is neither Ego nor Thou, the feeling is as of an abyss.

In general, throughout this book we have assumed that every reality is concernful: it is real as the object of appetite, emotion, or concern. So both the ancients and medievals held that "being" and "good" were interchangeable (but see below, Section 3). This is in opposition, of course, to the contemporary postivism, whose reality is neutral, but also to the analytic conception of "cathexis," that the excitement is attached to the object—a conception made plausible by the unusual charges of energy in fetishes, objects of reference, etc. Our view is that unconcernful-object and objectless-excitement are abstractions from the concernful figure of contact, which in the end and potentially from the beginning is the primary spontaneous awareness of reality. The abstractions seem to be pri-

---

*Compassion, the concern of the physician, seems to be precisely motivational and on-going. But it is not a motive. Compassion is the loving recognition-of-defect-as-potentially-perfect, and the on-goingness is the filling-out of the potentiality of the object. The concern itself is final and unchanging. (Analytically, it is interpreted as the refusal to resign to one's own loss, e.g., castration. So Jekels.) In the practice of compassion, it is not some interest of the "I" but the integration of the "Thou" that is in motion.

mary in experience if one judges from a background of unaware deliberateness and vague pain, as we shall discuss in the next chapter.

3: Example of Sexual Touch, etc.

Love aims at proximity, that is, the closest contact possible while the other persists undestroyed. The contact of love occurs in seeing, speech, presence, etc. But the archetypal moment of contact is sexual embracing. Here the actual spatial closeness spectacularly illustrates the diminution and unconcernfulness of the background. There is little background because there isn't room for one: the lively figure looms trying to dispense with background altogether, and all its parts are exciting. The figure is not an "object" of the "subject," for the awareness crowds into the touch. The "distant" senses are made to feel that they are touch (touching and touched), for a face fills the oval of vision and small sounds fill the hearing. It is not a moment for abstractions or images of other times and places; there are no alternatives. The speech is, so to speak, pre-verbal; what is important in it is the tone and the primitive concreteness of the terms. And the "close" senses, taste, smell, and touch make up much of the figure. Excitement and closeness of contact are felt as one and the same thing; more excitement is simply closer touch. And motion is finally spontaneous.

The vanishing of the body-background is even more remarkable. Toward the climax, the figure is composed of the two bodies; the sense of touching and being touched; but these "bodies" are now nothing but a system of contact-situations at the boundary; there ceases to be a sense of physiological organs underlying. Organic pains become unaware. Paradoxically, one's own body becomes part of the Thou, and finally the whole figure, as if the boundary were disattached and placed opposite.

This archetypal contact shows also the creativity of the self. At the height of awareness, the experience is novel, unique, and original. But when, at the orgasm, the boundary is "broken" and the self diminishes, one has the sense of a conservative instinctual gratification of one's own familiar body.

We see too that the contact is spontaneously transitory. The self works for its *completion* but not its *perpetuation*. When the process of figure-forming is complete and the experience becomes self-contained and the background vanishes, it becomes immediately obvious that the contact-situation as a whole is just one moment of the interaction of the organism/environment field.

The same characteristics of final contact are evident in eating, a contact by destruction and incorporation. What is tasted and chewed is lively and unique; but spontaneously it is swallowed, the figure vanishes, and assimilation is unaware.

Again, during an intense experience of a work of art it is felt to be not only inevitable in its working but also, strangely, the only possible work or at least the highest kind, and the experience of it inestimably valuable; that is, the background in terms of which we make comparative judgments has vanished.

(We have chosen our examples of contacting and final contact mainly from the appetites. Yet much, although not exactly, the same holds of such a contacting as annihilating. The figure in annihilating is the absence of the expelled object from the ground; at its height, therefore, one is left with no object of excitement but only the heavy breathing of the effort and a cold feeling of the self confronting the no longer interesting situation—unless there happens also to be a sense of triumph: with the glorification of the ego-ideal. In cold annihilation there is not, of course, any aftermath of growth. Nevertheless, psychologically at least, annihilating is a positive behavior and feeling, and one must therefore disagree with the ancients and medievals in the formulation we mentioned above that the reality is "good" (desirable), and evil a negation of reality; for the absence of the expelled is psychologically a reality; it removes a dread. We prefer to say, "reality is exciting or concernful.")

4: Post-Contact

The aftermath of contact (except annihilating) is accomplished growth. This process is unaware, and its details belong to physiology—to the extent that they are understood at all.

Depending on the kind of novelty that has been addressed and transformed, the growth has various names: increase in size, restoration, procreation, rejuvenation, recreation, assimilation, learning, memory, habit, imitation, identification. All these are the result of creative adjustment. The basic notion underlying them is a certain unification or made-identity in the organism/environment interaction; and this has been the work of the self. Food, where the "unlike" is made "like," is literally assimilated, "made like to." Learning, when it is digested and not swallowed whole, is said to be assimilated; it can then be used not otherwise than one's muscularity. With regard to perceptions, the philosophic usage has been the reverse: it is the seeing that becomes the same as the seen-color. Habits are "picked up from" our behavior in company, we have imitated or identified-with the others, and formed our personalities on their model. But we must not be deceived by the apparent reversal in language, for in every case there has been the destroyed, the rejected, the changed on the one hand, and going-out-to and being-formed-by on the other. Where the contact is by incorporation and the irrelevant part is practically disregarded, we speak of assimilation; yet of course the chemical elements persist, the waste is excreted and still exists, etc. Where the contact is by proximity or touch, and the irrelevant (rejected) part is still potentially interesting, as in perception and love, we speak of becoming the other or identifying-with. The aftermath of orgasm is procreation, and rejuvenation by a systemic release of tension. (Reich holds that there is also some biophysical nourishment.)

It is in considering the aftermaths of contact, the assimilations and identifications, that one can most appreciate the importance of the middle mode of spontaneity. For if the self had been merely active, it could not become also that other, it would merely project; if it were merely passive, *it* could not have grown, it would have suffered an introjection.

5: Passage from the Psychological to the Physiological

Psychologically, the passage from aware contact to unaware assimilation has a deep pathos. For the figure of contact filled the world, was excitement, all the excitement there was; but in the aftermath it is seen to be a small change in the field. This is the Faustian pathos, when one says, "Stay! thou art so fair!" but to effectuate this saying would be just to inhibit the orgasm, the swallowing, or the learning. But the self spontaneously goes on and extinguishes itself.

(It is at this point, as Rank has shown, that the basic neurotic mechanism of the artist comes into play. For the artist insists on the perpetuation, the "immortality," of himself, and therefore he projects part of himself into the material enduring medium of the work. But in this behavior he forfeits the possibility of final completion and is never happy. He must repeat: not the same work, but the process of making an artwork. It is this interruption and its attendant anxiety, and not the "guilt" of daring, that is the source of what Rank calls the "guilt of creating.")

The inhibition of the achieved climax is par excellence the figure of masochism: it is holding in the maximum excitement and wanting to be released from the pain of it by being forced, forced because the self is afraid to "die," as if the self were anything but just this transient contact. Then the height of love comes to feel the same as an invitation to death. Love-death is praised, as if it were the best love. But in fact the love-dying organically live on; the excitement fades; they try to recapture the fair moment and necessarily fail, for the now possible fair moment is quite different.

But although the increment of physiological growth

is small, it is absolutely sure; we may use it reliably
forever. One cannot be deceived by a creative adjustment. (So, pleasure, the feeling of contact, is always, in whatever form and under whatever conditions,
a *prima facie* evidence of vitality and growth. In ethics
it is not the sole criterion—there is no sole criterion
—but its occurrence is always positive evidence toward
a behavior, and its absence always raises a question.)
With regard to perception, the reliability of a creative
identification is universally admitted: the sensation
itself is irreducible evidence, though the interpretation
may be in error. Yet the same holds with regard to
learning, love, and other social identifications. But this
is not appreciated; on the contrary, the love we once
experienced is often later thought of as disgusting, the
opinions we used to hold are considered absurd, the
music we responded to as adolescents is dismissed
as sentimental, the loyalties of local-patriotism are abhorred. As Morris Cohen used to say, "If falling in
love is blind, falling out of love is dizzy." But such
reactions are a failure to accept the present actuality of
our achieved pasts, as if we were given to ourselves
in the present as anything but what we have become
and will go on to be. Clearly in such cases the contact
was never complete, the situation was not finished;
some inhibiting force was introjected as part of the
experience and is now part of the ego-concept against
which we are measuring ourselves. And now when
our past achievement, such as it was, is necessarily
different from our present aim, instead of being able
to use it as part of our present equipment, or to disregard it as irrelevant, we waste energy warding it off,
being ashamed of it, attacking it (for it is still an unfinished situation).

6: Formation of Personality: Loyalty

The aftermath of creative social contact is the formation of personality: group-identifications and viable
rhetorical and moral attitudes. The self seems to be-

come part of the Thou that it has grown into. (When the creativity has been interrupted and the inhibiting force has been introjected, the personality seems to be aping its fellows, to be imitating a speech and attitudes really alien and unbecoming to it; and this is indeed the case.)

Group-identification that has fulfilled needs and powers and is a source of strength for further action is the habit of loyalty, what Santayana called acceptance of the "sources of our being." Consider, for example, loyalty to a language. Every language adequately realizes elementary social needs, if one learns it in circumstances at all favorable. If it is a great language, like English, one's personality is deeply formed by its genius and literature; a writer feels his loyalty in the pleasure of writing English sentences. An Italian peasant immigrant, loyal to his childhood, often refuses to learn English, though his ignorance hampers his present life: it is that he was too quickly and thoroughly uprooted and too many of the old situations were unfinished. On the other hand, a German refugee from Hitler learns English in a few weeks and completely forgets German: he needs to blot out the past and speedily make a new life to fill the void.

In therapy, the so-called "regressions" are aware loyalties, and it is pointless to deny or denigrate what the patient has really felt as his own; the task is to find out the unaware unfinished situations that are taking energy from the possibilities of the present. The classical instance is the impossibility of "changing" homosexuals who have once gotten important sexual satisfaction, especially since they have creatively overcome many social obstacles in order to get it. The method is clearly not to attack the homosexual adjustment, for that has been the result of the self's integrative power, it is a proved felt contact and identification. The method must be to bring to light what the personality is unaware *alienating,* here the interest in the other sex, half the human beings in the world. That is, it is pointless to say, "Why do you act like an

11-year-old?" but it is reasonable to ask, "What is disgusting, immoral, dangerous in acting like a 12-year-old?" Whatever *is* acted has, in so far, been assimilated.

7: Formation of Personality: Morality

As aftermaths of contact, moral evaluations, judgments of proper behavior, combine two kinds of assimilation. (a) On the one hand, they are simply technical skills that one has learned, guesses as to what leads to success. As such they are flexible, subject to modification in changing circumstances. Every present problem is met on its merits. One's crystallized prudence is part of the ground from which one addresses the problem. (b) On the other hand, they are group-loyalties such as we have been describing: one acts in a certain way because it is the social expectation, including the expectation of one's formed personality. One's technique in a particular present case is modified by one's abiding choice to remain a member of the group, to use the group's technique. Usually the group's technique is less flexible than the individual's, and there is likely to be a certain conflict between these grounds of action. If this conflict becomes too marked too frequently, one has to decide that the group is irrational—is past-bound—and then either change the group's technique or abandon one's loyalty. Abandoning loyalty, one has to find a new loyalty, for sociality of some kind is always part of one's needs. It is in the conflict itself that one finds one's new allies.

So far there is no theoretical difficulty. But unfortunately in discussions of morals, these two conflicting grounds, the prudent and the loyal, are confused with two quite different kinds of evaluation, neither of which is an assimilation. (c) One of these is the new discoveries-and-inventions that occur during creation of anything. One finds that the old way, either what is sensible or what is customary, does not serve the creative function at all, rather one has to do *this*. Such evaluation is concernful and compelling; it goes beyond what one "wishes" according to one's achieved personality. It is the emerging figure, and on its emerging one must risk being absurd or lonely. In the aftermath, again, the new figure will be technique and will either be one's self-realization of loyalty to a new group or will lead and win itself a group. But at the moment of concern, the choice is daring, revolutionary, prophetic. And partly what confuses moral questions that could be simply the adjustment of individual and social techniques is the injection into them of a nostalgia for the prophetic and absolute, especially on the part of people who inhibit their creativeness. A moral choice that has long been learned and is a ground of ordinary behavior is discussed as if it were just now being invented by Ezekiel.

But (d) the chief cause of confusion is the usual morality of self-conquest: behavior is "esteemed" as "good" because of some introjected authority, or it is condemned as "bad" because one is attacking in oneself the impulse to similar behavior. Since Nietzsche this morality has been correctly analyzed as resentment; its effects are mostly annihilating and negative. One does not observe that a man who has been "good," who has not been to jail for half a century, is praised and given medals by his fellow-citizens for his virtue, shrewdness, and technique of living that have led to wonderful achievements; for the alien, introjected standards are creatively useless. But there is vindictive heat and force and punishment in the condemnation of the "bad." Indeed, the weak self-conquering personality lives most of its reality in the projection of scapegoats, which permits it to turn some aggression outward and feel something.

In creating something, there are concernful judgments of good and evil, that which advances the coming achievement and that which must be annihilated from the field; but in the aftermath the rejections, the "evil," are seen to be archaic, for in a new enterprise the rejected things are again likely possibilities. But in self-conquest, it is just the "bad," the excluded, that persists, for the vital urges to it recur and the aggression against it must be wielded continually.

8: Formation of Personality: Rhetorical Attitudes

Another kind of learning that forms personality is rhetorical attitude, one's way of manipulating interpersonal relationships, which can be observed by concentrating on one's voice, syntax, and manners. (See Chapter 7.) Such attitudes are complaining, bullying, being helpless, shiftiness, or forthrightness, give and take, fairness, etc. These are all techniques of manipulation, rapidly acquired by children who have a limited and specific audience to work on and soon find which means succeed and which fail. The protocol and etiquette of societies are similar. And when these attitudes are regarded as assimilations (as with one's loyalties or morals), the only issue is whether they are useful for a present problem, or whether they must be modified or discarded. If people strongly disesteem certain attitudes, e.g., shiftiness, it is because they are prone to be manipulated by them despite themselves; to other people the attitudes are simply ineffective and tiresome (although, of course, to be boring is also a powerful technique of punishing and distracting).

When a rhetorical technique is ineffective—when a therapist declines, for instance, to be moved by the patient's boring voice or crocodile tears—then it may simply be dropped; so we see children often laugh at their fraud and try something else. In such cases the technique is a good assimilation. In other cases, however, the awareness of one's technique rouses strong feelings or anxiety. Strong feelings when the "technique" is not really a technique at all, but a direct but imperfect expression (a "sublimation") of an important unfinished need: one chooses to bully because one needs to win, and is now again frustrated and angry; one chooses helplessness because one *is* helpless and is now again abandoned; or one is boring because one wants to be left alone.

But anxiety is roused when the voice one hears is not, after all, one's own voice, but the other speakers one has introjected: it is mother or father complaining, shouting, or being fair. This is again, as in false loyalty or resentful morality, the situation of self-conquest; and one is anxious because one again throttles, at the present moment, one's true identity, appetite, and voice.

9: Conclusion

In ideal circumstances the self does not have much personality. It is the sage of Tao that is "like water," assuming the form of the receptacle. The increment of growth and learning, after good contact, is certain, but it is small. The self has found and made its reality, but recognizing what it has assimilated it sees it again as part of a vast field. In the heat of creative contact, one says, "It is this, not that," and now, "It is only this, let us open our minds to that." That is, the pulsation of contact and its aftermath is the succession of the philosophic feelings that one has grasped the essential good, but that after all, as Bishop Butler said, "Everything is what it is and not another thing," including oneself. Whether such a process is "meaningful" or "worthwhile," or what it means, is not a psychological question.

Where the self has much personality, we have seen, it is because either it carries with it many unfinished situations, recurring inflexible attitudes, disastrous loyalties; or it has abdicated altogether and feels itself in the attitudes toward itself that it has introjected.

Finally, let us return to the relation of the psychological and the physiological. Assimilation, digested learning, technique, group-identifications constitute proper habits, in the sense that "habit is second nature." They seem to become a part of the non-conscious physiological self-regulation. With regard to assimilated nourishment, no-one would raise any question of this. With regard to obvious motor-habits, the "organic" nature of the learning is almost as evident. Learning to walk, for instance, would be considered first-nature and not habit at all; yet swimming, skating, cycling seem almost as organic and cannot be forgotten Catching a ball, again, seems hardly less so. To spea is organic; to speak the mother-tongue is hardly less so; and reading and writing again hardly less so. Therefore, it seems reasonable to define the physiological as the conservative, the non-aware, self-regulation, whether inherent or learned. The psychological is the shifting, transitory contact with novelty. The physiological "first nature," including non-aware neurotic interference with "first nature," has periodic recourse to contact, need for novelty. The physiological "second nature" is contacted aperiodically—e.g., available memory is drawn on as a result of external stimulation.

It is the organism and not the self that grows. Let us speculatively describe growth as follows: (1) After contact there is a flow of energy, adding to the energy of the organism the new elements assimilated from the environment. (2) The contact-boundary that has been "broken" now reforms, including the new energy and the "organ of second nature." (3) What has been assimilated is now part of the physiological self-regulation. (4) The boundary of contact is now "outside" the assimilated learning, habit, conditioned reflex, etc. —e.g., what is *like* what one has learned does not touch one, it raises no problem.

XIV

LOSS OF EGO-FUNCTIONS: I. REPRESSION; CRITIQUE OF FREUD'S THEORY OF REPRESSION

1: The Figure/Background of Neurosis

Neurotic behavior is also a learned habit, the result of creative adjustment; and like other assimilated habits is no longer contacted, because it presents no novel problem. What differentiates this kind of habit from others, and what is the nature of neurotic unawareness (repression) as distinct from simple forgetting and available memory?

In the process of creative adjustment we have traced the following sequence of grounds and figures: (1) Fore-contact: in which the body is the ground and its urge or some environmental stimulus is the figure; this is the "given" or id of the experience. (2) Contacting: accepting the given and drawing on its powers, the self goes on to approach, estimate, manipulate, etc. a set of objective possibilities: it is active and deliberate with regard to both the body and the environment; these are the ego-functions. (3) Final contact: a spontaneous, disinterested, middle mode of concern for the achieved figure. (4) Post-contact: diminishing self.

We saw also (12, 7) that at any stage the process could be interrupted, because of danger or inevitable frustration, and the excitement throttled, resulting in anxiety. The particular stage of interruption is important for the particular neurotic habit that is learned, and we shall discuss this aspect in the next chapter. But now let us consider how any interruption and anxiety leads also to an attempt to inhibit the original drive or response to the stimulus, for these are most available to control. There is thus set up a reverse sequence that we must explore.

501

(1) The deliberate effort to control is the ground. The figure is the inhibited excitation or response to stimulus; this is a painful feeling of the body. It is painful because the excitation seeks discharge in outgoing and the control is a contraction of the expansion (gritting the teeth, clenching the fists, etc.).

This figure-ground does not as such, of course, lead further. One relaxes the control and tries again. But supposing now the danger and frustration are chronic and one cannot relax the control; meantime there are other matters to attend to. Then,

(2) A new situation arises and the old situation is still unfinished. The new situation may be either a new stimulus or a distraction sought to lessen the pain, disappointment, etc. In meeting the new situation, the old unfinished situation is necessarily suppressed: one swallows one's anger, hardens oneself, pushes the urge out of mind. Yet in the new situation, the painful suppressed excitation persists as part of the ground. The self turns to cope with the new figure, but it cannot draw on the powers engaged in keeping down the suppressed excitation. Thus the ground of contacting the new figure is disturbed by the existence of the painful suppression, which is immobilizing certain of the ego-functions.

Beyond this, the sequence cannot develop. This is because the body cannot be annihilated. The suppressed urge belongs to the physiological self-regulation and conservatively persists, recurs acutely whenever sufficient tension accumulates or there is a stimulus, and always remains as a coloration of whatever looms in the foreground of interest. The excitation cannot be repressed but only kept out of attention. All further developments are again in the other direction, of confronting the new problem, except that the process is now hampered by the disturbed ground of the unfinished situation. This persisting disturbance prevents final contact in the new adjustment, for all concern is not given to the figure. It prevents the new problem from being addressed on its merits, for every new solution must also "irrelevantly" solve the unfinished situation. And perceptual and muscular powers are bound in maintaining the deliberate suppression.

The excitation cannot be forgotten; but the deliberate control can be forgotten and remain unaware. This is simply because, being a motoric pattern, after a while the situation is learned; if the inhibition is chronic, the means of effecting it are no longer novel and contacted; they are a kind of useless knowledge that would occupy the attention apparently without function. So long as nothing is to be changed in the ground inhibition, the self forgets how it is being deliberate, as it turns to new problems. The motor and perceptual powers involved in the inhibition cease to be ego-functions and become simply strained bodily states. In this first step, thus, there is nothing remarkable about the transition from aware suppression to repression; it is ordinary learning and forgetting how one learned it; there is no need to postulate a "forgetting of the unpleasant."

(Further, in every important case of repression, one quickly attends to quite different matters and therefore quickly forgets.)

But let us follow the process further, for as yet the means of inhibiting is an available memory. We have seen that any uncontacted habit is "second nature"; it is part of the body, not of the self. So our posture, whether correct or incorrect, seems "natural," and the attempt to change it rouses discomfort; it is an attack on the body. But unaware inhibiting has this peculiar property, that if the attempt is made to relax it, there is immediate anxiety, for the situation of excitement is revived, and promptly must be throttled. Suppose, for instance, the inhibited excitation is surprised by an unusual stimulus, or vice versa that the control is temporarily loosed by a therapeutic exercise: then the sight habitually dulled is threatened, it seems, with blindness, the ears ring, the muscle is threatened with a fatal cramp, the heart pounds, etc. The self, unaware that these are the effects of a simple contraction, and that all that is called for is to bear a slight discomfort, to locate the contraction and loosen it deliberately—

the self imagines that the body itself is in danger, and it responds with fright, throttling, and a secondary aware deliberateness to protect the body. It avoids the temptation, resists the therapy; being unaware close-mouthed against something savory but once dangerous, it reacts now with vomiting, as if the thing were poison. Further, since the nascent excitement is painful in any case, it easily lends itself to the extreme interpretation. The attitude and interpretation of defending the one-time ego-functions as if they were vital organs rather than learned habits, is reaction-formation. (Throughout this process there is evident the aggressive attempt to annihilate the more basic physiology.)

We are thus elaborating the following theory of repression: Repression is the forgetting of deliberate inhibiting that has become habitual. The forgotten habit becomes unavailable because of further aggressive reaction-formations turned against the self. What is not, and cannot be, forgotten, is the urge or appetite itself; but this persists as a ground of pain because undischarged and obstructed. (This is the "reversal of affect.") To the extent that the drive maintains its original quality and can enliven objects in the foreground, there are "sublimations," direct but imperfect gratifications.

2: Neurosis as Loss of Ego-Functions

Neurosis is the loss of ego-functions to the secondary physiology as unavailable habits. The therapy of neurosis, conversely, is the deliberate contacting of these habits through exercises graded so as to make anxiety tolerable. Some of these were set forth in the first part of this book.

As a disturbance of the self-function, neurosis lies midway between the disturbance of the spontaneous self, which is misery, and the disturbance of the id-functions, which is psychosis. Let us contrast the three classes.

The one who gives himself spontaneously may not achieve final contact: the figure is disrupted in frustration, rage, exhaustion. In this case he is miserable rather than happy. The harm his body suffers is starvation. His disposition is soured and he turns against the world; but he does not as yet turn against himself, nor have much sense of himself except that he is suffering, until he becomes desperate. The therapy for him must be to learn more practical techniques, and there must also be a change in social relations so that his efforts can bear fruit, and biding that, a little philosophy. This is the culture of the Personality. (This is a description of many small children who, however, are hard to make philosophical.)

At the other extreme is psychosis, the annihilation of some of the given-ness of experience, e.g., the perceptive or proprioceptive excitations. To the extent that there is integration at all, the self fills the experience: it is utterly debased, or immeasurably grand, the object of a total conspiracy, etc. The primary physiology begins to be affected.

Midway, neurosis is the avoidance of spontaneous excitement and the limitation of the excitations. It is the persistence of sensory and motor attitudes when the situation does not warrant them or indeed when no contact-situation exists at all, as a bad posture is maintained in sleep. These habits intervene in the physiological self-regulation and cause pain, exhaustion, susceptibility, and disease. No total discharge, no final satisfaction; disturbed by unfulfilled needs and unaware maintaining an inflexible grip on himself, the neurotic cannot become absorbed in his outgoing concerns nor successfully carry them through, but his own personality looms in awareness: embarrassed, alternately resentful and guilty, vain and inferior, brazen and self-conscious, etc.

Through the assimilation of experience under conditions of chronic emergency, the neurotic self has lost part of its ego-functions; the process of therapy is to change the conditions and provide other grounds of experience, till the self discovers-and-invents the figure, "*I* am deliberately avoiding this excitement and wielding this aggression." It may then go on again to a

spontaneous creative adjustment. (But, to repeat it
again, to the extent that the conditions of life inevitably
involve chronic emergency and frustration, the chronic
control will prove to be functional after all; the release
during the session of therapy will provide nothing but
an abreaction of rage and grief, or worse, vomiting up
of situations which one "can't stomach.")

3: Critique of Freud's Theory: I. Repressed Wishes

Our explanation, especially of repression, is so at
variance with Freud's that we must account for the
discrepancy, that is, account for his view as well as
give evidence for our own. For repression was the process that he studied most intensively, and it would be
possible to construct the entire system of Freudian
psychoanalysis using "repression" as the primitive term.

To Freud it seemed that the "wish," the excitation,
was repressed, whereas we hold it to be irrepressible,
though any particular thought or behavior associated
with the wish may be forgotten. He is then led into an
uncharacteristically complicated and admittedly difficult attempt to explain how the conservative organism
can inhibit itself. The entire system of "unconscious
thinking" and the Id that can never be experienced
are part of this attempted explanation—though like any
ad hoc entity it raises a host of new problems. Again,
Freud held that the contents repressed are both driven
away by the ego and attracted by the "unconscious,"
and he required also an unconscious censorship; whereas we hold that the attraction or censorship of the
contents is at variance with the facts, and that repression is sufficiently explicable by deliberate suppression
and simple forgetting *and* the spontaneous figure/
background activity of the self confronting new problems in the previous conditions.

It is evident that the inhibited excitations are not
repressed but on the contrary express themselves in
such a way that one must say they want to express
themselves, to develop. Under conditions of relaxation,
such as free-association or dozing, or again under

conditions of spontaneous concentration, such as art-working or lively conversation, at once all kinds of strange images, ideas, abortive impulses and gestures, restless aches and twinges, come to awareness and claim attention: the suppressed excitations that want to develop; and if by disinterested but directed concentration they are given language and muscular means, they immediately reveal themselves with full significance. Such tendencies are, of course, the bread-and-butter of any analytic session; how is it possible that Freud did not assign them weight as evidence for the irrepressibility of the id?

Consider a typical passage of Freud:

"Among the wish-impulses originating in the infantile life, indestructible and incapable of inhibition, there are some the fulfillment of which have come to be in contradiction with the purposive ideas of our secondary thinking. The fulfillment of these wishes would no longer produce an affect of pleasure, but one of pain: and it is just this reversal of affect that constitutes the essence of what we call 'repression.' "*

That is, regarded as "infantile," the impulses are incapable of inhibition, as we are claiming; later, they "contradict" other purposes, are therefore painful, and therefore repressed. But pleasure and pain are not ideas, they are the feelings of release or tension. What organic transformation is Freud envisaging by which the "contradiction" produces the change of affect? We are claiming, on the contrary, simply that the wish is painful because of the effort to inhibit it—an undischarged tension and a muscular restriction: this transformation is a matter of common experience.

Yet if what we are claiming is the case, then the entire aware experience continues to be colored by the *un*repressed pain. Obviously to Freud this did not seem to be so. Yet it is so. It does not seem to be so because we do not allow it to seem so when we are

---

*Sigmund Freud, *The Interpretation of Dreams,* trans. by A. A. Brill, Macmillan Co., New York, 1933, p. 555.

intent on going about our business with a stoic resignation and trying to make the best of the impulses that we do accept. The pain is there but suppressed: concentrate on your feelings and it at once colors everything. Freud is notoriously gloomy about the prospect of happiness in the human condition; yet he is not nearly so gloomy as necessary about the actuality of the human condition.

The disagreement here is also a verbal one, depending, like all important semantical differences, on a difference in the standard of what is desired: what shall we call "pain" and "pleasure"? To Freud, the dulled perception, deliberate motion, and controlled feeling of ordinary adult life is not "painful" but neutral. Yet compared with a standard of spontaneous behavior, it must be called at least "unpleasure": it is not neutral, for it is positively marked by restlessness, fatigue, dissatisfaction, resignation, a sense of incompletion, etc.

Note too in the above passage the implication that there is no physiological self-regulation, for the "infantile" impulses are random, incapable of inhibition, and purposiveness belongs to secondary thinking. This brings us to another reason why Freud thought the excitations were repressed. He persistently regarded certain *excitations* as infantile, as specifically bound to infantile situations and therefore to infantile thoughts and scenes; and indeed such situations and thoughts are recoverable, if at all, with extreme difficulty; they are not in the background of awareness. But as we have tried to show above (Chapter 5), *all* excitations are much more general in application; it is the changing objects and situations that define and specify them. The apparent essential connection with specific forgotten thoughts, evident when the repression of the thoughts is lifted, is due, we have argued, to the fact that it was in a certain situation that one deliberately restricted the excitation and suppressed it—and this attitude soon became habitual and forgotten; therefore, the first free development of the excitation on release of the inhibition stimulates an old memory as its available technique. It is not the memory that essentially frees the impulse, but the development of the impulse that stimulates the memory. Or to put this conversely, the spontaneous life is persistently more "infantile" than is allowed; the loss of the infantile is not an organic change but a deliberate suppression.

4. Critique of Freud: II. Dreams

Turning now to Freud's theory of the "attraction" of certain contents by the unconscious, let us consider the familiar example of the "fleeing" of the tail-end of a dream; for it is true that this does not seem to be merely pushed out of mind, but rather to be attracted as by an invisible magnet. Yet we must notice first of all that, in practice, to hold the dream one does not *pay* attention to it, but one attends to it disinterestedly, letting it come if it will, and this would be senseless if the dream were really attracted away.

The dream does not vanish by deliberate suppression; it is mainly the spontaneous synthesizing of the self that annihilates the dream as far as possible in the act of forming the simplest figure/background in the waking state: this is why the dream vanishes so effortlessly (the annihilation is spontaneous), and why, from the point of view of effortful introspection, the dream seems to flee—for the grounds of making the usual kind of waking effort are incompatible with the grounds of experiencing a dream. The simplest *possible* contact in usual waking experience spontaneously excludes the dream. Thus, to allow the dream, or any drive, to express itself, the only recourse finally is to alter the usual figure/background formation itself—to change the circumstances in which contact is possible, so that the dream also is a possible part of the contact. This is done by assuming the attitude of disinterest. The method is neither to try deliberately to remember nor to try to activate what is "unconscious," but to alter the grounds of the self's reality so that the dream too looms as real. Our dreams are "pushed away" by us and they "flee" from us because we ourselves are making a mistake about the nature of things; we cannot hold the dream because we refuse to take it as real.

The incompatibility of dream and usual waking-up is familiar. Waking up, a person begins to feel he is active, up and doing, about to move. But the dream belongs to the class of wishes that can be gratified just in immobile hallucinating of them; the beginning of muscular motion puts the dream to flight (this is interpreted as "censoring the wish before it can attain motor discharge"). More importantly, as in hallucination, the dream is excluded from what is conceived to be the real world. Hallucinations are not accepted as functions of oneself. (Yet children, of course, take their hallucinatory play as part of the real world; and among adults, vast expenditures of time and attention are devoted to art-works, other people's hallucinations. Only one's own dreams are disesteemed. Or consider the common attitude toward willful day-dreaming: it is taken as an escape, a flight from reality and obligation; but it is not so much an escape as an abuse: the wish in the daydream is, in the end, left vague and not used; it is not allowed to become concrete in active play nor is it used as an interpretation of one's intentions, as an intimation of real interest and vocation.) Still another property of the usual waking that excludes dreams is that it is verbal and abstractive—on awaking we at once verbalize our abstract purposes: "Where am I?" "What do I intend to do this morning?" "What time is it?" "What did I dream?"; our experience is organized by these abstractions. But the dream is concrete, non-verbal, sensory—"eidetic." In general, that is, the dream is not a possible experience not so much for its content but for its form.*

All of these factors operate especially strongly—so that the dream flees rapidly and is irrecoverable, rather than merely fading and losing dominance because ir-

---

*An excellent similar analysis of dream-forgetting is given by Schachtel in his essay "On Memory," in A Study of Interpersonal Relations, Hermitage Press, New York, 1949, pp. 3–49.

relevant—when the self is neurotic and there is already a strain in the usual relations of figure and ground because of unaware habits of inhibition. This strain is the system of reaction-formations defending the usual concept of the ego and of its body. Since the ground is habitually not empty but disturbed, to achieve any figure at all it is necessary to keep the background as empty and usual as possible; considerable energy of annihilation is given to this work. Confronted with the spontaneity of dreaming, the sanity of the self and the safety of its organism seem to be in acute danger. From this point of view we could regard the need to be up and doing, to orient oneself in time and place and purpose, to be alert, as so many spontaneous reaction-formations to meet the emergency of the dangerous dream-attitude. With so much artillery mobilized against it, the dream-thoughts are at once annihilated, and the dream-wish is strongly suppressed.

The dream flees and is pushed away, in sum, both because of the spontaneous figure/background formation possible in the conditions, and because of a deliberate decision as to what we will take reality to be. Otto Rank says that the Iroquois used to make the opposite decision: the dream was the real, therefore the task was to interpret the waking in terms of the dream rather than the dream in terms of the waking. To Freud, it would seem, it was childhood that was psychologically most real, for finally he interprets the dream not in terms of the waking (the day's remnants) but in terms of childhood situations. Let us consider this further.

5: Critique of Freud: III. Reality

To be clear about Freud's theory of repression, we must again consider his discussion of the real (see 3, 13 f.)

Freud distinguishes the "primary process" and the "secondary process" of thinking. A few passages will show the underlying similarity between what he is say-

ing and our propositions, and also the important differences.

> "The primary process strives for discharge of the
> excitation in order to establish with the quantity of
> excitation thus collected an *identity of perception;* the
> secondary process has abandoned this intention and has
> adopted instead the aim of an *identity of thought.*"*

We should say, the primary process—a unity of perceptual, motor, and feelingful functions that is not well
called "thinking"—*creates* a reality; the secondary process that abstracts from this unity is thinking that *reflects* the reality.

> "The conversion of affect (the essence of 'repression')
> occurs in the course of development. One need only
> think of the emergence of disgust, originally absent in
> infantile life. It is connected with the activity of the
> secondary system. The memories from which the un-
> conscious wish evokes a liberation of affect have never
> been accessible to the pre-conscious, and for that
> reason liberation cannot be inhibited. . . .

> "The primary processes are present in the apparatus
> from the beginning, while the secondary processes take
> shape only gradually through the course of life, inhib-
> iting and overlaying the primary, gaining complete con-
> trol over them probably only in the prime of life."**

> "The 'incorrect processes' dream-displacements, etc.
> are the primary processes of the psychic apparatus;
> they occur whenever ideas abandoned by the pre-
> conscious cathexes are left to themselves and can
> become filled with the uninhibited energy that flows
> from the unconscious and strives for discharge . . .
> The processes described as 'incorrect' are not really
> falsifications of our normal procedure, or defective
> thinking, but *the modes of operation of the psychic
> apparatus when freed from inhibition.*" (Italics ours) †

---

*Sigmund Freud, *The Interpretation of Dreams,* trans. by A. A. Brill,
Macmillan Co., New York, 1933, p. 553.
**Ibid., p. 555.
†Ibid., p. 556.

The primary process (making an identity of perceptual reality) is spontaneous contacting; but it comes to be equated, by Freud, with only the dream-processes. Art, learning and memory, growing up, are radically disjoined from the primary-process, as if all learning, and the deliberate control that comes with learning, could never be simply used and then released as the self again spontaneously acts. Then, of course, growing up necessarily involves the "conversion of affect," for learning, according to this concept, is *nothing but* inhibiting.

What led Freud to think of the secondary overlying the primary in this way, rather than of their healthy unity in a system of available memories? We may speak of reasons of theory, practice, and personality.

In theory, Freud had a misconception of reality springing from his acceptance of an erroneous psychology of consciousness. For if any orientation in reality is given in isolated sensa and percepts, and if any manipulation of reality is given by isolated motor-habits, then certainly in order to get a reality at all, there must be an abstract thinking process to add up the parts and reconstruct a whole. In this construction, all of the parts—the isolated percepts, propriocepts, habits, and abstract purposes—are grounded in inhibiting the unity of spontaneity. But apparently the only spontaneous wholes of contact that Freud could notice were the dream-processes, and these indeed give little orientation and no manipulation. But of course there are an indefinite number of non-hallucinatory spontaneous wholes; it is a question of correctly theorizing what occurs in experience, as the Gestalt psychologists and the pragmatists have done.

Practically, in therapy, Freud relied precisely on the dissociations of the patient; he forbade them to make sense or practice; so it was only the dreams that forcibly struck him as spontaneous wholes. (The transference, which was a spontaneous whole of practice, he persisted in regarding—as if embarrassed—as merely a remnant of childhood.) Then further, not only was

Freud's psychology of consciousness defective, but also his physiological psychology, for he conceived of random impulses, the isolated excitations of a mechanical organism. In our view the body is full of inherited wisdom—it is roughly adjusted to the environment from the beginning: it has the raw materials to make new wholes, and in its emotions it has a kind of knowledge of the environment as well as motivations of action; the body expresses itself in well-constructed purposive series and complexes of wishes. Leaving all this out of account, Freud was reduced to a purely verbal and not a psychosomatic therapy. The result of his practice, then, was that he could connect the dynamic spontaneous "thinking" that he noticed neither with the environment nor with the body; so he boldly staked out for it an independent realm, the "unconscious."

Yet he is not at all satisfied with this, but he keeps trying to say, "The dream-processes are *not* incorrect after all; *they* are the way to reality; instead it is I, precisely in the prime of life, who have lost the reality." And because he wants to say this, the whole system of Freudian psychoanalysis concerns itself with the "infantile." It does so correctly, because in childhood there was importantly an uninhibited process, giving a reality, which was not at the same time only dream. What was incorrect was the notion that later a new healthy entity developed, the secondary process, for that was the epidemic neurosis.

The notion of the "secondary process" is the expression of the loss of awareness by the self that *it* is exercising the inhibition, and therefore could also release it. The constraint is projected rather as the "harsh reality." And by a reaction-formation the spontaneous process is spitefully denigrated and becomes "merely" dreams and neurotic distortions, and all other spontaneous figure-formations are quite overlooked. And the dreams and symptoms, further, are again attacked, "interpreted," and reduced, rather than also taken as parts of vital reality and, indeed, essential in any creative operation. (This is Jung's critique.) And finally childhood is both denigrated and overestimated; it is overestimated when it is being considered as irrecoverably lost; it is denigrated in the therapy where the entire task of the analysis comes to be to recover this irrecoverable.

6: Examples of Repression: Insomnia and Boredom

Let us take up the thread of our own argument and give an example of repression.

In repression, we have said, the excitation persists in the background and colors all further formations with pain. The deliberateness of the inhibition is forgotten. In these conditions, the self turns to other creative adjustments and makes further efforts to keep the forgotten inhibiting forgotten. Acute insomnia illustrates this method of functioning at its simplest; for in the act of wooing sleep, the further creative adjustments are minimized, and the pain of the unfinished need is pervasively felt as distinct unpleasure, restlessness, and strain. But the meaning of the need is forgotten, for it is not allowed to develop and find orientation.

In insomnia, the self wants to relax and disintegrate, but an unfinished need keeps pulling it together. The very efforts to fall asleep then become means of keeping the need suppressed. First the insomniac closes his eyes, imagines boring scenes, etc. These deliberate imitations of sleep are of course irrelevant to the real need, which is not to sleep but to solve the unfinished problem; but they may be interpreted as a retroflection: he wants to bore that "other" who has the need and to put him to sleep. Then the insomniac starts on a process of dissociated fantasies and thoughts, all of which indeed bear on the suppressed problem, but he does not want to grasp the connection, and therefore the fantasies do not cohere into one wish but tormentingly succeed one another. It happens sometimes, indeed, that one such line of fantasy has the same affective meaning as the suppressed need, in which case the thoughts abreact part of the excitation and one falls into a light dream-haunted sleep; but soon awakes, if the tension again becomes very strong. A third stage is when the insomniac fixes and concentrates on some dummy cause for the sleeplessness, the howling dog, the noisy party downstairs; and he turns his aggression to annihilate this. The wish to annihilate an object is very close to the true underlying situation of trying to annihilate the problem, and so it spontaneously achieves great affect—it draws on the very energy that one is unaware powerfully exerting. So it happens that if this urge to annihilate is allowed to gain important dominance and lead to a violent action—throwing a shoe at the dog, pounding on the floor—there is a partial recovery of the ego-function. This can have alternative consequences: either one then has more control of the suppression and can make it stick sufficiently to fall asleep (in orthodox terms, the repression succeeds rather than fails); or vice versa, now that one has exhausted against the dummy some of the energy turned inward, one may suddenly accept the unfinished need as one's own. One gives up the effort of trying to sleep, gets up, admits that the party downstairs is attractive rather than distractive, or that it is not the howling dog but some other sound that one wants or fears to hear. The correct orientation leads to further relevant activity: one dresses and goes downstairs, writes the letter, or whatever it is.

Ironically, when one is not trying to sleep, when it is not "time" to sleep, the repression of the problem and the persistence of the excitation appear as inattention, boredom, fatigue (and sometimes falling asleep!). The dominant need cannot reach the foreground, but the figures in the foreground are disturbed, and since they cannot draw on full energy and are not attractive, attention lapses; no figure becomes bright. Because there is a wish to be elsewhere and doing something else (but one cannot recognize the wish because it is not allowed to develop), one feels merely that one wishes to be *not* here, *not* doing this. This is boredom. But the bored person forces himself to pay attention

—he exhausts himself in the effort to maintain the strained relation of the dull figure and the disturbed ground; soon he is overcome with fatigue and the eyelids droop. If the suppressed excitation is such as to be importantly gratified in fantasy, he may daydream or fall asleep and dream. But often, unfortunately, as soon as one gives in to the desire to sleep and lies down, then precisely the insomnia sets in.

7: "Sublimation"

Contrasting with the distractions that cannot become attractive and win attention are those that successfully organize an interesting activity. These are interests that draw on an excitation which cannot simply express itself because the meaning is repressed, but which "indirectly" satisfy the need. They are the so-called "sublimations"—interests that satisfy the need in "ways socially acceptable or even esteemed."

On the Freudian theory of the conversion of affect and, therefore, the repression of the excitation, the process of sublimation would be impenetrably mysterious, for if the organic wish is intrinsically changed, what is it that is satisfied by the substitute activity? On the theory we are presenting, there is no problem. Strictly speaking, there is no such special process as "sublimation" at all. What is called "sublimation" is a direct but imperfect satisfaction of the same need.

The satisfaction is imperfect because the loss of ego-functions in the unaware inhibiting prevents efficient creative adjustment; because the excitation itself is colored with pain, difficulty, masochism; and these color the satisfying interest; because the limitations operating make the interest always somewhat abstract and disconnected from the need; and because the inability to become spontaneous prevents a full discharge. Therefore, the sublimation is compulsively repetitious, the organism does not fully come to equilibrium, the need recurs too frequently. A good deal of masturbating illustrates these properties of sublimation.

Nevertheless, it is evident that the sublimation is not

a substitute but a direct satisfaction. Consider, for instance, the well-known interpretation that the art of the novelist is partly a sublimation of repressed infantile peeping and exhibition. (So Bergler.) Certainly the novelist does peep and exhibit. The question is what is repressed here? He satisfies his curiosity about the deeds, sexual and other, of his personages, who are often his acquaintances and very often his remembered family; he exhibits his own feelings and forbidden knowledge. The proof that nothing of this part is repressed is that he in fact feels guilty about doing it. But it will be objected that it is not these things but witnessing the primal scene and exhibiting his childish genitals that are repressed and sublimated, and the guilt is inherited from that era. It seems to us that this is a faulty interpretation of what occurred at that time: the childhood interest in the primal scene consisted of desirous curiosity about the doings of the persons most important to the child, and what he wanted was to exhibit his own nature and desires, and to take part. These are the very needs that he now directly satisfies —but the satisfaction is imperfect, for he is only telling a story, and not also sensing and doing.

For it is just the novelist who manages *not* to suppress these drives, but to get some direct satisfaction of them. A moment's reflection on the social effectiveness of many sublimations will show that they are really giving direct satisfaction; for it is the spontaneous and uninhibited that is powerful and effective and, in the end, esteemed. Let us give another, less usual, example. The power of a Gandhi to move millions by his famously childlike personality had as one of its important aspects his peculiar attitude toward food: when Gandhi refused to eat or agreed to eat, it was politically momentous. Now shall we interpret this as an infantile petulance? Then how was it so effective? But on the contrary, it was an extraordinarily direct keeping alive of the child's *true* feeling that it makes all the difference in the world under what conditions of love and hate one eats. Gandhi probably fasted not primarily as a calculated threat, but because under certain conditions food was nauseating to him. This spontaneous physiological judgment and consequent considered act, in a context not of the nursery but of the adult world where it is equally relevant but universally disregarded, touched every heart. It was effective not because it was symbolic or a substitute, but because it was a spontaneous response to an actuality.

The Freudian theory of "sublimation," however, was again the result of his too closely associating the persistent drives with their past situations and thoughts.

8: Reaction-Formation

Reaction-formation is the avoidance of the anxiety threatened by breakdown of the repression (through increase of the inhibited excitation or relaxation of the inhibition) by further attempts to annihilate the excitation or the temptations to it, and by strengthening the inhibition. The repression avoids the excitement; the reaction-formation avoids the anxiety of the throttled excitement—for this anxiety excitement seems even more dangerous than the original excitement was. Examples of annihilating the tempting stimulus or the excitation are avoidance, disgust, defiance, snobbery, moral condemnation; examples of strengthening the inhibition are righteousness, stubbornness, willful stupidity, pride.

If we leave behind the Freudian theory of the conversion of affect and the repression of the excitation, we no longer need to speak of "ambivalences," contrary feelings toward the same object in the same situation, as if the contraries existed on the same level and were both out-going feelings. (Such contraries, if they existed, would be explicable as incomplete conversion of affect: the thing that childishly gave pleasure does not yet give merely pain.) But it is much more likely that the contraries are dynamically related: one contrary is a reaction-formation against the other: what exists is a dynamic hierarchy of drive, inhibition of the drive, and "defense" of the inhibition, that is, further aggression against the drive and identification with an introject aggressing against it. For instance, consider the appetizing and the disgusting. The appetizing (tempting) is disgusting because the appetite is inhibited by closing the mouth tight: the disgust is a response to the forced feeding of a tight-closed mouth —but one has lost awareness of the fact that one could open one's mouth, the food would no longer be forced in, and there would be no need to vomit it out. At the stage of suppression, deliberate inhibition, the food is simply alienated from oneself, one does not identify with one's appetite for it; but at the stage of reaction-formation, one is no longer in contact with the food at all—the choice has nothing to do with the food, but with the forgotten interpersonal relations. So the recurrent appetite and the disgust do not form a true conflict; there is no real "ambivalence": the contraries are "I like this food" and "I won't eat something I don't like"; these are of course not incompatible, but the adjustment between them is impossible because of the repression.

From a therapeutic point of view, our society has an unfortunate hostility also to its usual reaction-formations, and in turn tries to annihilate them. The reason for this is the state of unequal social development that we have described previously (8, 3); a self-conquering society that also esteems the out-going and sexual. The reaction-formations are obviously annihilating and negative; and no one wants to own to them. Righteousness, obsessive cleanliness, thrift, stubborn pride, moral censure are ridiculed and disapproved; they seem small instead of grand. Just so, spite and envy—the aggressiveness of the powerless and the eros of the frustrated—are disapproved. It is only in crises, emergencies, that they are allowed to become foreground. Instead, all these attitudes are themselves replaced by an annihilating of the annihilating, and we get an empty politeness, good-will, loneliness, affectlessness, tolerance, and so forth. The result is that in therapy the relations of patient and therapist are at first too sensible; and it is necessary painfully to mobilize these reactive-traits and petty triumphs. The therapist would prefer the patient to come in like a good neurotic with strong moral convictions.

LOSS OF EGO-FUNCTIONS:
II. TYPICAL STRUCTURES
AND BOUNDARIES

1: Stratagem of Therapy of "Neurotic Characters"

In this final chapter, let us try to explain the most important neurotic mechanisms and "characters" as ways of contacting the actual on-going situation, whatever it happens to be during the therapy session. Neurotic behaviors are creative adjustments of a field in which there are repressions. This creativity will spontaneously operate in any on-going present; the therapist does not have to get under the "ordinary" behavior or trick it out of the way in order to reveal the mechanism. His task is simply to pose a problem which the patient is not adequately solving and where he is dissatisfied with his failure; then the need of the patient will, with help, destroy and assimilate the obstacles and create more viable habits, just as with any other learning.

We have located the neuroses as loss of ego-functions. In the ego-stage of creative adjustment, the self identifies parts of the field as its own and alienates other parts as not its own. It feels itself as an active process, a deliberateness, of certain wants, interests, and powers that have a definite but shifting boundary. Progressively engaged the self is as if asking: "What do I need? Shall I act it? How am I aroused? . . . What is my feeling toward that out there? . . . Shall I try for that? Where am I in relation to that? How far does my power extend? What means do I dispose of? Shall I press on now or hold back? What technique have I learned that I can use?" Such deliberate functions are spontaneously exercised by the self and are carried on with all the strength of the self, awareness and excitement and the creation of new figures. And ultimately, during close and final contact, the deliberateness, the sense of "I," spontaneously vanishes into the concern, and then boundaries are unimportant, for one contacts not a boundary but the touched, the known, the enjoyed, the made.

But during this process the neurotic loses his boundaries, his sense of where he is and what and how he is doing, and he can no longer cope; or he feels his boundaries as inflexibly fixed, he does not get on, and he can no longer cope. Therapeutically, this problem of the self is the obstacle to solving other problems, and is the object of deliberate attention. The questions now are: "At what point do *I* begin not to solve this simple problem? How do I go about preventing myself? What is the anxiety I am feeling?"

2: Mechanisms and "Characters" as Stages of Interruption of Creativity

The anxiety is the interruption of creative excitement. We now want to present the idea that the various mechanisms and "characters" of neurotic behavior may be observed as the stages of creative adjustment at which the excitement is interrupted. That is to say, we want to elaborate a typology from the experiencing of the actual situation. Let us discuss the advantages of such an approach and the properties of a typology that can be useful in therapy (for of course it is a unique person and not a type of disease that is being treated).

Every typology depends on a theory of human nature, a method of therapy, a criterion of health, a selected run of patients (see above, 4, 6). The scheme we shall offer here is no exception. The therapist needs his conception in order to keep his bearings, to know in what direction to look. It is the acquired habit that is the background for this art as in any other art. But the problem is the same as in any art: how to use this abstraction (and therefore fixation) so as not to lose the present actuality and especially the on-goingness

of the actuality? and how—a special problem that
therapy shares with pedagogy and politics—not to impose a standard rather than help develop the potentialities of the other?

(a) If it is possible to find our concepts in the
process of contacting, then at least it will be the actual
patient that is there, not the past history or the propositions of a biological or social theory. On the other
hand, of course, in order to be the means by which
the therapist can mobilize the learning and experience
of his art, these concepts must recognizably belong to
his knowledge of human upbringing and his somatic
and social theory.

(b) The actual situation is always, we must remember, an example of all the reality that there ever was or
will be. It contains an organism and its environment
and an on-going need. Therefore, we can ask the usual
questions concerning the structure of the behavior:
how does it cope with the organism? How does it cope
with the environment? How does it fulfill a need?

(c) Again, if we draw our concepts from moments
in a present process (namely its interruptions), we can
expect that, with awareness, these interruptions will develop into other interruptions; the on-goingness of the
process will not be lost. The patient will be found not
to have a "type" of mechanism, but indeed a sequence
of "types," and indeed all the "types" in explicable
series. Now the case is that in *applying* any typology,
rather than finding it in the actuality, one experiences
the absurdity that none of the types fits any particular
person, or conversely that the person has incompatible
traits or even all the traits. Yet what does one expect?
It is the nature of the creative—and so far as the patient has any vitality he is creative—to make its own
concrete uniqueness by reconciling apparent incompati-
bilities and altering their meaning.* Then instead of

---

*Let us reinforce this truism with an example from another human
discipline. A literary critic comes to a work with a system of *genres,* what
tragedy is, what farce is, etc. But he finds that not only are these incompatible types combined in *Henry IV, Hamlet, Romeo and Juliet,* but
that the very meaning of tragedy or comedy has been transformed in

attacking or reducing the contradictory traits in order to get at the "real" underlying character that the therapist guesses at (character-analysis), or of trying to uncover the missing connections to what must be the "real" drive (anamnesis), we need only help the patient develop his creative identity by his ordered passage from "character" to "character." The diagnosis and the therapy are the same process.

(d) For the ordered passage is nothing but the remobilizing of fixations into wholes of experience. The most important thing to remember is that every mechanism and characteristic is a valuable means to live if it can only go on and do its work. Now the patient's behavior, in therapy and elsewhere, is a creative adjusting that continues to solve a problem of chronic frustration and fear. The task is to provide him a problem in circumstances in which his customary (unfinished) solutions are no longer the most adequate possible solutions. If he needs to use his eyes, and does not because it is not interesting and safe to use them, now he will alienate his blindness and identify with his seeing; if he needs to reach out, he will now become aware of his muscular aggression against reaching out and relax it, etc.; but this is not because blindness and paralysis are "neurotic," but because they no longer achieve anything: their meaning has changed from technique to obstacle.

To sum up, we offer the following sketches of "character" as a kind of bridge between the therapy of the actual situation and the therapist's concepts. These characters and their mechanisms are not types of persons, but taken as a whole they are a description of the neurotic "ego" in process. So we try in each case to (1) start from a moment of actual interruption, (2) indicate the normal functioning of the interruption, (3) show how, against the background of repressions, it copes with the organism and the environment and

---

each unique whole. Now if this is true in dealing with simple musical and plastic media, how much more so when the patient has for his creations the entire range of human situations?

gives a positive satisfaction, (4) relate it to the cultural and somatic history. Finally (5) we discuss the sequence of characters when mobilized.

3: The Moments of Interruption

The question in the loss of ego-functions is, we saw, "At what moment do *I* begin not to solve this simple problem? How do I prevent myself?"

Let us return again to our schematized sequence of grounds-and-figures in excitement and the reverse sequence in inhibition (14, 1). In the neurotic inhibition the sequence was reversed and the body became a final object of aggression: the background is occupied by a repression, a chronic inhibiting that has been forgotten and is kept forgotten.* Against this ground, the present interruption (loss of ego-functions) occurs.

The difference in types consists in whether the interruption occurs

(1) Before the new primary excitation. Confluence.

(2) During the excitation. Introjection.

(3) Confronting the environment. Projection.

(4) During the conflict and destroying. Retroflection.

(5) At final contact. Egotism.

4: Confluence

Confluence is the condition of no-contact (no self-boundary) although other important interacting is go-

---

*The "repression," "sublimation," and "reaction-formation" mentioned in the preceding chapter are themselves, of course, normal adjustive functions. Normally, repression is simply a physiological function, the forgetting of useless information. Sublimation we have regarded as only a normal function, the imperfect contact possible in the average situation. The interesting case is reaction-formation. Normally, reaction-formation is the automatic emergency-response to a threat to the body: it is the class of such responses as playing dead, fainting, shock, panic flight, etc. All these seem to imply an immediate, and therefore indiscriminate and total, interaction between the physiological signal and the ego-functions of caution, unmediated by the usual sequence of contacting. Normally, the emergency-response seems to meet a commensurate threat—though often a slight injury leads to shock. When the threat has to do with the anxiety resulting from releasing a chronic and forgotten inhibiting, we speak of reaction-formation.

ing on, for instance physiological functioning, environmental stimulation, etc. We saw that normally the aftermath of contact, assimilation, occurs with diminishing self, and all habits and learning are confluent. The distinction between the healthy and the neurotic confluences is that the former are potentially contactful (e.g., available memory) and the latter cannot be contacted because of the repression. Yet obviously immense areas of relatively permanent confluence are indispensable as the underlying unaware background of the aware backgrounds of experience. We are in confluence with everything we are fundamentally, unproblematically or irremediably, dependent on: where there is no need or possibility of a change. A child is in confluence with his family, an adult with his community, a man with the universe. If one is forced to become aware of these grounds of ultimate security, the "bottom drops out," and the anxiety that one feels is metaphysical.

Neurotically, the present attitude—not recognizing the new task at all—is a clinging to unawareness, as if clinging for satisfaction to some achieved behavior, and as if the new excitation would snatch it away; but of course since that other behavior has been achieved and is habitual, there is no aware satisfaction in it, but only a sense of security. The patient sees to it that nothing new will occur, but in the old there is no interest or discrimination. The archetypal instances are unaware suckling or clinging to warmth and body-contact that are not felt but whose absence makes one freeze.

Toward the environment the attitude is to prevent the achieved behavior from being snatched away (by weaning). The jaw is set in the hanging-on bite of the suckling with teeth, who could go on to other food but won't; or one has a bear-hug in copulation; or maintains a death-grip in interpersonal relations. This muscular paralysis prevents any sensation.

So he meets the frustration and the fear. What is the satisfaction? In the framework of muscular paralysis and desensitization satisfaction is possible only in random spontaneity independent of the ego-surveillance altogether (hysteria). Much so-called regression serves as an out-going attitude in which the random impulses can find a language and a behavior; this involves a displacement of feelings and reinterpretation of the meanings of the satisfaction to make them appropriate. The regressive behavior is not neurotic in itself; it is simply prior to or outside the confluence. But the scattered satisfaction in it does not add up. And the bother is, of course, that in the "out-going" behavior similar difficulties arise—something demands to be contacted—and then he begins to cling again.

Culturally, the confluent responses will be on the most rudimentary baby-like or disjointed level. The aim is to get the other to make all the effort.

5: Introjection

The interruption may occur during the excitation, and the self then introjects, displaces its own potential drive or appetite with some one else's. Normally this is our attitude toward all the vast range of things and persons we are aware of but that do not make much difference one way or the other: conventions of speech, dress, city-plan, institutions. The neurotic situation is that in which the convention is coercive and incompatible with a lively excitation, and where in order to avoid the offense of not belonging (not to speak of further conflicts), the desire itself is inhibited—and the hateful environment is both annihilated and accepted by swallowing it whole and blotting it out. Yet unless human beings could imitate and assume a public uniform without much lively engagement, the great agglomerations of culture and cities of men that seem to belong to us would be unthinkable. Every natural (uncoercive) convention was at one time a spectacularly creative achievement; but we use most of them neither really assimilating them nor being crushed by them. For instance, it is only after years that a poet assimilates English; yet other persons speak it unneurotically enough. (The misfortune is that the common usage is taken for the essence.)

Neurotically the introjector comes to terms with his own frustrated appetite by reversing its affect before he can recognize it. This reversal is accomplished simply by the inhibiting itself. What one wants is felt as immature, disgusting, etc. Or conversely, if it is an impulse to reject something that is inhibited (an opposition to forced feeding), he persuades himself that the unwanted is good for him, is what he indeed wants, etc. But he bites it off without tasting or chewing it.

The attitude toward the environment is resigned (pelvis strongly retracted), and then childish and accepting. For it is necessary to have some personality, some technique, some desires. If he cannot identify himself and alienate what is not himself in terms of his own needs, he confronts a void. The social environment contains all the reality there is, and he constitutes himself by identifying with its standards, and alienating what are potentially his own standards. But the culture acquired with this attitude is always superficial, though it may be far-ranging. He will accept any authoritative position, even though it is the opposite of what he thinks he believes; there is even a secondary satisfaction in annihilating his previous authority; he is masochistically eager to be refuted. His own proper opinions are touchingly childlike, but because of the borrowed trappings they wear they seem affected and silly.

The out-going satisfaction of introjecting is masochism—nausea inhibited, jaws forced open in a smile, pelvis retracted, breath drawn in. Masochistic behavior is the possibility of creatively adjusting the environment in a framework of inflicting pain on oneself with the approval of one's false identifications. Intensifying the identification and turning further against the self, he indulges in sadistic biting, complaining, etc.

6: Projection

When the excitation is accepted and the environment confronted, there is emotion—the relating of appetite or other drive with a vaguely conceived object. If the interruption occurs at this stage, the result is projection: he feels the emotion but it is free-floating, unrelated to the active sense of the self that comes in further out-going behavior. Since the emotion does not spring from himself, it is attributed to the other possible reality, the environment—he feels it "in the air" or directed against himself by the other. For example, the patient is embarrassed by what the therapist is thinking of him. Yet normally, projection is indispensable. Projection into "thin air" is the beginning of gratuitous creativity (12, 4), that then goes on to make an objective correlative for the floating emotion or intuition; in ordinary creative adjustment, it is the factor of hallucination necessary in the first approaches. By intuition or prescience we are warned of or invited by the meaning not yet apparent. The neurotic projector, however, does not go on to identify the floating feeling as his own; rather he makes it definite by attaching it to somebody else, and this can result in ludicrous and tragic errors.

The typical instance of neurotic projection is that A has designs on B (erotic or hostile), but A inhibits his approaching; therefore he feels that B has designs on him. He avoids the frustration of the emotion by disowning that it is his.

Toward the environment, however, he presents (and exercises) an unmistakable attitude of provocation. What he deeply wishes is the approach and contact, and since he cannot take the steps, he tries to bring it about that the other does. So, not moving, he does not sit quiet, but he communicates by lying "in wait," in silence, sulking, brooding. Yet if the other reads the signal and does approach, intense anxiety is aroused.

What real satisfaction does he get? It is the acting out of the dreaded dramatic scene as in a dream. He chews it over. The brooding is full of highly colored thoughts. This is the activity possible to the self in the rigid framework of shutting out the environment, inhibiting the motor powers, and lying passively basking in free emotions. It is almost the figure of relaxation that induces hypnagogic images, except that instead of relaxation there is a framework of rigid muscles, so that the more feelingful and attractive the images become the more they become colored with pain and menace.

Culturally, the areas in which projections occur will be stupid, wrong-headed, suspicious—for at the point where the fantasies and feelings could begin to inform themselves with the environment and learn something, the excitement is throttled; and the anxiety, the menace, is likely to be attributed precisely to those who are most "objective," matter-of-fact. Much is made of abstract morality and sin. The more positive thinking abounds in far-fetched plans and future projects.

7: Retroflection

Suppose now the outgoing energies, of orientation and manipulation, are fully engaged in the environmental situation, whether in love, anger, pity, grief, etc.; but he cannot cope and must interrupt, he is afraid to hurt (destroy), or be hurt; he will necessarily be frustrated: then the engaged energies are turned against the only available safe objects in the field, his own personality and body. These are retroflections. Normally, retroflection is the process of reforming oneself, for instance correcting the impractical approach or reconsidering the possibilities of the emotion, making a readjustment as the grounds for further action. So we suffer remorse, regret; we remember, reconsider, etc. Recreating in fantasy the unattainable object, the desire may again rise and one satisfies it by masturbating. And more generally, any act of deliberate self-control during a difficult engagement is retroflection.

Neurotically, the retroflector avoids frustration by trying not to have been engaged at all; that is, he tries to undo the past, his mistake, his dirtying himself, his words. He regrets having encroached on the environment (excreting). This undoing is obsessive and repetitious in the nature of the case; for a reformation, like anything else, can be assimilated only if it comes

to include new environmental material; undoing the
past, he goes over the same material again and again.

The tangible environment of the retroflector consists
of only himself, and on this he wreaks the energies he
has mobilized. If it is a fear of destroying that has
roused his anxiety, he now systematically tortures his
body and produces psychosomatic ailments. If he is
engaged in an enterprise, he works unaware for its
failure. This process is often shrewdly managed to
give secondary results that achieve the original inhibited intention: e.g., in order not to hurt his family and
friends, he turns on himself and produces illness and
failure that involve his family and friends. But he gets
no satisfaction from it, but only further remorse.

The direct satisfaction of the retroflector is his sense
of active control, and of being busy with concernful
matters—for he is obsessively busy and he feels the
impact in his skin. His ideas and plans are often
well-informed, well-considered, and felt with extraordinary earnestness—but one is all the more baffled and
finally undeceived by the timidity and hesitation with
which they stop short of action. The orientation—the
sense of where he is in the situation—seems to be remarkable; until it becomes clear that the simple
practical possibility is being overlooked. There is considerable reminiscence and clouding of the actuality
by this means.

The direct satisfaction of retroflection may be observed when the drive is erotic, as in masturbating; the
masturbation is a kind of rape—for the body is likely
to be no more responsive to it than any other tangible
body in the environment; but the satisfaction belongs
to the aggressive hand, the sexual pleasure is irrelevant. (We may easily distinguish between this sadistic-
anal phase and the earlier introjective sadism grounded
in a felt masochism.)

8: Egotism

Lastly, when all the grounds for final contact are
adequately prepared, there is interruption of letting go

the control or the surveillance, of giving in to the behavior that would lead to growth, e.g., performing
the action that he can do and that the situation calls
for, or finishing off what he is making and leaving it.
This is a slowing-down of spontaneity by further deliberate introspection and circumspection, to make sure
that the ground possibilities are indeed exhausted—
there is no threat of danger or surprise—before he
commits himself. (For want of a better term, we call
this attitude "egotism," since it is a final concern for
one's boundaries and identity rather than for what is
contacted.) Normally, egotism is indispensable in any
process of elaborate complication and long maturation;
otherwise there is premature commitment and the need
for discouraging undoing. Normal egotism is diffident,
skeptical, aloof, slow, but not non-committal.

Neurotically, egotism is a kind of confluence with
the deliberate awareness and an attempted annihilation of the uncontrollable and surprising. The mechanism for avoiding frustration is fixation, the abstraction
of the controlled behavior from the on-going process.
The typical example is the attempt to maintain erection and prevent the spontaneous development of the
orgasm. By this means he proves his potency, that
he "can," and gets a satisfaction of conceit. But what he
is warding off is confusion, being abandoned.

He wards off the surprises of the environment (fear
of competition) by seeking to isolate himself as the only reality: this he does by "taking over" the environment and making it his own. His problem ceases to
be one of contacting some Thou for which he is concerned, but of multiplying sciences and acquaintances
and bringing more and more of the environment into
his scope and power in order to be himself irrefutable.
Such an "environment" ceases to be environment, it
does not nourish, and he does not grow or change.
So eventually, since he prevents experience from being
novel, he becomes bored and lonely.

His method of getting direct satisfaction is to compartment: by bracketing off an attitude that is achieved
and safe, he can regulate the quantity of spontaneity.

Every exercise of such deliberate control feeds his conceit (and contempt of the world). Given a certain amount of shrewdness and enough self-awareness not to make impossible demands on his physiology, the egotist easily transforms himself into the well-adjusted, modest, and helpful "free personality." This metamorphosis is the neurosis of the psychoanalyzed: the patient perfectly understands his character and finds his "problems" absorbing beyond everything else—and there will endlessly be such problems to absorb him, for without spontaneity and risk of the unknown he will not assimilate the analysis any more than anything else.

9: Summary

We may summarize these moments of interruption and their "characters" in the following scheme. (O is the aggression toward the organism, E toward the environment, and S the direct satisfaction possible in the fixation.)

Confluence: no contact with excitation or stimulus
    O: clinging, hanging-on bite
    E: paralysis and de-sensitized hostility
    S: hysteria, regression
Introjection: not accepting the excitation
    O: reversal of affect
    E: resignation (annihilation by identification)
    S: masochism
Projection: not confronting or approaching
    O: disowning the emotion
    E: passive provocation
    S: fantasy (chewing it over)
Retroflection: avoiding conflict and destroying
    O: obsessive undoing
    E: self-destructiveness, secondary gain of illness
    S: active sadism, busyness
Egotism: delaying spontaneity
    O: fixation (abstraction)
    E: exclusion, isolation of self

S: compartmenting, self-conceit
Repression
Reaction-Formation
Sublimation

(The above scheme may be proliferated indefinitely by combinations of the classes with one another, as "confluence of introjects," "projection of retroflects," etc. Of these combinations we may perhaps mention the set of attitudes toward the introjects—the super-ego: (1) the confluence with one's introjects is guiltiness, (2) the projection of introjects is sinfulness, (3) the retroflection of introjects is rebelliousness, (4) the egotism of introjects is the ego-concept; (5) the spontaneous expression of introjects is the ego-ideal.)

10: The Above Is Not a Typology of Neurotic Persons

To repeat it, the above scheme is not a classification of neurotic persons, but a method of spelling out the structure of a *single* neurotic behavior.

This is obvious on the face of it, for every neurotic mechanism is a fixation and every mechanism contains a confluence, something unaware. Likewise every behavior is resigned to some false-identification, disowns an emotion, turns aggression against the self, and is conceited! What the scheme means to show is the *order* in which, against the background of a threatened repression, the fixation spreads throughout the entire process of contact, and the unawareness comes to meet it from the other direction.

That there must be a sequence of fixation in the actual experience is evident, if we consider that at a certain moment one is in fairly good contact, is exercising one's powers and adjusting the situation, and yet a little later is paralyzed. The sequence may in fact be directly observed. The person walks in, smiles or frowns, says something, etc.: in so far he is vital, he has not lost his ego-functions and they are fully engaged. Then he becomes anxious—no matter what it is that is too exciting, it may be the other, a memory, the exercise, whatever. Instead then of proceeding to orient himself *further* (it is the furtherness, the on-goingness that is essential), he at once isolates himself and fixates the situation: he fixates the single achieved orientation. This is the "ego cut off from the self." But this "self-consciousness" at once makes him awkward; he upsets the ash-tray. He becomes muscularly rigid (turns on himself), and then he thinks that the other must take him for a consummate ass. He adopts this standard for his own and is ashamed, and the next moment he is dizzy and paralyzed. Here we interpret the experience as created by the spreading of the fixation.

But of course it could be regarded in the opposite way, as the spreading of the confluence. At the anxious moment, he is out of contact with the on-going situation—for whatever reason; he may want to be elsewhere, reject a hostile impulse against the other, etc. But it is his standard to be all there and attentive. What right do they have to judge him anyway! So he angrily upsets the ash-tray on purpose. Next moment he excludes the environment altogether and is sufficient unto himself.

Regarding the experience as the spread of the un-awareness, it would be hysteria; regarding it as the spread of the fixation, it would be compulsive. The hysteric has "too much spontaneity and too little control"; he says, "I cannot control the impulses that arise": the body looms in the foreground, he is swept by emotions, his ideas and inventions are capricious, everything is sexualized, etc. The compulsive over-controls; there is no fantasy, warm feeling or sensation, action is strong but desire is weak, etc. Yet these two extremes come always to the same thing. It is just because there is too little self, too superficial desire and too little spontaneity, that the hysteric organizes the experience apparently desired: the feelings are not dominant enough to energize the functions of orientation and manipulation—and thus these are pointless and seem to be "too little." But conversely, it is because the functions of control, orientation and manipulation, are too fixated and inflexible that the compulsive is inadequate to cope with his exciting situations; therefore, he cannot control his impulses and turns against them, and then his feelings seem to be "too little." The split of self and ego is mutually disastrous.

This must be so, for neurosis is a condition of both chronic fear and chronic frustration. Because frustration is chronic, desire does not learn to activate important practical functions, for a man bound for disappointment and grief will not engage with the environment seriously. Nevertheless, the frustrated desire recurs and sets going fantasies and finally impulsive acts that are practically ineffective; and so he is again unsuccessful, hurt, and subject to chronic fear. On the other hand, a man who is chronically fearful controls himself and directly frustrates himself. Nevertheless, the drive is not annihilated, but it is merely isolated from the ego; it reappears as hysterical impulse. The frustration, the impulsiveness, the fear, and the self-control all aggravate one another.

In any single experience, all of the powers of the self are mobilized to complete the situation as well as possible, either in a final contact or a fixation. The accumulation of such experiences during a life-history results in well-marked personalities, characters, and types. But still in every single experience, regarded as the peculiar act of self, all the powers are mobilized. And since in therapy it is the self that must destroy and integrate the fixations, we must consider a "typology" not as a method of distinguishing among persons, but as a structure of the single neurotic experience.

11: Example of Reversing the Sequence of Fixations

Let us invent an example* to illustrate a therapeutic sequence:

---

*The example is invented. In this book we have quite eschewed the use of "real" case histories. For unless these are conveyed with the color and concreteness of a novelist, they are not convincing. They are merely examples for an interpretation and the informed reader at once thinks of quite different interpretations and is annoyed that the author has left out the relevant evidence. Therefore it is preferable, we think, to give the intellectual framework directly, and omit the references to "reality."

Egotism

(1) Fixation: The patient is "potent"; he can do the exercise to his own satisfaction. The bother is that when it comes to the finale, of getting something out of it for himself, or thereby giving something to the therapist, he cannot let go. He becomes anxious. When his attention is called to the fact that he interrupts at this stage, he becomes aware of his conceit and exhibitionism.

(2) Retroflection: He reproaches himself for his personal failings. He adduces examples to show how his love for himself and showing off have stood in his way. He has no one to blame but himself. The question is asked: "Instead of reproaching yourself, whom would you like to reproach?" Yes; he wants to tell the therapist a thing or two.

(3) Projection: The sessions have been failing because the therapist does not really want to get on. He is using the patient; if the fee were higher, one would think his intention was to get money out of him. As it is, the situation is uncomfortable; no-one likes to lie there and be stared at. Probably the orthodox method is better, when the therapist is out of the way. The question is asked, "What is your feeling when you are stared at?"

(4) Introjection: He is embarrassed. The reason he shows off is that he wants the therapist to admire him; he considers him as a kind of ideal—in fact he had a fantasy about him (the opposite of the dream that was discussed). Question: "Am I really attractive to you?" No; but naturally one has to love, or at least be well-disposed to, a person who is trying to help you. This said with some anger.

(5) Confluence: He is angry because the experiments (see Part I of this book) are boring, senseless, and sometimes painful, and he is tired of doing them; he is getting disgusted with the therapy . . . At this he falls silent; he is not interested in making any further effort. The other must do it.

The therapist declines to cooperate and holds his peace. The patient suddenly feels that his rigid jaw is painful and he recalls, in the stillness, that his voice had come between his teeth. He closes his teeth.

Let us assume now that the energy bound in this confluent characteristic is available. During his silence he had been alternately guilty at not cooperating and resentful that the therapist did nothing to help him out (just like his wife). Now perhaps he sees that he has been imposing his own dependency unnecessarily; and he smiles at the picture it calls up. Nevertheless, the energy freed from the confluence will again be contacted and fixated according to the other characters. Thus:

Introjection: A man ought to be independent and do what he wants. Why shouldn't he look for other women? Question: "Is there anybody in particular you're interested in?"

Projection: He never had such thoughts before the therapy. He feels almost as though they were being put into his mind. "Really?"

Retroflection: It's the fault of his upbringing. He recognizes that censorious face on middle-class mothers, just like his own mother's. He embarks on a lengthy reminiscence. Question: "What about her now?"

Egotism: He understands everything perfectly. What people don't know won't hurt them. Just do it within the rules of the game. "Who's playing a game?"

Contacting the Situation: He'll try the experiment again now and see if he gets anything out of it.

12: Sense of Boundaries

The functioning of the ego, we have seen, can be described as a setting of boundaries of the self's interest, power, etc.; identifying with and alienating are the two sides of the boundary; and in any live contacting the boundary is definite but always shifting. Now in the therapeutic situation of deliberately contacting the character, what is the sense of the boundary?

Engaged in an interesting activity, the self contacts

its lost ego-functions as blocks, resistances, sudden failures. One identifies with the interesting engagement, that is on one side of the boundary; but what is alienated is not—as in normal functioning—uninteresting and irrelevant, but precisely alien, oppressive, uncanny, immoral, numb; not a boundary, but a limitation. The sense is not indifference, but unpleasure. The boundary does not shift with will or need, as one tries to see, remember, move; but remains fixed.

Regarded topologically, as fixed boundaries in the shifting organism/environment field, the neurotic characters we have been describing are as follows:

Confluence: identity of organism and environment.

Introjection: something of the environment in the organism.

Projection: something of the organism in the environment.

Retroflection: part of the organism made the environment of another part of the organism.

Egotism: isolation from both id and environment, or: organism largely isolated from environment.

There is an exact opposition in the way these situations are sensed by the neurotic need of keeping them fixed and by the creative self concentrating on them:

In confluence, the neurotic is aware of nothing and has nothing to say. The concentrating self feels hemmed in by an oppressive darkness.

In introjection, the neurotic justifies as normal what the concentrating self feels as an alien body it wants to disgorge.

In projection, the neurotic is convinced as by sensory evidence, where the concentrating self feels a gap in experience.

In retroflection, the neurotic is busily engaged where the concentrating self feels left out, excluded from the environment.

In egotism, the neurotic is aware and has something to say about everything, but the concentrating self feels empty, without need or interest.

It can be seen from this that the treatments of an area of confluence and of an area of egotistic fixation present opposite difficulties. The confluent darkness is too embracing; the self is routine; no novel proposal is accepted as relevant—just as in the hysterical behavior anything is likely to be momentarily relevant (there is no dearth of symptoms for the therapist to interpret to his own satisfaction).

Now in the history of psychoanalysis the extreme opposite of this condition has been taken as the health of the self, namely the stage of all ego that feels a boundary of possible contact everywhere. The essential self is defined as the system of its ego-boundaries; it is not seen that this is an on-going stage of the self. The temptation to such a theoretical conception is irresistible because in therapy the awareness of boundaries dissolves the neurotic structures, and the physician defines according to what works in therapy; further, any particular "problem" that arises in therapy can finally be met and "solved" in egotism by compartmenting it and employing all the ego-functions within this safe framework, without engaging the feelings at all. This is a condition of too heightened consciousness, that will never have brilliant creative flashes, but is quite adequate for therapeutic sessions. To the self, everything is potentially relevant and novel—there is a boundary everywhere and no limit to action—but nothing is interesting. He is psychologically "emptied out." This is, as we have said, the "analysis-neurosis"; it is likely that *any* method of therapy continued too long must give this result, which in antiquity was praised as the Stoic apathy, and among the moderns is taken for a "free personality"—but such freedom of the individual, without animal or social nature, or in perfect hygienic and juridical control of the animal and social nature, such freedom is, as Kafka said, a lonely and senseless business.

13: Therapy of Boundaries

For a concentration-therapy, the problem of contacting the lost ego-functions is no different from any other problem of creative orientation and manipulation, for the unawareness, or the unsatisfactory kind of awareness, is felt simply as another obstacle in the organism/environment field. It is necessary to need, approach, destroy, in order to identify, contact, and assimilate. It is not a question of recovering something from the past nor of rescuing it from behind an armor, but of making a creative adjustment in the given present situation. To complete the gestalt in the present situation it is necessary to destroy and assimilate the unawareness as an obstacle. The therapeutic exercises consist of sharp delineation and precise verbal description of the felt block or void, and experiment on it to mobilize the fixed boundaries.

From this point of view there is no mystery in the psychoanalytical miracle, that simple awareness is somehow cathartic, for the effort of concentrated awareness and mobilizing of the block entails destroying, suffering, feeling, and excitement. (The therapist, correspondingly, is a vastly important part of the present situation, but it is not necessary to speak of "transference," the attachment of repressed Oedipal energies, for the actuality contains both the confluence of dependency and the rebellion against it.)

Let us return then to the question of the patient that we started with: "At what point do I begin not to solve the problem? How do I prevent myself?" And now let us lay the stress not on the moment of interruption, but on the *begin* and on the *how*. Let us contrast the non-therapeutic and the therapeutic situation. Ordinarily, the self, trying to contact some interesting present actuality, becomes aware of the boundaries of its lost functions—something of the environment or body is missing, there is not enough strength or clarity. It nevertheless presses on and tries to unify the foreground, even though the neurotic structure looms in the background as an unfinished situation, unknowable, a threat of confusion and a threat to the body. The mounting excitement is throttled, there is anxiety. Nevertheless, the self persists in the original task and allays the anxiety by further blotting out the background with reaction-formations and proceeding with less and less of its powers. In the therapy, on the contrary, it is just the point of the interruption that is now made the interesting problem, the object of concentration: the questions are: "What hinders? What does it look like? How do I feel it muscularly? Where is it in the environment? etc." The mounting anxiety is allayed by continuing the excitement in this new problem; what is felt is some quite different emotion, of grief, anger, disgust, fear, longing.

14: The Criterion

It is not the presence of "inner" obstacles that constitutes the neurosis: they are simply obstacles. To the extent that a situation is alive, when the obstacles to creativity appear, the excitement does not diminish, the gestalt does not stop forming, but spontaneously one feels new aggressive emotions and mobilizes new ego-functions of caution, deliberateness, paying attention, relevant to the obstacles. One does not lose the sense of oneself, of one's synthetic unity, but it continues to sharpen, to identify itself further and alienate what is not itself. In neurosis, on the contrary, at this point the excitement falters, the aggression is not felt, one loses the sense of the self, becomes confused, divided, insensitive.

This factual difference, of continuing creativity, is the crucial criterion of vitality and neurosis. It is an independent criterion, generally observable and also introspectable. It does not require norms of health for comparison. The test is given by the self.

The neurotic begins to lose contact with the actuality; he knows it but he does not have techniques for continuing the contact; he persists in a course that gets him further from the actuality, and he is lost. What he must learn is to recognize sharply when he is no longer in contact, how he is not, and where and what the actuality now is, so he can continue contacting it; an "inner" problem is now the actuality, or probably the relation of an "inner" problem to the previous experiencing. If he learns a technique of awareness, to follow up, to keep in contact with the shifting situation, so the interest, excitement, and growth continue, he is no longer neurotic, no matter whether his problems are "inner" or "outer." For the creative meaning of the situation is not what one thinks beforehand, but it emerges in bringing to the foreground the unfinished situations, whatever they are, and discovering-and-inventing their relevance to the apparent present lifeless situation. When in the emergency the self can keep in contact and keep going, the therapy is terminated.

In the emergency, the neurotic loses himself. To live on a little, with diminished self, he identifies with re-active feelings, a fixated interest, a fiction, a rationalization; but these in fact do not work, they do not alter the situation, release new energy and interest. He has lost something of actual life. But the patient comes to recognize that his own functioning is part of the actuality. If he has alienated some of his powers, he comes to identify with his own alienation of them as a deliberate act; he can say, "It is I who am doing this or preventing this." The final stage of experience, however, is not a subject of therapy: it is for a man to identify with his concern for the concernful and to be able to alienate what is unconcernful.

In its trials and conflicts the self is coming to be in a way that did not exist before. In contactful experience the "I", alienating its safe structures, risks this leap and identifies with the growing self, gives it its services and knowledge, and at the moment of achievement stands out of the way.

INDEX

INDEX

READ TOMORROW'S LITERATURE—TODAY

The best of today's writing bound for tomorrow's classics.